P9-CES-663

IMAGINING THE HOLOCAUST

ALSO BY DANIEL R. SCHWARZ

AUTHOR

Reconfiguring Modernism: Explorations in the Relationship between Modern Art and Modern Literature (1997)

Narrative and Representation in the Poetry of Wallace Stevens (1993)

The Case for a Humanistic Poetics (1991)

The Transformation of the English Novel, 1890–1930 (1989, revised ed. 1995)

Reading Joyce's *Ulysses* (1987)

The Humanistic Heritage: Critical Theories of the English Novel from James to Hillis Miller (1986)

Conrad: The Later Fiction (1982)

Conrad: Almayer's Folly through *Under Western Eyes* (1980)

Disraeli's Fiction (1979)

EDITOR

The Secret Sharer (Bedford Case Studies in Contemporary Criticism) (1997)

The Dead (Bedford Case Studies in Contemporary Criticism) (1994)

Narrative and Culture (coeditor) (1994)

IMAGINING THE HOLOCAUST

Daniel R. Schwarz

St. Martin's Press
New York

IMAGINING THE HOLOCAUST. Copyright © 1999 Daniel R. Schwarz. All rights reserved. Printed in the United States of America. No part of this book may be used or reproduced in any manner whatsoever without written permission except in the case of brief quotations embodied in critical articles or reviews. For information, address St. Martin's Press, 175 Fifth Avenue, New York, N.Y. 10010.

ISBN 0-312-17303-2

Library of Congress Cataloging-in-Publication Data

Schwarz, Daniel R.
    Imagining the Holocaust / by Daniel R. Schwarz
        p.   cm.
    Includes bibliographical references and index.
    ISBN 0-312-17303-2 (cloth)
    1. Holocaust, Jewish (1939-1945), in literature. 2. Holocaust, Jewish (1939-1945)--Personal narratives--History and criticism. I. Title.
    PN56.H55.S35 1999
    809'.93358--DC21   99-19092
                                                                    CIP

Design: Acme Art, Inc.
First edition: October, 1999
10 9 8 7 6 5 4 3 2 1

For my wife, Marcia Jacobson
my sons, David and Jeffrey Schwarz
and my parents, Florence and Joseph Schwarz

CONTENTS

Acknowledgements viii

INTRODUCTION

The Ethics of Imagining the Holocaust: Representation,
Responsibility, and Reading 1

PART ONE
Memoirs

CHAPTER ONE

The Ethics of Reading Elie Wiesel's *Night* 45

CHAPTER TWO

Painful Memories: The Agony of Primo Levi 75

CHAPTER THREE

World into Words: *The Diary of Anne Frank* and
Sophie Goetzel-Leviathan's *The War from Within* 101

PART TWO
Realism

CHAPTER FOUR

Haunted by History: Tadeusz Borowski's *This Way for the Gas,
Ladies and Gentlemen* 129

CHAPTER FIVE

John Hersey's *The Wall*: Fiction as History in the
First Generation of Holocaust Fiction 143

CHAPTER SIX

Popular Fiction: Gerald Green's *Holocaust: A Novel of Survival
and Triumph* 161

CHAPTER SEVEN

Beyond the Camps: Kosinski's *The Painted Bird* 173

CHAPTER EIGHT

The Ontological Problems of Docufiction:
William Styron's *Sophie's Choice* 195

CHAPTER NINE

Keneally's and Spielberg's *Schindler's List*:
Realistic Novel into Epic Film. 209

PART THREE

Myth, Parable, and Fable

CHAPTER TEN

Schwarz-Bart's Mythopoeic and Historical Humanism:
The Last of the Just 239

CHAPTER ELEVEN

Aharon Appelfeld's Parables 249

CHAPTER TWELVE

Illuminating Distortion and Historical Cartoon:
Leslie Epstein's *King of the Jews* 271

PART FOUR

Fantasy

CHAPTER THIRTEEN

The Comic Grotesque of Spiegelman's *Maus* 287

CHAPTER FOURTEEN

Cynthia Ozick's Fables: "The Shawl" and "Rosa" 303

CHAPTER FIFTEEN

Bruno Schulz's Nightmare in *The Street of Crocodiles* and
Sanitarium under the Sign of the Hourglass and Cynthia Ozick's
Response in *The Messiah of Stockholm* 317

Works Cited and Discussed 339

Index 347

ACKNOWLEDGEMENTS

I wish to thank Gabriel Spitzer and Parichay Rudina for helping with indexing and proofreading. I wish to also thank Joe Cheung, , Anne Marie Ellis, Michelle Houle, Grace Jean, Dan Jossen, Jay Joshua Oppenheim, and Alexandra Vinograd who helped in various stages of this project. Robin Doxtater, Denise Huff, and Lisa Melton have assisted with secretarial tasks. I have enjoyed once again working with the able editors and staff at St. Martin's including my longtime friend Garrett Kiely, Karin Cholak, Amy Reading, Kristi Long, Maura Burnett, and, especially, Alan Bradshaw, the production editor. My greatest debt is to Marcia Jacobson, my insightful, supportive, and generous wife.

PERMISSIONS

Excerpts from *Night* by Elie Wiesel, translated by Stella Rodway. Copyright © 1960 by MacGibbon & Kee. Copyright renewed © 1988 by the Collins Publishing Group. Reprinted by permission of Hill and Wang, a division of Farrar, Straus and Giroux, Inc.

From *If This Is a Man (Survival in Auschwitz)* by Primo Levi, translated by Stuart Woolf. Translation copyright © 1959 by Orion Press, Inc., © 1958 by Giulio Einaudi editore S.P.A. Used by permission of Viking Penguin, a division of Penguin Putman Inc.

"In the Midst of Life," "Posthumous Rehabilitation," "The Survivor," and "Pigtail" are taken from *Tadeusz Różewicz: They Came to See a Poet*, translated by Adam Czerniawski. Published by Anvil Press Poetry in 1991.

From *Badenheim 1939* by Aharon Appelfeld, Dalya Bilu, Translator; reprinted by permission of David R. Godine, Publisher, Inc. Copyright 1980 by Aharon Appelfeld, Dalya Bilu, Translator.

From *The Age of Wonders* by Aharon Appelfeld, Dalya Bilu, Translator; reprinted by permission of David R. Godine, Publisher, Inc. Copyright 1981 by Aharon Appelfeld, Dalya Bilu, Translator.

From *The Complete Fiction of Bruno Schulz*, copyright 1989 by Ella-Podstolski Schulz; reprinted with permission from Walker and Company, 435 Hudson Street, New York 10014; 1-800-289-2553. All Rights Reserved.

From *The Painted Bird* by Jerzy Kosinski published by Grove Press, 1998. Permission granted by Scientia-Factum, Inc.

From *The Last of the Just* by Andre Schwarz-Bart. Used by permission of Georges Borchardt, Inc.

From *The King of the Jews* by Leslie Epstein. Used by Permission of the author.

"Discovery" by Hilda Schiff used by permission of the author.

From *This Way for the Gas, Ladies and Gentleman* by Tadeusz Borowski, translated by Barbara Vedder, Translation copyright © 1967 by Penguin Books, Ltd. Original text copyright © 1959 by Maria Borowski. Used by Permission of Viking Penguin, a division of Penguin Putnam, Inc.

Excerpts from Nelly Sachs "A Dead Child Speaks" and "O the Night of the Weeping Children" used by permission of Farrar, Straus, and Giroux, Inc.

Excerpts from *Holocaust*, by Gerald Green. Copyright © 1979, by Gerald Green; reprinted by permission of the author's agents, Scott Meredith Literary Agency L.P.

From Sophie Goetzal-Leviathan's *The War Within*, reprinted by permission of the publisher, the Judah Magnes Museum of Berkeley, California.

THE ETHICS OF IMAGINING THE HOLOCAUST: REPRESENTATION, RESPONSIBILITY, AND READING

POSTHUMOUS REHABILITATION
The dead have remembered
our indifference
The dead have remembered
our silence
The dead have remembered
our words

The dead see our snouts
laughing from ear to ear
The dead see
our bodies rubbing against each other
The dead hear
clucking tongues

The dead read our books
listen to our speeches
delivered so long ago
The dead scrutinize our lectures

join in previously terminated
discussions
The dead see our hands
poised for applause

The dead see stadiums
ensembles and choirs declaiming rhythmically

all the living are guilty

little children
who offered bouquets of flowers
are guilty
lovers are guilty
guilty are poets
guilty are those who ran away
and those that stayed
those who were saying yes
those who said no
and those who said nothing

the dead are taking stock of the living
the dead will not rehabilitate us

—Tadeusz Różewicz
Translated by Adam Czerniawski

I

I begin with a wonderful parable entitled "The Night Watchman" that is
found in *The New Mahzor*:

The Dubner Maggid taught: Prayer is not a device to arouse God,
to make him aware of us and our needs. God is always aware of us
and our needs. God is always aware. The true purpose of prayer is

to arouse *us*, to keep us aware of our obligations—toward our community, our people, our God, and even toward ourselves.

The Maggid gave this illustration: In the shtetl, the night watchman walks the streets and every hour on the hour calls out the time. The purpose for "calling out" is not to awaken the residents in the middle of the night. The purpose is to indicate that he, the watchman, is alert, tending to his tasks, and has not fallen asleep.

Prayer is a means of keeping us spiritually alert and morally awake. (*The New Mahzor* 698)

If I may borrow from the above, when we write—and read—about the Holocaust, we do so to arouse ourselves, to awaken our conscience, to keep our obligations to those who were lost, those who survived, and those of future generations. If we are Jews, we write about the Holocaust for our community, our people, and ourselves, but finally the concepts of "our people" and "our community" include not only Jews but all humankind. We are indeed playing the role of night watchmen reminding ourselves—and those to whom we feel an intellectual responsibility—to keep alert and attend to the necessary task of keeping the lessons of the Holocaust alive.

In this study, I want to address a number of questions: (1) Is the concept of a "fictive construct" disrespectful to the Holocaust, the events of which are all too true? (2) How does one discuss how memory transforms reality and words transform memory? (3) How can those of us who are not survivors write respectfully about the Holocaust since we cannot make amends through our writing for not being victims? (4) Why do those survivors and their kin and others immersed in Holocaust studies strongly object to films like *Schindler's List*, which, while twice told tales to the cognescenti, make Holocaust themes and images available to a general audience? Can those who are not Jews have a legitimate vision of the Holocaust? While survivors are most likely to use verisimilitude, surely there are other ways of engaging audiences effectively on the subject. (5) Why do some object to the use of fantasy, hyperbole, and illuminating distortion such as the little girl in red in Spielberg's film of *Schindler's List*, cartoon figures in Spiegelman's *Maus* or, in the Italian film *Life is Beautiful*, the legerdemain the father uses to disguise from his son what is actually occurring when they are sent to a camp? (6) Why do others object to *any* rendering of the Holocaust? (7) Can we define an ethics of Holocaust writing that accounts for rendering the horror of the original events—namely what happened to victims—while still meeting the responsibility of *persuading* a contemporary audience? How would such an ethics affect the aesthetics of representing the Holocaust?

As a scholar working in modernism, I want to understand the Holocaust writing in terms of twentieth-century intellectual and social history. As a formalist, I want to see how these narratives are constructed and what distinguishes them. Holocaust narratives draw upon history and recast it in narrative form. But history often depends on the lived experience of individuals. Just as autobiographical Holocaust narratives—diaries, memoirs, even meditative essays such as Levi's *The Periodic Table*—create a fictional order, so do Holocaust fictions depend often on actual events, or at least the verisimilitude of such. Surely we need to differentiate between memoirs and documentary fiction posing as memoirs, and between realistic novels and fables.

As a humanist, I want to show how these narratives are about humans, by humans, and for humans. I wish to examine how these narratives reclaim through language defining values, including a belief that we can communicate. I shall address major texts about the Holocaust from the position of a modernist scholar and literary critic. (At the outset we should acknowledge that when we discuss translations, our inquiry will address the English words on the page as if those words were the original text even if we occasionally do comment on the original text). I am not a Holocaust scholar but a literary critic. Drawing on a range of texts from diary to memoir to fiction, I wish to examine the narrative techniques and the relation between narrative and memory in Holocaust writers. But we need also examine these texts for a grammar of motives, for behavioral cause and effect, to learn why some people survived, why some refused to be demoralized, and why some, even when suffering deprivation, could still think of others.

How does one evaluate the body of Holocaust narrative? I have selected some of the best-known works, those that have contributed to how most educated people perceive the Holocaust. I have chosen for the most part major texts that have a wide readership and raise interesting narrative issues, but I have left out countless works that could have been discussed, most notably novels such as Leon Uris's *Mila 18* (1961), D. M. Thomas's *The White Hotel* (1981), David Grossman's *See Under: Love* (1989), and memoirs and testimonies such as *An Interrupted Life: The Diaries of Etty Hillesum, 1941–1943* (1983). To be sure, such a selection must be arbitrary, although I have consulted with colleagues. I did not use anything as crass as sales figures, but tried to locate pivotal and often-discussed texts. These works are addressed to a heterogeneous audience. Yet these books need to be judged on how they address Jews and non-Jews, and among Jews a distinction has to be made between how the books address survivors and their children and those who by luck of location or time missed the Holocaust. In considering the value of a text, we need to consider not only aesthetic questions and the accuracy and intensity of mimesis, but the rhetorical effect upon the intended audience. Thus, we may fault Styron in *Sophie's Choice* for not attending to Jewish sensibilities, even while focusing on the continued relevance of the Holocaust in American moral life in 1976.

Is the experience of women Holocaust writers and characters in the texts we will be discussing in the following pages different from that of males? Why, we might ask, are there more men than women writers of Holocaust memoirs and fictions? Is it because woman were thought less valued as skilled labor, and thus fewer *survived* the selections for the gas chambers? Is it inappropriate to survive physically, and is that itself an indication of moral compromise and complicity?

Each reader responds differently to a text, but as a Jew who was three years old when the death camps were discovered, Holocaust narratives— transmuting facts into fictional form—play a large part in my understanding of what transpired. Certainly Jews respond to the Holocaust differently than non-Jews do, and children of those Jews who survived their family's decimation respond still another way from the more fortunate Jews who, like myself and other American Jews, were protected by accidents of geography. Indeed, is it a particular feature of Holocaust narratives that Jews remember them differently from the way non-Jews do and that they enter our dreams and nightmares as if they were our own experience? We see ourselves in these ghetto places, these streets. In our nightmares, we are deported and suffer the horrors of the camps.

Thus I dream of myself within shtetls, camps, and confined circumstances, as a participant in the very world I am writing about. I awake in a cold sweat from dreams of being deported. I know, in some small way, the world I avoided by the luck of history and geography. What I wish to do is examine the texts that moved me and share with you that world of history's nightmare from the perspective of diverse powerful fictional and nonfictional visions. As the historical period of the Shoah recedes, imaginative literature will help keep those events alive. Do we not know more about the War of the Roses and the history of Britain from Shakespeare than from Holinshed's chronicles? If ever a past needs a human shape, it is the Holocaust; yet, as we shall see, putting a human shape on inhuman behavior challenges our ability to imagine evil and to represent it linguistically.

Our study of Holocaust narratives addresses inextricably related issues of aesthetics, ethics, and politics. We need to think about the ethics of reading Holocaust narratives; how do we suspend our daily selves and enter into the world of the unspeakable, how do we as scholar-critics write about that world? Can we relate some Holocaust narratives to modernism and others to postmodernism and see that while some, like Hersey's *The Wall* and Green's *Holocaust,* rely on controlling motifs and formal order, others, like Spiegelman's *Maus* and Kosinski's *The Painted Bird,* accommodate incongruity, disorder, and sequences that barely hold together. Is there an ironic relationship between the effort of Holocaust writing to reclaim the world of language of which the writers were deprived and modernism's emphasis on "art for art's sake"—art as an alternative to the chaos of life? Does the inherent conservatism of Holocaust literature in some way try to reattach itself to the very value system that tolerated right-wing politics and anti-Semitism, including such modernists figures as Pound, T. S. Eliot, Lawrence, and even Yeats? Is there a link between modernism's frequent celebration of technology (futurism, supremetism, constructivism), and the gruesome efficiency of the death camps and transport system?

Holocaust studies has not only developed in the wake of ethnic studies but has become a centerpiece, an essential field. In short, the study of the war against the Jews has become an industry. One can almost say it has the cachet that women's studies had a decade ago. Indeed, Jewish women who had obliterated that part of their identity when becoming active in the women's movement are now often in the forefront of those reexamining their Jewish roots and the Holocaust. The English journal *TLS,* which barely mentioned Jewish studies for decades—and that looked at Jews from a steep and icy peak—overflows with reviews and discussion. More than *The Sorrow and the Pity* and *Shoah,* Green's television series *Holocaust* and Spielberg's film *Schindler's List* have placed the Holocaust in the popular conscience. Generous donors underwrite Jewish studies the way they once underwrote Yeshivahs in Israel. Book publishers compete for Holocaust studies because they sell. Museums, photography, books, and films feed upon one another and whet the very appetite they are meant to sate. Psychoanalytic critics have focused on the effect of trauma upon the memory of survivors and how it effects the children of survivors.

Relating the reasons for revisiting the Holocaust trauma in France to the larger pattern throughout the world, Roger Cohen perspicaciously remarks:

> As a bloody century wanes, repentance is in vogue, a sort of global purging of the soul before the millennium. A world relatively becalmed, perhaps moderately bored, is confronting the upheavals of the past hundred years as a form of atonement. British colonialism, Nazism, Communist totalitarianism, apartheid: the candidates for expiatory examination are rich and varied. But nowhere, perhaps, is the process more fraught or obsessive than in France's contemplation of its treatment of the Jews during World War II.
>
> The forces pushing France toward an orgy of retrospection are similar to those at work elsewhere: the passing from power of the generation that lived the war years; the end of the cold war with its bending of truth to strategic imperatives; the odd moral magnetism of the number 2000, so evocative of a circle completed as to be an invitation to what Pope John Paul II has called "the purification of memory."
>
> Here, as in other countries, there appears to be an almost physical realization of the sheer weight of the century's slaughter, and the triumph of the ideology of human rights in a post-ideological age leads naturally to the examination of past brutality. (Cohen 1)

Is the contemporary obsession a return of the repressed? How do we account for the burgeoning interest in Holocaust studies? What is it about our time that has brought the Shoah to the fore? Is it in part what we might call the CNNing of the world so that now the Jewish global village can look into its past together, while forming an elaborate support group? Have the Europeans become a related codependent support group, responding to and reflecting on the Jewish angst, often by denying, sublimating, editing, reconfiguring, evading, and sometimes by sorting a little dirty laundry in public—for example, the 1997 Maurice Papon trial in France—so as to avoid our seeing the graves in the basement? As Michael André Bernstein writes:

> If anything can be concluded from the ceaseless outpouring of works in every genre and medium about the Nazi genocide, it is how central that cataclysm has become to the self-interrogation of the culture we inhabit today. Although among non-Jews the consensus evolved only very gradually, by now there is a surprisingly widespread sense that the Shoah constitutes the defining event of the Second World War, that the extermination of European Jewry was not merely one among many competing projects of the Third Reich, but rather the very essence of Nazism, and that the universe of the death camps created a decisive breach in the fabric of the modern world. Whether one invokes Habermas's formulation that in the Shoah "a deep stratum of solidarity between all that bears a human countenance was touched," or Terence des Pres's, "a new shape of knowing invades the mind," the motif of some lasting violation, a transgression of what we had previously imagined as humanly possible, is perhaps the most far-reaching of the Shoah's continuing after-shocks. The bleakness of Paul Celan's lines, "no one witnesses for the witness," haunts our consciousness, its indictment directed less at our refusal to listen to those who went through the death camps than at the more disturbing rupture in the very possibility of ever transmitting such experiences. ("Lasting Injury" 3)

Each country, including the United States, wrote its own version of postwar history, often to suit the needs of rebuilding its self-esteem. The cold war meant that history was distorted. We were told that the United States, England, and France won the war when in fact France was a defeated country complicit in the Holocaust. Decades passed before France began as a nation to reexamine its role and realize that only a comparative few partisans resisted the Vichy government while the vast majority cooperated with a government that rounded up and deported Jews beyond the Nazi demands. In the last few years, we have been learning about Switzerland's role in expropriating Jewish money after the war as well as laundering expropriated German money and harboring Nazi assets during the war. Finally, 50 years later, French war criminals such as Maurice Papon are brought to trial. Hardly a week goes by without new revelations from the repressed political past. In France after the Allied victory, 300,000 French collaborators were arrested and 7,037 were put to death. But then followed 25 years of silence before a period of reexamination—25 years after the war. Now after another silence, a new generation in France is seeing the past far differently from the way their parents or grandparents did. As Craig R. Whitney puts it:

> France did not come easily to willingness to go through with [Papon's] trial, which examines a subject that was long taboo—crimes committed in the name of France not just by egregious collaborators and disgraced Vichy leaders convicted of treason like Marshal Henry Philippe Petain who died in prison, and Prime Minister Pierre Laval, who was executed, but by anonymous civil servants and other French functionaries who stayed at their jobs.
>
> Many did terrible things that were later enfolded by a collective loss of memory in a nation all too eager to forget. For most of the last half-century the French, encouraged by the Resistance leader, Gen. Charles de Gaulle, President of France from 1958 to 1969, and other postwar leaders, cherished the belief that the ultimate responsibility of the Nazi occupiers and the illegitimacy of the Vichy regime absolved France from complicity in the crimes of the Holocaust.
>
> That has now clearly changed, as the bishops of the Roman Catholic Church in France showed last week in a statement of contrition asking forgiveness from the Jews of France for the Church's silence on measures taken against them during the war. A

moving ceremony last month to honor 18 foreign Jews arrested in a village . . . after a French informant tipped off the Gestapo provided further evidence of the change. (Whitney 1)

Does our intense interest in the Holocaust derive from a human fascination with the nature of evil, particularly evil that defies explanation? Milton, Blake told us, was of the devil's party without knowing it. Perhaps interest in the Holocaust is also stimulated by the realization that the last witnesses, the last voices, are dying, and we must listen to them. Survivors' children cannot offer the kind of testimony offered by the Video Archive for Holocaust Testimonies at Yale. It may be, too, a kind of secular millenarianism, a sense of an ending at the year 2000 that demands our taking stock of the central atrocity of the past and providing explanations for wherever we have been and where we are going.

There are contradictory modes of interpreting Holocaust narratives. The tendency to universalize Holocaust narratives into general human victimization or into the story of moral growth in trying circumstances has been criticized. Yet some, like Itzvan Déak, are impatient with specific memories of those who fail to mention the moral compromises necessary to survive. Others criticize the humanistic teleology of Holocaust narratives in which the teller returns—perhaps too easily—to an affirmation of life. But others find fault with the *angst* and loss of faith of those who abandon Jewish tradition and spiritual belief. Like the despair of Schwarz-Bart's *The Last of the Just*, the affirmative nature of Wiesel's *Night*—attributed to revisions Wiesel made at the behest of François Mauriac—are put under a critical eye. So sensitive was the editor of Goetzel-Leviathan's affirmative memoir *The War from Within* that she included as an appendix a scathing critique of the memoir by another survivor.

Not too long ago, I wrote a poem about meeting the aging daughter of Jim Thorpe. After revising and rewriting, I convinced myself that I had actually met this person rather than learning about her from someone else. At one point I actually told my wife that I had met this woman around whose memories and needs I structured the poem, but then she reminded me that I had imagined this incident. I want to take this as a parable for remembering and narrating the Holocaust; of course Holocaust memories have an infinite higher stake for the survivors whose memories are disrupted by trauma, nightmares, displacement, and guilt. Even the original experiences are mediated by hunger, fear, and physical and psychological abuse beyond our imagination. But memory distorts even as it records, seeks narrative patterning in its sense-making, and depends often on a repetition compulsion that wears tracks in the mind for subsequent sense impressions to follow. Memory breaks a trail, and in its iteration that complex path of understanding and misunderstanding deepens. Memory relies upon narrative to shape inchoate form and make that path into a road.

Survivors rely on memory and narrative to give their lives sense. Why, let us ask, do so many survivors write? Why, indeed did so many people in the ghettos write? As Sem Dresden writes in *Persecution, Extermination, Literature*:

> In each case, one has to start from the isolation in which the victims found themselves: contact with what then generally was called the outside world was almost completely cut, so communication in the normal sense of the word was impossible, or possible only by way of writing and without counting on an immediate reply. But while there could be no chance of reciprocity, there was a chance that records, reflections, and so on would, as was hoped, reach posterity, in spite of serious obstacles, in due course. . . . The individual feels himself, and indeed is, so greatly deprived of his freedom of movement and, more particularly, of his spiritual freedom, he is so mercilessly stripped and thrown back on himself in unexpected circumstances he cannot control that everybody is at a loss. What can serve as and is used as an expedient is found in writing, an activity that lies in the danger zone but is all the same difficult to control or prevent. The individual in a sense thus takes back his rights: the writer can show that in spite of all the attempts to rob him of his personality, he remains indestructibly who he is or even becomes somebody he would like to be and could be. (25, 27)

The Holocaust memoirist redeems himself and regains a semblance of coherence by means of his writing. Richard Terdiman writes:

> What we need now is a model of cultural and textual understanding that could conceive how the contents of our memory and our past

retain—and how they could assert—the capacity to ground or norm interpretations, so that the relativism of the latter might be brought into contact with a principled and nuanced complex of constraints. What could be the character of such interpretations formed by memory, but responsive to its representation and transformative nature? (Terdiman 352)

Holocaust studies begin and end with the questions, "How do we remember? How do we interpret?" As Terdiman argues:

> [M]emory is far from a unified or transparent register of our past. The pasts we carry but do not entirely cognize regularly rise to colonize our present. But once we admit the ways—whether subtle and subterranean, or entirely overt—by which this eerie domination of *now* by *then* can happen, then memory turns labyrinthine. At that point any notion of a self-identical and accessible subjectivity as the straightforward agent of interpretations of our lives—past *and* present—spins off into perplexities that disable the paradigms that might have seemed to credit the dominion of the hermeneutic. (346-347)

Istvan Déak has remarked how selective memory has shaped survivor's tales. He says facetiously of these memoirs: "Although many of his family members perish, the author's inner dignity and readiness to help others keep him alive. . . . It was almost always someone else, hardly ever himself, who stole a spoon, a needle, or a slice of bread from a neighbor, who lorded it over the prisoners or who escaped the gas chambers at the loss of a fellow inmate's life" (38). He mocks the pretense of total recall: "And who can believe that so many writers have perfect recall, enabling them to reproduce verbatim conversations they had, or overheard, half a century earlier?" (Déak, 38). Or as Terdiman puts it, "Yet for all this apparent centering of meaning in memory, memory's contradiction perversely exists" (347).

Finally, it is as if the very acts of memory and telling were the subject, the possibility that we can recall and narrate the unspeakable. It is the very ability to communicate, then, that is being validated when we speak about narratives that convey Holocaust horror in the *written word.*

In an argument that recalls the work of James E. Young's important *Writing and Rewriting the Holocaust*, Dresden makes an important distinction: "I shall begin at the beginning and be certain only that there exist writings that have been written and contain only words, that they differ from one another not on the basis of the reality they have to offer, but, perhaps, in the technique used in writing. It is there, perhaps, that literature as shaping force distinguishes itself from other, equally moving, writings" (Dresden 39).

When the New York City Museum of Jewish Heritage: A Living Memorial to the Holocaust opened in September 1997, some wondered whether there were, as Michael Kimmelman asked in the *New York Times*, "too many memorials, an abundance that inures people to the singularity of genocide: a saturation point in other words, when remembering permits forgetting?" (1). The same thing can be said about Holocaust studies. As Kimmelman notes, "Memories are sustained when they are unresolved" (26). One way we use our narrative is to step back from our needs, joys, and fears and try to give stability to self by finding structures out of which to create order and meaning. What Holocaust narratives do is rescue Jews from viewing anonymous photographs of victims—victims deprived of their humanity and reduced to the way the Nazis wanted to remember them—and to restore to them human dignity. It allows them the dignity of voice. We might think of Victor Frankl, author of *Man's Search for Meaning*, who as Herbert Muschamp wrote, "founded a practice he called logotherapy, based on his own experience as a survivor of a Nazi death camp. Mental health, Dr. Frankl argued, is contingent on our power to invest events with meaning" (Muschamp, "Museum Tells a Tale," 1). Muschamp continues, "In addition to everything else, the Holocaust was a crisis of meaning, a calamitous cognitive breakdown. What people knew—that Jews were being herded onto boxcars, in full and often thunderously approving public view—overwhelmed what they were able to believe: that a catastrophe of such magnitude was actually taking place before the eyes of the civilized world" (2).

We might recall the Book of Daniel, in which the Babylonian King Belshazzar—a tiny facsimile of Hitler in his persecution of Jews—is feasting and drinking from the sacred vessels that his father Nebuchadnezzar had plundered from the Jewish Temple in Jerusalem; suddenly a hand unattached to a body appears and writes mysterious words on the wall: "Mene, mene, tekel upharsin." But neither Belshazzar nor his followers can understand the words, which seem to be written in an unknown tongue. Desperate to know what has been written, Belshazzar summons Daniel, who has a reputation for wisdom. Daniel can read the words, which are in an early Semitic language, Aramaic, from which Hebrew is derived. Literally the words mean, "Numbered, numbered, weighed, and divided." But Daniel interprets these words as foretelling the destruction of Belshazzar and his kingdom. His reading is a prophecy: "God hath numbered thy kingdom, and brought it to an end; thou art weighed in the balances, and found wanting; thy kingdom is divided, and given to the Medes and Persians."

While Daniel's words "numbered, numbered, divided, and conquered" foretold the destruction of one despot terrorizing Jews, we modern Daniels already know of Hitler's demise and the Jews' survival. Are we not also like Daniel when we are called upon to interpret and to understand the incomprehensible that we confront in Holocaust literature? In one sense the Holocaust, like these mysterious words on the wall, will always elude us. Yet in another sense, Holocaust narratives—like Daniel's interpretative story—unravel mysterious and incomprehensible words and pronounce a verdict on events that have already occurred. The very fact that these buried texts speak to us of what happened shows us that Hitler did not eradicate Jewish life.

When we write 50 years later of those who wrote as survivors, we bear a moral responsibility because we become witnesses to witnesses. We may have read volumes of testimony, theories of how words recuperate or do not recuperate the past, and thought about the relation between history and memory. If we are Jews, we feel identification with fellow Jews, knowing that even if we lived outside Nazi control, members of our family—perhaps those we have heard of, perhaps those we do not even know existed—have perished. For me, reading the books I discuss in this study requires multiple optics. At times I feel as if I, too, were there in the camps as a witness; I feel the testimonies open my eyes to what the world sometimes would deny. But I also feel that the prior events, so distant, *must* continually be revived as a present. Yet to do that we need to explore memoirs and fictions to understand how and why imagining the Holocaust works not merely for the authors and their original audience, but for us 55 years later. How do we *imagine* the extermination of an entire civilization?

II

Let me look back from my current vantage point as someone who has taught English at Cornell for 30 years. When I was growing up in a community that was one-third Jewish, the Holocaust was a repressed subject. The child of an assimilated family, one that didn't talk much about the Holocaust, I was bar mitzvahed in a temple that my grandfather helped establish in a Long Island suburb, Rockville Centre. He knew not a word of Hebrew or Yiddish and, as were all my grandparents, was born in this country. If my memory is correct, the Holocaust was barely mentioned in the Conservative religious school I attended three times a week until my bar mitzvah at age 13. Why was the Holocaust a suppressed subject? Did American Jews feel they had something to be ashamed of because they did not prevent the destruction of their European counterparts? Did they fear provoking American anti-Semitism by special pleading? Was it that my parents' generation thought that children's sensibilities could not deal with the horrors of genocide?

Jewish silence mirrors the much more striking silence of the American community that, despite the Nuremberg trials and the gruesome pictures in *Life* magazine, chose to repress their guilt not only for assuming the role of helpless onlookers but even for their tacit complicity. We now know how much the American political leadership knew and how little they did about it. Thus a conspiracy of silence mirrored the ineffectuality and complicity of the American political establishment. The atrocities committed against blacks, particularly in the South, rightfully focused attention on civil rights, but there was surprising little linkage to the wartime persecution of Jews, notwithstanding the prominence of Jews in the Civil Rights movement in the fifties and sixties.

Much was made of my maternal grandfather and grandmother as Jewish elders and as Rockville Centre community elders, although in fact they moved back to Manhattan after the war. My mother's family was quite comfortable; my father's quite poor. My father was acceptable (I suspect barely) as an eligible Jewish male; my father's family moved to Rockville Centre to open a dry-cleaning business, one of many not-very-successful enterprises, and my mother's parents brought them clothes. Family pictures with my mother's parents and my father's mother are rather awkward-looking, as if they arrived from different worlds. Bar mitzvahed but not really educated in Jewish religious practices, my father was a CPA, a temple member, and did reasonably well economically, but he never had the elegance of my mother's parents. He was and is a frugal and prudent man.

Both of my grandfathers were German Jews. One grandmother, who was born in St. Louis in 1888, was a Polish Jew, but her family, like all my grandparents, emigrated to the United States at a time close to the Civil War. My mother's mother was descended from Hungarian Jews. As I am reminded when I visit Vienna and Budapest, some of my mother's cooking reflects her Austrian-Hungarian heritage. My mother learned it from her grandmother—my great-grandmother whom I never met—but who lived with her parents and managed the house while my grandmother went to work. About five years ago I saw photographs of my mother's forebears that were never before shown to me, of German Jews in German military uniforms, some born around 1800: my relatives, many of whom must have been left behind and whose children may have died in the Holocaust. My maternal grandfather was a formal man. Until I was ten I thought he took a shower with his tie on. My father's father, born in this country, insisted that his children learn German. I always imagine how German these Jews must have felt even here. What an irony!

While I had some sense of Jewish identity, my growing up was insulated from flagrant anti-Semitism and my friends were just as likely, if not more likely, to be non-Jewish as Jewish. I confronted my Jewish identity when in 1961-62 I spent my junior year in college in what was still postwar Europe; I saw the Anne Frank house, was approached by Jews with numbers on their arms who wanted to meet American Jews, and saw the shards of the Warsaw ghetto. As I drove through Germany a number of times, I slept in inexpensive small guest houses only to awake and see pictures of SS officers on the walls. My sons were bar mitzvahed. Among a small number of Jews in my English Department, I am the only member of the local temple, although I go only on the High Holy Days and never for more than part of the long Conservative services.

I suspect some of my memories are distorted by time and by the demands of narrative teleology that require coherent story. I remain an agnostic, but with deep spiritual (if I may use that term) ties to my Jewish heritage. Passover and Hanukkah mean a great deal as family holidays, and I light the candles on Friday night if I am home—if I remember. My visit to Israel in 1985-86, built around a lecture at Hebrew University in Jerusalem, accentuated my moderate Zionist sympathies. More and more, when I travel in Europe, I visit synagogues and Jewish sites and learn about Jewish history.

III

For several decades, Jewish scholars passionately taught and still teach Anglo-American literature but now many are rethinking whether these professional interests have repressed ethnic concerns. To be sure, *Partisan Review* and *Commentary* had many Jewish writers and argued for the importance of Bellow, Malamud, and Roth. But except for those at Columbia, the Jewish New York intellectuals including figures like Alfred Kazin, Irving Howe, and Leslie Fiedler—all of whose work was mostly on American literature—were considered academic outsiders by many in elite universities in the 1950s and 1960s. In the 1960s every Jewish graduate student knew the fairy tale of Fiedler, exiled in Missoula, Montana, where he wrote and taught before returning to the East to the State University of New York at Buffalo. While making a substantial reputation based primarily on one important book, *Love and Death in the American Novel* (1960), Fiedler thumbed his nose at the academic establishment and parochial historical criticism and what he saw as the narrow formalism of the New Criticism. Published when he was in his forties, the book was embraced by younger academics and graduate students as relevant to overlooked themes and issues.

At a time when the relevance of literary study was being increasingly called into question by rampant McCarthyism and, later, the Vietnam War, the antiwar protest movement, and the resulting fissures between university and society, Fiedler's book argued that literary study was central to our lives. Fiedler's bold discussion of psychosexual and political issues fulfilled the desire of younger academics for a more lively and engaged critical discourse. For Fiedler, literary criticism is, as he writes in an encomium to his mentor, William Ellery Leonard, "an act of total moral engagement, in which tact, patience, insolence, and piety consort strangely but satisfactorily together; nor can anyone who once listened to him believe that the truth one tries to tell about literature is finally different from the truth one tries to tell about the indignities and rewards of being the kind of man one is—an American, let's say, in the second half of the twentieth century, learning to read his country's books" (Preface, *Love and Death in the American Novel*, n.p.).

Why do assimilated Jewish scholars of different theoretical persuasions who used to discuss passionately Wordsworth and Hardy in the halls now discuss passionately their Jewish pasts and their common interest in Holocaust studies? How do we account for the return of the repressed and the sublimated? Is it because these Jews became tired of "cross-dressing" to gain acceptance in Anglophile English departments within prestigious universities?

When I did my graduate work in English studies, a project such as this book would have been a passport to obscurity. Now it has become the fashionable subject. Jewish scholars—such as Geoffrey Hartman—who decades ago made their careers in English or language studies have returned to their origins. Jewish members of other university departments pride themselves on being part of Jewish studies programs. When and why did this cross-dressing end for Jews in prestigious English departments? For one thing, ethnic studies made it permissible to own one's past; for another, cultural and ethnic studies expanded dramatically the range of what one could address in one's courses and research. In the wake of African American, Asian American, and Native American ethnic consciousness, it became permissible for Jews to discuss their past. That Jewish students wanted courses in their history was demonstrated by the numerical success of Holocaust courses and other Jewish studies courses.

Certainly major English departments in the sixties and seventies were dominated by Anglophile preoccupations. In graduate school many of us read anti-Semitic poems by Eliot and Pound, and barely noticed, or pretended not to notice, that anti-Semitism was not disruptive of the formalist rubric of organic form. We pretended to be part of that imaginary audience of ideal readers on which New Criticism and Aristotelian criticism depended, little realizing that those ideal readers were WASPs. We immersed ourselves in elaborate and arcane Christian theological debate to understand Milton or Hawthorne without reflecting that we were part of a different tradition, but perhaps we took secret satisfaction in the fact that Milton knew Hebrew. Perhaps, too, we took pleasure in knowing that the exegetical tradition of literary criticism resembled the nuances of Talmudic studies, or what we—as assimilated Jews—imagined Talmudic study to be.

Raised in a Jewish home in New York, one distinguished academic wrote on Flannery O'Connor at Berkeley and "identified," as she puts it, with O'Connor's Southern Catholicism rather than with her own marginal situation as a Jew in a gentile universe. When I arrived at Cornell, I encountered in the English department older colleagues who had experienced anti-Semitism and were wary of being "too" Jewish. My generation, too, was taught not to be too Jewish; as another colleague put it, "As a graduate student, I was taught not to walk around with a Hebrew National salami hanging out of my pocket." Virtually none of my Jewish colleagues had synagogue affiliation; some gave almost surreptitiously to the UJA (United Jewish Appeal), while others of Jewish parentage denied their Jewish heritage. One, whose father had been at CCNY with my father, responded tartly to a UJA solicitation, "You must not assume from my name that I have Jewish origins."

As they reach 50 or so and perhaps realizing that their professional lives have not so many years remaining, Jewish scholars begin to go back to their own heritage and history. In some ways, our—for am I not speaking of myself?—collective cultural silence in the Anglophiliac world of English departments has poignantly (and maybe, we should say, pathetically) mirrored that of some survivors who tried to bury the past. I am thinking of survivors who seem to have successfully put behind them the concentration camp universe, only to find out that the experience cannot be repressed or sublimated. Now some of us want to use the skills we have learned, to reconnect to our European antecedents, whether they be emigrants generations ago or Holocaust survivors. Jews realize that the discontinuity in their history created by mass destruction left not only an absence of specific people, a human loss, but also a generational gap—indeed, an epistemological gap—in their actual and metaphorical lineage. We want to close the gaps in the vertical relations not only with our parents but with our children as well. Realizing perhaps that our own survival depended on a geographic accident, we want to understand the plot that might have been. In Anne Frank's pictures we see our children, our nieces and nephews. We try to build bridges in our memory from our world to the Holocaust's inexplicable erasure of history as well as from our world to what might have been had European Jewry continued to flourish—and we inevitably fail in both endeavors.

IV

Even while providing documentation and testimony, historic perspectives at first inevitably used language to domesticate, naturalize, and confine the Holocaust. We might recall Cynthia Ozick's comments in "Who Owns Anne Frank?," an article that objects to her being turned into an idealized and universal adolescent:

> Yet any projection of Anne Frank as a contemporary figure is an unholy speculation: it tampers with history, with reality, with deadly truth. "When I write," she confided, "I can shake off all my cares. My sorrow disappears, my spirits are revived!" But she could not shake off her capture and annihilation, and there are no diary entries to register and memorialize the snuffing of her spirit. . . . She was designated to be erased from the living, to leave no grave, no sign, and no physical trace of any kind. Her fault—her crime—was having been born a Jew, and as such she was classified among those who had no right to exist: not as a subject people, not as an inferior breed, not even as usable slaves. The military civilian apparatus of an entire society was organized to obliterate her as a contaminant, in the way of a noxious and repellent insect. (76)

Ozick reminds us how the Holocaust was transformed and domesticated in Otto Frank's editing of the diary and in the Broadway dramatization by the husband-and-wife team of Frances Goodrich and Albert Hackett: "Where the diary touched on Anne's consciousness of Jewish fate or faith, they quietly erased the reference or changed its emphasis. Whatever the specific they made generic. The sexual tenderness between Anne and the young Peter van Daan was moved to the forefront. Comedy overwhelmed darkness. . . . " (Ozick, "Who Owns Anne Frank?" 85). The Hannukah religious liturgy was minimized and the Zionist aspirations of Margot, Anne's sister, disappeared. Ozick objects not only to how the diary was edited and received, but how it was taught as a text about the universal experience of a young adolescent growing up in difficult circumstances.

Otto Frank himself had omitted adolescent musings on sexuality. The German edition's translator, Anne Liebe Schütz, further edited the diary to minimize criticism of the Germans; Ozick quotes Schütz: "A book intended after all for sale in Germany cannot abuse Germans" (82). Ozick comments on the diary's most famous sentence:

> Yet the diary's most celebrated line (infamously celebrated, one might add)—"I still believe, in spite of everything, that people are truly good at heart"—has been torn out of its bed of thorns. Two sentences later (and three weeks before she was seized and shipped to Westerbork), the diarist sets down a vision of darkness:
>
> "I see the world being slowly transformed into a wilderness, I hear the approaching thunder that, one day, will destroy us too, I feel the suffering of millions. . . . In the meantime, I must hold on to my ideals. Perhaps the day will come when I'll be able to realize them!" (81)

Ozick angrily complains how the historically ironic "truly good at heart" shibboleth has been distorted:

> Why should this sentence be taken as emblematic, and not, for example, another? "There's a destructive urge in people, the urge to rage, murder, and kill," Anne wrote on May 3, 1944, pondering the spread of guilt. These are words that do not soften, ameliorate, or give the lie to the pervasive horror of her time. Nor do they pull the wool over the eyes of history. (81)

Ozick reminds us, too, that Anne Frank's diary has been misread as a conventional testimony of a middle class adolescent experiencing mild *angst*, while in fact it should be read as a "story of fear. . . . Betrayal and arrest always threaten. Anxiety and immobility rule" (78).

Thus the story of Anne Frank becomes a miniature of how the Holocaust is not only domesticated and naturalized but also debated and reinterpreted. Finally, the diary reveals as much about the reader as the writer. Otto Frank is only the first of a series of "readers" of the originating experience; Meyer Levin, and later, the Hacketts and Lillian Hellman are the next group; but we too are part of the sequence. And is this not true for each reader-interpreter of Holocaust texts? And does not the ethics of reading require trying to put ourselves both inside and outside the texts?

V

One point of departure must be Adorno's famous dictum: "After Auschwitz to write a poem is barbaric." His point was that aesthetic principles "transfigure" and strip of its horror "the unimaginable ordeal" (quoted in Howe, 28). As Howe writes,

> Through a dramatic outburst he probably meant to focus upon the sheer difficulty—the literary risk, the moral peril—of dealing with the Holocaust in literature. It was as if he were saying, "Given the absence of usable norms through which to grasp the meaning (if there is one) of the scientific extermination of millions, given the intolerable gap between the aesthetic conventions and the loathsome realities of the Holocaust, and given the improbability of coming up with images and symbols that might serve as 'objective correlatives' for events that the imagination can hardly take in, writers in the post-Holocaust era might be wise to be silent. Silent, at least, about the Holocaust." (29)

Adorno said that it was barbaric to write *poetry*—which we should understand as a metaphor for imaginative literature—after Auschwitz. But in truth it is barbaric *not* to write poetry, in part because if we do not write imaginative literature, how can there be a post-Holocaust era? We must write about the Holocaust because, as Kenneth Seeskin points out, "Silence can be taken for acquiescence or, in some circles, lack of interest" (Lang 111); put another way, those that perished rely on us to speak. Words have instrumentality when the word *Jew* becomes a fact or thing, a star to be worn, a reason to be defiled. Words also have materiality when they fictively render that process into a text that lives in its effects on others. Narrative provides an order, a sequence, an explanatory concatenation that represents in mediated form a prior reality. Narratives shape events with meaning, purpose, and teleology. Narratives have words and a voice. Because of its witnesses, actual and imaginative, the Holocaust lives as narratives that become part of our lives.

Holocaust literature is the voice of those who all along believed in the ethical and aesthetic dimensions of literature and culture and are once again being heard. Leslie Epstein, author of *King of the Jews,* has argued that "our very idea of what the Holocaust was . . . depend[s] upon what artists make of it" (Lang 269); while Epstein's words may seem hyperbolic, they are nevertheless more and more true as the survivors pass away and the written and oral records that they leave behind become necessarily the material for future imaginative reconstructions. Claude Lanzmann notes, "The destruction of Europe's Jews cannot be logically deduced from any . . . system of presuppositions. . . . Between the conditions that permitted extermination and the extermination itself—the *fact* of the extermination—there is a break in continuity, a hiatus, an abyss" (Howe 28). But it is the artistic rendering of the Holocaust that will keep it alive in the imagination particularly as memoirists dwindle. The word and the image have rescued the Holocaust from oblivion even if they cannot bring back its victims. Fifty years later the Holocaust lives because the Nazis' genocidal efforts to erase all traces of a people and to deprive the Jews of their private selves have been flouted by word and image.

Let us look briefly at the issues raised by Lanzmann's *Shoah* ("annihilation" in Hebrew), a film of epic length and incredible force that was released in 1985 but that he compiled, produced, and edited over a period of eleven years. We shall see that this film not only introduces major *topoi* that recur in our texts, but some of the ethical questions about how the Holocaust has been and should be rendered. The film is an extended exploration of the scorched memories of the victims and the repression of the perpetrators and the bystanders and witnesses who were complicit by their silence. Smoking incessantly, speaking gently, Lanzmann zealously follows the tracks of history; indeed, we are struck by how the railway transports of humans are so much a part of the retrieved memory of the Shoah's victims and perpetrators. Gathering a huge array of historical evidence intermingled with Raul Hilberg's historical commentary, Lanzmann is a character in his own film: he asks leading questions; fleshes out details; adds at crucial moments in his conversations a quiet and encouraging "Yes"; listens intently, when he uses interpreters, to their words; and tries to ingratiate himself with his witnesses, speaking especially slowly and graciously to surviving Polish and German witnesses—including those who participated as guards and security police—so as to win their confidence, make them comfortable, and engage them in dialogue. His very involvement and subjectivity within his epic film emphatically remind us that there can be no one perspective on these events.

Lanzmann is like a district attorney methodically presenting evidence of past crimes to the grand jury of his viewers. Lanzmann even hunts down some of the living perpetrators. While it has been objected that the film is his personal *J'accuse* rather than a historical document, is it not both? That the editing to nine and a half hours from some 240 hours reflects his personal engagement and excludes material that he did not want to use—including large parts of interviews—reflects the historian's making choice of evidence. Focusing on the extermination of Jews—the very essence of the final solution—rather than the historical context, *Shoah* is a work of art reflecting the perspective of one man who relentlessly shows the pain of victims and the lack of remorse of the perpetrators. But within that single perspective is a complex chorus of voices showing us that history is composed not merely of the actions of the powerful but of the behavior of ordinary people and their retrospective views of it. Rather than having one homogenized voice, history has many voices. As Lanzmann moves from place to place and country to country, he is effective as a character engaged in an Odyssean journey of sense making.

For Lanzmann, the death camps are at the center of a series of concentric circles that radiate outward—circles that include pictures of Polish villages and the countryside where these killings took place, the transport system and the trains that even now continue to run through Poland, the current lives of surviving victims and participants and the places they now live, and the presence of Raul Hilberg, the historian living in Vermont, whose commentaries play an important role.

To be sure Lanzmann is also a deft psychologist; that he shapes his interviews—even when using his Polish interpreter—to probe memo-

ries, to uncover repressed and displaced constructions within his interviewees' psyches, to reenact traumatic experiences, and to locate
epiphanic moments makes the film more compelling. At times he unites
viewer, interviewee, and audience in a redemptive moment; at other
times he joins the audience in asking us to observe the irony of self-
indicting words from a steep and icy peak. And often he achieves the
complex response of sympathy and judgment when we hear about Jews
forced to participate in carrying out German orders.

Lanzmann gradually reveals how the Germans' conquest of Poland
and the extermination of Jews depended in part on how they appropriated language. They renamed the places of rural Poland with German
names. Thus the town of Oswiecim—which had a flourishing Jewish
community since 1250 and had before the Holocaust 7000 Jews and 12
synagogues—became Auschwitz. We learn from witnesses that in
November 1942, the Gestapo used forced labor of Jewish workers to dig
up the bodies of those gassed from the Vilna ghetto. They were forced
to work with their bare hands and were beaten; they were not allowed
to call the bodies that they excavated from burning "victims" or
"corpses," but rather had to call them *"figuren"* (dolls), or *"schmatten"* (rags).
The Germans wanted to erase all traces of what had happened. As Simon
Srebnik tells us, the dust or powder of Jewish bodies was put in bags and
thrown into the river. After inflicting the ultimate silence, as the Pole Jan
Piwonski and others remind us, the surviving Germans now refuse to
speak. When Lanzmann films Oberhauser, another Nazi factotum,
serving beer in a Munich beer hall, hiding behind dark glasses, and
unwilling to be interviewed or acknowledge a picture of his superior
Wirth, does he not make an eloquent statement about how those who
had appropriated language now would appropriate the silence they once
inflicted on the Jews?

In some ways the very lack of archival footage of Holocaust
material in *Shoah* and the very ordinariness of the current lives of
surviving victims, perpetrators, onlookers, and, yes, interviewers,
interpreters, and cameramen, make what occurred all the more overwhelming. We realize our commonality as mortal human beings taking
pride in a nice house (as one Polish family who lives in what was once
a Grabow Jew's house) or enjoying mountain air (as one former Nazi
now does). Because English subtitles clearly do not include all the

words we hear on screen of those whom he interviews—words translated from Polish, English, and German to French and back to English—one wonders what one does *not* read in the English subtitles. After Lanzmann promises a former Treblinka guard, Franz Suchomel—whom he gets to describe how the Treblinka killing system worked—that he will not reveal his name, he does so. To create a comfortable chatty environment between himself and former Nazis like Suchomel and a security guard at Treblinka named Schlapper, he has his crew film some of the interviews with former Nazis from a remote truck. In blurry black and white, the grainy texture of these pictures distances the figures.

In addition to criticizing him for being too much a character in his supposed documentary, other questions too have been raised about Lanzmann's ethics of inquiry. For example, some have complained that Abraham Bomba, who survived because he was the barber of Treblinka, is depicted cutting hair in Israel even though he was in fact a retired barber. But is this not an example of a film director creating an artistic affect by his selection and arrangement, in this case juxtaposing a careful haircut with the one minute Bomba took to take off all the hair from those awaiting the gas chambers? Jan Karski, who was sent to the West to tell the world what was occurring, complains that most of his interview was cut, but is not this the privilege of the filmmaker? Lanzmann has also been faulted for the accuracy of the translations from Polish to French, particularly those of Barbara Janica, who may not have understood French perfectly and may have missed the questions Lanzmann wanted her to ask the Poles and the answers she translated back into French for him.

The first part focuses more on the gassing in trucks at Chelmno, and the gradual development of the camps at Auschwitz, Treblinka, Sobibor, and, to a lesser degree Belzec, which Camp Commandant Wirth had used as what Suchomel calls a "laboratory" for Treblinka. Gradually, in Part One, we see how history insists on revealing the secrets of the "final solution" buried under the surface of the beauty of contemporary rural Poland, evoked in the opening scenes, and the hum and buzz of daily life in the Poland of the 1980s. The juxtaposition of the natural beauty and the quiet community life of the 1980s with the historical horror compellingly emphasizes the magnitude of what occurred. That these functionaries—the guards such as Franz Suchomel; Jan Piwonski, who was the assistant railroad switchman at Sobibor; and the man who was second in command of the Warsaw Jewish ghetto—survive and speak about their experiences as if they were simply talking about pedestrian jobs is most effective. Lanzmann juxtaposes his pictures of the contemporary landscape and community life with the memories of Jewish survivors of a rich culture. Thus we see desecrated cemeteries in Lodz and the town of Auschwitz or the Jewish community of Wlodava—a community that ended up in the Sobibor death camp. At Sobibor, explains Piwonski, the same tracks are still there and nothing has changed. In the Polish forest now it is quiet, but as Piwonski tells us, once there were screams, explosions, and gunshots; yet, he recalls, too, that after the transports arrived and the passengers were gassed, a preternatural silence prevailed. Sometimes the Jewish memories of the Holocaust come first and then we have interviews with Poles living in these places. The cumulative testimony of witnesses identified by name become engraved on the geography. Often we hear testimony and see pictures before the speaker is identified.

The very pace of *Shoah's* nine and half hours becomes its argument. Weaving a rich tapestry of pictures and words, Lanzmann focuses on discovering what happened to millions of Jews in rural Poland during World War II. Watching *Shoah* straight through or maybe even over two days enables us to understand the enormity of the war against the Jews, its geographic and technological range, and the number of people required to carry out the task, including enslaved Jews who were forced to do the Germans' bidding. As we see the film taking shape and gathering in intensity, we put aside our misgivings about its length and structural looseness and begin to discover recurring themes and characters. We understand that no matter what its length, the film will always be incomplete, open-ended, and invite further testimony. But is that not part of Lanzmann's point about the need for a continually evolving multivocal history based on individual witnesses self-dramatizing their own roles? With each viewing *Shoah* becomes more compelling. Even if at first those of us who have read widely in Holocaust narratives and history think we are inured to a retroactive view of the Holocaust, the very nominalism, the slow accumulation of detail, overwhelms us. For suddenly a picture, a striking detail, awakens our sensibility and jars us from our complacency: the crematoriums; the functionary serving beer who won't be interviewed; or Henrik Gawkowski, the man who drove the transport trains to Treblinka station and then pushed with his locomotive the trains into the death camp of Treblinka. Gawkowski, who heard screams behind him and is now on a train with the camera crew, claims that he was bribed with vodka and was often drunk—as if that were a partial justification. We see Mr. Borowi, whose land abutted and still abuts Treblinka and hear his voice describing how he had continued farming his land. When we hear how village acquaintances of Borowi talk about how one got used to the "awful screams," we realize that we must not allow ourselves to *get accustomed* to the Holocaust.

What is most impressive is the passionate intensity and, at times, surprising gentleness of some of the survivors (such as Simon Skrebnik, one of the two Chelmno survivors). But equally revealing are some of the interviews with the obtuse functionaries who participated in the atrocities or pretended to be oblivious to them and whose words become nuanced by their very stupidity and denial. We hear the tendency of Germans and Poles to blame the worst behavior on the Ukrainians. But the Jewish interviews are not without their ambiguity. When Filip Muller, who stoked the Auschwitz ovens, tells us, "I was ready to do whatever I was told," we hear resonances of the Germans' excuse that they were only following orders and we think of Jewish Kapos with whips and Jewish policemen in Lodz and Warsaw committing atrocities at the behest of the Germans in exchange for extra food or other favored treatment.

Lanzmann reminds us that words conceal as well as reveal. We hear the interview with the German chief traffic officer for the railroad of the Reich. This man speaks of "resettlement trains," and says, "of course I didn't know [until the end of 1944] . . . [I] was strictly a bureaucrat. . . .We knew nothing, not a clue." He even raises the possibility that the extermination did not happen—before inconsistently saying the Poles knew and could talk about it. The aforementioned Franz Suchomel, one of the guards, describes how Treblinka worked when it was "operating at full capacity," before its capacity for killing was upgraded by more efficient means. Jews waited on the ramp for two or three days because the gas chambers could not "handle the load." Dead bodies from transports "were stacked like wood." Suchomel speaks of Jews who would rather be shot than touch rotting and decomposing bodies from the gas chambers, bodies gruesomely resting next to the gassing facilities. He seems pleased to discriminate between Auschwitz as a "factory" and Treblinka, where by 1942, after the new crematoriums were installed, 3,000 Jews a day were gassed in a "primitive but efficient line of death." Lanzmann deftly gives us the human voices of Treblinka victims in the form of the witnessing testimony of Abraham Bomba, the barber of Treblinka, and the Czech Jew Richard Glazer as they discovered how the annihilation of Jews was taking place in Treblinka. Glazer tells about the "sorting place for the belongings of the gassed." Bomba tells about how "in one second" the concept of family ceased immediately. Both Bomba and Glazer speak of suicides in the barracks. Glazer speaks of the slaughtering process as a "manufacturing" of bodies.

Lanzmann stresses how normal life continued for those outside the Warsaw ghetto and for most of the German and Polish population during the war. We are reminded about this when, after we see the subtitle "Berlin," we see a couple dancing and a woman's voice tells us that in Berlin Jews were rounded up and put in a large dance hall. We might even think of the festive if decadent city of Christopher Isherwood's Berlin stories and their adaptation in *Cabaret*.

Chelmno ("Kulmhof" during the German occupation) is a major focus of the first half of *Shoah*, a film originally shown in two parts. Chelmno was the first place where gas was used; beginning in 1941, 400,000 people were executed. In places like Kolo, which the film shows, Jews were rounded up and taken to the synagogue. But even in the first half, the death camps play an important role. Almost as if to blur the differences in place or to give an overview of what occurred, the film in its early hours moves rapidly without subtitles or clear transitions from Treblinka (where the Warsaw ghetto inhabitants were transported for killing) to Auschwitz to Sobibor. It is as if the dizzyingly rapid change of venue mimes the emotional vertigo of the surprised and confused Jews when by rail they arrived at the camps—thinking, hoping that they were being only "resettled."

Lanzmann presents three very different interviews to give us a sense of how the Jews at Chelmno castle disappeared. Using the remote truck, he interviews Franz Schalling, a former security guard at Chelmno castle, who describes the gassing of Jews with "exhaust fumes" piped into a van. He also explains how he had been asked to sign a document not to speak about what he soon learned was called "the final solution to the Jewish problem." Mordechai Podchlebnik, one of the Jewish workers at Chelmno and one of two Chelmno survivors, gives the victims' perspective. Under the illusion that they were being taken to "delousing centers," the Jews were herded and, when reluctant, beaten into the gassing vans. Podchlebnik, whom we saw earlier, is always smiling. He tries to forget and prefers not to talk about Chelmno. Lanzmann asks why he smiles all the time. Revealing his smile as a masque for his continuing pain, Podchlebnik finally breaks down when recalling how he placed his dead wife in a grave and asked that he himself be killed.

The color pictures of the outside of Schalling's apartment show that he is now living comfortably and contrast with the pictures taken of the interview from the remote truck, pictures that are in black and white as if to capture the texture of the newsreels that first exposed the Holocaust. Finally, Lanzmann gives us a third perspective, that of an elderly German settler in Chelmno: Mrs. Michelsohn, wife of the Nazi, speaks of Chelmno castle as a place "for housing and delousing of Poles"—before Lanzmann provokes her to recall that Poles and Jews were different and that Polish Jews were exterminated. She complains about *her* concerns at the time, namely the sanitary conditions—the lack of toilets—in the "primitive" area where she was settled.

Simon Srebnik, one of two survivors from Chelmno, who at the time of the filming was 47, opens the film singing in a canoe as he returns to Chelmno and Grabow, a still rural Polish town twelve miles from Chelmno, where a prosperous Jewish community once flourished. A simple, handsome man, he survived a bullet in the head. He returns to the geography where he had sung German songs along the river to amuse the Gestapo. The Gestapo had turned him into a privileged mascot who had been taught to sing songs for the Germans about girls "welcoming" soldiers. But the events engraved on his memory are of extermination. In the opening scene, as he walks in the place where two thousand Jews were gassed every day, he describes the gas vans, and how "no one left here." That, while Lanzmann is conducting interviews, other older citizens are peering out the windows behind curtains, mirrors the way that the citizens might have responded when their Jewish neighbors were being deported and when, as one interviewee recalls, Germans tossed kids by their legs into trucks.

Lanzmann's self-dramatized role as a character within his documentary is important in the Grabow scenes. Before taking us to Grabow, a town now devoid of Jews, he reads a letter written by the rabbi of Grabow, Jacob Schumann, to friends in Lodz telling them that Jews are being shot and gassed, a letter that ends with a prayer that the Creator look after the Jews. Lanzmann then raises his head, looks outward to his imagined audience and, speaking directly into the camera, concludes: "The Creator of the Universe did not protect the Jews of Grabow." We see how he wins the confidence of his interviewees by flattery when he tells his interpreter, Barbara Janica, to tell one family who is living in a house formerly owned by Jews that "They live in a lovely house." Lanzmann juxtaposes the religious procession celebrating the Virgin Mary with their hostility toward Jews; he interviews the celebrants on that very day. He focuses on the religious procession to remind us how the Jewish presence has been stamped out.

At one point, toward the end of Part One, the unassuming Simon Srebnik stands outside the church where Jews were rounded up before gassing. In a community barren of Jews, where the synagogue has now become a furniture warehouse and where Poles live in the fine houses built and decorated by Jews, Srebnik stands with Poles, some of whom justify the extermination of the Jews as retribution for Christ's death. Others justify it by arguing that Poles were killed also or that the Jews were the "richest." One Grabow woman says that the townswomen were glad to see the Jewish women go because the Polish men were attracted to them; she claims that the Jewish women thought only of beauty and clothes and had more time to primp. Another says they were unattractive and stank because they were tanners. In a chorus of living anti-Semitism, others say: "Jews and Germans ran Polish industry," "Jews are dishonest," "All Poland was in Jewish hands," "[T]hey exploited Poles . . . by imposing their prices."

After we see Auschwitz for the first time, we learn that it was a Jewish town from which Jews were "expelled and resettled" before they were returned for gassing. At one point, 100,000 bodies from Auschwitz were dug up and burned. In 1942 it was transformed from a labor camp to an extermination camp, but even before the gassing there were crematoriums for disposing of bodies. Germans moved into the area around Auschwitz, and I. G. Farben located a massive factory there. Birkenau, Auschwitz's counterpart camp, was originally a labor camp; there, Russian prisoners provided slave labor. The camp was to hold 120,000 people in barracks that had no inside toilets. Himmler turned to Jews as slave laborers when Goering overruled his using Russian prisoners of war as slave labor. Unlike the other death camps, in Auschwitz Zyklon B rather than carbon monoxide was used.

Some Poles claim to have given—at great risk to themselves—the Jews water when the trains arrived. Mr. Borowi and other Poles in Treblinka make much of their "heroic" behavior. Given the testimony on the part of the Jews of Polish indifference and complicity, and given that some of them repeat anti-Semitic shibboleths, do we believe that the Poles gave them water at risk to themselves? An eloquent witness, Abraham Bomba—who is interviewed on his boat in Israel as if to emphasize that, yes, the survivors, although scarred, have made new lives—claims that the Poles were glad that the Jews were taken away. He recalls, too, how the Germans took valuables from the Jews in exchange for the promise of water and never brought any water. Other Poles claim with great pride to have signaled the Jews arriving in transports to Treblinka station that they were going to die by moving their hands across their throats. But is not Lanzmann implying that this is a pathetic intervention on the part of the Poles? For, we ask, what could the victims *do* with these admonitions? Richard Glazer speaks of seeing a boy make the warning gesture, and we may think of Spielberg's appropriating the gesture in *Schindler's List.* Yet, ironically, when Gawkowski, the man driving the train, wipes the sweat from his neck, he repeatedly moves his hand across his throat in a gesture that suggests throat cutting. What this shows is not only the ambiguity of a gesture now claimed to have been an act of heroism, but possibly how the latent iteration of repressed trauma—what Freud calls the *repetition compulsion*—inadvertently surfaces in Gawkowski's psyche. For us contemporary viewers, that inadvertent gesture could be our response to the desserts of those who participated or stood by while annihilation took place.

VI

The imaginative energy of Holocaust fictional narratives, transmuting facts in the crucible of art, has become more and more prominent a part of how the collective memory of the Holocaust is shaped and survives. As the Holocaust Museum in Washington, D.C., shows us, it is when Holocaust history is personalized and dramatized, when abstractions and numbers give way to human drama, that the distance between us and the victims closes. In a sense Holocaust narratives rescue language from its perversion in such terms as "final solution" or the sign over the inside of the Auschwitz gates, *Arbeit Macht Frei* ("Work will make you free")—an obscene falsehood suggesting that the purpose of the concentration camp was to reform inmates who would then earn their freedom. As Lawrence Langer observes, "the habit of verbal reassurance, through a kind of internal balancing act, tries to make more manageable for an uninitiated audience (and the equally uninitiated author?) impossible circumstances" (*Holocaust Testimonies* 2).

Why were Jews, it is often asked, so compliant with the Holocaust and what effect did that compliance have on subsequent narratives? Jews learned to accommodate their trials and terrors to their history and to see their perils as reiterations of the Destruction of the Temple or the Persecution of the Just Men. Sidra DeKoven Ezrahi perceptively notes: "as the Jews came to live more and more within the elastic bounds of their own internal discourse, the significant historical and geographic coordinates of collective life were located in the suspended time and place of sacred texts, and a lamentation tradition based on archetypal rather than historical memory evolved. . . . The destruction that gave rise to a state of geographical and spiritual exile is balanced by the promise of ultimate redemption" (Lang 139). Certainly the *topoi* of redemption is enacted not only in the presence of Israel in *Schindler's List* (particularly Spielberg's film version), and in Lanzmann's *Shoah* as well as in the Palestine Agency in Green's *Holocaust*, but also even in the very survival of Jews in the United States and Europe and in such diverse texts as Sophie Goetzel-Leviathan's *The War from Within*, Wiesel's *Night*, Epstein's *King of the Jews*, and Spiegelman's *Maus*.

Yet Epstein and, to a lesser extent, Appelfeld and Spiegelman use what Ezrahi has called the "parodic, subversive mode" of creating Holocaust fiction, one that departs from the pattern of suffering followed by redemption (Lang 141). Life in the camps and ghettos, we learn from reading Holocaust narratives and history, was far more complex than we realize. Many of the people remaining in the ghetto opposed the Jewish fighters in the Warsaw ghetto because they thought they could survive better in bunkers if the Nazis didn't know they were in hiding. Déak writes approvingly of Todorov's *Facing the Extreme: Moral Life in the Concentration Camps*: "In the concentration camps, Todorov argues, moral values inevitably conflict with the need to ensure one's own survival, and suffering can make some people better while it degrades others" (Déak 39). As Déak notes, Levi's friend Lorenzo brought him soup every day and perhaps inspired him to "quiet acts of compassion and heroism." Not everybody became demoralized, and "survival was often a question of mutual assistance and community" (Déak 39). That is surely the lesson of Green's fictional partisans in *The Holocaust* and his fictional version of the actual Sobibor rebellion. Déak reminds, too, of what is obvious in Levi, Borowski, and in Spiegelman's *Maus* books, namely that: "Privilege, rank, and power were important words in the camps. . . . The concentration camp, whether at Auschwitz or Siberia, fostered an immensely complex social hierarchy in which some thrived, others survived, and others died" (40). When we recall how Levi writes of a cook's dipping the soup ladle deeper or prisoners having work details as chemists—or recall the shoemakers in Spiegelman's *Maus*—we can see the power of privilege. The Jewish prisoners formed the Sonderkommando—the squad who kept the gas chambers cleaned, who met the trains, and who were eventually shot. Gilbert summons the words of one of the Sonderkommando: "Our kommando always numbered five hundred—we knew, for example, that although Jews had built the camp and installed the death engine, not one of them now remained alive. It was a miracle if anyone survived for five or six months in Belzec" (Gilbert 417).

Perhaps the Sonderkommando's words remind us that it is the *word* that redeems and gives moral meaning to human history. Irving Howe writes, "Holocaust writings often reveal the helplessness of the mind before an evil that cannot quite be imagined, or the helplessness of the imagination before an evil that cannot quite be understood. This shared helplessness is the major reason for placing so high a value on the memoir, a kind of writing in which the author has no obligation to do anything but, in accurate and sober terms, tell what he experienced and witnessed" (30). What Holocaust fiction needs to do, according to Leslie Epstein, author of *King of the Jews*, is "to show what life in the ghettos and camps was really like—that is, reproducing, re-creating, restoring to life, in such a way that the reader feels a sense of connectedness, not dispassion and distance, least of all horror and repugnance, to the events and the characters that, Lazarus-like, are called back from the dead. Indeed, if I might anticipate my final argument, I would go so far as to say that while the historians and rabbis surely seek, and often find, meaning and understanding, they cannot instill the peculiar sense of responsibility that the novelist can—the sort of responsibility for creation that might alone (and here you must forgive me for a vision of pie in the sky) bring about the kind of political change that would make another Holocaust less certain, more unlikely" ("Writing about the Holocaust," Lang 264-65).

The difficulty in reading about the Holocaust has been remarked. Thus, Sidra DeKoven Ezrahi notes, "[T]he distorted image of the human form which the artist might present as but a mirror of nature transformed can hardly be contained within the traditional perimeters of mimetic art, because, although Holocaust literature is a reflection of recent history, it cannot draw upon the timeless archetypes of human experience and human behavior which can render unlived events familiar through the medium of the imagination" (*By Words Alone* 2-3). As such an "exception," Ezrahi continues, "the representation of the Holocaust in art is essentially an oscillation and a struggle between continuity and discontinuity with the cultural as well as the historical past" (*By Words Alone* 4). Perhaps we should say that Holocaust narratives have become a genre with its own archetypes and its own cultural continuity.

VII

I am focusing on the relationship between how narratives are told (their aesthetics) and how they mean (their hermeneutics). I am interested, too, in how they mean differentially for diverse audiences. I see telling as a crucial act, all the more crucial because of the trauma of the originating cause. Because we can never trust memory fully, in narration effects (how a teller presents himself or herself) sometimes *precede cause* (the explanation for why a narrator is the person he or she is.) Originally, Holocaust testimonies like those of Wiesel, Levi, and Anne Frank spoke of the unthinkable. Later fictional narratives such as Hersey's *The Wall*, which documented day-to-day life in the ghettos, were effective at opening the doors to Holocaust hell. Perhaps as time passed we have become somewhat anaesthetized to concentration camp realism and that realism has become slightly clichéd. The exaggerations of Kosinski raised the stakes in the popular imagination beyond which it was hard to go. The mythic and metaphoric rendering of the Holocaust in works such as Epstein's *King of the Jews* and Spiegelman's *Maus* books show how we no longer think of Holocaust narratives as objective truths or events but as the dramatized consciousness of those seeking meaning and explanations, or as dramatizations of the mind seeking appropriate words and images to render experience that seems to defy understanding. But, it might be argued, this makes Holocaust writing no more than a special case of all writing. Perhaps in 1999, metaphoric Holocaust novels written at a distance may work better for us. Even earlier, a book such as *The Last of the Just,* which combined mythic and epic overview with a kind of apocalyptic vision manqué and alternated heightened and realistic language, effectively appealed to the desire for context and scope. The strand of hyperbole looks back immediately to Kafka and Schulz, and earlier to a Jewish tradition that emphasized parable and folk tale—to writers such as Sholem Aleichem—to illustrate values.

While *The Diary of Anne Frank, Night,* and Levi's *Survival at Auschwitz* established the high seriousness and intense attention to the actual facts that we expect if not require of Holocaust narratives, Appelfeld's mocking fables, Spiegelman's comics, Epstein's caricatures and dreamscapes, and Schwarz-Bart's use of myth and legend to structure his narrative are all departures from traditional naturalism and realism. Paradoxically, their very efforts to depart from mimesis break down and show how the searing reality of the Holocaust resists these innovative forms. And it is this tension between putative formal solutions and inchoate resistance that is at the very center of these authors' artistic accomplishment. These more experimental authors acknowledge that representing the Holocaust—like all narrative representations—is a fiction, an illuminating distortion. But paradoxically, their reversion to documentary techniques—for example, the unexpected photographs in *Maus*—and specific detailed testimony of the death camps demonstrate an inner resistance to aesthetic decisions that undermine formal realism or solemnity; they may fear—perhaps unconsciously—that such aesthetic decisions risk dishonoring the dead and trivializing the Holocaust.

It may be that Holocaust narratives enable us to enter into the subjective world of participants and to respond to historical events from their perspective; by walking in their shoes, sharing their pain and fear within the hypothesis "as if," the reader of Holocaust texts lives uniquely in fictive universes. The limits of our language, Wittgenstein taught us, are the limits of the world; the search for fictions to render the Holocaust, the quest for form and meaning, is different in degree but not kind from other artistic quests, and it does no dishonor to memory to say so. If the Nazis succeeded in turning words into charred bone and flesh, skeletons that survived in terror, bodies almost completely deprived of their materiality, then writing about the Holocaust paradoxically restores the uniqueness of the human spirit by restoring the imaginative to its proper place and breathes new life into the materiality of victims and survivors. Were the victims to remain numb and mute, they would remain *material* without soul as well as participate in an amnesia that protected the culprits.

Each of the books I shall be discussing depends on the *power* of content and most depend on aesthetic minimalism. In his essay "After the Holocaust," Appelfeld has written that "the problem, and not only the artistic problem, has been to remove the Holocaust from its enormous, inhuman dimensions and bring it close to human beings" (Lang 92). Unlike other art, which requires intensification, he argues that the Holocaust "seems so thoroughly unreal" that we "need to bring it down to the human realm" (Lang 92). In a folk version of the suffering, lamentation, and redemption in Jewish biblical and actual history, shtetl Jews learned that falling down and getting up needed to be one motion if they were to survive. Each of our texts tells of individuals reclaiming their private identity and imagination, and that reclamation is a secularization of the traditional redemption *topoi.*

The intelligibility of history, even the place of evil in history, depends on reconfiguring it in imaginative and aesthetic terms. Many of our texts encode catastrophe without resort to apocalyptic visions. Writers as diverse as Primo Levi, Elie Wiesel, Aharon Appelfeld, Tadeusz Borowski, John Hersey, and, yes, Anne Frank and Jerzy Kosinski all understand that, as Langer puts it, "the Holocaust does little to confirm theories of moral reality but much to question the reality of moral theories" (198). They understand that, as Langer puts it, "Auschwitz permanently destroyed the potency of the sedative we call illusion" (*Holocaust Testimonies*, 4). All of these writers understand how we domesticate the implausible and unthinkable into experiences within our ken. What these works have in common is brevity, a spare style, a childlike vision of the adult world, an ingenuousness through which horrors are realized, the desire to humanize an experience without losing its mythic quality, and a structural principle that ostentatiously highlights and foregrounds some episodes at the expense of others. Each traces the gradual devolution of an organic community in the face of the Nazi parasite.

Most of our texts begin in a pedestrian world of apparent normalcy, within a seemingly stable culture. What follows is usually a progressive narrative of disruption and deterioration, a teleology of unweaving the strands of individual and cultural constructions, until Jews are faced with unspeakable horrors of hunger, starvation, deportation, disease, crematoriums, and death marches. In Wiesel's case the very emphasis on graphic details paradoxically has the fabric of a dreamscape. It is as if imagining the Holocaust requires metaphors and parables. Of course, different writers choose different approaches. *Night* and *Survival at Auschwitz* are memoirs, but they exist on the borderland between fact and fiction. In each, the artist shapes his vision into a coherent form, highlighting some episodes that have value in terms of his structure, while discarding or giving minimal attention to others. Dresden makes an important distinction between chronicle and diary:

> Like the chronicle, the diary progresses in time, but while the chronicle chooses to do so and could possibly refrain from following temporal order or change it, the diary is forced to fulfill the chronological requirement. We are dealing here with a series of events that can be described and discussed freely in many respects, but with respect to the order of which little or nothing can be changed. It is a fundamental given that a diary is committed to following the normal progression of time. (29)

He further discriminates between memoirs and diaries:

> These memoirs have in common with diaries the fact that the authors speak of their own experiences and take themselves as

starting-point. In that respect, both forms of writing have the same kind of authenticity. But while the writer of a diary is on the spot, the writer of memoirs implicitly has been on the spot. His presence belongs to the past and he writes about a time that is past perfect, even though he may use notes or even diary entries he made at the time. One thing is characteristic of this form, however, and not only where war memoirs are concerned: memory and distance in time always change the data that are available and falsify, as it were, the reality of the past, for they have an apologetic purport that originates not in the past reality but in the present time, which obtrudes in the interpretation of the events. (31-32)

Perhaps all Holocaust fiction is disguised autobiography. The personal is rarely far from Holocaust texts, whether they purport to be autobiographical or not. Whether in autobiography or fiction, surviving children—Kosinski, Wiesel, and Appelfeld—tell stories in which they struggle with trauma and try to rescue themselves from history. In language reaching back and reconnecting with Shoah, they strive to reestablish a lineage, a paternity to which the self has a link, and try to wrench themselves from history even while acknowledging history. Wiesel is twelve in 1941, and his is the story of adolescence. Appelfeld was born in 1932 and, as a young boy, after his mother was killed, escaped from a labor camp. Kosinski, we now know, invented himself, and in a much less flagrant way, Appelfeld recreated himself as an Israeli novelist. Schwarz-Bart is a survivor but chooses a mythic approach to give shape and order to the history he has lived through; he imagines the end of a centuries-old family line, even as we hear his voice establishing another one. The son of a survivor, born in 1948, Spiegelman discovers a new genre, uniting cartoons with documentary as he seeks to overcome mental illness and alienation and to discover himself.

What the aforementioned writers are implicitly arguing is that to know ourselves we have to write ourselves, make a record. All are fictions—more or less stories about personal and historic memory. And Spiegelman's cartoons are no different. He treasures the notes and tapes he makes in interviews with his father because by telling the story of his father, he tells his own story and thus better understands himself. His artist-narrator's greatest rage is at his father for destroying his mother's wartime memoirs.

What is striking about Appelfeld's *Badenheim 1939* is that its characters suffer short-term amnesia—because of their inability to face the reality of their circumstances—and are unable to weave the concatenation of events into a narrative. They are caught out of time and out of language when the external fantasy of the seasonal vacation becomes the internal fantasy—or vacation from memory and consciousness—of amnesia and escape. If individual amnesia is a grotesque vacating of self, is not cultural amnesia the vacating of history? Lacking memory, the people of Badenheim don't know themselves. Yet are they not metonymies for those who refuse to address the realities in which they live? Do they not remind us that writing is recovery, return of memory, a reestablishing dialogue between self and world?

Our procedure will be to start with the most autobiographical of texts, *The Diary of Anne Frank*, Wiesel's *Night*, and Levi's *Survival at Auschwitz*, and then move to postwar memoirs like Levi's *The Reawakening* and Goetzel-Leviathan's affirmative reminiscence, *The War Within*. What is a testimony? *Webster's Dictionary* defines it as a "declaration or statement meant to establish a fact, especially one made under oath by a witness in a court" but also as an "affirmation." While Goetzel-Leviathan's text is most ostentatiously an affirmation of life, in more muted terms so are the texts of Levi, Wiesel, and Anne Frank. And there is an aspect of testimony to Wiesel's and Levi's memoirs—and perhaps in the sense of the first *Webster* definition—to most Holocaust fiction. In the Levi chapter we shall move to more allusive and allegorical nonfiction like *The Periodic Table* before taking up realistic fictions posing as autobiography like Kosinski's *The Painted Bird* and Borowski's *This Way for the Gas, Ladies and Gentlemen*. Dresden comments on Borowski, reminding us that literary techniques such as ambiguity and indirection are important and that we need consider these texts as narrative art:

> So what Borowski expresses in the title can be summarized as follows: in one short, brief sentence that of course was never spoken, he catches the gas and the politeness, and thus, by means of standard expressions, brings together total contrasts. The whole produces a frightful effect, because an innocent and widely

accepted manner of speaking is slightly altered and adjusted to fit a situation in which it does not fit at all. One may think of the sarcastic cynicism that in all likelihood is there, or of the irony that is clearly present. But first and foremost, attention should be given to the distancing and especially to the indirectness that evokes the gassing, as it were, and maybe [sic: not] only evokes it but accepts it as a "fact of life." (48)

We then turn to such realistic fictions as John Hersey's *The Wall*, Green's *Holocaust*, and Keneally's *Schindler's List*. James E. Young noted of Holocaust documentary fiction:

> [B]y mixing actual events with completely fictional characters, a writer simultaneously relieves himself of an obligation to historical accuracy (invoking poetic license), even as he imbues his fiction with the historical authority of real events. By inviting this ambiguity, the author of documentary fiction would thus move the reader with the pathos created in the rhetoric of historically authentic characters, even as he suggests the possibility that both his events and those in the world are fictional. ("Holocaust Documentary Fiction: The Novelist as Eyewitness" 201-202)

But, we shall ask, does the ontology of *Sophie's Choice* (one of his examples of documentary fiction) work? The pressure of fact and history, I think, cries out and overwhelms the fictive ontology. Young continues:

> Several other questions arise at this point. First, why is the writer of Holocaust fiction so forcefully compelled to assert the factual basis underlying his work? That is, why is it so important for [some] novelists to establish an authoritative link between their fictions and the Holocaust experiences they represent? Second, to what extent are this literature's dramatic interests, and its supposed documentary interests, served in such claims to historical authority? And how does the perception of authority in the Holocaust novel affect the way readers approach and respond to Holocaust fiction? That is, can Holocaust documentary fiction ever really document events, or will it always fictionalize them? . . . The

difference between fictional and nonfictional "documentary narratives" of the Holocaust may not be between degrees of actual evidential authority, but between the ontological sources of this sense of authority: one is retrieved and one is constructed wholly within the text as part of the text's fiction. As it was for the diaries and memoirs, the operative trope underpinning the documentary character of Holocaust fiction is the rhetorical principle of testimony or witness, not its actuality. ("Holocaust Documentary Fiction" 202, 212)

Finally, we take up allegorical fiction like Schulz's *Cinnamon Shops* and Appelfeld's *Badenheim 1939* and *The Retreat*, the mythopoeic *The Last of the Just*, the fable *King of the Jews*, and the illuminating distortions in Spiegelman's cartoons in the *Maus* books. We shall look at the strand of Holocaust fiction that seeks to transcend realism and looks for imaginative and innovative forms of knowing to render the Holocaust. Spiegelman as cartoonist, Epstein as Rabelaisian entertainer, and Appelfeld as chronicler of a make-believe resort town all choose to set themselves obliquely at odds with traditional mimesis. They use a kind of metaphorical narrative at odds with traditional realism. Just as Spiegelman depicts the Germans as cats harassing the Jewish mice, Appelfeld finds his metaphors in "Sanitation workers" harassing the residents and guests of a mysteriously contaminated Jewish resort. Many of our writers adhere to a kind of minimalism—to, as Raul Hilberg puts it, "the art of using the minimum of words to say the maximum" ("I Was Not There" 23); they avoid trivialization and respect the need for silence. As we shall see, the tension between speaking and silence, between reclaiming life by means of language and images in the face of stories of extermination and torture, is a recurring theme of Holocaust narratives and a crucial component of their forms.

PART ONE

MEMOIRS

CHAPTER ONE

THE ETHICS OF READING ELIE WIESEL'S *NIGHT*

FROM A DEAD CHILD SPEAKS
My mother held me by my hand.
Then someone raised the knife of parting. . . .
—Nelly Sachs
(Translated by Ruth & Matthew Mead)

The survivor . . . is a disturber of the peace. He is a runner of the blockade men erect against knowledge of "unspeakable" things. About these he aims to speak, and in so doing he undermines, without intending to, the validity of existing norms. He is a genuine transgressor, and here he is made to feel real guilt. The world to which he appeals does not admit him, and since he has looked to this world as the source of moral order, he begins to doubt himself. And that is not the end, for now his guilt is doubled by betrayal—of himself, of his task, of his vow to the dead. The final guilt is not to bear witness. The survivor's worst torment is not to be able to speak.

—Terence Des Pres,
The Survivor: An Anatomy of Life in the Death Camps, 42-43

I

In considering ethical reading, I want to suggest that we differentiate between an *ethics of reading* and an *ethics while reading*. For me, an ethics of reading includes acknowledging who we are and what are our biases and interests. An ethics *of* reading speaks of our reading as if, no matter how brilliant, it were proposing some possibilities rather than vatically providing the solution to Daniel's prophetic reading of handwriting on the wall; it means reading from multiple perspectives, or at least empathetically entering into the readings of those who are situated differently. For me, an ethics while reading would try to understand what the author was saying to her original imagined audience and both why and how the actual polyauditory audience might have responded and for what reasons. An ethics *while* reading is different from but, in its attention to a value-oriented epistemology, related to an ethics of reading. An ethics *while* reading implies attention to moral issues generated by events described within an imagined world. It asks what ethical questions are involved in the act of transforming life into art, and notices such issues as Pound's or Eliot's anti-Semitism and the patronizing racism of some American nineteenth- and early twentieth-century writers. What we choose to read and especially what to include on syllabi has an ethical dimension. Thus, I will choose to select other Conrad works for my undergraduate lecture course than the unfortunately titled *The Nigger of the "Narcissus."*

Let me tentatively propose five stages of the hermeneutical activities involved in ethical reading and interpretation. Even while acknowledging that my model is suggestive rather than rigorous, I believe that we do perceive in stages that move from a naive response or surface interpretation to critical or in-depth interpretation and, finally, to understanding our readings conceptually and ethically in terms of other knowledge. Awareness of such stages enables us to read ethically. My stages are:

1. *Immersion in the process of reading and the discovery of imagined worlds.* Reading is a place where text and reader meet in a transaction. As we open a text, we and the author meet as if together we were going to draw a map on an uncharted space. We partially suspend our

sense of our world as we enter into the imagined world; we respond in experimental terms to the episodes, the story, the physical setting, the individualized characters as humans, and the telling voice. While it has become fashionable to speak dismissively of such reading as "naive" or the result of the "mimetic illusion," in fact how many of us do not read in that way with pleasure and delight—and with ethical judgments? Who of us would be teaching and studying literature had we not learned to read mimetically?

2. *Quest for understanding.* Our quest is closely related to the diachronic, linear, temporal activity of reading. The quest speaks to the gap between "What did you say?" and "What did you mean?" In writing, as opposed to speech, the speaker cannot correct, intrude, or qualify; she cannot use gestures or adjust the delivery of her discourse. Because in writing we lack the speaker's help, we must make our own adjustments in our reading. As Paul Ricouer notes, "What the text says now matters more than what the author meant to say, and every exegesis unfolds its procedures within the circumference of a meaning that has broken its moorings to the psychology of its author" (191). We complete the sign of the imagined world by providing the signified, but no sooner do we complete a sign than it becomes a signifier in search of a new signified. In modern and postmodern texts, our search for necessary information will be much more of a factor than in traditional texts. In this stage, as we are actively unraveling the complexities of plot, we also seek to discover the principles or worldview by which the author expects us to understand characters' behavior in terms of motives and values. Moreover, we make ethical judgments of intersubjective relations *and* authorial choices.

3. *Self-conscious reflection.* Reflection speaks to the gap between "What did *you* mean?" and "What does *that* mean?" Upon reflection, we may adjust our perspective or see new ones. What the interpretive reader does—particularly with spare, implicatory modern literature—is to fill the gaps left by the text to create an explanatory text or *midrash* on the text itself. As Iser puts it, "What is said only appears to take on significance as a reference to what is not said; it is the implications and not the statements that give shape and weight to the meaning" (Suleiman and Crosman, 111). While the reader half-

perceives, half-creates his original "immersed" reading of the text, he retrospectively—from the vantage point of knowing the whole—imposes shape and form on his story of reading. He discovers its significance in relation to his other experiences, including other reading experiences, and in terms of the interpretive communities to which he belongs. He reasons posteriorly from effects to causes. He is aware of referentiality to the anterior world—how that world informs the author's mimesis—and to the world in which he lives. He begins—more in modern texts, but even in traditional texts—to separate his own version of what is really meant from what is said, and to place ethical issues in the context of larger value issues.

Here Todorov's distinction between signification and symbolization is useful: "Signified facts are *understood*: all we need is knowledge of the language in which the text is written. Symbolization facts are *interpreted*: and interpretations vary from one subject to another" (Suleiman and Crosman 73). A problem is that in practice, what is understood or judged by one reader as signified facts may require interpretation or a different ethical judgment by another.

4. *Critical analysis.* As Paul Ricouer writes, "To understand a text is to follow its movement from sense to reference, from what it says to what it talks about" (214). In the process, we always move from signifier to signified; for no sooner do we understand what the original signifiers signify within the imagined world than these signifieds in turn become signifiers for larger issues and symbolic constructions in the world beyond the text. And we respond in terms of the *values* enacted by the agon and, as with Eliot's and Pound's anti-Semitism, resist where texts disturb our sense of fairness.

While the reader responds to texts in such multiple ways and for such diverse reasons that we cannot speak of a correct reading, we can speak of a dialogue among plausible readings. Drawing upon our interpretive strategies, we reflect on generic, intertextual, linguistic, and biographical relationships that disrupt linear reading; we move back and forth from the whole to the part. As Ricouer writes: "The reconstruction of the text as a whole is implied in the recognition of the parts. And reciprocally, it is in constructing the details that we construe the whole" (204). My responses to my reading are a function of what I know, what I have recently been reading, my last experience of reading a particular author, my knowledge of the period in which she wrote as well as the influences upon her and her influence on others, *and* my current values. My responses also depend both on how willing I am to suspend my irony and detachment and enter into the imagined world of the text and on how much of the text my memory retains.

5. *Cognition in terms of what we know.* In a continuation of our fourth stage, we return to the original reading experience and text and subsequently modify our conceptual hypotheses about genre, period, author, canon, themes, and, most of all, *values.* We integrate what we have read into our reading of other texts and into our way of looking at ourselves and the world. Here we consciously use our values and our categorizing sensibility—our rage for order—to make sense of our reading experience and our way of being in our world. In the final stage, the interpretive reader may become a critic who writes his own text about the "transaction" between himself and the text—and this response has an ethical component. Novels raise different ethical questions, ones that enable us to consider not only how we would behave in certain circumstances, but also whether—even as we empathetically read a text—we should maintain some stance of resistance by which to judge that text's ethical implications.

II

Let us now turn to our example. Elie Wiesel begins *Night,* his fictionalized autobiographical memoir of the Holocaust, with a description of Moshe the Beadle, an insignificant figure in a small town in Transylvania who taught the narrator about the cabbala: "They called him Moshe the Beadle, as though he had never had a surname in his life. He was a man of all work at a Hasidic synagogue. The Jews of Sighet—that little town in Transylvania where I spent my childhood—were very fond of him. He was very poor and lived humbly. . . . He was a past master in the art of making himself insignificant, of seeming invisible. . . . I loved his great, dreaming eyes, their gaze lost in the distance" (1). But Moshe is expelled in early 1942 because he is a foreign Jew, and is not heard of for several months. He unexpectedly returns to tell of his miraculous escape from a Gestapo slaughter of Jews in the Polish forests. But no one believes him. Moshe cries: "Jews, listen to me. . . . Only listen to me" (5). Everyone assumes that he has gone mad. And the narrator—still a young boy—recalls asking him: "Why are you so anxious that people should believe what you say? In your place, I shouldn't care whether they believed me or not" (5).

Let us consider the significance of Moshe the Beadle. For one thing, Wiesel is using him as metonymy for himself in his present role as narrator who is, as he writes, calling on us to listen to his words as he tells his relentless tale of his own miraculous escape from the Nazi terror. Implicitly, he is urging us that it is our ethical responsibility not to turn away from the witnessing voice—Moshe, Wiesel himself, indeed all those who have seen specifically the Holocaust, and by extension man's inhumanity to man, whether it occurs in Kosovo, Bosnia, Northern Ireland, or Somalia.

Night is a narrative that traces the dissolution of the Jewish community in Sighet, the ghettos, deportations, concentration camps, crematoriums, death marches, and, ultimately, liberation. Distilling memoir into narrative form, *Night* traces the growth of adolescent courage and the weakening, questioning, and—notwithstanding his praying during the death march—finally the loss of religious faith. Wiesel's original Yiddish title for *Night* was *Un di velt hot geshvign*, or, in English, *And the World Remained Silent.* He distilled 862 pages to the 245 of the published Yiddish edition and Jérôme Lindon, the French publisher, further edited it to 178 pages. I am interested not in indicting Wiesel for transforming his nominalistic memoir into novel-istic form, but in how, in response to publishing circumstances and perhaps his own transformation, he reconfigured an existential novel about the descent into moral night into a somewhat affirmative reemergence to life. While the narrator is a fifteen-year-old boy, Wiesel was born in 1928 and would have been sixteen for most of the 1944-45 period. Is not this age discrepancy one reason why we ought to think of *Night* as a novel as well as a memoir?

Another more important reason *Night* is a novel is that there was a substantive change from the original Yiddish text submitted in 1954, months before Wiesel met Mauriac, and 1958 when the French version was published. In 1956, it was volume 117 of a series on Polish Jews entitled *Dos polyishe yidntum* (Polish Jewry). Wiesel's title was *Un di velt hot geshvign*. Naomi Seidman writes of the Yiddish text:

> What distinguishes the Yiddish from the French is not so much length as attention to detail, an adherence to that principle of comprehensiveness so valued by the editors and reviewers of the Polish Jewry series. Thus, whereas the first page of *Night* succinctly and picturesquely describes Sighet as "that little town in Transylvania where I spent my childhood," *Un di velt* introduces Sighet as "the most important city [*shtot*] and the one with the largest Jewish population in the province of Marmarosh." The Yiddish goes on to provide a historical account of the region: "Until the First World War, Sighet belonged to Austro-Hungary. Then it became part of Romania. In 1940, Hungary acquired it again." And while the French memoir is dedicated "in memory of my parents and of my little sister, Tsipora," the Yiddish names both victims and perpetrators: "This book is dedicated to the eternal memory of my mother Sarah, my father Shlomo, and my little sister Tsipora—who were killed by the German murderers."
>
> The Yiddish text may have been only lightly edited in the transition to French, but the effect of this editing was to position the memoir within a different literary genre. Even the title *Un di velt hot geshvign* signifies a kind of silence very distant from the mystical silence at the heart of *Night*. The Yiddish title indicts the world that did nothing to stop the Holocaust and allows its perpetrators to carry on normal lives; *La Nuit* names no human or even divine agents in the events it describes. From the historical and political specificities of Yiddish documentary testimony, Wiesel and his French publishing house fashioned something closer to mythopoetic narrative (5).

What Seidman calls the "mythopoetic narrative," I would call a novel with a central agon, a structure of affects, a narrative voice, an imagined narratee (the implied listener to the narrator), and an ending that transforms, modifies, and reformulates what precedes.

Whether a novel or memoir, *Night* depends upon and affirms the concept of individual agency, for the speaker tells a wondrous and horrible tale of saving his life and shaping his role as Witness, perhaps our Daniel. As Terence Des Pres writes:

> Silence is the only adequate response, but the pressure of the scream persists. This is the obsessive center of Wiesel's writing: his protagonists desire a silence they cannot keep. . . . The conflict between silence and the scream, so prominent in Wiesel's novels, is in fact a battle between death and life, between allegiance to the dead and care for the living, which rages in the survivor and resolves itself in the act of bearing witness. . . .
>
> Silence, in its primal aspect, is a consequence of terror, of a dissolution of self and world that, once known, can never be fully dispelled. But in retrospect it becomes something else. Silence constitutes the realm of the dead. It is the palpable substance of those millions murdered, the world no longer present, that intimate absence—of God, of man, of love—by which the survivor is haunted. In the survivor's voice the dead's own scream is active. (36)

In *Night* we see dramatized the process of the narrator's developing into his role of ethical witness in the face of historical forces that would obliterate his humanity, his individuality, and his voice. Notwithstanding the grotesque efficiency of Nazi technology in the death camps—especially the gas chambers and crematoria—the narrator re-creates himself through language. In the sense of the technological fulfillment of an ordered state that subordinated individual rights to the national purpose of the State, Nazi ideology has been thought of as a product of industrial and technological modernism. For those, like Wiesel, who have experienced the Holocaust first hand, for whom Auschwitz is not a metaphor but a memory, language is more than the free play of signifiers. For these people and others on the political edge, their very telling—their very living—testifies to will, agency, and a desire to survive that resists and renders morally irrelevant simple positivistic explanations arguing that an author's language is culturally produced.

One might ask why Wiesel writes. For one thing, it is to bear witness; for another, it is an act of self-therapy; for a third, it is a kind of transference; and as the dedication stresses ("In memory of my parents and of my little sister, Tzipora"), it is an act of homage. Furthermore, in psychoanalytic linguistic terms, the narrator's telling is a resistance to the way in which the word "Jew" was culturally produced to mean inferior people who were progressively discounted, deprived of basic rights as citizens, labeled with a yellow star of David, imprisoned, enslaved, and killed. We might recall how all male German Jews were required to take the middle name "Israel," all females the name "Sarah."

Cultural modernism, as James Clifford notes, takes "as its problem—and opportunity—the fragmentation and juxtaposition of cultural values" (117). Wiesel's novel/memoir *Night* is an essentialist rejection of that fragmentation and juxtaposition even as its form records in fragments the grotesque consequences in Europe of their occurrence. According to Wiesel, "the Holocaust in its enormity defies language and art, and yet both must be used to tell the tale, the tale that must be told" (Muschamp, "Shaping a Monument's Memory" 1). The very opening, "They called him Moshe the Beadle," is a storyteller's invitation to step into another world. As with any life writing, the selection and arrangement into narrative blur the line between fiction and fact, and the inclusion of dialogue, recalled at an immense distance of years, contributes to the novelistic aspect of his memoir.

Wiesel explains in his essay "An Interview Unlike Any Other" why he waited ten years to write his memoir:

> I knew the role of the survivor was to testify. Only I did not know how. I lacked experience, I lacked a framework. I mistrusted the tools, the procedures. Should one say it all or hold it all back? Should one shout or whisper? Place the emphasis on those who were gone or on their heirs? How does one describe the indescribable? How does one use restraint in re-creating the fall of mankind and the eclipse of the gods? And then, how can one be sure that the words, once uttered, will not betray, distort the message they bear?
>
> So heavy was my anguish that I made a vow: not to speak, not to touch upon the essential for at least ten years. Long enough to see clearly. Long enough to learn to listen to the voices crying inside my own. Long enough to regain possession of my memory.

Long enough to unite the language of man with the silence of the dead. (*A Jew Today*, 15)

Night is a spare, rough-hewn text that is an eloquent testimony depending on human agency and ethical commitment. *Night* reminds us, too, that the concept of author-function as a substitute for the creating intelligence does not do justice to the way in which language and art express the individual psyche. Readers will recall that the book's signification depends on a taut structure underpinning an apparently primitive testimony and depends, too, on its spare, even sparse style. Its eloquence derives from its apparent ingenuousness. Yet *Night* speaks on behalf of meaning, on behalf of will—the will to survive, the will to witness—and on behalf of language's signification. *Night* eloquently reminds us of a grotesque historical irony, namely that with its use of modern technology and Enlightenment rationality, Western man's progress led to the efficiency of the Nazi transport system, Nazi work camps, and Nazi gas chambers. *Night* is a text that resists irony and deconstruction, and cries out in its eloquence, pain, and anger as it enacts the power of language. The text traces the death of the narrator's mother, a sister, and finally, his father; it witnesses an encroaching horrible moral night, a night that includes the speaker's loss of religious belief in the face of historical events. Notwithstanding his religious upbringing, Wiesel parts company from those who, as Dawidowicz explains, accept the Holocaust as God's will:

For believing Jews the conviction that their sacrifice was required as a testimony to Almighty God was more comforting than the supposition that He had abandoned them altogether. To be sure, God's design was concealed from them, but they would remain steadfast in their faith. Morale was sustained by rabbis and pious Jews who, by their own resolute and exalted stance, provided a model of how Jews should encounter death. (308)

Perhaps we should for a moment think of the Wiesel's text as a physical object and note its slimness, its titleless chapters, its breaks between anecdotes. We wonder what could be added in those white spaces—whether his loss of faith, for example, is gradual? But the slim volume, the white spaces, become a kind of correlative or metonymy to emptiness, to his "starved stomach" (50). The short paragraphs give a kind of cinematic effect, as if the paragraphs were frames in an evolving film. The very simplicity—the almost childlike quality—of the imagery gives the work its parabolic quality.

Wiesel draws upon a tradition of prophetic hyperbole: "Never shall I forget that night, the first night in camp, which has turned my life into one long night, seven times cursed and seven times sealed. . . . Never shall I forget those moments which murdered my God and my soul and turned my dreams to dust. Never shall I forget these things, even if I am condemned to live as long as God Himself. Never" (32). The camps dissolve traditional morality and replace it with extreme conditions that make the struggle to survive the only value. Thus the death of his father "frees" him to save himself; he is at once "free at last" and emotionally anaesthetized: "nothing could touch me any more" (106-107). We might recall the words of Lucy Dawidowicz:

> The wish to live, the inability to believe in one's own imminent death, the universal human faith in one's own immunity to disaster—all these factors conspired to make the Jews believe that resettlement, not death, was the fact. "At bottom," wrote Freud, "nobody believes in his own death." Not gullibility, or suggestibility, but universal human optimism encouraged them to believe in the deceptions that the Germans perpetrated. In the process of repressing and denying the overpowering threat that confronted them, perceptual distortion and skewed interpretation based on wishful thinking managed to reconcile the illogic and inconsistencies of their fears and hopes. Without accurate information, without corrective feedback from authoritative sources on the course of events, their isolation helped give credence to their distorted and distorting evaluation of their predicament. This mechanism of denial, this arming oneself against disquieting facts, was not pathological, but, as psychologists point out, a tool of adaptation, a means of coping with an intolerable situation in the absence of any possibility for defensive action. The alternative was despair, the quiet stunned reaction of the defeated. (306)

Wiesel's text is written in the biblical style in which highlighted moments full of significance are presented without the careful concatenation of events we find in the realistic novel. Yet he has an eye for details that may owe something to his journalistic career in the years prior to meeting Mauriac. The biblical style owes itself to his being steeped not only in the Old Testament—a text that pays little attention to background or setting and eschews gradual introductions of its heightened and sublime moments—but also in a Talmudic tradition by which parabolic anecdotes are used to illustrate important themes. Rather than gradual change, he experiences loss of faith as an epiphanic moment when he sees Jews saying Kaddish for themselves. Unlike in the realistic novel or memoir, we cannot relate his role of passionate witness to a grammar of specific causes such as his father's tears: "For the first time, I felt revolt rise up in me. Why should I bless His name? The Eternal, Lord of the Universe, the All-Powerful and Terrible, was silent. What had I to thank Him for?" (*Night* 31).

Assuming in its form—especially its prophetic voice—an ethical narratee, *Night* also demands an ethical response. By that I mean a real attention to issues that pertain to how life is lived within imagined worlds. Truth in novels takes place within the hypothesis "as if," which is another way of saying that, as we think about our reading, we are never completely unaware of the metaphoricity of literature. At one time, some critics may have naively ignored the metaphoricity of language and confused characterization with actual human character. But have not some theorists reached the other pole of willfully denying analogies to human life and naively repressing the possibilities of significance? We shall see that Holocaust fiction—like *Night*—has an ethical narrator, demands an ethical reader, believes at least hypothetically in essential truths, insists on strong analogies to life lived within the Holocaust, and has faith that language signifies.

Rereading *Night* is a powerful experience, one that requires self-conscious reflection about how language can rescue meaning from the moral vacuum surrounding Holocaust events. What strikes the reader is its efficiency as a work of art. Derived, as we have seen, from a much longer Yiddish typescript, the precise, lucid, and laconic telling is in ironic juxtaposition to the historical complexity in Europe, but it is appropriate for the simple cause and effect of annihilating an entire people. Such stark imagery as that with which he described a work detail— "we were so many dried up trees in the heart of a desert"(35)—is all the more effective for its spareness. Wiesel has written:

> There are some words I cannot bring myself to use; they paralyze me. I cannot write the words "concentration," "night and fog," "selection," or "transport" without a feeling of sacrilege. Another difficulty, of a different type: I write in French, but I learned the language from books and therefore I am not good at slang.
>
> All my subsequent works are written in the same deliberately spare style as *Night*. It is the style of the chroniclers of the ghettos, where everything had to be said swiftly, in one breath. You never knew when the enemy might kick in the door, sweeping us away into nothingness. Every phrase was a testament. There was no time or reason for anything superfluous. Words must not be imprisoned or harnessed, not even in the silence of the page. And yet, it must be held tightly. If the violin is to sing, its strings must be stretched so tight as to risk breaking; slack, they are merely threads.
>
> To write is to plumb the unfathomable depths of being. Writing lies within the domain of mystery. The space between any two words is vaster than the distance between heaven and earth. To bridge it you must close your eyes and leap. A Hasidic tradition tells us that in the Torah the white spaces, too, are God-given. Ultimately, to write is an act of faith. (*Memoirs* 321)

The English translation of *Night* was published in the United States in 1960 by Hill and Wang; it sold only a few thousand copies in its first few years. Wiesel recalls,

> As for *Night*, despite Mauriac's preface and the favorable reviews in the French, Belgian, and Swiss press, the big publishers hesitated, debated, and ultimately sent their regrets. Some thought the book too slender (American readers seemed to prefer fatter volumes), others too depressing (American readers seemed to prefer optimistic books). Some felt its subject was too little known, others that it was too well known. In short, it was suggested over and over again that we try elsewhere. Refusing to lose heart,

Georges [Borchardt, a New York literary agent] kept trying. In the
end Hill and Wang agreed to take the risk. (*Memoirs* 325)

Although the basic unit of form is the retrospective memory of the
teller who writes after a ten year hiatus, the book is also organized around
a number of motifs. The most important is the loss of faith in the face of
evidence that God can or will do nothing to prevent the Holocaust. Young
Wiesel has a transvaluation of faith to disbelief and unbelief. He loses all
illusions about a purposeful world. As Naomi Seidman puts it: "In the
description of the first night Eliezer spends in the concentration camp,
silence signals the turn from the immediate terrors to a larger cosmic
drama, from stunned realism to theology. In the felt absence of divine
justice or compassion, silence becomes the agency of an immune, murderous power that permanently transforms the narrator" (1).

Let us continue our critical analysis. As if the narrator were
struggling to stay alive, as if he were having trouble breathing, the
unnumbered and untitled chapters get shorter; the last three of nine
chapters take up only seventeen pages. That he moves, on occasion, to
a postwar retrospective gives the reader the sense, as in Marlow's
narration in Conrad's *Heart of Darkness*, that his memory is struggling with
the narrative and that at times he needs to avoid the horrors. Wiesel's
breaks between anecdotes have the same effect, as if a pithy anecdote
were all the narrator could *stand* to tell before being overcome. The
recurring term "empty" reminds us of how, except for the will to live, his
life had become a negation—that is, an absence of love, comfort, health,
food. But in the retelling it reminds us of how he has become spiritually
anaesthetized *and* how he has left behind everything he had on the
written page. The verbal correlatives to "empty" include "night" and
"never" and of course anticipate the survivors' credo, "Never Again."

Never shall I forget that night, the first night in camp, which
has turned my life into one long night, seven times cursed and
seven times sealed. Never shall I forget that smoke. Never shall I
forget the little faces of the children, whose bodies I saw turned
into wreaths of smoke beneath a silent blue sky.

Never shall I forget those flames which consumed my faith
forever.

> Never shall I forget that nocturnal silence which deprived me,
> for all eternity, of the desire to live.(32)

The observant young boy who at the outset wished to be initiated into the mysteries of the cabbala feels the "void" of unbelief; the void is the alternative to the plenitude of belief (66, 93).

> Why, but why should I bless Him? In every fiber I rebelled. Because He had had thousands of children burned in His pits? Because He kept six crematories working night and day, on Sundays and feast days? Because in His great might He had created Auschwitz, Birkenau, Buna, and so many factories of death? How could I say to Him: "Blessed art Thou, Eternal, Master of the Universe, Who chose us from among the races to be tortured day and night, to see our fathers, our mothers, our brothers, end in the crematory? Praised be Thy Holy Name, Thou Who hast chosen us to be butchered on Thine altar?" . . .
> This day I had ceased to plead. I was no longer capable of lamentation. On the contrary, I felt very strong. I was the accuser, God the accused. My eyes were open and I was alone—terribly alone in a world without God and without man. Without love or mercy. I had ceased to be anything but ashes, yet I felt myself to be stronger than the Almighty, to whom my life had been tied for so long. (64, 65)

III

Our ethics of reading require that we look back and understand how the themes organize the agon. The title motif of *Night* is moral death, or historical void. Antithetical to light and its association with understanding—the Enlightenment of Europe—and with inner faith and wisdom, night is the dominant pattern around which the novel is organized. In *Night*, death is the antagonist, an active principle present at every moment. During the death march from Auschwitz, Wiesel recalls: "Death wrapped itself around me till I was stifled. It stuck to me. I felt that I could touch it. The idea of dying, of no longer being, began to fascinate me. Not to exist any longer. Not to feel the horrible pains in my foot. Not to feel anything, neither weariness, nor cold, nor anything. To break the ranks, to let oneself slide to the edge of the road" (82). During the transport to Buchenwald, he remarks, "Indifference deadened the spirit. Here or elsewhere—what difference did it make? To die today or tomorrow, or later? The night was long and never ending" (93). Yet, as Des Pres writes, Wiesel's narrative gives the lie to indifference and moral nights:

> Survivors do not bear witness to guilt, neither theirs nor ours, but to objective conditions of evil. In the literature of survival we find an image of things so grim, so heartbreaking, so starkly unbearable, that inevitably the survivor's scream begins to be our own. When this happens the role of spectator is no longer enough. But the testimony of survivors is valuable for something else as well. By the very fact that they came to be written, these documents are evidence that the moral self can resurrect itself from the inhuman depths through which it must pass. These books are proof that human heroism is possible. (Des Pres, 49-50)

At first, we recall, night is juxtaposed with day, but gradually it devours day: "The night was gone. The morning star was shining in the sky. I too had become a completely different person. The student of the Talmud, the child that I was, had been consumed in the flames. There remained only a shape that looked like me. A dark flame had entered into my soul and devoured it" (*Night*, 34). That last sentence I just quoted contains a major motif. Night becomes something that nullifies and obliterates; finally night overwhelms light, language, and meaning:

> The days were like nights, and the nights left the dregs of their darkness in our souls. The train was traveling slowly, often stopping for several hours and then setting off again. It never ceased snowing. All through these days and nights we stayed crouching, one on top of the other, never speaking a word. We were no more than frozen bodies. Our eyes closed, we waited merely for the next stop, so that we could unload our dead. (94-95)

On the death march, when he recalls that "the night had now set in. The snow had ceased to fall" (88), his words are rich with metaphorical meaning. We recall his words as he is leaving Buna: "The last night in Buna. Yet another last night. The last night at home, the last night in the ghetto, the last night in the train, and, now, the last night in Buna. How much longer were our lives to be dragged out from one 'last night' to another? (79). Night threatens everything, even the cosmos: "Night. No one prayed, so that the night would pass quickly. The stars were only sparks of the fire which devoured us. Should that fire die out one day, there would be nothing left in the sky but dead stars, dead eyes" (18).

Another important image is that of fire and burning. When during the death march he feels his infected foot "burning," we recall Madame Schächter's delirious yet prophetic nightmare on the train to Auschwitz:

"Jews, listen to me! I can see a fire! There are huge flames! It is a furnace!"

It was as though she were possessed by an evil spirit which spoke from the depths of her being. (23)

Note how fire and death are associated with night. Her words turn out to be all too true:

"Jews, look! Look through the window! Flames! Look!"

And as the train stopped, we saw this time that flames were gushing out of a tall chimney into the black sky.

Madame Schächter was silent herself. Once more she had become dumb, indifferent, absent, and had gone back to her corner.

We looked at the flames in the darkness. . . .

We jumped out. I threw a last glance toward Madame Schächter. Her little boy was holding her hand.

In front of us flames. In the air that smell of burning flesh. It must have been about midnight. We had arrived—at Birkenau, reception center for Auschwitz. (25-26)

Within Wiesel's dramatization of Madame Schächter's psyche are the warnings of Moshe, the rumors of cremation, the anxiety about sons and husbands being deported early. But she also is part of the prophetic and mystical tradition when she foresees the fire. Of course, the very meaning of the word Holocaust is the complete destruction of people or animals by fire, *and* an offering, the whole of which is burned.

As in other Holocaust texts, hunger is a dominant theme in Auschwitz. The narrator recalls that he soon "took little interest in anything except my daily plate of soup and my crust of stale bread. Bread, soup—these were my whole life. I was a body. Perhaps less than that even: a starved stomach. The stomach alone was aware of the passage of time" (50). After a hanging that the prisoners are forced to watch before they are allowed to eat, he recalls: "I remember that I found the soup excellent that evening" (60). Or, after another hanging, this time of a young boy he knew who took half an hour to die:

> Behind me, I heard the same man asking:
> "Where is God now?"
> And I heard a voice within me answer him:
> "Where is He? Here He is—He is hanging here on this gallows . . . "
> That night the soup tasted of corpses. (62)

We might ask whether the last sentence is a metaphor or a searing actuality because he had feelings for the boy who had been hanged. Is "soup" that "tasted of corpses" a tactile transference of his feelings to his senses or vice versa? We recall Des Pres's words about how survival depended on fulfilling basic needs at the cost of ethics:

> To oppose their fate in the death camps, survivors had to choose life at the cost of moral injury; they had to sustain spiritual damage and still keep going without losing sight of the difference between strategic compromise and demoralization. Hard choices had to be made and not everyone was equal to the task, no one less than the kind of person whose goodness was most evident, most admired, but least available for action. (*The Survivior* 131)

Another motif is the father-son tie, one that is so essential in Jewish life. Within the horrors of the Holocaust, these bonds threaten to dissolve. In an awful scene after the evacuation of Auschwitz, when Wiesel and his father are being transported to Buchenwald, they see a son fight his father for bread:

> "Meir. Meir, my boy! Don't you recognize me? I'm your father . . . you're hurting me . . . you're killing your father! I've got some bread . . . for you too . . . for you too. . . ."
> He collapsed. His fist was still clenched around a small piece. He tried to carry it to his mouth. But the other one threw himself upon him and snatched it. The old man again whispered something, let out a rattle, and died amid the general indifference. His son searched him, took the bread, and began to devour it. He was not able to get very far. Two men had seen and hurled themselves upon him. Others joined in. When they withdrew, next to me were two corpses, side by side, the father and the son.
> I was fifteen years old. (96)

On another occasion, a son—a *pipel*, that is, a boy belonging to the Kapo—beats his own father for not making his bed well (60). Whenever Wiesel thinks fleetingly of his father as a burden, he feels pangs of guilt. Indeed, his loyalty to his father is among the text's most touching motifs. He rejects the terrible advice of "the head of the block": "Don't forget that you're in a concentration camp. Here, every man has to fight for himself and not think of anyone else. Even of his father. Here, there are no fathers, no brothers, no friends. Everyone lives and dies for himself alone. I'll give you a sound piece of advice— don't give your ration of bread and soup to your old father. There's nothing you can do for him. And you're killing yourself. Instead, you ought to be having his ration" (105). But after a fraction of a second in which he found himself agreeing with this advice, he recalls running "to find a little soup to give my father. But he did not want it. All he wanted was water" (105). In contrast to Wiesel's devotion to his father, the son of another inmate, Rabbi Eliahou, "wanted to get rid of his father! He had felt that his father was growing weak, he had believed that the end was near and had sought this separation in order to get rid of the burden, to free himself from an encumbrance which could lessen his own chances of survival" (87).

While Wiesel's narrative is informed by retrospective guilt for not saving his father, we ask what more could the son have done? Isn't Wiesel's guilt disproportionate to his behavior? In a way, the father represents the tradition from which he has departed, the man he would have been. His early perceptions are informed by his Jewish upbringing. Describing the SS officer when he arrived at the barracks, he writes as if the German were stamped with the mark of Cain, who would kill his brother: "An SS officer had come in and, with him, the odor of the Angel of Death. . . . A tall man, about thirty, with crime inscribed upon his brow and in the pupils of his eyes" (35-6). His father is the eternal flame to which he returns as a boy and to which his memory returns in the telling.

One terrible irony is that the bad luck of a choice Wiesel and his father made is a cause of their worst days: "I learned after the war the fate of those who had stayed behind in the hospital. They were quite simply liberated by the Russians two days after the evacuation" (78). But how could he and his father have known that if they only stayed behind in the hospital that they could have been liberated two days later and that his father would have lived? The dramatic action is filled with missed chances: the opportunity of emigrating to Palestine (6); the missed warning of the Hungarian police inspector because they did not open the window in time: "It was not until after the war that I learned who it was that had knocked" (12); the maid Martha who could have hidden them in her village; and, of course, Moshe's warning. Palestine becomes the anti-tale, the utopian alternative to what is occurring. He meets two brothers in Auschwitz with whom he shares dreams of leaving Europe for Haifa: "Having once belonged to a Zionist youth organization, they knew innumerable Hebrew chants. Thus we would often hum tunes evoking the calm waters of Jordan and the majestic sanctity of Jerusalem. And we would often talk of Palestine" (48).

Transformation is as much a theme here as it is in Kafka. By showing us how life was in Sighet at the outset, we can see the terrible transformation in young Wiesel and his father. When he writes of the masquerade of clothes before the death march, we think of the clown motif in Picasso and the grotesque carnival in Ensor: "Prisoners appeared in strange outfits: it was like a masquerade. Everyone had put on several garments, one on top of the other, in order to keep out the cold. Poor mountebanks, wider than they were tall, more dead than alive; poor clowns, their ghostlike faces emerging from piles of prison clothes! Buffoons!" (79). When we see his father as a virtual corpse—broken in spirit, a *musulman*—before dying, we realize how little time has passed since he was a respected and cultured fifty-year-old senior member of the Jewish community of Sighet, a man consulted about public and private matters.

As in Primo Levi's *Survival in Auschwitz*, recurring memorable characters, employed in relationship to the evolving plot, give the text unity. For example, when Elie and his father arrive in the barracks of Gleiwitz, he recalls meeting Juliek, the violinist who plays Beethoven in violation of the German prohibition against Jews playing German music: "I could hear only the violin, and it was as though Juliek's soul were the bow. He was playing his life. The whole of his life was gliding on the strings— his lost hopes, his charred past, his extinguished future. He played as he would never play again" (90); Juliek is dead in the morning. We recall other figures Wiesel uses to weave the narrative together into a meaningful pattern: Madame Schächter with her prophetic nightmares; Idek, the psychotic Kapo; Rabbi Eliahou; Meir Katz, the healthy giant who finally gives up and dies; the faceless cynic in the hospital who says, "I've got more faith in Hitler than in anyone else. He's the only one who's kept his promises, all his promises, to the Jewish people" (77).

Wiesel occasionally moves to the present as when he tells us what he learned after the war about the liberation of Auschwitz, when he speaks of the man who knocked on the window to warn his family or the women throwing coins to the poor in Aden, or when he concludes his testament with a searing bridge across time:

> One day I was able to get up, after gathering all my strength.
> I wanted to see myself in the mirror hanging on the opposite wall.
> I had not seen myself since the ghetto.
> From the depths of the mirror, a corpse gazed back at me.
> The look in his eyes, as they stared into mine, has never left me. (109)

The mirror as a reflection of the inner self—the other self—is a recurring image in modernism, but the mirror is also a traditional image of realistic representation in the Western tradition. By his act of writing, Wiesel rejects the corpse as his double. In both cases, he makes a rhetorical gesture that positions himself within Western culture and away from his iconoclastic position as witness or as one of the humble anonymous Lamed Vov or Just Men. As Seidman puts it, "In the final lines of *Night* when the recently liberated Eliezer gazes at his own face in a mirror, the reader is presented with the survivor as both subject and object, through his inner experience and through outward image of what he has become" (3). But when we note how different this is from the original ending, we begin to place our reading in the context of what we now know. In his 1995 *Memoirs: All Rivers Run to the Sea*, Wiesel recalls the original ending before Lindon edited it:

> The book ended this way (I only quote it for its relevance today):
> I looked at myself in the mirror. A skeleton stared back at me. Nothing but skin and bone.
> It was the image of myself after death. It was at that instant that the will to live awakened within me.
> Without knowing why, I raised my fist and shattered the glass, along with the image it held. I lost consciousness.
> After I got better, I stayed in bed for several days, jotting down notes for the work that you, dear reader, now hold in your hands.
> But . . .
> . . . Today, ten years after Buchenwald, I realize that the world forgets. Germany is a sovereign state. The German army has been reborn. Ilse Koch, the sadist of Buchenwald, is a happy wife and mother. War criminals stroll in the streets of Hamburg and Munich. The past has been erased, buried.
> Germans and anti-Semites tell the world that the story of six million Jewish victims is but a myth, and the world, in its naïveté, will believe it, if not today, then tomorrow or the next day.
> So it occurred to me that it might be useful to publish in book form these notes taken down in Buchenwald.
> I am not so naïve as to believe that this work will change the course of history or shake the conscience of humanity.
> Books no longer command the power they once did.

Those who yesterday held their tongues will keep their silence tomorrow.

That is why, ten years after Buchenwald, I ask myself the question, Was I right to break that mirror? (*Memoirs*, 319-320)

He questions whether his breaking the mirror as an affirmation of his decision to live is appropriate. Seidman comments:

By stopping when it does, *Night* provides an entirely different account of the experience of the survivor. *Night* and the stories about its composition depict the survivor as a witness and as an expression of silence and death, projecting the recently liberated Eliezer's death-haunted face into the postwar years when Wiesel would become a familiar figure. By contrast, the Yiddish survivor shatters that image as soon as he sees it, destroying the deathly existence the Nazis willed on him. The Yiddish survivor is filled with rage and the desire to live, to take revenge, to write. Indeed, according to the Yiddish memoir, Eliezer began to write not ten years after the events of the Holocaust but immediately upon liberation, as the first expression of his mental and physical recovery. In the Yiddish we meet a survivor who, ten years after liberation, is furious with the world's disinterest in his history, frustrated with the failure of the Jews to fulfill "the historical commandment of revenge," depressed by the apparent pointlessness of writing a book. (7-8)

But should we not also notice how Seidman, too, especially in the last of the above sentences, appropriates Wiesel for her own purposes, namely to indict Wiesel and his successors for eschewing a rhetoric of revenge. As Seidman puts it, "*Un di velt* does not spell out what form this retribution might take, only that it is sanctioned—even commanded—by Jewish history and tradition" (6).

IV

We continue to our final phase of hermeneutics—cognition in terms of what we know—when we turn to the introduction to the French edition.

Originally, when Wiesel was a young unknown, François Mauriac, a French Catholic Nobel Laureate, not only helped him get his book published in France but also wrote the introduction, which, with its Christian meditation on the narrator's loss, became part of the text:

> And I, who believe that God is love, what answer could I give my young questioner, whose dark eyes still held the reflection of that angelic sadness which had appeared one day upon the face of the hanged child? What did I say to him? Did I speak of that other Jew, his brother, who may have resembled him—the Crucified, whose Cross has conquered the world? Did I affirm that the stumbling block to his faith was the cornerstone of mine, and that the conformity between the Cross and the suffering of men was in my eyes the key to that impenetrable mystery whereon the faith of his childhood had perished? Zion, however, has risen up again from the crematories and the charnel houses. The Jewish nation has been resurrected from among its thousands of dead. It is through them that it lives again. We do not know the worth of one single drop of blood, one single tear. All is grace. If the Eternal is the Eternal, the last word for each one of us belongs to Him. This is what I should have told this Jewish child. But I could only embrace him, weeping. (*Night*, x-xi)

The introduction frames the book in a Christian context and implies a different set of beliefs. Mauriac was the kind of cultural icon who gave legitimacy to Wiesel's novel. It was as if today a young writer were being published under Wiesel's auspices. In 1963, as Wiesel notes in his *Memoirs*, Mauriac wrote in his newspaper column: "Someday Elie Wiesel will take me to the Holy Land. He desires it greatly, having a most singular knowledge of Christ, whom he pictures wearing phylacteries, as Chagall saw him, a son of the synagogue, a pious Jew submitting to the Law, and who did not die, 'because being human he was made God,' Elie Wiesel stands on the borders of the two testaments: he is of the race of John the Baptist" (271).

There can be no doubt that Mauriac's introduction to *Night* shapes the response of some readers into a more Christian reading. For example, when a child is among three condemned prisoners,

Christian students see the parallel to a crucifixion scene, and see the longer and slower death of "a child with a refined and beautiful face" as a Christ figure (*Night* 60). Yet didn't Wiesel mean the scene as a *challenge* to the original Christian readers, most of whom (whether Poles or French or others) had either remained silent or done far worse while *night* engulfed Europe? In his memoir he distances himself from Mauriac's teleology: "Where I come from and from where I stand, one cannot be Jew and Christian at the same time. Jesus was Jewish, but those who claim allegiance to him today are not. In no way does this mean that Jews are better or worse than Christians, but simply that each of us has the right, if not the duty, to be what we are" (*Memoirs* 271).

Mauriac appropriates *Night* to his own theology:

> The child who tells us his story here was one of God's elect. From the time when his conscience first awoke, he had lived only for God and had been reared on the Talmud, aspiring to initiation into the cabbala, dedicated to the Eternal. Have we ever thought about the consequence of a horror that, though less apparent, less striking than the other outrages, is yet the worst of all to those of us who have faith: the death of God in the soul of a child who suddenly discovers absolute evil?. . . . It was then that I understood what had first drawn me to the young Jew: that look, as of a Lazarus risen from the dead, yet still a prisoner within the confines where he had strayed, stumbling among the shameful corpses. (*Night* viii-ix)

But I doubt whether Wiesel has really written a *novel* that fulfills the paradigm of rebirth and resurrection—"of a Lazarus risen from the dead," to use Mauriac's words. Moreover, Wiesel speaks to us as a twenty-six-year-old adult, not as a child. Is Mauriac's construction not only a Christian appropriation of *Night's* angst, but, no matter how well meant, an ethical transgression? It is as if, for Mauriac, Wiesel is the Christ child, an archetype for all victims whose suffering is redemptive. Seidman writes:

> The friendship between the older Christian and younger Jew began, then, with Wiesel relinquishing his aim of manipulating

Mauriac for Jewish purposes and turning, in all sincerity, to the man himself. With the psychological shift, Wiesel began his transformation from Hebrew journalist and (still unpublished) Yiddish memoirist to European, or French writer. . . . The French reworking of *Un di velt hot geshvign* and Mauriac's framing of this text together suggest that *La Nuit*—read so consistently as authentically Jewish, autobiographical, direct—represents a compromise between Jewish expression and the capacities and desires of non-Jewish readers, Mauriac first among them. (13, 14)

She concludes:

Was it worth "unshattering" the mirror the Yiddish Elie breaks, reviving the image of the Jew as the Nazis wished him to be, as the Christians prepared to accept him, the emblem of suffering silence rather than living rage? In the complex negotiations that resulted in the manuscript of *Night*, did the astonishing gains make good the tremendous losses? It is over this unspoken question that the culture of Holocaust discourse has arisen and taken shape. (16)

V

What is the grammar of cause and effect within Wiesel's testament?

To a contemporary reader, historical ironies abound. Why did the Germans continue to persecute Jews when they needed every resource to stem defeat? Was it an attempt on the part of a compulsive if not psychotic collective group psychology—or should we say *psychopathology?*—to shift blame and erase evidence? Why did they use Jewish slave labor mostly for useless tasks and systematically starve that labor? As Des Pres puts it,

But here too, for all its madness, there was method and reason. This special kind of evil is a natural outcome of power when it becomes absolute, and in the totalitarian world of the camps it very nearly was. The SS could kill anyone they happened to run into. Criminal *Kapos* would walk about in groups of two and three, making bets among themselves on who could kill a prisoner with a single blow. The pathological rage of such men, their uncontrollable fury when rules were broken, is evidence of a boundless desire to annihilate, to destroy, to smash everything not mobilized within the movement of their own authority. And inevitably, the mere act of killing is not enough; for if a man dies without surrender, if something within him remains unbroken to the end, then the power which destroyed him has not, after all, crushed everything. (*The Survivor* 59)

Finally Wiesel confronts the horrors of the Holocaust and insists on bearing witness (and resisting Mauriac's Christian gloss). For some, Wiesel's text has been an antidote to the way that Anne Frank's story had been manipulated to "glorify," as Bruno Bettelheim puts it, "the ability to retreat into an extremely private, gentle, sensitive world, and there to cling as much as possible to what have been one's usual attitudes and activities, although surrounded by a maelstrom apt to engulf one at any moment" (*Surviving and Other Essays* 247). In the play and film, we hear Anne's voice from beyond saying, "In spite of everything, I still believe that people are really good at heart," but Bettelheim argues passionately that this statement is not supported or justified in Anne's diary: "This improbable sentiment is supposedly from a girl who had been starved to death, had watched her sister meet the same fate before she did, knew that her mother had been murdered, and had watched untold thousands of adults and children being killed. This statement is not justified by anything Anne actually told her diary" (*Surviving and Other Essays* 250).

But, of course, we see Anne's last word as ironic because she has been killed. Bettelheim is quite harsh in his judgments:

Those Jews who submitted passively to Nazi persecution came to depend on primitive and infantile thought processes: wishful thinking and disregard for the possibility of death. Many persuaded themselves that they, out of all the others, would be spared. Many more simply disbelieved in the possibility of their own death. Not believing in it, they did not take what seemed to them desperate precautions, such as giving up everything to hide out singly; or trying to escape even if it meant risking their lives in doing so; or preparing to fight for their lives when no escape was possible and death had become an immediate possibility. (*Surviving and Other Essays* 251)

In an essay entitled "Freedom from Ghetto Thinking," Bettelheim defines "ghetto thinking": "to believe that one can ingratiate oneself with a mortal enemy by denying that his lashes sting, to deny one's own degradation in return for a moment's respite, to support one's enemy who will only use his strength the better to destroy one. All that is part of ghetto philosophy" (*Freud's Vienna and other Essays* 261). For him the Franks embody ghetto thinking:

> The Frank family created a ghetto in the annex, the Hinter Haus, where they went to live; it was an intellectual ghetto, a sensitive one, but a ghetto nevertheless. I think we should contrast their story with those of other Jewish families who went into hiding in Holland. These families, from the moment they dug in, planned escape routes for the time when the police might come looking for them. Unlike the Franks, they did not barricade themselves in rooms without exits; they did not wish to be trapped. In preparation, some of them planned and rehearsed how the father, if the police should come, would try to argue with them or resist in order to give his wife and children time to escape. Sometimes when the police came the parents physically attacked them, knowing they would be killed but thus saving a child. (*Freud's Vienna and other Essays* 270)

Bettelheim, who himself eventually committed suicide, writes in his essay "Surviving" how the survivor "knows very well that he is not guilty, as I, for one know about myself, but that this does not change the fact that the humanity of such a person, as a fellow being, requires that he *feel* guilty, and he does. This is a most significant aspect of survivorship" (*Surviving,* 297). Bettelheim reminds how, while the foremost condition for survival was luck, other factors helped, such as, to quote Bettelheim,

> correctly assessing one's situation and taking advantage of opportunities, in short, acting independently and with courage, decision and conviction. . . . Survival was, of course, greatly helped if one

had entered the camps in a good state of physical health. But most of all, as I have intimated all along, autonomy, self-respect, inner integration, a rich inner life, and the ability to relate to others in meaningful ways were the psychological conditions which, more than any others, permitted one to survive in the camps as much a whole human being as overall conditions and chance would permit. ("Owners of their Faces," *Surviving* 109)

Whether we agree with Bettelheim and whether we chide him for letting his rage distort and appropriate Anne Frank's text as Mauriac and Seidman have appropriated Wiesel's, his words give us some sense of how difficult it is for readers of Holocaust texts to respond ethically to such a searing and heart-rending narrative of memory, trauma, and literary imagination as *Night.*

CHAPTER TWO

PAINFUL MEMORIES:
THE AGONY OF PRIMO LEVI

FROM O THE NIGHT OF THE WEEPING CHILDREN!
O the night of the weeping children!
O the night of the children branded for death! . . .
—Nelly Sachs
(Translated by Michael Hamburger)

I

My book is not about how and why the Holocaust occurred, but about how it is imagined and narrated in literary texts. I want to use Levi's metaphor as "a dream within a dream" to describe the kinds of phantasmagoric tales included in my study (*The Reawakening* 208). For these narratives shaped by trauma are special kinds of memories that have meaning, as Conrad's narrator says of Marlow's tales in *Heart of Darkness*, "not inside like a kernel but outside, enveloping the tale which brought it out only as a glow brings out a haze" (*The Portable Conrad* 493). One of our inquiries will be whether these texts *mean* in the same way as other texts; like all texts, they reveal as they conceal, but enact in their telling and agon a structure of affects for readers. Do they mean in their resonances and explanations differently from other texts and, if so, how? Is that difference one of degree or kind? Does our knowledge of the apocalyptic nature of the Holocaust, its onerous weight on every page, change the way we read and respond? All reading is a function of who we are, and while those personally touched by the Holocaust respond differently, are their responses to texts necessarily more intense than others? Do texts, for some, cause trauma and short-circuit responses? Are Holocaust texts that pull together the personal, political, and ethical more effective?

Primo Levi's *Survival in Auschwitz* (1958; first published in 1947 without "The Canto of Ulysses" chapter), which originally appeared in English under the more accurate translation of the Italian title *Se questo e un uomo*, as "If this is a Man," *The Reawakening* (1963), *The Periodic Table* (1975), *Moments of Reprieve* (1979), and *The Drowned and the Saved* (1986), a book published a year before his 1987 suicide, are not novels but memoirs. For Levi, his months in the camps were what Conrad's Marlow refers to in *Heart of Darkness* as "the culminating point of my experience" (*The Portable Conrad* 496). The way in which the mind remembers and organizes experiences and how memory deploys language to make sense are the foci of his work. In *The Periodic Table*, Levi writes: "It seemed to me that I would be purified by recounting . . . by writing I found peace for awhile and I felt myself anew again" (*The Periodic Table* 151). Levi's recurring theme is the therapeutic, purifying function of language. Levi believes in language. In the camps, language had been reductive, destructive, and persecuting, but his narrating and witnessing language has the capacity to be vital: "So I realized that the German of the Lager—skeletal, howled, studded with obscenities and imprecations—was only vaguely related to the precise, austere language of my chemistry books, or to the melodious, refined German of Heine's poetry that Clara, a classmate of mine, used to recite to me" (*The Drowned and the Saved* 97). When he hears that *Survival in Auschwitz* will be translated into German in 1959, he writes: "I had written the book in Italian, for Italians, for my children, for those who did not know, those who did not want to know, those who were not yet born, those who, willing or not, had assented to the offense; but its true recipients, those against whom the book was aimed like a gun were they, the Germans. Now the gun was loaded. . . . Before they had been oppressors or indifferent spectators, now they would be readers: I would corner them, tie them before a mirror. The hour had come to settle accounts, to put the cards on the table. Above all, the hour of colloquy" (*The Drowned and the Saved* 168). His German translator did not understand the language of the camp: *"per force* he did not know the degraded, often satanically ironic jargon of the concentration camps. . . . I wanted that in that book, particularly in its German guise, nothing should be lost of its harshness and the violence inflicted on the language, which for that matter I had made an effort to reproduce as best I could in my Italian original" (*The Drowned and The Saved* 172).

Language is the protagonist of Levi's books, the means by which he seizes light from darkness. For him, it is the means of creation and understanding, the one antidote to chaos. His imprisonment in Auschwitz was all the worse because he didn't understand Yiddish and had only a primitive ability to communicate, notwithstanding a specialized version of scientific German. He writes of the loss of language experienced by those who did not know German: "[W]e who, not knowing German, were reduced to the condition of deaf mutes: in a way, if I may put it like this, that was spiritual rather than material." For a German Jew it "was a barbaric jargon that . . . scorched his mouth when he tried to speak it" (*The Drowned and the Saved* 135). Silence was the means of German control of the camp's terrible secret; the purpose of the pitiful resurrections was to *speak* the secret: "In the intentions of the insurgents they were supposed to achieve another, more concrete result: to bring the terrifying secret of the massacre to the attention of the free world. Indeed, those few whose enterprise was successful, and who after many more depleting vicissitudes had access to the organs of information, did speak. But, as I mentioned in my introduction, they were almost never listened to or believed. Uncomfortable truths travel with difficulty" (159). Silence was enforced by what he called "Useless Violence" in the chapter of that name in *The Drowned and the Saved.*

Levi refused to write a preface to the German edition of *Survival in Auschwitz* as if, as a metonymy for what its speakers had once done to him, he wanted to resist German efforts to control his language. He had written in *Survival in Auschwitz: The Nazi Assault on Humanity,* "Nothing belongs to us anymore; they have taken our clothes, our shoes, even our hair; if we speak, they will not listen to us, and if they listen, they will not understand. They will even take away our name: and if we want to keep it, we will have to find in ourselves the strength to do so, to manage somehow so that behind the name something of us, of us as we were, still remains" (22). He wants the German translation to stand naked and exposed, without intervention, before his audience; but he reprints a letter to his translator: "I was expected to raise my voice, climb on the podium, change from witness to judge, preacher; set forth theories and interpretations of history; divide or set apart the pious from the impious; pass from the third person to the second. . . . I do not believe that man's life necessarily has a definite purpose; but if I think of my life and the aims I have until now set for myself, I recognize only one of them as well defined and conscious, and it is precisely this, to bear witness, to make my voice heard by the German people, to 'answer' the *Kapo* who cleaned his hand on my shoulder, Dr. Pannwitz, and those who hung Ultimo [all people described in *Survival in Auschwitz*] and by their heirs" (*The Drowned and the Saved* 173-74). He speaks to the Germans, in part, because: "I repeat: the true crime, the collective, general crime of almost all Germans of that time was that of lacking the courage to speak" (*The Drowned and the Saved* 182). Note the anger of one of his responses to German letters he recieved: "If I were a judge, even though repressing what hatred I might feel, I would not hesitate to inflict the most severe punishment or even death on the many culprits who still today live undisturbed on German soil or in other countries of suspect hospitality; but I would experience horror if a single innocent were punished for a crime he did not commit" (*The Drowned and the Saved* 184-85).

Levi's memoirs focus on the moment when, as Sidra DeKoven Ezrahi puts it, "*Haftling* 174517 begins to rediscover his humanity, to combat by the powers of imagination and analogy the absurdity of his condition" (Ezrahi, *By Words Alone* 18). Levi is a witness; his *agon* is telling. As an Italian Jew, more Italian than Jew, he experiences Eastern Jews—Jews other than those with whom he is familiar—as an awakening. Levi is conscious of memory as a protagonist giving shape, but also of the role of imagination in his writing: "It is possible that the distance in time has accentuated the tendency to round out the facts or heighten the colors: this tendency, or temptation, is an integral part of writing, without it one does not write stories but rather accounts" (*Moments of Reprieve* 11). He is conscious of how memory enables him to give shape to the past, and writing enables him to give words to that shape: "Well, it has been observed by psychologists that the survivors of traumatic events are divided into two well-defined groups: those who repress their past *en bloc,* and those whose memory of the offense persists, as though carved in stone, prevailing over all previous or subsequent experiences. Now, not by choice but by nature, I belong to the second group. Of my two years of life outside the law I have not forgotten a single thing. Without any deliberate effort, memory continues to restore to me events, faces, words, sensations, as if at that time my mind had gone through a period of exalted receptivity, during which not a detail was lost" (*Moments of Reprieve* 10-11). Self-conscious about acts of writing, Levi understands that the complex trialogue among memory, imagination, and words *is* the subject of his memoirs: "[T]he task of transforming a living person into a character ties the hand of the writer. This happens because such a task, even when it is undertaken with the best intentions and deals with a respected and loved person, verges on the violation of privacy and is never painless for the subject. Each of us, knowingly or not, creates an image of himself, but inevitably it is different from that, or, rather, from those (which again are different from one another) that are created by whoever comes into contact with us. Finding oneself portrayed in a book with features that are not those we attribute to ourselves is traumatic, as if the mirror of a sudden returned to us the image of somebody else: an image possibly nobler than ours, but not ours" (*Moments of Reprieve* 149). For the memoirist, as opposed to the novelist, the author's narrative quest is to rediscover the factual underpinnings of experience. Yet as readers we know that this quest is an epistemological Zeno's paradox because the essential facts are not only always evanescent and dependent on a particular experiential temporal-spatial perspective when the originating events occurred, but distorted and refracted through memory.

II

We might examine parallels between Levi and Tadeusz Borowski, the subject of chapter four. Both committed suicide, Borowski in 1951, Levi in 1987. They both were in Auschwitz. After liberation, each went through a number of repatriation camps—Levi in the Soviet Union, Borowski in Germany. But while Borowski's narrator lives in cynicism, Levi's lives in hope. Borowski's Tadeusz insists that the camp is the *only world* and everything beyond it is an illusion; he is an antihero and sometimes collaborator. Levi finds solace in small gestures of humanity and believes in a world beyond the camps. Thus Levi writes of Lorenzo, a man who befriended him in the camps:

> [A]n Italian civilian worker brought me a piece of bread and the remainder of his ration every day for six months; he gave me a vest of his, full of patches; he wrote a postcard on my behalf to Italy and brought me the reply. For all this he neither asked nor accepted any reward, because he was good and simple and did not think that one did good for a reward. . . . I believe that it was really due to Lorenzo that I am alive today; and not so much for his material aid, as for his having constantly reminded me by his presence, by his natural and plain manner of being good, that there still existed a just world outside our own, something and someone still pure and whole, not corrupt, not savage, extraneous to hatred and terror; something difficult to define, a remote possibility of good, but for which it was worth surviving. . . . But Lorenzo was a man; his humanity was pure and uncontaminated, he was outside this world of negation. Thanks to Lorenzo, I managed not to forget that I myself was a man. (*Survival in Auschwitz* 109, 111)

In a sense, that act of generosity defines Levi's relationship to his reader; recall that the Italian version title translates as "What Is a Man?"

As Lawrence Langer has remarked, "[T]he survivor account . . . in the very process of forming a narrative with words, adopts a procedure that makes it impossible to avoid some kind of teleology, a view of experience invested with meaning and purpose" ("Interpreting Survivor Testimony," Lang 26). Narrative provides an order, a sequence, an explanatory concatenation that represents in mediated form a *prior reality*. Narratives shape events with meaning, purpose, a teleology. Narrative has words and a voice. Narrative represents what it describes, but the telling inevitably distorts the original events. The mature perspective is often overwhelmed by memory of the past, even as it tries to keep its distance. Thus what is represented is a *telling* rather than unmediated reality.

Sidra DeKoven Ezrahi has remarked: "[A]s the Jews came to live more and more within the elastic bounds of their own internal discourse, the significant historical and geographic coordinates of collective life were located in the suspended time and place of sacred texts, and a lamentation tradition based on archetypal rather than historical memory evolved. . . . The destruction that gave rise to a state of geographical and spiritual exile is balanced by the promise of ultimate redemption" ("Considering the Apocalypse," Lang 139). In Holocaust narratives the narrator often takes on one or more traditional Jewish roles: the Just Man of the legendary *Lamed Vov*; the Righteous Man; the Witness; the Prophet; the rabbinical interpreter. Often the speaker during his telling trajectory occupies a number of these positions. But while he partakes of all of the above, he is primarily the self-conscious and at times self-accusing Guilty Survivor of Pogroms. We see other archetypes, too: the figure who has descended into hell only to return—for example, the one who has lived with Levi in a moral hell where, as he puts it, "there is no why" (*Survival In Auschwitz* 25).

In *Modernity and the Holocaust*, Zygmunt Bauman argues that the "lesson of the Holocaust is the facility with which most people, put into a situation that does not contain a good choice . . . argue themselves away from the issue of moral duty . . . adopting instead the precepts of rational interest and self-preservation" (206). While Bauman is speaking of the Germans, collaborators, and bystanders, and not the victims, Levi makes clear that at times the victims of necessity need adopt the morality of the victimizers.

Let us recall some basic historical background. While Italy had racial laws, it was only after the fall of Mussolini and the German occupation of northern Italy that Jews were deported from Italy. Gilbert writes,

> On 16 September 1943, less than seven weeks after the fall of Mussolini, as German forces occupied all but the southern tip of Italy, the first twenty-four Jews had been deported from Merano, in northern Italy, to Birkenau. Even though allied forces, fighting in the south of Italy, were forcing the Germans back towards Rome, the deportation of Jews was a high priority for the German occupying power. Of the thirty-seven thousand Jews who suddenly found themselves in danger, only a few hundred managed to escape over the mountain passes to Switzerland. In Italy itself, several thousand found refuge in Catholic homes and institutions. (Gilbert 622)

In late 1943, after being arrested while fighting with Partisans, Levi is deported from his native Turin to Auschwitz. He spends ten months in Auschwitz. Because of his training as a chemist, he is spared from the gas chambers. Levi is assigned to a synthetic rubber plant at Buna—a plant that *never* produced any synthetic rubber—where he learns how to steal and connive: "I was reliving—*me*, a respectable little university graduate—the involution-evolution of a famous respectable dog, a Victorian, Darwinian dog who is deported and becomes a thief in order to live in his Klondike *Lager*—the great Buck of *The Call of the Wild.* I stole like him and like the foxes: at every favorable opportunity but with sly cunning and without exposing myself" (*The Periodic Table* 140). To his retrospective horror he recoils from a civilized university student to a savage whose only concern was self-survival. Martin Gilbert has written of Buna: "On the day after the Cologne raid, at Monowitz, just to the east of Auschwitz, the first of a series of forced labour camps was opened for the construction of a massive synthetic oil and rubber factory, the Buna works. One of the labour camps was for Jews. Known as Auschwitz III, it drew off thousands of Jews from Birkenau, or Auschwitz II. If these Jews could survive the harsh conditions of work, the starvation and the brutality, they could hope to survive the war, and several thousand did so, unlike the hundreds of thousands of adults sent to Chelmno, Sobibor and Belzec, where all, whether 'able-bodied' or not, were gassed" (Gilbert, *The Holocaust* 353-54).

As Langer puts it in *Holocaust Testimonies,* "[F]or many, Auschwitz permanently destroyed the potency of the sedative we call illusion" (*Testimonies* 4). Not only is the very fabric of civilization torn, but the ability to create and sustain fictions of order and morality fails. *Survival in Auschwitz* is a retrospective memoir of Levi's year at Auschwitz: "The book has been written to satisfy this need: first and foremost, therefore, as an interior liberation. Hence its fragmentary character: the chapters have been written not in logical succession, but in order of urgency. The work of tightening up is more studied, and more recent" (*Survival in Auschwitz* 6). It shows how the camps systematically deprived humans of their identity, and how for survivors, *deprival* is a more apt term than *survival:* "Imagine now a man who is deprived of everyone he loves, and at the same time of his house, his habits, his clothes, in short, of everything he possesses: he will be a hollow man, reduced to suffering and needs, forgetful of dignity and restraint, for he who loses all often easily loses himself. He will be a man whose life or death can be lightly decided with no sense of human affinity, in the most fortunate of cases, on the basis of pure judgment of utility. It is in this way that one can understand the double sense of the term 'extermination camp,' and it is now clear what we seek to express with the phrase: 'to lie on the bottom'" (*Survival in Auschwitz* 23).

Levi obsessively focuses on the search for food, and he describes the tricks and ruses necessary to procure food in detail. As if to remind his comfortable readers of the difference between the Lager—his term for the concentration camp—life and our comfortable life in which food is taken for granted, he writes of his daily struggles with the pervasive condition of hunger and how the prisoners think and talk about food constantly. Auschwitz deprived Levi not only of clothes and food but of the sense of belonging—to use his later metaphor in *The Periodic Table*—to the "affinity" of human elements, that is, the human periodic table:

> A man is normally not alone, and in his rise or fall is tied to the destinies of his neighbours; so that it is exceptional for anyone to acquire unlimited power, or to fall by a succession of defeats into utter ruin. Moreover, everyone is normally in possession of such spiritual, physical and even financial resources that the probabilities of a shipwreck, of total inadequacy in the face of life, are relatively small. And one must take into account a definite cushioning effect exercised both by the law, and by the moral sense which constitutes a self-imposed law; for a country is considered the more civilized the more the wisdom and efficiency of its laws hinder a weak man from becoming too weak or a powerful one too powerful. . . . But in the Lager things are different: here the struggle to survive is without respite, because everyone is desperately and ferociously alone. (*Survival in Auschwitz* 80)

Levi understands that while luck is a major, and perhaps the most important component, those who survived are not necessarily morally the best, but those who are most committed to surviving—often for political and religious reasons—are those who make the most of every opportunity. In the camps, one must learn to think of oneself as a community of *one*. The next important unit is a friend or two, who looks out for you as you do for him, and with whom you share small good fortune like extra food or water.

The Hitler years, which devastated Europe, as Levi recalls them, "were characterized by widespread useless violence, as an end in itself, with the sole purpose of inflicting pain, occasionally having a purpose, yet always redundant, always disproportionate to the purpose itself. . . . Thinking back. . . . one feels torn between two opinions: Were we witnessing the rational development of an inhuman plan or a manifestation (unique in history and still unsatisfactorily explained) of collective madness? Logic intent on evil or the absence of logic? As so often happens in human affairs, the two alternatives coexisted" (*The Drowned and the Saved* 106). Work had the purpose of being "afflictive": "Work was not paid; that is, it was slave work, one of the three purposes of the concentrationary system, the other two being the elimination of political adversaries and the extermination of the so-called inferior races. . . . Their work must be afflictive: it must leave no room for professionalism, must be the work of beasts of burden—pull, push, carry weights, bend over the soil. This too is useless violence: useful only to break down current resistance and punish past resistance" (*The Drowned and the Saved* 120, 121). What he testifies to in his books is the desecration of European civilization. While he *creates* by means of his words, he describes the process of destruction wrought by the Germans: "All the buildings had been subjected to a Teutonically methodical devastation and plundering; the German armies in flight had carried away everything that could be carried: locks, bars, railings, the entire lighting and heating plant, the water pipes, even the fence posts. Not a nail had been left in the walls. The tracks and sleepers of a near-by railway junction had been torn up: with a special machine, the Russians told us" (*The Reawakening* 123).

At the very center of *Survival in Auschwitz* is what we might call the ironic subversive mode of rendering the Holocaust. By that I mean a narrative that, in the guise of recalling the past, at times proposes an alternative context that looks toward values of a different, more stable, and presumably more noble era. It is the method by which such modern writers as T. S. Eliot in *The Waste Land* and James Joyce in *Ulysses* measure a bankrupt present with a supposedly more noble past (although the past in those texts is also called into question). Thus in the allusive chapter of *Survival in Auschwitz*, "The Canto of Ulysses," the voice from "that age-old fire" of Hell is that of Ulysses, but it is also that of the speaker caught in the symbolic fires of the

Holocaust and the threat of the real fire of the crematorium. The speaker quotes Dante's depiction of a hubristic Ulysses who does not know his limitations: "Think of your breed; for brutish ignorance / Your mettle was not made; you were made men, / To follow after knowledge and excellence" (*Survival in Auschwitz* 103). Ulysses, we realize, is a trope not only for both the prisoners seeking to maintain their humanity, but ironically the imprisoning Germans, who in their hubris believed that their "breed" made them a special case with their own rules and who are finally reduced by events to history's playthings. While Levi finds respite from his plight in literature, in memory, and in values, his escape into literary imagination is only temporary, a rare moment between the tick and the tock of the relentless German prison machine. In a sense the "Canto of Ulysses" chapter, added to the 1958 Einaudi edition, is an audition for the allusive method of *The Periodic Table*, in which human events are consistently compared with chemical elements rather than with literary and mythic antecedents.

In *The Drowned and The Saved*, Levi writes:

> After forty years I am reading in *Survival in Auschwitz* the chapter entitled "The Canto of Ulysses." It is one of the few episodes whose authenticity I have been able to verify . . . because my interlocutor of that time, Jean Samuel, is one of the book's few surviving characters. . . . At that time Dante did not interest him; I interested him by my naive and presumptuous effort to transmit Dante to him, by my language and my confused scholastic reminiscences in the space of half an hour with the soup poles on our shoulders. . . . I would really have given bread and soup, that is, blood, to save from nothingness those memories which today with the sure support of printed paper I can refresh whenever I wish and gratis, and which therefore seem of little value.
>
> Then and there they had great value. They made it possible for me to reestablish a link with the past, saving it from oblivion and reinforcing my identity. They convinced me that my mind, although besieged by everyday necessities, had not ceased to function. They elevated me in my own eyes and those of my interlocutor. They granted me a respite, ephemeral but not hebetudinous, in fact liberating and differentiating; in short, a way to find myself. (*The Drowned and The Saved* 139-140)

Culture has provided him with value, with a continuity to the past, with his linguistic heritage. Ironically, the *Ulysses* canto is about Odysseus who, after returning home to Ithaca from his long voyage to Troy, becomes the evil counselor leading his followers on a fatal second voyage. Homer's Odysseus is a domestic figure who longs for home. Dante's Ulysses—the Latin name for Odysseus—is confined to Hell because of spiritual pride and intellectual hubris. He has been an evil counselor who persuaded his comrades to follow him to destruction. He is something of a Faustian hero seeking knowledge and experience in undiscovered worlds. After returning to their home, Ulysses and his followers sailed westward until they reached a mysterious mountain, the Mount of Purgatory, before suddenly drowning. As he is being led through the Inferno by Virgil, the poet of the fall of Troy, the flight of Aeneas, and the founding of Rome, Dante would hardly have been predisposed to admire the man whose intellect had devised the stratagem that led to the Greeks conquering Troy.

For Dante, Ulysses represented the potential of the analytic intelligence for wiliness, deception, and, ultimately, evil. Ulysses explains to Dante and Virgil why he was compelled to resume his travels and turn his back on his family responsibilities: "[N]either fondness for my son, nor reverence for my aged father, nor the due love which would have made Penelope glad, could conquer in me the longing that I had to gain experience of the world, and of human vice and worth."

While Sander Gilman argues that Levi redefines himself from an Italian chemist to a Jewish writer, I would argue that he never forgets his dual Jewish-Italian heritage. Yet Gilman perceptively remarks, "Language becomes the very subject of Levi's life after the camps. . . . [T]his tongue was what Levi later called 'Lager jargon.' It consisted of fragments of the language of the murderers, combined with bits and pieces of the languages of the victims and some words which were created only in 'the camps'" (Gilman, "To Quote Primo Levi" 140). Levi has an ambivalent attitude toward Eastern Jews but discovers a tie to all Jews in being persecuted. "Levi constructs his contradictory understanding of the idea of Yiddish as simultaneously the valid and invalid, clean and polluted, clarifying and obfuscating language of the Jews" (Gilman, "To Quote Primo Levi" 158).

The Periodic Table, written much later, brilliantly relates events in his life to the periodic table. While the theme of disruption and loss is never far from the surface, and an elegiac tone informs the entire work, the narrative is less disruptive and more organic. Yet Levi still uses the vocabulary of loss, absence, emptiness, if in a sparer, more controlled way. Levi is burdened by the guilt of surviving, and that may have been a factor contributing to his suicide in 1987:

> At a distance of thirty years I find it difficult to reconstruct the sort of human being that corresponded, in November 1944, to my name or, better, to my number: 174517. I must have by then overcome the most terrible crisis, the crisis of having become part of *Lager* system, and I must have developed a strange callousness if I then managed not only to survive but also to think, to register the world around me, and even to perform rather delicate work, in an environment infected by the daily presence of death and at the same time brought to a frenzy by the approach of the Russian liberators, who by now were only eighty kilometers away. Desperation and hope alternated at a rate that would have destroyed almost any normal person in an hour. (*The Periodic Table* 139-40)

As if he were a chemical element, Levi thinks of himself in terms of a number that defines his time of arrival, his place in the death system.

Since events at Auschwitz and some of the characters recur, one can regard *The Periodic Table* as a sequel to *Survival in Auschwitz*. In some ways *The Periodic Table* is a midrash to *Survival in Auschwitz*, an explanatory commentary on the original experience. In a process akin to pentimento, *Survival in Auschwitz* continually peeks through *The Periodic Table*. We might recall Lanzmann's interview with Itzhak Zuckerman in *Shoah*: "If you could lick my heart," ventured Zuckerman, "it would poison you" (Langer, *Testimoniess*, 37). That *periodic* suggests *parodic* for an English reader stresses that the text's basic trope—the organization of chemical element within groups, families, and periods as an image for diverse human qualities—is an example of the ironic subversive mode of discourse in which the author-narrator displaces his rage. For Levi the periodic table is not only the basis for the semiotics of matter, a semiotics that has its own self-regulating structure with its own rules, but the periodic table is also a metaphor for the alphabet of a language. Indeed, for Levi the periodic table is a language and epistemology that enable him to understand better his life and times. "Rhyming" matter and experience, thoughts and language are his foci. Levi is interested in the etymology of languages. Like the elements in the periodic table, etymologies differ, but each has common properties. Yet beneath the apparent differences in etymology, grammar, and syntax, language is a common denominator of humanity that binds its speakers together. In fact, he discovers that among the diverse nationalities in the concentration camp—diverse nationalities of Jews gathered together and speaking different languages—one could imagine a *periodic table* of Jews.

Levi speaks of the language of Jewish-Piedmontese in *material* terms: "Its historical interest is meager, since it was never spoken by more than a few thousand people; but its human interest is great, as are all languages on the frontier and in transition. In fact it contains an admirable comic force, which springs from the contrast between the texture of the discourse, which is the rugged, sober, and laconic Piedmontese dialect, never written except on a bet, and the Hebrew inlay, snatched from the language of the fathers, sacred and solemn, geologic, polished smooth by the millennia like the bed of a glacier" (*The Periodic Table* 8). Conquering matter can take the form of mastering chemistry *or* language: "That conquering matter is to understand it, and understanding matter is necessary to understanding the universe and ourselves; and that therefore Mendelev's *The Periodic Table*, which just during those weeks we were laboriously learning to unravel, was poetry, loftier and more solemn than all the poetry we had swallowed down in liceo; and come to think of it, it even rhymed! That if one looked for the bridge, the missing link, between the world of words and the world of things, one did not have to look far: it was there, in our Autenrieth, in our smoke-filled labs, and in our future trade" (*The Periodic Table* 41-42). The first passage defines the optative relation between his chemical and his human investigations—including his probes into his own behavior and deep memory—and his poignant belief (or wish) that science will create an enclave from history.

Just as, Levi implies, Sandro, the man who taught him how to climb, conquers mountains, so the chemist comes to terms with the elements and the writer with words: all are human triumphs. Yet Levi is aware of the limitations of words, particularly to describe Sandro, whose physicality made him forget for a short time "the nightmare weighing on Europe" (*The*

Periodic Table 45): "Today I know that it is a hopeless task to try to dress a man in words, make him live again on the printed page, especially a man like Sandro. He was not the sort of person you can tell stories about, nor to whom one erects monuments—he who laughed at all monuments: he lived completely in his deeds, and when they were over nothing of him remains—nothing but words, precisely" (*The Periodic Table* 48).

Levi's melancholy tone prevails throughout *The Periodic Table* as he recalls that he comes from modest stock, and that after the war he becomes a commercial chemist, a *useful* person—a cog in the postwar Italian machine—but one on the margins in every phase of his life. Humility at times approaches self-denigration, survival touches self-deprivation. Levi begins *The Periodic Table* with a paragraph about inert gases, and then uses those gases as a metaphor for his ancestors: "[T]here is no doubt that they were inert in their inner spirits, inclined to disinterested speculation, witty discourses, elegant, sophisticated, and gratuitous discussion. It can hardly be by chance that all the deeds attributed to them, though quite various, have in common a touch of the static, an attitude of dignified abstention, of voluntary (or accepted) relegation to the margins of the great river of life. Noble, inert, and rare: their history is quite poor when compared to that of other illustrious Jewish communities in Italy and Europe" (*The Periodic Table* 4).

Levi uses the synchronic and diachronic historical contexts to place his own personal tragedy. In *The Periodic Table* the personal gradually becomes subsumed by the political when encroaching fascism in his native Piedmont transforms the essential *elements* of national and personal life: "Writing sad, crepuscular poems, and not all that beautiful, while the world was in flames, did not seem to us either strange or shameful: we proclaimed ourselves the enemies of Fascism, but actually Fascism had had its effect on us, as on almost all Italians, alienating and making us superficial, passive, and cynical" (*The Periodic Table* 128). He traces the awakening of his historical awareness, in part because Aryan laws have declared Jews "different": "'[T]hey' had declared us 'different,' and different we would be; we took sides but kept out of the stupid and cruel Aryan games, discussing the plays of O'Neill and Thornton Wilder, climbing the Grigne slopes, falling a bit in love with each other, inventing intellectual games, and singing the lovely songs Silvio had learned from some of his Waldensian friends. As to what was happening during those same months in all of Europe occupied by the Germans, in Anne Frank's house in Amsterdam, in the pit of Babi Yar near Kiev, in the ghetto of Warsaw, in Salonika, Paris, and Lidice: as to this pestilence which was about to submerge us no precise information had reached us, only vague and sinister hints dropped by soldiers returning from Greece or from the rear areas of the Russian front, and which we tended to censor" (*The Periodic Table*, 129). Once again, Levi writes of how he sought refuge in the imaginative word of literature, as he later would in the art of writing the texts we are discussing.

The Periodic Table has become, we realize, a map of how Levi *knows*, an essential epistemological and semiotic tool for ordering his life. He begins his concluding chapter, "Carbon," by calling his book a "micro-history, the history of a trade and its defeats, victories, and miseries" rather than calling his book a memoir or an autobiography (*The Periodic Table* 224). Just as nature speaks to most of us, so the elements speak to him. He weaves a putative journey about an atom of carbon that eventually becomes part of his own brain cell—a chemical odyssey to the place where his brain functions to produce words: "This cell belongs to a brain, and it is my brain, the brain of *me* who is writing; and the cell in question, and within it the atom in question, is in charge of my writing, in a gigantic minuscule game which nobody has yet described. It is that which at this instant, issuing out of a labyrinthine tangle of yeses and nos, makes my hand run along a certain path on the paper, mark it with these volutes that are signs: a double snap, up and down, between two levels of energy, guides this hand of mine to impress on the paper this dot, here, this one" (*The Periodic Table* 232-33). Does not Levi's later suicide make the prior passage all the more poignant?

The Periodic Table shows us, as Spiegelman does in the *Maus* books, how indirection can bring the subject of the Holocaust to life as much as graphic memoir. Somewhat anticipating Spiegelman's bestiary in the *Maus* books, Levi sustains, throughout his unnumbered chapters named for elements, a comparison between the elements and human behavior. Indeed its epigraph is a Jewish proverb, "Troubles overcome are good to tell." (Perhaps the subtitle to Spiegelman's sequel, *Maus II, And Here My Troubles Began,* owes something to Levi's epigraph for *his* sequel.) The dense interweaving of the personal and historical give both the *Maus* books and *The Periodic Table* their special quality. While *The Periodic Table* is a memoir, the anecdotes—really carefully structured stories—become, like the beginning three first-person stories of *Dubliners*, universal in their meaning; and like *Dubliners* too the stories change their focus from youth to adolescence to maturity. *The Periodic Table*, like *A Portrait of the Artist as a Young Man*, also has aspects of the bildungsroman and kunstlerroman, and takes a novelistic shape with a progressive movement from boyhood in prewar Italy to maturity in postwar Italy.

Levi's memory is not heroic; as Langer puts it, "Heroic memory searches for a moral vision, a principle supporting the idea of the individual as responsible agent for his actions" (*Holocaust Testimonies* 186). Levi dramatizes the return of his humanity at liberation but also how the inflicted pain continues. The last chapter of *Survival in Auschwitz* is just that: a story of survival, not liberation, and its last sentence expresses a hope that he will see one of the companions with whom he survived after the Germans flee. In the last book published in his lifetime, *The Drowned and the Saved*, he wrote: "In the majority of cases, the hour of liberation was neither joyful nor lighthearted. For most it occurred against a tragic background of destruction, slaughter, and suffering. Just as they felt they were again becoming men, that is, responsible, the sorrows of men returned: the sorrow of the dispersed or lost family; the universal suffering all around; their own exhaustion, which seemed definitive, past cure; the problems of life to begin all over again amid the rubble, often alone" (*The Drowned and the Saved* 70-71). Levi's text speaks to the memory as narrative, as testimony to past events that it re-creates according to its own needs.

III

The Reawakening (1963; translated 1965) covers the period after Levi's liberation from Auschwitz in January 1945. Drawing upon the metaphor of rebirth in spring, it begins with a chapter entitled "The Thaw." On January 27, the first Russians arrive to liberate the camp: "So for us even the hour of liberty rang out grave and muffled, and filled our souls with joy and yet with a painful sense of prudency, so that we should have liked to wash our consciences and our memories clean from the foulness that lay upon them; and also with anguish, because we felt that this should never happen, that now nothing could ever happen good and pure enough to rub out our past, and that the scars of the outrage would remain within us for ever, and in the memories of those who saw it, and in the places where it occurred and in the stories that we should tell of it" (*The Reawakening* 16-17).

Levi understands that the Holocaust is the alpha and omega of his life, that everything is affected and shaped by that experience. He thinks of himself as an ancient mariner who has the burden of telling. He entitles the book *The Reawakening*, in part because in *Survival in Auschwitz* he speaks of a dream-state between conscious and unconscious life:

> My dream stands in front of me, still warm, and although awake I am still full of its anguish: and then I remember that it is not a haphazard dream, but that I have dreamed it not once but many times since I arrived here, with hardly any variations of environment or details. I am now quite awake and I remember that I have recounted it to Alberto and that he confided to me, to my amazement, that it is also his dream and the dream of many others, perhaps of everyone. Why does it happen? Why is the pain of every day translated so constantly into our dreams, in the ever-repeated scene of the unlistened-to story?
>
> While I meditate on this, I try to profit from the interval of wakefulness to shake off the painful remnants of the preceding sleep, so as not to compromise the quality of the next dream. (*Survival in Auschwitz* 54)

The Reawakening is about the reawakening of self *and* of Western civilization. It is a journey home, but, as the map preceding chapter 1 reminds us, it is a journey fraught with detours and misdirection. Instead of going west and south, he goes north and even at one point east. Levi finds the Russians far less hostile than the Germans and somewhat idealizes them in terms of the classical myths that give him stability: "They were cheerful, sad and tired, and took pleasure in food and wine, like Ulysses' companions after the ships had been pulled ashore. And yet, under their slovenly and anarchical appearance, it was easy to see in them, in each of those rough and open faces, the good soldiers of the Red Army" (*The Reawakening* 59-60).

After almost nine months since the camp's liberation and more than thirteen months in the camps, eleven in Auschwitz, he arrives home exhausted. In the final chapter, entitled "The Awakening," he is moved to self-searching and self-questioning interrogatives: "And how much had we lost, in those . . . months? What should we find at home? How much of ourselves had been eroded, extinguished? Were we returning richer or poorer, stronger or emptier? We did not know; but we knew that on the thresholds of our homes, for good or ill, a trial awaited us, and we anticipated it with fear. We felt in our veins the poison of Auschwitz, flowing together with our thin blood; where should we find the strength to begin our lives again, to break down the barriers, the brushwood which grows up spontaneously in all absences, around every deserted house, every empty refuge" (*The Reawakening* 206). For Levi is also the analytic chemist of emotion: "Nostalgia is a fragile and tender anguish, basically different, more intimate, more human than the other pains we had endured till then—beatings, cold, hunger, terror, destitution, disease. Nostalgia is a limpid and clean pain, but demanding; it permeates every minute of the day, permits no other thoughts and induces a need for escape" (*The Reawakening* 144).

The subject and structuring motif of *The Reawakening* is the disconfirmation, the postponement, the reformulation of dreams, plans, and hopes. Our interior narratives console, and Levi had found consolation in the equation of liberty with perfection and with the potential for reestablishing community with his fellow humans. By contrast, the Greek Mordo Nahem's code is one of self-survival, without dependence on anyone, and his concept of work includes activities that others might call theft and fraud: "The basis of his ethic was work, which to him was a sacred duty, but which he understood in a very wide sense. To him, work included everything, but with the condition that it should bring profit without limiting liberty. . . . [He] considered reprehensible . . . any relationship of employment, [and] any services, even if they were well paid, he lumped together as 'servile work'. But it was not servile work to plough your own field, or to sell false antiques to tourists at a port. (*The Reawakening* 47). Levi comments: "It is common knowledge that nobody is born with a decalogue already formed, but that everyone builds his own either during his life or at the end, on the basis of his own experiences. . . . The Lager had happened to both of us; I had felt it as a monstrous upheaval, a loathsome anomaly in my history and in the history of the world; he, as a sad confirmation of things well known.

'There is always war', man is wolf to man: an old story" (*The Reawakening* 52). Even in moments of despair, Levi holds out the hope of a better alternative. Yet he has an inkling of the pollution of his dream when, in his Eastward journey after the war, a Polish lawyer speaks of him to her compatriots as a political prisoner rather than as a Jew who had been persecuted: "I had dreamed, we had always dreamed, of something like this, in the nights at Auschwitz: of seeking and not being listened to, of finding liberty and remaining alone" (*The Reawakening* 55).

A major theme of the months of wandering is exile: "I was overcome—as if a dike had crumbled—by a new and greater pain, previously buried and relegated to the margins of my consciousness by other more immediate pains: the pain of exile, of my distant home, of loneliness, of friends lost, of youth lost and of the host of corpses all around" (*The Reawakening*, 18); the parallel again is to the *Odyssey*, the tale of the wily adventurer who must make his very home from exile. As he leaves Auschwitz in a "feverish torpor," he looks back, as if he were leaving Troy, at the special sign on "the gate to slavery, on which one could still read the three, now hollow, words of derision: '*Arbeit Macht Frei*', 'Work Gives Freedom'"(*The Reawakening* 20-21).

Each of the episodes of *The Reawakening* is structured to end in an epiphany. For example, after describing D'Agata's obsessive and near psychotic fear of bugs in the last of his anecdotes entitled "The Dreamers," Levi writes: "At first, these habits of his had been derided; was his skin thinner than ours? But then compassion had prevailed, mixed with a trace of envy; because, of all of us, D'Agata was the only one whose enemy was concrete, present, tangible, capable of being fought, beaten, crushed against the wall" (*The Reawakening* 105). Characteristically, as in the prior passage, Levi finds moments of humanity in his objective yet touching description of his physically and emotionally crippled fellow prisoners: the paralyzed child, Hurbinek; the 15-year-old Hungarian Henek, who cared for Hurbinek, and who had been a Kapo in the children's block: "When there were selections at the children's Block he was the one who chose. Did he feel no remorse? No: why should he? Was there any other way to survive?" (*The Reawakening* 27). Kleine is a 12-year-old whose delirium reflects his imprisonment— even after he is freed—in part because he had been perhaps the sex slave of the Lager-Kapo.

It is as if Levi were in a dream-state, occupying a world between looking and seeing. As Langer writes,

> The permanently corrupting influence of such experiences inspired survivors, too, with recurrent collective dreams that later provided many writers with material for an imaginative universe existing between the bounds of fantasy and reality. Elsewhere Levi has commented on one peculiarity of the dream-phenomenon in l'univers concentrationnaire: . . . Levi's dream-state is a "ladder between the unconscious and the conscious," in which he tries to explain to friends and members of his family the essential truth of his camp experience—the railway cars, the train whistles, the hard wooden beds, the hunger, the lice, the beatings, the blood. (The Holocaust and the Literary Imagination 50-51)

In The Reawakening, Levi continues the dream metaphor; as Langer writes: "[T]he cosmic enemy becomes life itself, absorbed into the landscape and the atmosphere, pervading everything, an indefinable threat, always there to disturb one's waking hours and hover over one's dreams, announcing the impossibility of an episode at the very moment it occurs, deceptively reassuring at the instant of extremity, when the options of oblivion and eternity disrupt the 'real' until the imagination can no longer acknowledge what it once considered 'real'" (The Holocaust and the Literary Imagination 51). Notice how in the last chapter of The Reawakening, entitled "The Awakening," Levi describes his return in terms of the repetition of an association of feeling that Freud associates with trauma: "It is a dream within a dream, varied in detail, one in substance. I am sitting at a table with my family, or with friends, or at work, or in the green countryside; . . . yet I feel a deep and subtle anguish, the definite sensation of an impending threat. And in fact, as the dream proceeds, slowly or brutally, each time in a different way, everything collapses and disintegrates around me, the scenery, the walls, the people, while the anguish becomes more intense and more precise. . . . I am in the Lager once more, and nothing is true outside the Lager. . . . Now this inner dream, this dream of peace, is over, and in the outer dream, which continues, gelid, a well-known voice resounds: a single word, not imperious, but brief and subdued. It is the dawn command of

Auschwitz, a foreign word, feared and expected: get up, 'Wstawàch'" (*The Reawakening* 207-208). At times *The Reawakening* is an ironic title for a text that asks how nostalgia can become present suffering and how past trauma can overwhelm the present. Levi learns of the fate of the 29 others who had been deported with him, of whom only five survived gassing; even they are now dead.

Let us consider in the above passage how "nothing is true outside the Lager." Could not that one sentence stand as a metaphor for my study of Holocaust narratives? Like a gaseous nebula in the cosmos, this experience expands implicitly to fill Levi's entire universe. The dream becomes a metaphor for the process by which the mind tries to find a meaning in memory, to shape a narrative from the mind's mental universe.

Levi sees his role as witness, as heir to the biblical tradition of those who are compelled to speak by a combination of righteousness, responsibility, and moral urgency: "[I]f I had not lived the Auschwitz experience, I probably would never have written anything. I would not have had the motivation, the incentive to write. . . . It was the experience of the Camp and the long journey home that forced me to write. I did not have to struggle with laziness, problems of style seemed ridiculous to me, and miraculously I found the time to write without taking even one hour away from my daily professional work" (*The Reawakening* 230). With his references to such epic antecedents as *The Odyssey* and *The Divine Comedy*, he places the Lager experience in a Western context, but he cannot sustain the effort to use mythic methods to give shape and significance to the moral anarchy he observes. He is our Virgil taking us through Hell. His very reserve is a source of eloquence. He draws upon specific personalities to produce a Dantesque gallery of people, including the aforementioned Greek Mordo Nahum and the Italian Cesare, who lived mostly in the morally gray area. They are almost like medieval gargoyles. Levi comments in metaphorical terms that sees Nahum as "alone wolf" and Cesare, joyous and cunning, as "a child of the sun" (*The Reawakening* 80).

The Reawakening is a temporal journey through time in which it stands as the postwar *Odyssey* to *The Iliad* of the earlier war narrative, *Survival in Auschwitz*. Levi's first-person narrator—a surrogate for himself, but also an archtypical figure plays the role of a modern Odysseus consigned within a vertical axis to perpetual hell; *The Drowned and the*

Saved exists on a more temporal, horizontal axis in which he places characters on a spectrum of those who survived and those lost in the secular hell of the camps. Interestingly, he attributes his being an intellectual today to the camp experience: "I may be an 'intellectual' today, even though the word fills me with vague discomfort; I certainly was not one then, because of moral immaturity, ignorance, and alienation; and if I became one later on, paradoxically I owe that precisely to the Lager experience" (*The Drowned and the Saved* 132).

Primo Levi's *Moments of Reprieve* (1979) complements *Survival in Auschwitz* (1947) and *The Reawakening* (1963). The book contains what he calls "paralipomena" of his two "books of chronicles." These are stories written on different occasions that testify not only to the human spirit but also to the power of memory (note the title) to reshape odd moments, chance encounters, and intermittent bonding into patterns of meaning; as Levi puts it, "each of them is centered on one character only, who never is the persecuted, predestined victim, the prostrate man, the person to whom I had devoted my first book, and about whom I had obsessively asked myself if this was still a man. The protagonists of these stories are 'men' beyond all doubt, even if the virtue that allows them to survive and makes them unique is not always one approved of by common morality" (*Moments of Reprieve* 10). In the anecdotes comprising *Moments of Reprieve*, Levi has a double optics; on one hand, he has a morality to judge right and wrong even in the camps; but on the other, circumstances may justify any means to survive. Thus of the naiveté of Band who learns to steal after initial reluctance, he writes with a gently amused envy, "Besides, I soon realized that Band had a unique talent for happiness. Oppression, humiliation, hard work, exile—all seemed to slide off him like water off a rock, without corrupting or wounding him, indeed purifying and enhancing in him his inborn capacity for joy . . . " (*Moments of Reprieve* 51).

Levi wants to generalize the ghetto experience, to propose that the ghetto is life itself, and that the ghetto of life is an island from death "Like Rumkowski [the morally bankrupt leader of the Lodz ghetto and the subject of Leslie Epstein's *King of the Jews*, which we shall discuss in a later chapter] we too are so dazzled by power and money as to forget our essential fragility, forget that all of us are in the ghetto, that the ghetto is fenced in, that beyond the fence stands the lords of death, and not far away the train is waiting" (*Moments of Reprieve* 172). But even as we contemporary readers may resist the grim metaphor of the waiting train, we notice that it contains the seeds of Levi's subsequent suicide. Speaking of Avrom, the partisan, Levi writes of Avrom's trying to recapture the past in Hebrew that he has not fully mastered: "In this language, which is new to him, he has set down his memories in the form of bare and unpretentious notes, veiled by the distance of time and space. . . . It is to be hoped that [these notes] will find someone who will restore them to the full breath of life. . . . " (*Moments of Reprieve* 123). With his book of "paralipomena," has not the narrator himself restored Avrom and others like him?

In *Moments of Reprieve*, Levi's style is almost of the Yiddish folk tale; as Nicholas Patruno writes: "Levi's sober, lean style is reflective of a mind guided by reason and civility. Through his emphasis on clarity, his dispassionate approach, and his accurate observations (honed by his scientific training), he left emotional responses to the reader" (*Understanding Primo Levi* 5). Perhaps in *Survival in Auschwitz*—which, we recall, in its first English edition more accurately translates his Italian title, *Se questa e un uomo*, as "*If This Is a Man*"—he wished to be blessed, like Coleridge's Ancient Mariner, with the power of speech to pour out his heart as a witness. However, by the time he wrote *The Periodic Table*, Levi knew the place of restraint, irony, understatement. *Moments of Reprieve* lacks the fragmentary, seemingly untutored style and structure of *Survival in Auschwitz*. From the outset, he sees himself as a successor to Dante, a Virgil taking us through the modern inferno. Levi is a modern Dante who will read the hermeneutics of history. He knows he himself and other survivors never "wash our consciences and our memories clean from the foulness that lay upon them" (*The Reawakening* 16).

Why are Levi's books among the most effective Holocaust narratives? For one thing, they reveal his stance of presumed objectivity, which he attributes to his scientific temperament. Yet, he observes human behavior not as part of general rules but of wondrous particulars to be observed. From his observations, to be sure, he proposes tentative hypotheses or discursive formations, but they are flexible to new data and by no means rigid or doctrinaire. He is an Aristotelian who lives in the ineluctable modality of the visible; generalizations are based on what he has observed. He writes what he knew then, leaving out details and data that he may have learned afterward. As he puts it in the "Afterword" to *The Reawakening*: "Precisely for this reason, when describing the tragic world of Auschwitz, I have deliberately assumed the calm, sober language of the witness, neither the lamenting tones of the victim nor the irate voice of someone who seeks revenge. I thought that my account would be all the more credible and useful the more it appeared objective and the less it sounded overly emotional; only in this way does a witness in matters of justice perform his task, which is that of preparing the ground for the judge. The judges are my readers" (210).

CHAPTER THREE

WORLD INTO WORDS:
THE DIARY OF ANNE FRANK AND SOPHIE GOETZEL-LEVIATHAN'S *THE WAR FROM WITHIN*

I

To place our discussion of Wiesel, Levi, and Anne Frank in a historical context, I begin this chapter with a quote from Martin Gilbert:

> The systematic attempt to destroy all European Jewry—an attempt now known as the Holocaust—began in the last week of June 1941, within hours of the German invasion of the Soviet Union. This onslaught upon Jewish life in Europe continued without respite for nearly four years. . . .
>
> Jews perished in extermination camps, execution sites, ghettos, slave labour camps, and on the death marches. The testimony of those who survived constitutes the main record of what was done to the Jews during those years. The murderers also kept records, often copious ones. But the victims, the six million who were done to death, could leave no record. A few fragments of diaries, letters and scribbled messages do survive. But in the main, others must bear witness to what was done to the millions who could never tell their own story. (18)

The Diary of Anne Frank (published in 1947 in Holland as *Het Achterhuis,* "The House Behind" and in the United States in 1952) is probably the best known and most widely read Holocaust diary-memoir. As my discussion of Ozick's response in the introduction demonstrated, how we read this text tells something about ourselves. Yet it is a dialogic text that speaks in many, and at times contradictory, voices. *The Diary of Anne Frank* is a story of how Anne increasingly sees herself as a marginalized Jew, as *other,* as belonging to a group singled out for persecution, deprived of her complete personal and cultural identity and given another. At times we hear the voice of political and spiritual eloquence: "Who has inflicted this upon us? Who has made us Jews different from all other people? Who has allowed us to suffer so terribly up till now? It is God that has made us as we are, but it will be God, too, who will raise us up again. . . . We can never become just Netherlanders, or just English, or representatives of any country for that matter, we will always remain Jews, but we want to, too." (April 11, 1944; 221; unless otherwise indicated, cited passages are from the 1952 Doubleday edition).

How many assimilated Jews, reading this book in the 1950s as a child or young adolescent—as I did—became more conscious of their own Jewish identity?

The Frank family fled German persecution for Holland only to find themselves caught up in the maelstrom after Germany invaded Holland. After Otto Frank, Anne's father and the lone survivor from his family, returned from the camps, he was given the diaries by Miep Gies, who had taken care of the family in hiding and who found and hid the diaries after the Nazis arrested the eight Jews who were hiding. It is worth noting that Anne rewrote most of her dairy before capture. Otto Frank typed the diaries, and made some additions and corrections; as Frank wrote in 1949: "The text was edited at the request of the publishing house. Some unimportant changes were made with my agreement. In addition some passages were left out, again with my agreement. These were entries by my daughter which it was felt might cause offense to the readers. Thus, for instance, the penultimate paragraph of the Dutch version of the entry on January 5, 1944, was a slight abbreviation of the typescript and the original version, in that the story of the two girls touching each other's breasts was omitted; that passage, however, was included in the German edition without objection" (*The Diary of Anne Frank,* The Critical Edition, prepared by the Netherlands State Institute for War Documentation, 1989, 69). Gerrold Van Der Stroom explains: "Anne Frank wrote two versions of her diary, the second being based on the first. In addition she also wrote *Verhaaltjes en gebeurtenissen uit het Achterhuis (Tales from the Secret Annexe)*, referred to in short as the *Tales*. It was on the basis of these manuscripts that the first Dutch publication of her diaries, *Het Achterhuis*, was brought out in 1947" (*The Diary of Anne Frank: The Critical Edition* 168).

As Berteke Waaldijk summarizes the text's history:

Anne Frank started to rewrite her diaries at the end of May 1944. In the next 2 months, she rewrote almost all her diary entries of the 2 previous years. She must have been writing feverishly, rewriting up to 10 pages a day, while also adding new entries. After the Frank family had been deported, the rewritten version and parts of the original entries were found by a woman who had helped the family while in hiding. In 1945, she returned them to Otto Frank, Anne Frank's father, when it became obvious that Anne would never return. With the help of others, Otto Frank edited the diaries and made them into one text. After initial rejections by a few publishers, the diary of Anne Frank was published in 1947 as *Het Achterhuis* (The Secret Annexe). Translations followed and *The Diary of a Young Girl*, usually called *The Diary of Anne Frank* in English, became world-famous. (Waaldijk 328-29)

We might recall the prefatory comment to the 1952 English edition:

Het Achterhuis, the Dutch title of this book, refers to that part of the building which served as a hiding place for the two families who took shelter there between 1942 and 1944. *Achter* means "behind" or "in back of" and *huis* is Dutch for "house." In Amsterdam's old buildings the apartments overlooking a garden or court may be divided from those overlooking the street, thus providing two separate suites within the same apartment. Het Achterhuis or, literally, "the house behind" is situated on the Prinsengracht, one of the city's canals.

To simplify the English text, we have called that part of the house the Secret Annexe, although it is not an annex in the proper sense of the word. (*Anne Frank: The Diary of a Young Girl* 5)

The 1952 translation is in idiomatic English; for example Anne purportedly writes: "I explained all this carefully to Dussel. But one thing amazed me: he is very slow on the uptake" (Nov. 19, 1942; 64).

Dating from June 12, 1942 to August 1, 1944, the diary is the story of a young girl's life from 13 to 15. Anne objectifies the diary's imagined addressee as "Kitty," as a listening other who will respond empathetically: *"I hope I shall be able to confide in you completely, as I have never been able to do in anyone before, and I hope that you will be a great support and comfort to me"* (9). The diary opens with her wishes that she will have an empathetic other in whom to confide. Thus she gives the diary the name of a pet, "kitty." The entries are in the form of epistles, to "Dear Kitty," and signed "Yours, Anne." Her goal is to express her "real feelings" (January 22, 1944; 152). As she matures, she imagines an increasingly sophisticated narratee in "Kitty"—a narratee who becomes a polyauditory listener, responding to a tale of racial persecution, family deprivation, and adolescence. "I want to write, but more than that, I want to bring out all kinds of things that lie buried deep in my heart. . . . And now I come to the root of the matter, the reason for my starting a diary: it is that I have no such real friend. . . . In order to enhance in my mind's eye the picture of the friend for whom I have waited so long, I don't want to set down a series of bald facts in a diary like most people do, but I want this diary itself to be my friend, and I shall call my friend Kitty" (June 20, 1942; 13).

II

Anne Frank's diary begins as a search for self-definition *and* intimacy. In his 1841 notebook, Henry David Thoreau wrote, "My journal is that of me which would else spill over and run to waste" (quoted in Michael Frank 1). What is striking about *The Diary of Anne Frank* is that it is like most diaries—writing at a brief retrospective interval—and that it affords a record of the evolution of the writer's mind. Thus, each subsequent entry modifies the prior one. Entries become tentative formulations, discursive hypotheses, which are modified, undermined, and reformulated. The writing *is* the agon. What is different from a retrospective memoir is that, like a serial novel that would be published in tiny episodes and numbers, we are aware of the continuing possibility of unwriting and rewriting. Yet, not only does the rereader know the outcome—her capture, deportation, her death—but so do many first readers. Finally, every page is historically framed by the Holocaust. For the historical circumstances are always there, a pentimento peeking through. It accompanies our reading. Thus the writing and rewriting has a strong effect of pathos on the reader. The words struggle against the inevitability of history—our knowledge of not only what awaits her but what in fact *awaited* her—and we feel sadly her impotence and *ours* to prevent the inevitable even as we admire her courage and vitality.

When reading diaries we peek into pages supposedly not meant for our eyes. We play a performative role in discovering a private script and, by reading that script give it life. Anne Frank wrote because she needed to make a record of her self as a way of understanding herself, but did she ever believe that her diary would be read? Probably, for Anne situates herself in a world with a future; ironically readers learn she is the victim of the final solution. We see her struggle with words as a metaphor for her struggle to survive and vice versa. She finds refuge in words—refuge from her personal disappointment in establishing relations with the other inhabitants, except her father at the outset and Peter later—and both of these relationships seem to be, in part, self-created. Her need for a narrative to make sense of her life while it was taking unexpected turns, to retain the structures of family and intimate life on which she had relied, struggles with the narrative of actuality. As space and liberty become constricted, she often uses verbs of speaking, writing, and listening, as if the importance of words expands in her entrapped universe. How often do we find that communication is almost as crucial as food to alleviate suffering in Holocaust fictions?

By establishing control over words, Anne, the self-described "chatterbox" begins to establish coherent form over an inchoate self, to build a coherent identity. But she longs for the world beyond: "But most of all, I long for a home of our own, to be able to move freely and to have some help with my work again at last, in other words—school" (July 23, 1943; 102). Diaries ask the reader to complete the story, to provide historical nexus, to provide a bridge between entries. Yet, the reader must resist putting in plot where there isn't one. Just as in Civil War and other prisoner-of-war diaries, we see in Anne Frank's diary complaints of selfishness, petty thievery, ill manners, rudeness, and spite.

By contrast, memoirs depend on a different kind of memory; the intervening years of experience and psychological damage—blocking, dulling, or distorting events—play a role in shaping narratives. Memoirs are a mixture of autobiography and history. Memoirists are concerned with how they will be remembered and how to present themselves in a favorable light, but diarists write for the moment. (Of course, that we have Anne's *rewritten* diary gives it an aspect of memoir.) In Anne's writing to the moment, we see a dialogue between hope and fear, between self-immersion and historical awareness, between adolescent naiveté and insightful understanding of human behavior, and between specific Jewish consciousness and more universal human responses.

In Bakhtinian terms, *The Diary of Anne Frank* is a heteroglossic text in which different voices dialogically contend; these voices represent strands of a developing coherent self, strands that are at times inchoate, as the diary becomes much more defined. As diverse voices contend in her writing, we need not only to hear them but to understand how they contend: the adolescent girl drawing upon her expectations of upper-middle-class life, the historical perspective of a young Jew whose family is victimized by racial laws; the voice of a young girl observing the sociology of eight people in self-imposed exile and hiding; the evolving voice of a young girl coming to terms with her sexuality; the voice of a maturing adult in confinement and reduced economic circumstances. In this dialogic contention of voices is the rich meaning of a text that reveals as it conceals, conceals as it reveals.

The Diary of Anne Frank has a double teleology: (1) the growth of an adolescent, and (2) the political demise of the Jews in Europe, with the Frank's family representative of those facing the terror of the Holocaust. We must read with a double optics as we discover both the conventional memories seen from the perspective of a child and the wrenching drama as a child comes to terms with the searing actuality of a grotesque adult world that she has had no part in creating.

Some first readers may ask not only what will happen to her but also how much longer can she hide and will it be long enough to outlast historical circumstances. Even if some readers do not know that she died of typhus in Bergen-Belsen in March 1945, or assume that she was gassed, how many have ever read Anne Frank without knowing how the historical plot unfolds? Many if not most read the teleology of her development and growth, knowing the counter-teleology of her deportation and demise. "Our many Jewish friends are being taken away by the dozen. These people are treated by the Gestapo without a shred of decency, being loaded into cattle trucks and sent to Westerbork, the big Jewish camp in Drente. Westerbork sounds terrible: only one washing cubicle for a hundred people and not nearly enough lavatories. . . . If it is as bad as this in Holland whatever will it be like in the distant and barbarous regions they are sent to? We assume that most of them are murdered. The English radio speaks of their being gassed" (October 9, 1942; 49-50).

Notwithstanding the passages about deportation, Anne Frank's diary confines the Holocaust mostly to family life in the annex. Within the confined world in which she writes, Jews may be deprived of the privileges of citizenship, but they are not gassed. The dramatic irony is we know about that world beyond, but she does not. We meet Anne before she and her family, who left Germany for Holland, go into hiding but after Hitler has instituted racial laws. She tells us that her father was thirty-six when he married her mother, who was then twenty-five. Her sister Margot was born in 1926 in Frankfort-on-Main, and she followed on June 12, 1929. The family emigrated to Holland in 1933, where her father was appointed Managing Director of Travies N.V. She outlines the history of the persecution of Jews in Holland beginning with the 1938 pogroms, including decrees stipulating that Jews must wear a yellow star, that Jews are banned from trams and are forbidden to drive. Jews are only allowed to do their shopping between three and five o'clock and then only in shops that bear the placard "Jewish shop" (See June 20, 1942; 13, 14). Well before going into hiding she had been placed in a Jewish secondary school and been forbidden to visit her Christian friends.

Anne Frank's diary has in some curricula become an *annex* to the horrors of the Shoah. The omission of the more uncomfortable scenes and images of the Holocaust may have helped it find a place in curricula for public schools, where it has become an appropriate tale for school children whose young sensibilities supposedly must be protected from the terrors of the Holocaust. Anne at times speaks with a sanitized diction that keeps the Holocaust at bay and, that, for naive readers (and school boards in the 1950s and 1960s) provided a comfortable way of dealing with horrific events. Thus, if one disregards or minimizes the historical passages and the contextual knowledge we bring to the text, one can *think* one is experiencing the Holocaust without engaging in its unpleasantness. Surely, one of the book's appeals to generations of schoolteachers and pupils is its almost saccharine sweetness, but some of that apparent sweetness gives way to more complex emotions such as a competitive rivalry with her mother: "I am becoming still more independent of my parents, young as I am, I face life with more courage than Mummy; my feeling for justice is immovable, and truer than hers" (April 11, 1944; 222).

The Diary of Anne Frank may have been reviled by those who wished to find vestiges of liberal humanism and Enlightenment promise in the postwar era, but for some it provided a comfortable human alternative to the camp photographs and books such as *Night* or *Survival in Auschwitz*. Anne's naive meditations may even grate upon those who seek other than a humanistic scenario, but she is aware that God may be no more than anthropomorphized conscience: "People who have a religion should be glad, for not everyone has the gift of believing in heavenly things. You don't necessarily even have to be afraid of punishment of death; purgatory, hell, and heaven are things that a lot of people can't accept, but still a religion, it doesn't matter which, keeps a person on the right path. It isn't the fear of God but the upholding of one's own honor and conscience" (July 6, 1944; 270). Or take her ingenuous willingness to entertain the causes of anti-Semitism, before avowing "Anti-Semitism is unjust. . . . The cause of this hatred of the Jews is understandable, even human sometimes, but not good" (May 22, 1944; 252, 253).

Anne's politics are naive—yet logical *and* maddeningly humanistic: "I don't believe that the big men, the politicians and the capitalists alone, are guilty of the war. Oh no, the little man is just as guilty, otherwise the peoples of the world would have risen in revolt long ago! There's in people simply an urge to destroy, an urge to kill, to murder and rage, and until all mankind, without exception, undergoes a great change, wars will be waged, everything that has been built up, cultivated, and grown will be destroyed and disfigured, after which mankind will have to begin all over again" (May 3, 1944; 237). Even as we know how compliant some "little" men were and how many murdered the Jews in the camps and during the "actions" by death squads, yet others, Anne reminds us, such as "our vegetable man" did resist (May 25, 1944; 254). Her voice is what the survivors of the Western humanistic enlightenment perspective want to hear. According to this ethos, dominant in the 1950s, notwithstanding the threat of atomic warfare, mankind is evolving upward, coming together, and resolving differences between cultures—between Christian and Jew—and *that* is the lesson we *need* find in the Holocaust. It may even be that the view of the Holocaust as a grotesque wrong turn is an optative response to the fear of a cataclysmic atomic bomb exchange between superpowers.

III

Yet we should understand that the continuing appeal of the diary depends upon its multivocal and polysemous quality. Anne is alternately passionate and ruminative, restlessly gregarious and introspective. Melissa Muller's *Anne Frank: The Biography* (1998) fleshes out Anne's life and summarizes five missing pages that Otto Frank suppressed. According to Muller, these pages are sympathetic to Anne's mother, whom Anne saw as trapped in a marriage of convenience. But, while acknowledging the importance of Muller's discovery we must not forget Anne's rapid oscillations in tone and attitude toward her fellow annex denizens and the fundamental honesty with which she recorded her feelings at a given moment. Nor should we forget that she wished to isolate her mother and think of herself as sharing a special intimacy and rapport with her father. When we recall that her collection of favorite photos on the attic wall included Greta Garbo and Ray Milland, we should not be surprised about her propensity for dramatizing family nuances in large strokes.

A major *topos* of Holocaust fiction is the voice of the survivor; it is the dream of redemption fulfilled. That survivors caught in the flotsam and jetsam of the historical morass—Wiesel, Levi, Rachael Apt in *The Wall*, Art Spiegelman's father Vladek—live to extract meaning creates a teleology of hope to which we cling when we read other Holocaust texts in which the voice perished and only words survive. Yet, when we read about Cynthia Ozick's Rosa, Vladek Spiegelman, and especially Primo Levi and Tadeusz Borowski—both of whom were suicides—do we ever forget the ineradicable damage that survives with the victims? The voice of the victim who survives, like Anne Frank, if only in her words, also has its redemptive energy—but only if we as rereaders desperately desire an alternative counterplot and find ourselves repressing our knowledge of Anne's demise.

Some will object to Anne's apparent superficiality and how she has inculcated socially encoded stereotypes of females, as when, while in a school restricted to Jews, she needs to write an essay for being a chatterbox, and argues that her talkativeness is an "inherited" quality (June 21, 1942; 17). While she makes these arguments to please a male teacher, she constructs a self within the diary that is open, evolving, flexible, and increasingly poised. We might smile ironically when she writes two years later: "I have one outstanding trait in my character, which must strike anyone who knows me for any length of time, and that is my knowledge of myself. I can watch myself and my actions, just like an outsider. The Anne of every day I can face entirely without prejudice, without making excuses for her, and watch what's good and what's bad about her. The 'self-consciousness' haunts me, and every time I open my mouth I know as soon as I've spoken whether 'that ought to have been different' or 'that was right as it was'" (July 15, 1944, 274-275). She has found a self in the face of challenges: "I didn't want to be treated as a girl-like-all-others, but as Anne-on-her-own-merits" (July 15, 1994; 276). She has lived in close quarters with seven other unprotected people. She has seen immature quarrels and selfishness.

Most of the entries take place in the last 14 months of the Frank family's hiding. Anne's sanguine response mirrors that of the Jews in Europe during the late thirties and early forties. Anne's family is assimilated; they celebrate St. Nicholas Day and Hanukkah, but for her "St. Nicholas Day was much more fun" (December 7, 1942; 68). Anne finds her individuality apart from her father. She gradually individuates from her idealized father, and turns toward Peter as a putative intimate who might replace the magical but illusory Kitty. At first it may seem that Anne's diary is as much a drama of adolescence as it is a Holocaust fiction, but it is adolescence culturally shaped by historical conditions: "For a long time I haven't had any idea of what I was working for any more; the end of the war is so terribly far away, so unreal, like a fairy tale. If the war isn't over by September I shan't go to school any more, because I don't want to be two years behind" (April 4, 1944; 210). She understands the emerging self-immersion of the desperate adults, which she renders in the following ironic metonym for self serving behavior: "I, I, I . . . !" (March 14, 1944; 188). Yet she herself is not immune from the vertical pronoun. At times, we are struck by her nominalism and focus on the minutiae of everyday life. At other times she seems self-immersed in adolescent mood swings. But at best—and often in the same entry—she captures the anxious fantasies of encroaching horror: "Sometimes I wander by the roadside, or our 'Secret Annexe' is on fire, or they come and take us away at night. I see everything as if it is actually taking place, and this gives me the feeling that it may all happen to me very soon" (November 8, 1943; 127).

The "Secret Annexe" with its regimented routine is a pathetic parody of the camps they are trying to avoid. Even in her ingenuousness, she understands some of the ambiguity: "If I just think of how we live here, I usually come to the conclusion that it is a paradise compared with how other Jews who are not in hiding must be living. Even so, later on, when everything is normal again, I shall be amazed to think that we, who were so spick and span at home, should have sunk to such a low level. . . . For instance, ever since we have been here, we have had one oilcloth on our table which, owing so much use, is not one of the cleanest " (May 1, 1943; 91). In a sense, they *imprison themselves* when they go into hiding; after a few months, she writes: "I can't refrain from telling you that lately I have begun to feel deserted. I am surrounded by too great a void" (November 20, 1942; 66).

Gradually her perspective narrows to the tiny world of the secret Annexe and the relationships there, including her love for Peter Wessel: "Peter has touched my emotions more deeply than anyone has ever done before—except in my dreams" (April 28, 1944; 232-3). Unlike the concentration camp testimonies of Elie Wiesel and Levi that we have been discussing, in *The Dairy of Anne Frank,* as Rachel Fedman Brenner remarks: "The Annexe . . . attained a semblance of normalcy which helped insist on continuing faith in humanism" (105). The diary is the self-revealing narrative of a precocious and often confused teenager who enjoys flirtation and her budding adolescence: "I believe that it's spring within me, I feel that spring is awakening, I feel it in my whole body and soul. It is an effort to behave normally, I feel utterly confused, don't know what to read, what to write, what to do, I only know that I am longing" (February 12, 1944; 164). Her awakened sexuality becomes a magnet for Peter.

She is not only sexually precocious but at almost 15 wants more emotionally from seventeen-year-old Peter than he seems able to give: "Oh, I'll never reach Peter like this. Who knows, perhaps he doesn't like me at all and doesn't need anyone to confide in. Perhaps he only thinks about me in a casual sort of way" (February 19, 1944, 170). It is worth noting that the entries omitted by Otto Frank deal with her sexual experience. As she nears 15, she is desperately lonely and needs Peter as an empathetic other to replace her father: "When he said he didn't need any friends how harsh the words sounded to my ears. . . . Oh, Peter, if only I could help you, if only you would let me! Together we could drive away your loneliness and mine!" (March 6, 1944; 180). Later she asserts with some ambiguity: "I don't get any satisfaction out of lying in each other's arms day in, day out, and would so like to feel that he's the same" (April 18, 1944; 227). She has the impulse of the desperate: "[W]e are shut up here, shut away from the world, in fear and anxiety, especially just lately. Why, then, should we who love each other remain apart?" (April 17, 1944; 226). We are not sure Peter has been transformed, but we have no external evidence to refute her changed view of him except her reports of his reactive and clumsy responses. At times she is the passive female awaiting the approval of the accepting prince who might have the capacity to transform her as if by magic. The flirtation is not merely an emotional oasis, but also insulates her from boredom and loneliness.

Berteke Waaldijk argues:

> Most of the passages left out (in the published version prepared by Otto Frank) refer to Anne's experiences as a woman. They have to do with her body, menstruation, and sexuality, her conversing with Peter about sex, and her relationship to her mother. Other parts were deleted because they were deemed uninteresting for a post-war audience; these include the occasional dirty jokes Anne recounted in her diary and references to books she read. One such deletion concerns a reference to a famous Dutch woman novelist, Ida Boudier-Bakker. . . . Anne praises her description of a family, but confesses that she is not interested in the writer's feminism. (330)

The English version contained a franker discussion of sexuality than the Dutch version;" thus in the January 5, 1944, letter that was originally omitted, Anne writes:

> Sometimes, when I lie in bed at night, I have a terrible desire to feel my breasts and to listen to the quiet rhythmic beat of my heart. . . . I already had these kinds of feelings subconsciously before I came here, because I remember that once when I slept with a girl friend I had a strong desire to kiss her, and that I did do so. I could not help being terribly inquisitive over her body, for she had always kept it hidden from me. I asked her whether, as a proof of our friendship, we should feel one another's breasts, but she refused. I go into ecstasies every time I see the naked figure of a woman, such as Venus, for example. . . . If only I had a girl friend! (January 5, 1944; 143-144)

While it has been objected that the later dramatization of the diary by Albert Hackett and his wife Frances Goodrich turns Anne into even more of a representative figure of Western humanism that ignores her Jewishness, Sander Gilman argues that "Anne Frank was typical of assimilated Jews. . . . She does not speak with a Jewish accent, does not mix bits of Hebrew in her discourse" (Sander Gilman, *Jewish Self-Hatred* 349-50). Of course, finally, we have not her speech, only her writing, and we live with the knowledge that her voice is stilled. She grows as a person with a strong personal ethics and a writer who gradually gives narrative shape to her entries. The play, which won the 1955 Pulitzer Prize, takes her subjective adolescent feelings and gives them a public voice that belies the intimacy of the diary. And it further stresses the story as an adolescent coming-of-age story. It highlights the personal conflicts at the expense of a day-to-day tedium and small events that are given vitality by her ingenuous imagination. It diminishes our awareness of history, which we, as objective readers, need to bring to our diary reading.

In *The Informed Heart*, Bettelheim has noted how the Frank family's denial prevented their escape routes or alternative plans. Viewed retrospectively, the very pedestrian nature of confined routines without teleology foreshadows her capture and death. As Brenner remarks, "The meticulous listing of regular schedules, activities, and arrangements communicates the desire to hold onto the semblance of normalcy; it is as if the account of the routine could fend off the invading futility of hiding" (114). She continues: "Divested of everything that connects them to the past, deprived of the future, the inhabitants of the Annexe follow their daily schedules which, increasingly, turn into perfunctory, repetitious, and meaningless motions" (115). Yet Anne's diary implies the possibility of a good ending in a better world. Does she not write: "In spite of everything I still think people are good at heart"? She is the Candide of Holocaust literature. Her fantasy world of Western humanistic values, family unity, adolescent innocence, logical planning to survive, integrity, and courage are undermined by actual events. The world beyond the annex parallels the underground world in which they live—just as in *Notes from Underground*, except there the speaker, the diarist, is as corrupt or more so than the world he critiques. Lawrence Langer has noticed how *Anne Frank: The Diary of a Young Girl* is the antithesis of *Night* "in its premises, in the nature of the experience it narrates, and its conclusion" (*The Holocaust and the Literary Imagination* 76). "But her *Diary*, cherished since its appearance, as a celebration of human courage in the face of impending disaster, is in actuality a conservative and even old-fashioned book which appeals to nostalgia and does not pretend to concern itself with the uniqueness of the reality transforming life outside the attic walls that insulated her vision" (77). Her optimism is enclosed by walls that insulate her even while it imprisons her. Yet, she too, like the Wiesel surrogate, his younger self in *Night*, is separated from community, isolated by history, and—unlike him—finally killed.

As we close our discussion of *Anne Frank: The Diary of a Young Girl*, let us return to Martin Gilbert's words: "Unable to conceive of his own death, a man, even when surrounded by the death of others, grasps at any hope or rumour that might distance him from the realisation that he himself might be marked out for death. Any rumour which confirms that death might not be in prospect is acceptable. It was this psychological mechanism, the impossibility of conceiving of one's own death, that gave the hopeful rumours their force, and laid the groundwork for the deceptions that were to come. . . . [O]nce it had proved impossible for the Jews who witnessed these horrors to enter into the pathology of their persecutors, then it was possible for hope also to survive, which the full realisation of what was taking place would long before have destroyed" (333).

At the end, before their capture, we hear Anne's characteristic resilient optimism: "[W]ar going wonderfully" (June 30, 1944; 268). There is often an historical ingenuousness to her comments; as retrospective readers aware of the historical plot, we see with grim irony her account of the attempt on Hitler's life: "Perhaps the Divine Power tarried on purpose in getting him out of the way, because it would be much easier and more advantageous to the Allies if the impeccable Germans kill each other off" (February 21, 1944; 279).

IV

It was the Jews alone who were marked out to be destroyed in their entirety: every Jewish man, woman and child, so that there would be no future Jewish life in Europe. Against the eight million Jews who lived in Europe in 1939, the Nazi bureaucracy assembled all the concerted skills and mechanics of a modern state: the police, the railways, the civil service, the industrial power of the Reich; poison gas, soldiers, mercenaries, criminals, machine guns, artillery; and over all, a massive apparatus of deception. (Gilbert 824)

We know that Anne Frank died in Bergen-Belsen a few weeks before liberation. I want to discuss a memoir by a survivor of Bergen-Belsen who was almost certainly in the camp when Anne died. I have in mind Sophie Goetzel-Leviathan's short Holocaust memoir *The War From Within*, a book written retrospectively while she is recovering from her tribulations in May 1945. I could have chosen to discuss more widely read texts such as *An Interrupted Life: The Diaries of Etty Hillesum, 1941-1943,* or Alicia Appleman-Jurman's memoir *Alicia: My Story*, but I would like to call attention briefly to one eloquent voice that has not been much heard, a voice that speaks of the "wretched state of the Dutch Jews" who are beset by typhus at the very time Anne Frank was sent from Auschwitz to Bergen (Goetzel-Leviathan 69).

The memoir was not published until 1987; while naive in its workmanship and lacking the artistic organization of Wiesel's *Night* or Levi's Holocaust memoirs, the speaker gives us a sense of what it was like to live amidst the maelstrom of the Holocaust. Her memoir contains familiar *topoi*: the invasion of Poland by the Germans, the gradual deterioration in the quality of life, the Warsaw ghetto and its gradual disintegration, the claustrophobic cosmology of the camps where life is reduced to a Darwinian struggle for survival, hunger as a metaphor for deprivation, the sense that her experience is a dream, the missed opportunities to escape, the conversion to indifference and cynicism and/or to an anaesthetized state, and the *counterconversion* back to life. Barbara Foley has written in her essay "Fact, Fiction, Fascism: Testimony and Mimesis in Holocaust Narratives":

> First, the author describes life before deportation; then, the shock, disbelief, and despair of losing all one's relatives and being cast into the pit of the camp; then, the gradual process of adaptation and survival; finally, the departure from the camp and the return to a life that can only parody "normality." Innocence, initiation, endurance, escape—such is the pattern repeated in memoir after memoir, a kind of negative mirror of the traditional autobiographical journey toward self-fulfillment. And after the description of escape, a silence—more chilling, in a way, than the silence following the last page of a Holocaust diary. (338-339)

Looking back from her 1945 vantage point, Goetzel-Leviathan sees her transformation: "I am no longer myself" (9). As Langer writes in *Holocaust Testimonies*: "Written accounts of victim experience prod the imagination in ways that speech cannot, striving for analogies to initiate the reader into the particularities of their grim world. This literature faces a special challenge, since it must give most readers access to a totally unfamiliar subject" (18-19). What, we might ask, is meant by the term "testimony"? *Webster's Dictionary* defines *testimony* as a "declaration or statement meant to establish a fact, especially one made under oath by a witness in a court" but also as an "affirmation" and Goetzel-Leviathan's text is both, for she does affirm life. We might recall Langer's words in his conclusion to *Holocaust Testimonies*:

Part of the unreconciled understanding resulting from this investigation, what I earlier labeled a threatening and perhaps a treacherous one, is this: the Holocaust does little to confirm theories of moral reality but much to question the reality of moral theories. We can of course dismiss this historical moment as a terrible but temporary aberration, during which human nature veered off course for a time but then rediscovered its true compass and restored direction to its moral voyage. But we do this only by ignoring the hundreds of voices of former victims, the details of whose memories frustrate such a placid view. Their shrunken moral universe, full of ambiguities concerning the basis for personal conduct, mocks conceptual efforts, from Plato to the present, to determine the relationship between duty and the good life, what it is right to do and what it is good to be. . . . What are we to learn from this interlude in history, during which moral intuitions so often were useless because physical and psychological constraints like hunger, illness, fear, despair, and confusion created an unprecedented nonethical environment immune to the promptings of those intuitions? One of the unavoidable conclusions of unreconciled understanding is that we can inhabit more than one moral space at the same time—witnesses in these testimonies certainly do—and feel oriented and disoriented simultaneously. Another is that "damaged personhood" is one of the inevitable prices we pay for having lived in the time of the Holocaust, *provided* we acknowledge our active role as audience to the content of these testimonies. Indeed, it would be more than ingenuous to contend that the sources of such personhood in the twentieth century must be confined to this particular atrocity alone. History inflicts wounds on individual moral identity that are untraceable to personal choice or qualitative frameworks— though the scars they leave are real enough, reminding us that theoretical hopes for an integral life must face the constant challenge to that unity by self-shattering events like the Holocaust experience. (198, 201)

In the Prologue to *The War From Within*, Goetzel-Leviathan acknowledges the need for giving life new meaning by means of words:

Now that the war is over and a terrifying period is past, memories appear like the first shoots of spring when the early winds blow. The war had lasted five years and eight months, but for us it was an eternity. It had taken hold of our lives and plumbed in us depths whose very existence we neither knew nor suspected. Now that it is over, we ask ourselves whether we are able to give life new meaning. Many take up the pen. Will I be among them? Will I, dare I write? (xi)

In her memoir, we hear the teleology of a survivor who looks forward to renewed life and who frames her text with an epigraph from Schiller:

> Dear friends,
> It cannot be disputed that
> There were better times than ours,
> And that a noble people once lived;
> Even if history
> Could be silent about it,
> A thousand stones taken from
> The womb of the earth speak,
> But it is gone; it has disappeared,
> This wonderful generation,
> And we, we live!
> The hours belong to us;
> The living have the right! (x)

She concludes her brief memoir with lines from Goethe:

> For as long as you do not have
> this: "death and birth,"
> You are but a gloomy guest
> On the dark earth. (88)

Rather than turn her back on German culture, her evocation of Schiller and Goethe shows that her identification with a German Romantic and humanistic tradition has—at least from her perspective—sustained her. Had she survived, one wonders whether Anne Frank—with her characteristic resilience—would have affirmed her rebirth to life.

Despite the teleology of rebirth and affirmative ending, including her romantic faith in the restorative powers of nature, we wonder if Goetzel-Leviathan, who was alive when the memoir was published in 1987, had been haunted by recurring nightmares after 1945. In fact the text's editor tells nothing of Goetzel-Leviathan's life after the book had been written except that she was residing in Jerusalem in 1987. Has Goetzel-Leviathan ever exorcised completely the deep memory that haunts her immediately after liberation?

> We had thought that after two or three weeks on an adequate diet, I would recover completely, but we were wrong. I eat heartily now, but I still have pain in my right side. My hands tremble to such a degree that I can hardly hold a cup of coffee or spread butter on bread. I cannot sleep. I hear the cries that reached us from the concentration camp near Belsen; they ring in my ears. If I close my eyes, I see corpses piled high and behind them I see the flames of the crematorium. I am tormented by the fear that the Germans will return to drive us out of the village. I know this is impossible, but fear remains within me, and no amount of reasoning can allay my anxiety. (78)

The War From Within is a serious, honest tale in which Goetzel-Leviathan speaks about her own inner turmoils, including what we would now call a nervous breakdown after her husband returns from prison in 1940. Throughout she uses the present tense as if she were keeping a diary:

> The winter of 1940 passes. Coal is scarce, but the winter proves to be fairly mild. In spring, there is an outbreak of typhus in the Mokotow jail. Forty-five of the sixty inmates in my husband's cell have typhus. Most of them die. The jail is in quarantine. No mail is allowed in or out. A large number of prisoners are transported to Auschwitz and similar destinations. Money and influence are needed to remain in Warsaw, but the eight months of my husband's imprisonment are nearly over. I am terribly lonely. The last weeks are almost the worst. *We wait and wait.* On the thirtieth of April, he is due to come home.

It is the thirtieth of April. The room is clean. My daughter wears a brown silk frock; I wear a black dress. From early morning on, I wait and watch at the window, but the morning and the afternoon pass. Evening draws near and something like despair takes hold of me. (27)

By putting us by means of the present tense in *her* time, she captures the complicity of Jews as well as the manic pitch of some of those who know that their last days may be approaching: "Life goes on at a wild and crazy pace. Never, since the war began, have the Jews taken to spending so much on vodka and food. *Eat, drink, and be merry, for tomorrow we die.* Mothers, who only three weeks ago had their children torn away from them, now become quite different women. Some laugh and drink; others dance. They drink and dance away the memory of the holocaust" (42). The use of the present enables her both to freeze—to isolate—her past in an indeterminate time and to give it for her readers the intensity of a living, searing present. Thus when Goetzel-Leviathan describes in 1945 her life in Bergen-Belsen, her voice is not in the past tense but in the present tense as if she were still living in the harrowing present of concentration camp ontology:

These are terrible days for us. We are tortured by uncertainty and racked by hunger. Instead of bread, we get raw potatoes— which we cook with straw and wood. We use the women's washroom, where we have made small stoves out of old tin cans. Both the men and the women cook here. Women use the bathrooms and wash at the end of the washroom while the men cook. No one cares. Hunger reduces us all to the same shameless level. *Homo homini lupus est.* Man is a wolf. We are ready to devour one another. Our hunger is fearful as it is unbearable. (71-72)

Like Levi in *Survival in Auschwitz*, Goetzel-Leviathan feels that her experience is a dream: "A feeling comes over me which I am to feel often during the course of the war; it is a feeling that all this is a completely unreal dream. I watch the dream unfold before me like a film, but it does not concern me. During the most frightening episodes yet to come, this feeling will produce in me an icy composure and calm" (4). She recalls her brother's death in an air raid, her brother-in-law's disappearance (perhaps in Russia, but she will never know), her mother's and father's death, her sister-in-law going in the wrong direction at a selection:

> The director and the Jew have to decide who can work and who can be spared. They shout "Left!" to those who are useful, and "Right!" to those who are not. The one word *left* or *right* decides between life and death. Left indicates that one can go on living a bit longer; right, that one is to die. In the last few days, we have found out that "Resettlement in the East" is not a journey to a work place at all, but rather, a journey to death. . . . *My sister-in-law is in the crowd awaiting judgment. "Left!" They shout at her, but, in the excitement of the moment, she is so confused that she turns to the right. She sees her error and tries to retrieve it at once, but it is in vain. A German strikes her across the face with a whip, and she is taken off to the transit area and her death.* (38)

Her understated objective voice reports her memories, including the complicity of the Jewish employee, who works with the director. In the above passage we might note the italics that she uses for interior monologues and, occasionally (and perhaps inconsistently) for recalling the words of others. The italics have the function of calling attention to the observing self *within*: the interior self implied by the title.

Goetzel-Leviathan came from a comfortable Polish family, a family of German-Jewish ancestry not so different from Anne Frank's family, and she had traveled in Europe before the war. She met her husband in Paris, and worked at a Quaker school in England. For a time her husband's position in the Judenrat protects her: "[M]y husband received a so-called 'cast-iron letter' from the office of the German Commissar for Jewish Affairs. This letter stated that as an employee of the commissar's administration, neither he nor his family nor any of his staff were to be taken for 'resettlement'" (33). Yet, as she and her husband soon learn, there is no such thing as absolute protection. Before they leave the ghetto, they smuggle their child out, and she writes with some irony: "Many Christians will take Jewish children into custody in return for good Jewish money" (35). She dramatizes her gradual awareness of the Jews as the *hunted* and laughs at her companion's fastidiousness when they are being harbored by Christians: "Dr. A hesitates until he plucks enough courage to lie beside a strange woman for the first time in his life. *O doctor, doctor, what a funny man you are. Long ago we ceased to be men and women; we are simply hunted, persecuted, fearful people"* (54).

She and her husband leave the ghetto and are harbored by Christians before being tricked into getting transported to Bergen-Belsen. Although that camp lacks gas chambers, she struggles with hunger and, again like Levi in *Survival in Auschwitz*, she speaks almost obsessively of food:

> The food continues to deteriorate. The "turnip-soup" is mainly water, but it is often revoltingly bitter. More and more frequently, it is brought at nine in the morning. . . . How long is it since we slept in a comfortable bed? How long since we sat in a chair, ate a meal, dressed respectably, or went to the theater? We live like beasts. All sense of decency is gone, and our eating bowls serve other purposes at night. No one has the strength to go outside. . . . None of us can sleep because of our hunger. We throw ourselves on the food like wild animals and nibble on raw beets all day long, which we are given instead of bread. (70, 71)

A recurring theme of Holocaust memoirs is that of hunger and obsession with food. The women of the Theresienstadt even wrote fantasy recipes. American Civil War prisoner diaries—diaries often of terrifying deprivation—are also preoccupied with food. Food becomes a necessity for sustaining life itself as well as a way of connecting with prior periods of life when food was an intermittent pleasure. *In Memory's Kitchen: A Legacy From the Women of Terezin* re-creates from memory culinary marvels from a time when the inmates had sufficient food and lived in a family and community. The text was recorded by Maria Pachter, who on Yom Kippur 1944 died of starvation. As Rochelle Mancini has written of the recipies:

> Often incomplete and even incoherent, they bespeak memories clouded by cold and constant hunger. They are heroic attempts to fend off that same deprivation, an act of courage and pride in recalling times of relative plenty. . . . [T]he forced discipline of recalling recipes amid starvation was also an act of defiance, and

a refusal to give up. . . . All (the recipes) are a demonstration of
the desire to pass on something personal of importance, and the
act of sharing and recording for posterity itself an expression of
assurance that the Nazis would fail and that there would always
be Jews to carry on the cultural heritage. (18-19)

That many of the recipes are over the top shows in the camp inhabitants
the play of fantasy and life affirming ebullience, as well as a desire to
share in festive pleasures with those who might read the text. While
Theresienstadt is not Auschwitz nor even Bergen-Belsen, where Goetzel-
Leviathan finds herself, the *topos* of hunger occurs in our narratives.

In her memory we hear two competing selves—one part immersed
in the horror from which the speaker has emerged, the other desperately
trying to find sense and meaning in her current life. We might recall a
distinction made by Lawrence Langer in *Holocaust Testimonies*:

Deep memory tries to recall the Auschwitz self as it was then;
common memory has a dual function: it restores the self to its
normal pre- and postcamp routines but also offers detached portraits, from the vantage point of today, of what it must have been
like then. Deep memory thus suspects *and* depends on common
memory, knowing what common memory cannot know but tries
nonetheless to express. . . . One effect of common memory, with its
talk of normalcy amid chaos, is to mediate atrocity, to reassure us
that in spite of the ordeal some human bonds were invaluable.
(Langer 6, 9)

As in the better known memoirs and fictions, Goetzel-Leviathan
becomes anaesthetized; partly because she has typhus, she does not at
first recover: "Ever since my stay in camp, feelings elude me. I am numb,
and rejoice at nothing. Everything seems so empty" (82-83). And she
feels that she is still in the grip of outside control: *"Now we are actually free,
but if it is not the Germans, then it is the Americans who order us to leave. When will
we finally have a home from which no one will oust us?"* (80). We recall Levi's *The
Reawakening* and its tale of purgatory as he struggles to return home.

Although hers is a harrowing tale of persecution and survival, the
editor, Rebecca Fromer, has included a paragraph-long Addendum from a

Birkenau-Auschwitz survivor, Daniel Bennahmias, which curtly dismisses the possibility of emerging from *his* experience with her ebullience:

> To those of us who were in Birkenau-Auschwitz, the events in this account read like a romance, a fantastic tale of innocence and privilege wherein, due to circumstance and circumstance alone, it was possible to maintain some semblance of human sensibility, for within its pages there yet remains the distillation of civilized behavior and manifestations of a culture and a world, an existence outside of the concentration camp. We, who had been stripped of our smiles, could neither indulge evocations of *la vie Parisienne*, nor of the poets; men may have thoughts of man, but we, who had been brought into collusion with the instruments of death, had no such solace. We had attained the sub-human depths where all worlds are lost save for a vast sea of indifference. The currents that allowed the writer to remain within the childhood of consciousness swept us into the maelstrom, and, in that vortex, the veneer if not the illusion of self is stripped to the bone. Past conditioning and concepts of good and evil lies necessity, sheer, naked, raw, uncaring, operational necessity, and no man survives that with his innocence intact. Remember, then, this is but one of many tales; the dead, who have no voice, might have had other stories to tell.
>
> Daniel Bennahmias,
> *Sonderkommando* (May, 1944-January, 1945),
> Birkenau-Auschwitz (April 11, 1944-January 18, 1945). (89)

Gilbert reminds us what Bennahmias's task was: "No selection was made to keep alive those capable of work: only a few hundred were chosen to be part of a *Sonderkommando*, or 'Special Commando', some employed in taking the bodies of those who had been gassed to the burial pits, others in sorting the clothes of the victims and in preparing those clothes and other belongings for dispatch to Germany" (Gilbert 308-9).

Bennahmias is speaking of Goetzel-Leviathan's writing the memoir in St. Maur, near Paris, in May 1945 and reveling in her current comfortable setting:

The three of us have found living quarters. Micky plays happily in the country with French children, and my husband, who is kept busy in Paris, visits Micky and me every other day or so. I have seldom been as happy as I now am at St. Maur. I am delighted by the graciousness of the hospitality offered me, and take pleasure in the serenity to be found within the walls of this handsome old house. I sit in the dining room with its carved furniture, drink French wine, and eat French cuisine. The harmony of the French tongue fills my ears. Here there is peace and noble culture. Here I soon find the road back to a normal life. (86)

For Bennahmias, there can be no reconfiguring of experience into a teleology of hope, no oasis to relieve pain and guilt. His response is an example of the kind of ethical questions Holocaust fictions raise; to Bennahmias, Goetzel-Leviathan has no right to the claims of reality and truth. To this she might respond with words from her Prologue:

If the sandy soil of Treblinka could speak—if it could bear witness to all that happened—how it would shriek and groan under the weight of a fearful bloodbath! But, you see, the sandy wastes of Treblinka are silent and we, the few, must speak. (xi)

To some, her resilience and optimism—"to give life new meaning"—and her belief in words may seem fey but, as we have seen, what follows reveals her complexity.

PART TWO

REALISM

HAUNTED BY HISTORY: TADEUSZ BOROWSKI'S *THIS WAY FOR THE GAS, LADIES AND GENTLEMEN*

Born in 1922, Tadeusz Borowski was a Polish survivor of Auschwitz and Birkenau. His family lived in the Soviet part of Ukraine and, after being declared class enemies, were deported to Siberia in 1926. He remained with an aunt until the parents were released in 1932 and were reunited with their children. They were exchanged for communists imprisoned by the Polish government. When the Nazis arrived, he continued his education underground. A few weeks before he and his fiancée were arrested he mimeographed his first book of poems, *Wherever the Earth*, which, as Jan Kott has written in his introduction to the Penguin edition of *This Way for the Gas, Ladies and Gentlemen*: "predicted in classical cadences the extermination of mankind. Its dominant image was that of a gigantic labor camp" (pp. 14-15). As an Aryan, he survived in the camps and worked his way up the camp hierarchy. Like Levi, Borowski went through repatriation camps, Levi in the USSR, he in Germany. His stories about Auschwitz began to appear when he was 26. As Piotr Kuhiwczak writes,

> When Borowski's two collections of short stories appeared, *Pozeg-nanie z Maria* (Farewell to Maria) and *Kamienny swiat* (World of Stone), in 1948, and later in other European languages, they caused

considerable sensation. Here was a writer who, as Jan Kott writes, "judged European tradition and its level of civilization in the context of Auschwitz, while everyone else described and judged Auschwitz in the context of European tradition and its level of civilization." For Borowski, Auschwitz was neither a historical anomaly nor a temporary breakdown of civilized customs. (401)

His despair is the result of the events his speaker describes. Later, he embraced social realism and became a prominent writer in Stalinist Poland before becoming disillusioned and committing suicide on July 1, 1951.

The collection entitled *This Way for the Gas, Ladies and Gentlemen* in English comes from two collections that appeared in Poland in 1948. The book has a scant 160 pages in the edition I read, and the chapters have no numbers. Borowski's stories of the camp are grim, spare, searing, and honest in self-revelation. He is a witness, a Daniel, speaking to all those who need to be roused to the implications of what occurred. For Borowski, as Sidra DeKoven Ezrahi writes, "literature must function as a vehicle of preservation, as a medium through which the experience of victimization becomes part of the collective consciousness; . . . he rejects pure aesthetics as frivolous at best and the cooptation of evil into culture at worst" (53). But I would argue that the transformation of memory into narrative cannot ignore aesthetics. Indeed, the subtitle of my entire study might be "The Aesthetics of Transformation."

The voice of *This Way for the Gas, Ladies and Gentlemen* is Borowski's fictional surrogate, a Polish prisoner, who, while suffering indignities, is not immune to anti-Semitism. As Jan Kott has written, "Borowski's Auschwitz stories are written in the first person. The narrator of three of the stories is a deputy Kapo, Vorarbeiter Tadeusz. The identification of the author with the narrator was the moral decision of a prisoner who has lived through Auschwitz—an acceptance of mutual responsibility, mutual participation, and mutual guilt for the concentration camp" (Kott 21-22). In the final story, "The World of Stone," the narrator explains how he has become inured to emotional feeling and insensitive to difference, but he does so in passionate language that recalls the violence and indifference to human life in the camps, particularly in the image of the cosmic gale leaving human bodies strewn everywhere: "Sometimes it seems to me that even my physical sensibilities have coagulated and stiffened within me like resin. . . . Through half-open eyes I see with satisfaction that once again a gust of the cosmic gale has blown the crowd into the air, all the way up to the treetops, sucked the human bodies into a huge whirlpool, twisted their lips open in terror, mingled the children's rosy cheeks with the hairy chests of the men, entwined the clenched fists with strips of women's dresses, thrown snow-white thighs on the top, like foam, with hats and fragments of heads tangled in hair-like seaweed peeping from below. And I see that this weird snarl, this gigantic stew concocted out of the human crowd, flows along the street, down the gutter, and seeps into space with a loud gurgle, like water into a sewer" (178-179). Yet the speaker in the last sentence of "The World of Stone" eloquently if hyperbolically turns his back on despair: "For I intend to write a great, immortal epic, worthy of this unchanging, difficult world chiselled out of stone" (180).

The opening of the first and title story, "This Way for the Gas, Ladies and Gentlemen," takes us into a world where the fortunate who meet the transports thrive at the expense of those who arrive to be gassed or made slave laborers. Words are deprived of their expected meaning and a new language is created. The first story introduces us to a world where words metamorphose into new words. Terms like "Muslim" and "Canada" indicate the special camp discourse. "Canada" designated well-being in camp, specifically the temporarily privileged few who unload the transports of people heading for the gas chambers and thus can take some of the prisoners' possessions. "Muslims" are those who lacked the strength or the wiles to survive. The speaker, Vorarbeiter Tadeusz, is part of the "Canada" crew and wonders what happens if there are no more transports; his friend, Henri responds: "'They can't run out of people, or we'll starve to death in this blasted camp. All of us live on what they bring'" (31). Humans are reduced to predatory animals. Hearing a Rabbi "wailing, loudly, monotonously," one of the fortunate prisoners who meets the transports explains: "'Can't somebody shut him up? He's been raving as if he'd caught God himself by the feet'" (32). The speaker's tone—informed by his memory of the situation—is unmitigated cynicism. The most narrow kind of self-interest motivates human behavior because the alternative is the gas chambers. He remembers and reports, despite his desire to repress: "Motor cycles drive up, delivering S.S. officers, bemedalled, glittering with brass, beefy men with highly polished boots and shiny, brutal faces. Some have brought their briefcases, others hold thin, flexible whips. This gives them an air of military readiness and agility"(35). It is the juxtaposition of normality with the reality of what is actually happening that makes the story work. The transport arrives: "A huge, multicoloured wave of people loaded down with luggage pours from the train like a blind, mad river trying to find a new bed. But before they have a chance to recover, before they can draw a breath of fresh air and look at the sky, bundles are snatched from their hands, coats ripped off their backs, their purses and umbrellas taken away" (37-38).

As Kuhiwczak writes: "It is not surprising, then, that the narrator of Borowski's short stories, an antihero and semi-collaborator called Tadeusz, keeps reminding us that the concentration camp is the only real world, and everything beyond the wire fences is a temporary illusion. To this real world the moral standards imported from outside do not apply" (Kuhiwczak 401).

The drama of language—the "verboten" of power versus the help-lessness of the victims—comes through even in translation. Just as the power corrupts the Germans, so it corrupts the prisoners of "Canada." Thus the narrator speaks of feeling fury rather than pity: "I am not sorry they're going to the gas chamber. Damn them all! I could throw myself at them, beat them with my fists. It must be pathological, I just can't understand. . . ." His companion, Henri, who is an amorally cynical doppelgänger, responds: "Ah on the contrary, it is natural, predictable, calculated. The ramp exhausts you, you rebel—and the easiest way to relieve your hate is to turn against someone weaker. Why, I'd even call it healthy. It's simple logic, *compris?* "(40) The camps become a morally claustrophobic closed universe in which anything is possible. As Kuhiwczak writes,

> While forcing on us the darkest side of civilization, Borowski wants to give the impression that he presents things as they are, and therefore his narrative voice attempts to be calm and factual. But on many occasions this almost nonchalant detachment breaks down. Tadeusz, who is initially very excited to be allowed to participate in the selection of a new transport of prisoners with all the food and money they bring to the camp, suddenly vomits and refuses to

unload the cattle trucks. A Block Elder from another story passionately raises the question of what future punishments the inventors of the concentration camps should be subjected to. Now and again we encounter scenes and sentences which convince us that Borowski's cool detachment is only the mask behind which he attempts to hide his guilt, anxiety, and inability to make sense of his painful experience. The heavy condemnation of European civilization contained in his stories does not strike us as a detached theoretical statement. Apart from extreme bitterness, it also expresses the writer's longing for a different order of things. (402)

The opening story stresses how life can be reduced to a survival of the fittest where conventional morality gives way to the rule of the jungle. After the work, after he vomits, the speaker valorizes the camp as a refuge from his own death even as he is part of the machinery of countless deaths: "I lie against the cool, kind metal and dream about returning to the camp, about my bunk, on which there is no mattress, about sleep among comrades who are not going to the gas tonight. Suddenly I see the camp as a haven of peace. It is true, others may be dying, but one is somehow still alive, one has enough food, enough strength to work" (48). Borowski wants us to understand the mentality of those who survive in this closed universe; while the camp functionary-speaker sees the camp as a "haven," where "one is somehow alive"— note the impersonal pronoun to distance the first person involvement— he also understands the terrible ironic distinction between, on the one hand, the victims' plans for a future and, on the other, the prisoner's life expectancy of a few minutes as well as their reduction to a resource for treasure hunters, who will extract valuables for shipment to Berlin: "The lights on the ramp flicker with a spectral glow, the wave of people— feverish, agitated, stupefied people—flows on and on, endlessly. . . . They do not know that in just a few moments they will die. . . . Experienced professionals will probe into every recess of their flesh, will pull the gold from under the tongue and the diamonds from the uterus and the colon. They will rip out gold teeth. In tightly sealed crates they will ship them to Berlin" (Borowski 48-9). Ezrahi notes, "The concentration camp is a world without exit and, unless one clings to a chronological or ideological structure or to metaphorical or mythical forms of escape, there can be no organizing principle to point the way out. Borowski rejects the very notion of such a principle. 'I do not know whether we shall survive,' he writes in one story, 'but I like to think that one day we shall have the courage to tell the world the whole truth and call it by its proper name'" (*By Words Alone* 52).

Zeugma is the trope Borowski's narrator, Vorarbeiter Tadeusz, uses to describe the transport systems. Interchangeably trucks take lumber, cement, people to the crematoria: "Trucks drive around, load up lumber, cement, people—a regular daily routine" (34). When the latter cars open, the narrator describes the dehumanizing process: "People . . . inhumanely crammed, buried under incredible heaps of luggage, suitcases, trunks, packages, crates, bundles of every description (everything that had been their past and was to start their future). Monstrously squeezed together, they have fainted from heat, suffocated, crushed one another. Now they push towards the opened doors, breathing like fish cast out on the sand" (37). In this horrifying context, the cliché and childlike metaphor of "fish cast out onto the sand" functions well.

Borowski's narrator, Vorarbeiter Tadeusz, speaks in the present as if memory erases the preterit and creates a searing present. At first he writes as if he were one of the victims, but gradually we see that as one of these who meets the transports, he is also one of the perpetrators—a prisoner, to be sure, but one who, in the grim survival of the fittest economy of the death camps, lives at the expense of others. When the prisoners are liberated, they turn on their tormentors, as he describes in the grim anecdote entitled "Silence," in which one of the oppressors is trampled to death. Within Borowski's grotesque imagined world, violence is understandably contagious.

Borowski makes aesthetic choices for his imagined witness, based on their potential effect to awaken his audience to what they may have ignored, repressed, or never known. Giving a story the shocking title "This Way for the Gas, Ladies and Gentlemen" is an aesthetic choice. Narrating in the present, as if his "I/eye" were a camera, is another. His speaker is not Jewish and not in the same jeopardy as those he observes; that is why I demur slightly from Ezrahi's provocative statement, "Borowski is the writer with whom, in a sense, Holocaust literature begins and ends" (72). What Ezrahi means, I think, is the complicity, the transformation of prisoners into the oppressors' instruments, the use by prisoners of the oppressor's discourse: "You see, my friend, you see, I don't know why, but I am furious, simply furious with these people—furious because I must be here because of them. I feel no pity"(40).

We see the metaphoricity of Borowoski's narrator's imagination, the reduction of feeling, the apparent objectivity that struggles with memory's horror. "The morbid procession streams on and on—trucks growl like mad dogs. I shut my eyes tight, but I can still see corpses dragged from the train, trampled infants, cripples piled on top of the dead, wave after wave . . . freight cars roll in, the heaps of clothing, suitcases and bundles grow, people climb out, look at the sun, take a few breaths, beg for water, get into the trucks, drive away. And again freight cars roll in, again people'" (41). Inhumanity grows by accretion; guards shoot recalcitrant children. As they relentlessly transport those who go to the chambers, trucks become metonymies for the corpses: "Trucks, loaded with people, start up with a deafening roar and drive off amidst the wailing and screaming of the women separated from their children, and the stupefied silence of the men left behind" (38). The blond woman who moves the speaker's humanity recalls the recurring *topos* in Holocaust narratives of human sounds punctuating and anticipating the silence of death: "In the silence that settles over nature at this time of day, the human cries seem to rise all the way to the sky" (45).

Ezrahi remarks, "Borowski is a chronicler of the small acts of compliance, of despair, of cowardice—and, occasionally, of bravery—that myriads of men performed as they 'passed through' Auschwitz; as each character is silenced by the 'cremo' or removal to a different station, another comes to take his place. That each of Borowski's stories is narrated from a different point of view is reflected in the language itself" (*By Words Alone* 58-59). Yes, Borowski's speakers are different in each story while sharing a common bond of having lived through the Holocaust. But they depend on the oscillating distance between Borowski and his created narrator, who is at once an orderly and a labor Kommando somewhat insulated from the worst deprivations, and a surrogate who expresses Borowski's guilt and disgust with what he observes. At some points, his speaker seems hardened and cynical, as when he is a predatory Kapo meeting the incoming train and complains that "dammit, they'll run out of people" (31). Again, we see words deprived of their communicative function. The Polish narrator passively—almost catatonically—responds to a question of one of these people: "What's going to happen to us" with "I don't know. I don't understand Polish" before adding: "It is the camp law: people going to their death must be deceived to the very end" (37). But the very use of the present tense in the retrospective telling illustrates his crises of conscience and belies the casualness of his response. As Ezrahi compellingly writes, "Borowski's stories constitute a concrete realism which emanates from within a violated universe, which lays bare the victim's own form of adaptation to the situation in which he finds himself. The narrator is not the architect of and in most instances does not actually espouse the sadistic norms which prevail in this universe; even in his debasement he may not abandon the human image altogether—nevertheless, he is a part of his story, a prisoner of the reality he describes" (By Words Alone 51).

The story entitled "A Day at Harmenz" begins on a pastoral note, which is soon revealed as ironic: "The shadows of the chestnut trees are green and soft. They sway gently over the ground, still moist after being newly turned over, and rise up in sea-green cupolas scented with the morning freshness. The trees form a high palisade along the road, their crowns dissolve into the hue of the sky" (Borowski 50). The story includes seven anecdotes of greed, pettiness, and self-survival; the brief paragraphs resemble newspaper reports documenting in spare journalistic prose how the camps depend on a cycle of violence. The speaker, whose name is Tadek, a diminutive of Borowski's own first name, is judgmental and belligerent to Becker, a man who committed crimes at another camp but is starving. The speaker gets 16 loaves of bread from Warsaw and is clearly far better off than the Jews. The Unterscharfuhrer abuses the Kapo, who in turn abuses other prisoners. The narrator closes this seven part tale with the observation that the writing of his story confirms as much as the selection: "What a curious power words have. . . . Here in Auschwitz even evil words seem to materialize" (80). The prisoners' work is a charade. Workers move spades but shovel nothing unless they are being watched by guards. "The limbs move like those of marionettes—absurd, angular" (63). In what the speaker calls an "inferno"—recalling Levi's Dante echo in "The Canto of Ulysses" in Survival in

Auschwitz—humans scrounge to survive. But whenever possible, the empty spades swing up and down.

Perhaps the crucial insight, one that for a moment, undermines the telling, is the last line of by far the longest story, "Auschwitz, Our Home (A Letter)," a kind of grim parody of the Tristan-Isolde relationship that takes the form of letters written from the men's to the women's barracks of Auschwitz. After the narrator has heard a grotesque fantasy of a new way to burn people, the narrator comments: "But this is a monstrous lie, a grotesque lie, like the whole camp, like the whole world" (142). As Lawrence Langer writes,

> Like Camus, Borowski is outraged by man's acquiescence to forces that dehumanize, humiliate, and ultimately destroy him; but in this passage he appears even more apprehensive over the possibility of the reader's failing to recognize the implications of such acquiescence—hence his angry outburst. It is almost as if he feared too great a success for his literary art: the ostensible indifference in the tone of the speakers inculcates a comparable detachment in the reader, and creates the danger of his "passing by" without acknowledging the insidious change that has been wrought in the characters. The "monstrous" and "grotesque lie" that Borowski denounces, abruptly compels us to face the horrible fact that we too may have been seduced into accepting the abnormal as normal, intellectually conscious of the atrocities in the background but emotionally relieved that they happen to "others," not the characters we are concerned with (nor, by psychological extension, with ourselves)—abruptly we are wrenched from the detachment of contemplating a narrative, to an awareness of the narrative's roots in history: and with a shock we rub our imaginative eyes and try to sort out our responses, half literary, half real. (*The Holocaust and the Literary Imagination* 90-91)

The story is an epistle to his beloved who is in the women's camp. The choice of the epistolary technique in "Auschwitz, Our Home (A Letter)" by which the persona Vorarbeiter Tadeusz frames his responses as a letter to his beloved—a Polish woman partisan whom he had last seen at the Pawiak prison—gives the speaker a human voice: "You know, it feels very strange to be writing to you, you whose face I have not seen for so long. At times I can barely remember what you look like—your image fades from my memory despite my efforts to recall it. And yet my dreams about you are incredibly vivid; they have an almost physical reality. A dream, you see, is not necessarily visual. It may be an emotional experience in which there is depth and where one feels the weight of an object and the warmth of a body" (102-103). As we have seen already, the *topos* of a character finding refuge in dreams, and sometimes confusing dreams and reality, recurs in Holocaust narratives. Even in the intimacy of love letters—accompanied by the almost tactile memory of physical presence and past touches—the camp cannot be left behind for a moment of tenderness or passion. Indeed, the memory of her presence gives way to an image of physical degradation.

In the chapter "Auschwitz, Our Home (a Letter)," the speaker is a medical orderly—one of ten, he writes, "selected" (note the irony of the word) out of 20,000 at Birkenau. With dismay, he writes of the grim life, the routines of insanity, the lack of resistance:

> Today, having become totally familiar with the inexplicable and the abnormal; having learned to live on intimate terms with the crematoria, the itch and the tuberculosis; having understood the true meaning of wind, rain and sun, of bread and turnip soup, of work to survive, of slavery and power; having, so to say, daily broken bread with the beast—I look at these civilians with a certain indulgence, the way a scientist regards a layman, or the initiated an outsider. . . .
>
> Why is it that nobody cries out, nobody spits in their faces, nobody jumps at their throats? . . . What is the mystery? This strange power of one man over another? This insane passivity that cannot be overcome? Our only strength is our great number—the gas chambers cannot accommodate all of us. (111-113)

In the preceding passage, the speaker writes at first as one who seems to be somewhat protected by his position as an orderly and his not being Jewish. He looks at the "civilians" in the camp from a detached distance as if he couldn't become like them. But not even the brief tender recollection of dancing intimacy with the woman to whom he writes can erase the searing reality that Auschwitz is an efficient death machine organized to dehumanize and, finally, kill. By the conclusion he realizes only the thinnest wall of positional assurance protects him, and he speaks of all prisoners, himself included, in the collective third person as potential victims of the gas chamber. He sees the Auschwitz prisoners as slaves who are heirs to those who built the Egyptian pyramids and Greek statues, products of "human sweat, blood and hard labour": "We are laying the foundation for some new, monstrous civilization" (131-132). Auschwitz is a kind of parody of Western history and culture that he evokes only to remind us that ancient cultures too had a human cost and might be more of a foreshadowing than we would admit of the current terrors. Questioning the shibboleths of western culture, he concludes with a dismissal of the aesthetic as a category; for Borowksi's surrogate and our narrator, the concepts of beauty and ethical ideals are anachronistic in the face of what he has learned about human nature, and the terrible silence that supports it.

While Borowski's narrator understands that his wiliness enables his own life to continue as countless thousands walk to their death, we feel, too, his grim self-hatred and guilt for surviving while the motion of the camp moves almost magnetically to the gas chambers and crematoria, although some are allowed to walk beyond them on a second road to the concentration camp: "Each day, as I got up in the morning to scrub the hospital floors, the people were walking—along both roads. Women, men, children. They carried their bundles. When I sat down to dinner—and not a bad one, either—the people were walking" (84). Yet the speaker accepts this phantasmagoric death walk; he learns to live by his wits, learns how to survive, learns how to connive to keep himself alive: "One thing we have learned well about anatomy: at the camp you are not likely to trip if you stand on the shoulders of men who have influence" (120). Because barter is essential to survival, he develops an acquisitive temperament. But we hear a tortured, divided self, a self-loathing individual who knows that he is building a morally and emotionally insulated wall between himself— observer, functionary, aware of his primitive comforts—and those "walking," moving toward death.

The organization of Auschwitz replicates the hierarchy of the Nazis—but here the snobbery is of those who have the old numbers. The speaker is bitterly ironic about the jealousy of those who speak of "Auschwitz, our home" (100)—and yet Birkenau may be worse than Auschwitz because "you would understand why they look down with contempt and pity on their colleagues from Birkenau—where the barracks are made of wood, where there are no pavements, and where, in place of the bathhouses with hot running water, there are four crematoria" (101). Barely disguised is his outrage at the psychological conditions—the traumatized state in which one looks for external correspondences for chaotic internal feelings—that would enable people to make such a comparison, and he switches to a personal tone that acknowledges, even in his retelling, the need for an oasis of feeling.

It is a characteristic of Holocaust narratives to oscillate radically between the harsh realities of the outer world and descriptions of dehumanization, on one hand, and, on the other, an effort to find a space for interiority and human feeling. It is what creates a space between the telling and the told—an ethical and emotional space, and yet that momentary space is always threatened by the invasion of the actual. Borowski's detachment and distance reveal as they conceal his outrage. As Langer writes: "However extraordinary the imaginative efforts of the writer to disguise his theme with the garments of literary invention. . . . He can never totally conceal the relationship between the naked body and the covering costume, the actual scars of the Holocaust and the creative salves that often only intensify pain" (*The Holocaust and the Literary Imagination* 91).

We might recall Langer's prior comment:

> It would seem—and generally it was so—that of all the stylistic techniques available for representing the experience of atrocity, naturalistic dialogue would be the least effective, since the subject itself was so unnatural, so extraordinary, so resistant to the graphic efforts of unmanipulated prose. Yet as we have seen, even in the concentration camps the sun rose daily, men and women awoke to face their ordeal—and if some did not, but died quietly (or noisily) in their sleep, this too came to be part of an expected routine. Most accounts of the Holocaust—quite properly—emphasize the abom-

inations, though these would seem even more execrable if they could be highlighted by a kind of verbal chiaroscuro, in which horror is embedded like chips of mosaic in a clay of commonplace behavior. (*The Holocaust and the Literary Imagination* 89)

I am arguing that as we move away from the Holocaust, the matrix of naturalistic verisimilitude becomes less effective than illuminating distortions, parables, and mythic history *because* the memoirs and diaries for survivors and historical novels have become part of our *felt* knowledge.

In Borowski's Auschwitz universe humans become cogs in a machine, a commodity to be used and discarded. Words become instruments to survive, not a means to express feelings. Figures of speech become luxuries, but luxuries that when introduced are often all the more effective. Often the metaphors are drawn from the Holocaust experience. Take the brief anecdote entitled "The Supper," in which Russian soldiers are murdered by the SS under the auspices of a sadistic Kommandant, while the other prisoners are made to stand and watch for 17 hours before being sent to bed without dinner: "A dark, gusty wind, heavy with the smells of the thawing, sour earth, tossed the clouds about and cut through your body like a blade of ice. . . . Several bluish lamps, swaying to and fro on top of high lamp-posts, threw a dim light over the black, tangled tree branches reaching out over the road, the shiny sentry-shack roofs, and the empty pavement that glistened like a wet leather strap. The soldiers marched under the circle of lights and then disappeared again in the dark. The sound of their footsteps on the road were coming nearer" (152-153). Note the language of terror from the wind's "cut[ting] through your body," to the threatening anthropomorphized trees, the brutal "leather strap," and, finally, the ominously approaching soldiers. As Ezrahi comments, "To the extent that rhetoric or eloquence serves to mitigate fact or to integrate it into a larger scheme, the persistence in this literature of a factuality which does not allow for transcendence through metaphor is a reinforcement on the literary level of the brutal inexorability of concentrationary reality" (*By Words Alone* 55). While Borowski himself actually behaved heroically, according to his fellow prisoners, his fictional narrators bear the burden of a searing guilt, for he sees himself as a collaborator. He demonstrates how each human, moving towards the crematorium, is reduced to a caricature, a phrase. Gradually, human life is reduced to a struggle for survival in which teeth and talons dominate.

CHAPTER FIVE

JOHN HERSEY'S *THE WALL*: FICTION AS HISTORY IN THE FIRST GENERATION OF HOLOCAUST FICTION

John Hersey's *The Wall* (1950) is a moving docufiction and epic novel of the Warsaw ghetto. The story of the ghetto has been oft told; yet, even when read by someone steeped in this literature, it is surprising how full a fictional account Hersey presents. That he did not have the opportunity to read the later historical accounts of Raul Hilberg, Lucy Dawidowicz, Nora Levin, and Martin Gilbert makes his novel quite amazing in its depth and understanding. Hersey was a non-Jewish journalist who exhaustively researched his subject to produce a compelling work of popular fiction, albeit one perhaps a tad longer than necessary and slightly repetitious. Hersey focuses on individual acts of resistance and, later, the heroic rebellion, but he does not give credit to the Jewish acceptance of divine will. It is easy to patronize Hersey's popular novel from our contemporary vantage point, but it is more profitable to inquire why such a book fulfilled the needs and desires of its audience. Sidra Dekoven Ezrahi's comment on *The Wall*, which she groups with the play adaptation of *The Diary of Anne Frank* and the "Docudrama" *Holocaust*, seems unduly dismissive and harsh:

> Because of the appeal to the authority of history, of objective veracity
> rather than the imagination as the channel and arbiter of reality, this

borderline art form becomes a component in the cultural perception of major events, ultimately resisting the application of literary standards just as it resists the judgment of historical accuracy. According to Maurice Samuel, such a novel as Hersey's cannot be read as an isolated fictional episode but as an incident along a historical and cultural continuum; the ultimate question, for Samuel, is how the story of the Warsaw Ghetto is "establishing itself in the Jewish People." The fictional "documentation" of Jewish history provided in these novels stereotypic responses which were compatible with a general avoidance or attempted redress of "unacceptable reality." (Ezrahi, *By Words Alone* 35-36)

To understand Ezrahi, we need to pursue her objections somewhat further:

Even the rubric under which the horrors of those years are subsumed—the *Holocaust*—may be regarded as something of an evasion through verbal encapsulation. It is derived from the Greek word for whole-burnt and is meant, presumably, to suggest the extent and even the "manner" of the death of the Jews of Europe. Yet the word *holokautoma*, which refers in the Septuagint to the "burnt offering" in the Temple of Solomon, raises problems through the sacrificial connotation that it attaches to the death of the Jews of Europe and which is, unfortunately, consistent with a prevailing Christian reading of Jewish history. (The nomenclature that has been adopted in the Jewish world does not carry the same affirmative theological overtones but, rather, signifies the enormity of the rift in Jewish history and culture brought about by the destruction of the European Jewish community.) Minimally, the diffuse imagery and the facile and associative vocabulary reflect a tendency in European and American culture to circumscribe the events, to allocate to them a place and a function in human history, and to confine the madness which threatens to impinge on a "reconstructed" world. (Ezrahi, *By Words Alone* 2)

She fears that redefining the Holocaust in terms of Western humanism corrupts the Holocaust by the wrong kinds of telling and eviscerates the mystical Jewish culture by which much of Eastern European Jews lived. Ezrahi also fears that the actual events lose their terrible pathos in the face of the domesticating energy of realism and putative verisimilitude and realism:

> Even the most vivid presentation of concrete detail and specificity, the most palpable reconstruction of Holocaust reality, is blunted by the fact that there is no analogue in human experience. The imagination loses credibility and resources where reality exceeds even the darkest fantasies of the human mind; even realism flounders before such reality. . . . The very presentation of a systematic *explanation*, or the assignment of one form or another of social or psychological "meaning" to the camp experience constitutes a code by which writers, in particular those who did not share the experience, can reconstruct it. Yet for others, primarily those who were close to the events themselves, it may be precisely in its *resistance* to conceptual abstraction, to psychological reductionism, that art as a version of historical memory can provide form without fixing meaning, insight without explanation, for the recovered events (Ezrahi, *By Words Alone* 3, 4)

Unlike Hersey, Keneally, and even Anne Frank, others of our writers such as Schwarz-Bart, Wiesel, and Levi see the Holocaust in a tradition of Jewish values, but whether we can say that one way of presenting the Holocaust is better than another, as Ezrahi argues, is moot. In fact, as we are observing in this study, there are many diverse traditions, and not only Anne Frank, but Keneally and Hersey draw upon them. Furthermore, Ezrahi argues:

> The challenges that the Holocaust presented to a traditional Jewish world view and theodicy were not automatically resolved by such actions as the Warsaw uprising or the Treblinka revolt, even if these are viewed as preludes to the establishment of the Jewish state. What distinguishes most of the Hebraic writing is the *internal* struggle with traditional responses to catastrophe. The varying interpretations of Jewish history which Hebraic writers offer delineate the boundaries of cultural experience and shape the very form

of their art. For all of them, again, the ultimate appeal—and the ultimate recourse—is to Jewish principles of order and faith, not to objective "history."

But the unambiguously heroic reading of history, based on the claim to factuality, is more palatable to popular sentiment which is a reservoir of faith in the triumph of courage over meekness, of progress over stasis. The commercial success of the novels of Steiner, Uris, and Hersey was a phenomenon not limited to the vagaries of popular fiction but, like the dramatized version of *The Diary of Anne Frank* and the television "docudrama" "Holocaust," can be seen as an index of the penetration of the Holocaust into the consciousness of those who had not experienced it. (Ezrahi *By Words Alone* 35)

Hersey's *The Wall* is shaped by a humanistic teleology that wishes to overcome the grotesque cultural differences it describes. The book uses the techniques of the discovered manuscript, buried by a historian and archivist—Noach Levinson—in the Warsaw ghetto, and edited and arranged by an imaginary editor. The catalyst for Hersey's imagination was probably the diary of Hillel Seidman and the archives coordinated by Emmanuel Ringelblum and the Oneg Shabbat group he led, archives that were uncovered in 1946. According to Nora Levin:

> The activities of the Oneg Shabbat were another [form of the battle against annihilation]. With a foreboding of imminent catastrophe, the leaders of Oneg Shabbat decided to take steps to protect their archives. During the massive exterminations in July, preparations were made to seal the materials in crates and bury them. On August 3, they were buried at 68 Nowolipki and 34 Swietojerska. (Levin 324)

While Ringelblum was in part the model for Levinson, some of the material that became *Notes from the Warsaw Ghetto* was not discovered until December 1950, after Hersey's novel was published.

Within Hersey's fictional universe, Levinson is a writer and famous scholar who wrote books entitled *The Diaspora* and *The Customs*. A lonely man, an outsider, an observer of life who finds community, family, and commitment within the ghetto, Levinson grows from a misanthropic figure who writes, "I seem increasingly to dislike everyone. Hence my surprise at feeling well-disposed toward [Dolek] Berson" (*The Wall* 40). Levinson tells Berson: "I am happier in the ghetto than I was before. I have many friends now, and my mind has been opened up to all sorts of new things" (*The Wall* 163). Hersey creates an imaginary editor whose "Editor's Prologue" scrupulously explains his method: "After consultation with others, the editor decided it would be wisest to use for the most part only those passages which concerned the members of the 'family' which Levinson joined, and a few others. . . . In the case of each note, the reader will find first the date of the events therein described, and then the date of Levinson's entry. Levinson was careful in every note to designate his source, and these attributions have been kept. Where the note was based on his own observation or opinion, he used, and this volume uses, the initials N.L. The reader will notice that a number of passages are marked with a star (✡). The passages are all taken from the context of a series of interviews that took place on May 9-10, 1943" (*The Wall*, 9-10).

Writing to the fiction editor after the war, Rachel Apt tells of Levinson's strength of character in the sewer culvert during the final escape from the burning ghetto: "I got from him a wonderful feeling of warmth and understanding, and even of gentle humor, and although we discussed the most intimate matters, I felt that it was all perfectly in accord with our mood and with the situation" (*The Wall* 682). In the Editor's Prologue, the editor has quoted a letter of Rachel's: "He was a queer man, but we loved him. Until he joined our 'family' he was all alone. He had never developed ties of any kind, and he had no relatives. Thus he had plenty of time for work" (*The Wall* 7-8). Even as the ghetto is decimated he proposes rules for the survival as if one could control destiny: *"Those men will survive the physical hardships of ghetto life who manage, each day, to expend a few less calories than they take in"* (*The Wall* 430).

In the novel Levinson is one of those who escaped, but he did not survive the war. His recording of conversations supposedly explained how he knows everyone's intimate feelings, but he would need to have been a tape recorder to get these conversations right. The artifice of the diary does create problems. As Barbara Foley, one of the few critics who appreciates the merit and importance of *The Wall*, remarks: "[I]n places the artifice is perhaps overly visible, since Levinson occasionally has to introduce a rather cumbersome testimonial apparatus in order to report scenes at which he was not present" (Foley 352). How Levinson, even as a Judenrat official, could have known so much defies probability, notwithstanding the fictional editor's explanation that Levenson became obsessive in his task of historian: "He came to feel that anything that happened to any Jew belonged in his notes. In the midst of the most commonplace conversations, Levinson might be seen sitting there taking notes" (*The Wall* 7).

In 1950, historical fiction posing as fact accomplished the effect Hersey sought, for his novel helped reawaken the anesthetized American—and even some elements of assimilated Jewish—consciousness which, after the Nuremberg trials, became preoccupied with the cold war and wanted to repress the American role of neglecting the atrocities. Hersey writes to give a fictional version of historical cause and effect as it impacts upon a particular group of people living in the Warsaw ghetto. As David Sanders makes clear, Hersey immersed himself in Holocaust material:

> When he began work on this, he soon learned that there existed a flood of diaries, organization records, statistics, medical histories, and songs about the Warsaw ghetto, and that very little of all this would ever be translated. Undertaking to read what he could, he also engaged two translators to read from the original Polish and Yiddish onto a wire recorder in rapid English. Most of his time for the next several months was spent listening to these recordings. They changed all his plans and reversed his established habits of approaching materials. His translators had relatives who had died in the ghetto, and their sight translating turned them into involuntary story-tellers as they began to skip, summarize, and add their own impassioned comments on the documents. The process gave Hersey the illusion of felt experience, instead of seeing a documentary. (50)

It is noteworthy that Hersey's concept of the Jew is of an ideal universal man and draws upon humanist as opposed to observant Jewish stereotypes. He eschews the tradition of mystical faith and elaborate ritual. He is very conscious of writing for both the American Jewish community and for a liberal democratic postwar audience of Americans who have participated in the war effort and want to find meaning in historical events. For example, his principle narrator, Levinson, mocks the passivity of the ultra-orthodox who believe they are in God's hands and that they should be glad because they are going "to the Messiah": "I saw two men, evidently Hasids, but clean-shaven now, having quite a merry theological discussion, hurling quips and quodlibets at each other's head. . . . Right next to these bliss ridden Hasids there lay an insane, naked old man on the floor" (*The Wall* 390, 392). In the process of writing the novel, Hersey, we know, watched Levinson's choruses become more and more dominant until Hersey realized that Levinson *must* become his sole narrator.

Hersey dramatizes diverse responses to crises. As the size of the ghetto is shrunk by vindictive German destruction as well as by the ravages of bombing by the allies, a wide diversity of people come together in increasingly crowded circumstances; these people are drawn to one another not only by human needs for nourishment, companionship, sympathy, common values, but also by propinquity, serendipity, and fear. According to Nora Levin:

> Hunger raged through the Ghetto, more acutely felt than physical pain or the two bitter winters the Ghetto lived through. In May 1940, Ringelblum heard an eight-year-old boy scream madly: "I want to steal, I want to rob, I want to eat. I want to be a German!" Three months later, he wrote: "At a funeral for the small children from the Wolska Street orphanage, the children from the home placed a wreath at the graves with the inscription: 'To the Children Who Have Died from Hunger—From the Children Who Are Hungry." There was a day and night obsession with food; women tore at each other for a crust of bread. (Levin 220)

Within these conditions, the concept of "family" expands to become almost tribal. The German authorities also closed streets and sections from the ghetto area, and herded the Jews into smaller and smaller areas. As Gilbert notes, "Behaviour which in normal times was of no particular significance had become, in the Nazi perspective, a crime, and crimes, by their nature, have to be punished. Step by step, and by means of 'rules', 'regulations', 'laws'—the terminology of civilized life—the conqueror, with the full power of enforcement, created a logical corridor into a bizarre world of cruelty and injustice" (Gilbert 98).

Within the "family" to which the heroic figures Rachel Apt and Dolek Berson, as well as Levinson, belong are an array of figures; all are frightened but some find the resources to think of others while some are self-immersed. Rachel's father undoes his circumcision and bribes his way out of the ghetto, only to become, if he lives at all, a servant to Germans. Rachel and Halinka, his daughters, grow while his son Stefan joins the Jewish police and becomes a moral dwarf who thinks mostly of himself and beats other Jews into submission: "Stefan was beating the miserable marchers with his wooden club, cursing them, occasionally shoving them: the handsome young man seemed possessed by some bestial, sadistic Other Self whom Berson had never met" (*The Wall* 300-301).

In the ghetto's worst months, between July and December 1942, Ringelblum wrote an undated entry in his *Notes from the Warsaw Ghetto*:

THE SIGNS OF MODERN SLAVES

1. Numbered and stamped.

2. Live in barracks—without their wives.

3. Wives and children removed, because slaves don't require families.

4. Walk in crowds, not individually.

5. Beaten and terrorized at work.

6. Inhuman exploitation (agreement at Schultz's [?]) like coolies.

7. Ban on organization of any kind.

8. Ban on any form of protest or sign of dissatisfaction.

9. Every slave dependent for his life on his master and the [master's] Jewish assistant. At any moment a man can be sent to the Umschlagplatz.

10. The murderous discipline, and the sending of workers to forced [labor] camps because of lateness as happened at Schultz's.

11. Compulsion to work, even [when worker is sick] with temperature.

12. Worse off than slaves, because *they* must look after their own food.

13. Confiscation of property from a dead worker's family, because the right of inheritance has been abolished.

14. Locked inside the residential block.

15. Ban on leaving your apartment and walking in the street after work hours.

16. Limitation of personal freedom, of movement.

17. *Worse than slaves,* because the latter knew they would remain alive, had some hope to be set free. The Jews are *morituri*—sentenced to death—whose death sentence [has been] postponed indefinitely, or has been passed.

18. The sick and the weak are not needed, so ambulatory clinics, hospitals, and the like have been liquidated. (Ringelblum, 319-320)

As the ghetto becomes smaller because of the deportations, terrible moral decisions confront the inhabitants. For example, Mordecai Apt has to choose between his wife and his wife's mother, and the mother heroically chooses to volunteer for deportation long after it is known deportation means Treblinka and that Treblinka is a death camp. The conflict between the belonging to a specific Eastern Jewish culture and the Western Europe post-Enlightenment perspective of educated Jews takes place within the community and within many of the cosmopolitan Jews, like Dolek Berson.

As conditions worsen, surprising figures like the homely and obviously named Rachel Apt (for "aptitude") and Berson develop their potential. Originally Berson seems to Levinson "a drifter [who] lets life carry him along in its stream" (*The Wall* 11). The narrator traces Berson's gradual moral awakening. Berson had been passive; now he becomes active. He becomes morally responsible and is killed in the final escape. His moral "sound" is indicated by his concertina—which during the uprising seems to be everywhere: "[W]e in the bunker jumped to our feet when we heard, startlingly close at hand, the proud strains of *Hatkiva* [Note. Editor. 'Hope,' the Jewish national anthem], played on the concertina" (605). Berson is tempted by a sense of superiority when he sees the "parade of poverty stricken Jews" in the first deportation. But his compassion overcomes his snobbery: "What right had they to advertise the depths to which Jews could be driven? Quickly Berson's hatred surged over the threshold into the place of compassion and became mixed up with compassion and at last was wholly converted into compassion: and he wept . . . with great racking sobs" (*The Wall* 301). But religious faith and even Jewish cultural values are absent from Berson's transvaluation of values. That within *The Wall* how one responds to crises is measured in terms of Western humanistic values typifies the responses in American and Western European culture to the Holocaust in the 1950s and is responsible for the way *The Diary of Anne Frank* and *Night* were originally received. "[Berson] says he has noticed in himself a general quickening of all his faculties. He says he feels that he is more mature, more dependable, and more available (in the sense that a friendly man is available and a cold and self-centered one is not) than he has ever been; he feels as if he has suddenly found himself. . . . Berson is humble about these sensations he has had; he says he doubts them and interrogates them constantly, fearful lest they be illusory or mere conceit" (*The Wall* 410).

The *Wall* is divided into six parts. Part One begins after Hitler's conquest of Poland, when the wall is constructed to protect the Poles against a typhus epidemic supposedly sweeping through the Jewish community. According to Nora Levin, "By October 16, 1940, 140,000 still-dispersed Jews were ordered to move in with the 240,000 Jews already inside the Ghetto. This move concentrated almost 400,000 people within one hundred square city blocks. A third of Warsaw's population was crammed into 2.4 percent of the total area of the city. The new migrants carried all of their worldly goods into the Ghetto by hand or cart" (Levin 207). Incredibly, the Jews must pay for the wall that encloses them. As Levin notes, "It was Heydrich who ordered the ghettoization of Jews in the East. It was also Heydrich who, six weeks after the invasion of Russia, was given sweeping authority to organize the 'final solution' of the Jewish question, the Nazi euphemism for annihilation." (Levin 58). Levinson traces the history of the ghetto as hunger rages and murders of innocent Jews becomes commonplace; finally, deportations to concentration camps and, for the most part, to gas chambers decimate the ghetto.

The novel's final part deals with the uprising of the Z.O.B. and escape of a tiny group through the sewers. Perhaps some contemporary readers will find the conclusion, with its moral epithets, sentimental and reductive. The ghetto wall is the central image. Perhaps with some sense of how the creation of the wall is a grotesque parody of the creation story in *Genesis*, Hersey has Levinson recall the creation of the wall in April 1940: "This wall is not just a fence or a marker. This wall is actually intended to keep human beings from passing. At the bottom, there are small gutter drainage holes—too small for the smallest human infant to get through. . . . The occupation authorities are building this wall as they do everything else—section by section, episode after episode, separately, without apparent sequence" (*The Wall* 88-89). Hersey's prose reflects his journalistic background; he evokes visual impressions of what it is to live behind a wall. His detailed, unadorned prose is that of keen observer, the creation of someone who spent many years as reporter for the magazine *Time* and knew *Time*'s understated style. His unit of prose is more the paragraph than the striking phrase or allusion. He tells his story with a sense of Warsaw's geography and with an eye for extrinsic detail; in the above passage he uses accretions of phrases that give a sense of the turmoil. He can pull together disparate data in synthesizing paragraphs and set the part in relation to the whole. Even when the focus is on group or family, he never loses sight of the ghetto as a whole. Historical scope—the ability to imagine how a place functions—rather than fully developed round characterization is Hersey's strength. Finally, Hersey's Levinson is a reporter whose lucid style reflects the clarity and precision of his mind. Levinson observes changes in behavior and their effects on political, social, and personal situations, but he does not probe deeply into his characters' psyches.

Yet, as the novel continues, Hersey becomes interested in Levinson, his principle narrator, as a character. Levinson vacillates between being a self-dramatizing narrator and a journalist. He plays two somewhat contradictory roles in what Barbara Foley calls the "pseudofactual mode" of the Holocaust novel (Foley 351). As character he embodies the particular witness expressing his subjective response; as archivist and historian he embodies the general and more objective perspective.

Levinson the narrator-character has a passionate desire to belong, which he hides behind his early mask as detached outsider, and he develops a deep love for Rachel Apt. His story is a version of a conversion, from withdrawal and isolation to community, from detachment to commitment, from marginalized outsider to someone capable of passionate love. In both his capacities—as a character and as a historian—we as modern readers are aware of his rhetorical performance, even though Hersey's docufiction focuses on external events and how characters are caught in their web. Contemporary readers are used to seeing words as mirrors into the speaker's psyche; we seek to weave a narrative around the voice of a man who changes and evolves. We know that in first-person narrative, effect *causes* cause, and we seek to know from what perspective—or personal effect—the historian is explaining events. We want to know how consciousness of an audience shapes his self-presentation and how his persona filters events through his experience. Certainly Levinson is conscious of how he presents himself to his imagined audience.

Finally the wall has become a metaphor for a paradoxical relationship between insiders and outsiders. In this case, it is the outsiders, the others, who are in the dominant position and the insiders who are isolated and quarantined and imprisoned. Yet somehow the humanity of some insiders survives and flourishes. After tiny remnants of the ghetto fighters escape, Mordecai Apt speaks of the wall as an idea: "There are two ways of looking at the wall between Jews and gentiles: from the inside and from the outside: there is much to be said on both sides. On the one hand, it can be said that the actual masonry is done by the Jews: the Jews mix the mortar and lay the bricks and complain about the wall, but are sometimes glad to have it. On the other hand, it is the *goyim* who oblige the Jews to build the wall and who supply most of the materials for it; and they are very smug about its existence: without ever going inside it, they assume it is better to be outside and to keep the Jews inside" (*The Wall* 694). By emphasizing the human aspirations of the Jews more than their religious priorities and faith, Hersey creates a teleology of cultural homogeneity that would reach out to his audience and tear down the invisible bricks that perpetuated the walls of cultural separation between Jew and gentile in America and among survivors in Western Europe.

Levinson makes fun of those who pin their hopes on vague rumors, and gives one of the "family" members the name Rabbi Goldflamm (as in "flim-flam"): "Like all of the rabbi's rumors, the one he wanted Berson to hear this evening was circumstantial. It was to the effect that President Roosevelt had sent a cable two days before to Commissioner Haensch, declaring that the United States had opened its immigration quotas without limit for Jews, and that the Germans were to regard the Jews in the Warsaw ghetto as prisoners of war and were to make arrangements to exchange them for German soldier-prisoners by way of Istanbul." (*The Wall* 410-11) We might recall Martin Gilbert's words that I quoted before: "Unable to conceive of his own death, a man, even when surrounded by the death of others, grasps at any hope or rumour that might distance him from the realisation that he himself might be marked out for death" (Gilbert 333).

Prior to the uprising, Ringelblum in his *Notes from the Warsaw Ghetto* defines the mood when only 10 percent remain; he writes under the title "Why Were 10 Percent of the Jews of Warsaw Allowed to Remain?"

Hence the bitter pessimism dominating the Jewish populace. *Morituri*, that is the best description of our mood. Most of the populace is set on resistance. It seems to me that people will no longer go to the slaughter like lambs. They want the enemy to pay dearly for their lives. They'll fling themselves at Them with knives, staves, coal gas. They'll permit no more blockades. They'll not allow themselves to be seized in the street, for they know that work camp means death these days. And they want to die at home, not in a strange place. Naturally, there will only be a resistance if it is organized, and if the enemy does not move like lightning, as [They did] in Cracow, where, at the end of October, 5,500 Jews were packed into wagons in seven hours one night. We have seen the confirmation of the psychological law that the slave who is completely repressed cannot resist. The Jews appear to have recovered somewhat from the heavy blows they have received; they have shaken off the effects of their experiences to some extent, and they calculate now that going to the slaughter peaceably has not diminished the misfortune, but increased it. Whomever you talk to, you hear the same cry: The resettlement should never have been permitted. We should have run out into the street, have set fire to everything in sight, have torn down the walls, and escaped to the Other Side. The Germans would have taken their revenge. It would have cost tens of thousands of lives, but not 300,000. Now we are ashamed of ourselves, disgraced in our own eyes, and in the eyes of the world, where our docility earned us nothing. This must not be repeated now. We must put up a resistance, defend ourselves against the enemy, man and child. (Ringelblum 326)

In a crystallizing moment of Hersey's novel during the ghetto uprising, Levinson defines Jewishness not in religious term, but in terms of Western humanism:

> *Jewishness is that which makes the Jews, in eras of national independence, feel free and enables them to fashion institutions as embodiment of their national creative will. Jewishness is, in such times, joy, ecstasy, zestful living.*
>
> *Jewishness is that which creates, in troubled eras, institutions for defense, for prevention of danger, for protecting itself and its members. Jewishness is, in such times, a call to battle and a challenge to heroism.*
>
> *Jewishness is that which must, in times of dependence and weakness, retreat into its shell, conserve its resources, endure in silence, and wait for better days. Then Jewishness is hope and pain, messianic dreams, and other-worldliness. Then it demands real sacrifice* (The Wall 614; italics in original).

When a few Germans are killed at the beginning of the uprising, Levinson writes of his feeling that "this was victory. . . . I am moved because of the loneliness of this fighting figure in the ghetto. He stands alone. What has the conscience of the world ever done for him? Nothing. What will it ever do for him? Nothing. Why should I be moved?" (The Wall 584).

Hersey takes a harsh view of the Judenrat and the Jewish police whose duties, as Gilbert reminds us," included guarding the gates of the ghetto with German and Polish policemen, directing traffic in the ghetto streets, guarding post offices, soup kitchens and community offices, detecting 'and suppressing' smugglers, and driving the growing number of beggars from street to street" (Gilbert 133). Levinson is himself a minor functionary of the Jewish ghetto administrative estab-lishment, but he observes with dismay the complicity of the Judenrat and Jewish police with the Nazis. According to Jacob Sloan's introduction to Ringelblum's *Notes from the Warsaw Ghetto*:

> *It was the Nazi practice to force the Jews themselves to administer the discriminatory decrees that produced their suffering. A veteran Jewish community leader, Adam Czerniakow, was called to the Gestapo on October 4, 1939, and ordered to appoint a new Jewish Council to supplant the old, limited Jewish Community Council of Warsaw. . . . The new Jewish Council was to be a government-in-miniature, but without a trace of independence. It was the Council's duty to furnish the work battalion demanded by the Occupying force; to maintain peace and order (through an Ordnungsdienst, or Law and Order Service, consisting of Jewish policemen); to train skilled workers; to attend to sanitation and medical needs—particularly to combat epidemics.* (Ringelblum 4; italics are Sloan's)

As I mentioned, Ringelblum's *Notes from the Warsaw Ghetto* were discovered in the late 1950s after Hersey's novel was written, but Hersey had access to much of the archives that Ringelblum and his Oneg Shabbat group had buried. The *Notes* are even more severe on the role the Jewish police played in the final major deportations.

> And now people are wracking their brains to understand how Jews, most of them men of culture, former lawyers (most of the police officers were lawyers before the war), could have done away with their brothers with their own hands. How could Jews have dragged women and children, the old and the sick, to the wagons—knowing they were all being driven to the slaughter? There are people who hold that every society has the police it deserves, that the disease-cooperation with the Occupying Power in the slaughter of 300,000 Jews—is a contagion affecting the whole of our society and is not limited to the police, who are merely an expression of our society. Other people argue that the police is the haven of morally weak psychological types, who do everything in their power to survive the difficult times, who believe the end determines all means, and the end is to survive the war—even if survival is bound up with the taking of other people's lives. (Ringelblum 330)

Within Hersey's fictive universe, the ghetto's social strata mirrors that of other communities, notwithstanding the movement of the social wheel of fortune: "Those who managed to bring wealth into the ghetto with them, and who have conserved what they brought, still enjoy the respect and resentment their privileged position gave them before. . . . A man's address is still more or less a key to his social standing. Manners and education still make a certain amount of difference: an impoverished family of high breeding and training sneers self-consolingly at vulgar *arrivistes*. . . . Energy and enterprise are rewarded with surprising rapidity, and the scythe swings fast, too, to cut down those who let themselves grow apathetic and unvigilant. Unexpected jobs turn out to be the rewarding ones. For instance: janitorships" (*The Wall* 189). Originally, the well-to-do had separate streets and livable, if modest, apartments. When the deportations get in high gear, membership in the Judenrat or Jewish police or work in certain factories connected to the German war effort become more important than wealth. Finally, the ability to survive, physical strength, and courage, wiliness, and judgment replace material values.

By contrast, Hersey dramatizes Rachel Apt's great courage and refusal to leave when she is offered a chance of escape by a Jewish organization outside Nazi Europe. In the person of Rachel Apt, Hersey has created a strong woman character—perhaps one of the most genuinely heroic woman in the books I am discussing. But Hersey—or his surrogate narrator, Levinson—makes a great deal of Rachel's homeliness as if her looks were *why* she became "little mother" to the large ghetto family and as if only beautiful women can become—as she finally does with Berson—loved. One could ascribe this to a semi-reliable narrator's naiveté, if others in the novel did not buy into this 1950s commodification of women according to appearance and sexual attractiveness.

The Wall began a tradition of Holocaust realism, of reconstructing history. As Ezrahi puts it:

> In their reliance on meticulous reconstruction based on research, such novels exemplify a form of realism or naturalism which posits as morally acceptable the appropriation of the Holocaust through the autonomy and primacy of facts and the function of those facts in constraining imagination and personal fantasy. The tension between internal accountability to the imagination and external

accountability to the victims expresses the heart of the dilemma of
Holocaust literature in America. . . . The insular response of
postwar Jewish writers to the events in Europe was the first
indication of a tendency to extract a universal moral message out of
the particularistic experience and to explore the relevance of such
experience for post-Holocaust man. (Ezrahi, *By Words Alone* 216)

Hersey's realistic impulse would have been helped by a map of the
Warsaw ghetto of the kind that Jacob Sloan provides in his edition of
Ringelblum's *Notes from the Warsaw Ghetto* or some of the maps that
accompany Spiegelman's *Maus*. Yet what Hersey does do is remind us
that, as Martin Gilbert writes: "It was the Jews alone who were marked
out to be destroyed in their entirety: every Jewish man, woman and
child, so that there would be no future Jewish life in Europe. Against the
eight million Jews who lived in Europe in 1939, the Nazi bureaucracy
assembled all the concerted skills and mechanics of a modern state: the
police, the railways, the civil service, the industrial power of the Reich;
poison gas, soldiers, mercenaries, criminals, machine guns, artillery; and
over all, a massive apparatus of deception" (Gilbert 824). *The Wall*
dramatically enacts Gilbert's comment on resistance, and makes us
understand how Hersey conceived the project of his fictional Levinson
as an act of resistance. We see Hersey's use of the recurring *topos* of
language as resistance during the Holocaust and as a testimony of Jewish
historical survival if not redemption in the ensuing years.

CHAPTER SIX

POPULAR FICTION:
GERALD GREEN'S *HOLOCAUST*:
A NOVEL OF SURVIVAL
AND TRIUMPH

The German Nazis, then, did not discard the past; they
built upon it. They did not begin a development; they
completed it. In the deep recesses of anti-Jewish history,
we shall find many of the administrative and psychological tools with which the Nazis implemented their
destruction process. In the hollows of the past, we shall
also discover the roots of the characteristic Jewish
response to an outside attack.

—Raul Hilberg, *The Destruction of the*
European Jews 4

Holocaust is a novel written by Gerald Green, who first wrote the 1978
teleplay *Holocaust* for NBC, a production that popularized the Holocaust
in the American imagination. The teleplay served an important purpose
in raising American consciousness about the events of the thirties and
early forties in Europe and giving felt life to the abstractions of Holocaust
death numbers. It brought to life visually, if somewhat reductively, what
it was like to live in the ghettos and camps and what might have
motivated the oppressors to perpetrate crimes against humanity.

Writing of the popularization of the Holocaust, Ezrahi remarks:

There does seem to be a tendency on the part of middlebrow writers such as Steiner, Green, Uris, and Hersey to attempt to compel the reader's interest by the use of the documentary imperative; the "true story" commands a kind of automatic reverence and attention that the truly creative writer has to marshal all the powers of the imagination in order to achieve. But these writers are, additionally, catering to an attitude in which the ambiguities of history and the challenge to ethnic pride are resolved by heroic epic, and the documentary form, accommodating itself to ideological postures and minimal creative responsibilities, easily lends itself to such purposes. This popular version of the heroic epic is an affirmation of a simple causality in Jewish History. (*By Words Alone* 34)

Holocaust is not a very good novel, but examining it may tell us why other Holocaust books work. Moreover, it does seek the geographic and historical inclusiveness that the prior texts we have examined sometimes lack. It seeks to present individual lives within the fabric of a grammar of historical cause and effect and seeks balance between the general, objective supposedly factual perspective and the nominalistic subjective perspective of imagined characters caught in the maelstrom of events they cannot control or understand. Calling this kind of novel "pseudofactual," Barbara Foley has written, "The pseudofactual mode provides the unified image of a fictive realm but challenges the autonomy of this realm. While it projects an imagined world in its totality, in its local effects it substitutes historical probabilities for literary ones, and thus instantly reminds the reader of the text's relation to the historical world" (Foley 351).

To be sure, at times Green trivializes the Holocaust by creating wooden and stereotypical characters, stilted and implausible dialogue, reductive dichotomies, and silly fantastic discussion among the German leaders about how the Holocaust took philosophic shape and form. It also includes the use of anti-Semitic stereotypes, not only by Green's Germans but by some of Green's Jews themselves. Indeed, the book—more than the teleplay—patronizes Holocaust victims. This may be because in the teleplay the facial expressions and the background give the words a visual context.

Green's novel depends on simplistic explanations and pop psychology. Dorf, Heydrich's lieutenant, seeks a father figure because his own father, a socialist and economic failure, had committed suicide and was not a successful father. His sex life with his wife, Marta, improves in passion as he becomes powerful. The plot depends on implausible coincidences in which the two major characters and their families intersect at opportune times, as when Rudi Weiss and Helena meet Hans Helms meets in Russia outside Kiev and, after they have saved his life, are betrayed by him. The Americanized dialogue in this scene is also typical: "Rudi, give me a break" (188), "You lousy, lying bastard . . . we risked our necks for you" (190).

While Ezrahi lumps Green with Hersey, the latter created in 1950 an imagined ontology that gave a thick texture to the Warsaw ghetto. By contrast, in his novel, Green cinematically jumps around in a way that does not give the reader a plausible interior life for the characters or a feel of what it was like in places that gave way to grotesque moral assumptions and where life was reduced to a quest for survival. We may often be put off by Green's clumsy style, including the diction and syntax of B movies or sitcoms. Sometimes Green's prose is execrable: "I remarked that I might have trouble paying the doctor bills, and she responded that if Dr. Weiss was so happy to see me again, and even recalled my father's stollen, he'd certainly trust me until I found work. Marta is ever the optimist, the planner, the one who looks ahead and sees things getting better" (19). Or recall this dialogue: "In the kitchen I said to Anna, 'Mama always has her way.' 'Maybe 'cause she's always right'" (34). Or take Marta's soap operatic response to Dorf's rapid rise, as reported in his diary: "Marta kissed me, threw her arms around me. 'Oh, Erik. I'm so happy for us. And you once sneered at—what did you call it? Police work! Look how you've succeeded!'"(53). This is the careless prose of harlequin romance rather than the dense texture of a thoughtful mind. The grammar of motives is simplistic and the historical explanations are reductive, although at times this seems appropriate for insane Nazi behavior under the guise of rational policy. The Nazi characters' grammar of motives—personal, political, and logical—is that of the insane asylum; one thinks of the film *Sling Blade*. While this may be Green's point, others have done it in a more deft and nuanced way.

At times the political rhetoric is implausible, even though it works in the close-ups and quick fade-outs of the teleplay. Thus we are asked to believe in the following dialogue between Dorf and Eichmann:

"Oh, that you're a hard-working, loyal aide to the chief of the Gestapo and the Security Service. A sort of house intellectual. I must tell you, Dorf, Heydrich's memoranda are infinitely more readable since you took over."

"You're baiting me, Major."

"Not at all. I love the substitute words you've developed for us. Code words, as it were." He seemed to savor the sound as he spoke. "'Resettlement,' 'relocation,' 'special handling.' Marvelous synonyms for getting rid of Jews." (71)

Rudi Weiss is a Jewish hero rather than a victim. He may owe something to the Jews in *The Wall*. Green would certainly have read Raul Hilberg's controversial indictment of Jewish passivity in his 1961 *The Destruction of the European Jews:*

> Much has been said and much has been written about the *Judenräte*, the informers, the Jewish police, the *Kapos*—in short, all those persons who deliberately and as a matter of policy cooperated with the Germans. But these collaborators do not interest us so much as the masses of Jews who reacted to every German order by complying with it automatically. . . .
>
> Thus, over a period of centuries the Jews had learned that in order to survive they had to refrain from resistance. Time and again they were attacked; they endured the Crusades, the Cossack uprisings, and the Czarist persecution. There were many casualties in these times of stress, but always the Jewish community emerged once again like a rock from a receding tidal wave. The Jews had never really been annihilated. After surveying the damage, the survivors had always proclaimed in affirmation of their strategy the triumphant slogan, "The Jewish people lives [*Am Yisrael Chaj*]." This experience was so ingrained in the Jewish consciousness as to achieve the force of law. The Jewish people could not be annihilated.
>
> Only in 1941, 1942, and 1943 did the Jewish leadership realize that, unlike the pogroms of past centuries, the modern machine-like destruction process would engulf European Jewry. But the realization came too late. A two-thousand-year-old lesson could

not be unlearned; the Jews could not make the switch. They were
helpless. . . .

The Jews, in short, did not always have to be deceived; they
were capable of deceiving themselves; the Jewish repressive mechanism could work independently and automatically. In the minutes of
the Vienna Jewish war invalids' conferences we discover the same
significant absence of direct references to death and killing centers
that we have already noted in German correspondence. (666-667)

I quote at such length to show the Zeitgeist to which Green aggressively
reacted when he created Weiss as heroic Jew. *Holocaust* depends on a
juxtaposition of Rudi Weiss's retrospective narration with the diary of
Eric Dorf, an SS lawyer who is Heydrich's right-hand man. Dorf is a
shrewd young lawyer who rises to power by providing the necessary
euphemisms for Heydrich. We might recall Gilbert's account of Heydrich's words at the infamous January 20, 1942 Wannsee conference:

> The struggle waged against the Jews "so far," said Heydrich,
> had first involved the expulsion of the Jews "from various spheres of
> life of the German people" and then the expulsion of the Jews "from
> the living space of the German people." Now, following "pertinent
> prior approval of the Führer," the "evacuation of the Jews to the
> East" had emerged "in place of emigration" as a "further possible
> solution." But both emigration and evacuation, he pointed out, were
> to be considered "merely as a measure of expediency," from which
> experience could be gained which would be of importance "in view
> of the approaching final solution of the Jewish question."
>
> Heydrich then explained that this "final solution" concerned,
> not only those Jews who were already under German rule, but
> "some eleven million Jews" throughout Europe. (Gilbert 280)

Rudi Weiss, the Jewish narrator, is an athletic German Jew—a
family anomaly—who leaves Germany and finally joins up with Jewish
partisans in the Ukraine. Weiss writes his story in 1952 after marrying a
sabra and moving to Israel, where he lives on a kibbutz with his *sabra*
wife, Tamar. As he explains in the Prologue, he has gotten Erik Dorf's
diary from his uncle:

These diaries are of a fragmented and desultory nature. Oftentimes, Erik Dorf did not even date his entries, but fortunately he did mention enough places and dates in his rambling account so that I have been able to determine at least the month for each entry. . . . I never knew Major Erik Dorf, but in one of those crazy coincidences with which those dreadful years are filled, he and his wife had at one time been *my father's patients* in Berlin. Three years after my father had taken care of him and his family, this same Erik Dorf was signing orders and establishing procedures that would lead to the murder of Karl, my parents, my Uncle Moses—and six million other innocents. (3)

Weiss's opening tone—one that often recurs in the novel—is of a teacher who is giving a lesson to Jews and gentiles alike.

Anticipating the scope and range of Schwarz-Bart's *The Last of the Just,* Green wants his story to be representative and involve a cross-section of Jewish experience in several countries and venues, including the Warsaw ghetto and several camps: Buchenwald, Auschwitz, Sobibor, Theresienstadt. Weiss, the teller, has lost his entire family and his wife except for a sister-in-law's nephew. The novel begins on August 1, 1935—six weeks before the Nurenburg laws—with the wedding of Karl Weiss and a Catholic girl named Inga Helms. Anti-Semitism was lurking even before the Nuremberg laws. In *The Destruction of the Jews,* Raul Hilberg has traced Nazi antecedents to Luther:

The picture of the Jew which we encounter in Nazi propaganda and Nazi correspondence had been drawn several hundred years before. Martin Luther had already sketched the main outlines of that portrait, and the Nazis, in their time, had little to add to it. . . . Luther's treatise about the Jews was addressed to the public directly, and, in that pouring recital, sentences descended upon the audience in a veritable cascade. Thus the passage:

"Herewith you can readily see how they understand and obey the fifth commandment of God, namely, that they are thirsty bloodhounds and murderers of all Christendom, with full intent, now for more than fourteen hundred years, and indeed they were often burned to death upon the accusation that they had poisoned water and wells, stolen children, and torn and hacked them apart, in order to cool their temper secretly with Christian blood."

And:

"Now see what a fine, thick, fat lie that is when they complain that they are held captive by us. It is more than fourteen hundred years since Jerusalem was destroyed, and at this time it is almost three hundred years since we Christians have been tortured and persecuted by the Jews all over the world (as pointed out above), so that we might well complain that they had now captured us and kill us—which is the open truth. Moreover, we do not know to this day which devil has brought them here into our country; we did not look for them in Jerusalem." (8-9)

Green has Weiss retrospectively recall the Jews's plight in the year 1935:

> We were Jews, already a marked people. Thousands of Jews had already left Germany, their businesses and properties stolen by the Nazis. There had been outbreaks of beatings on the street, humiliations, demonstrations. But we had stayed on. My mother always insisted that Hitler was "another politician," an upstart who would be put in his place soon enough. She was certain that things would get better. Her family had been in the country for centuries, and she felt more German than any flag-waving bully in the street. (8)

Already his father, a physician, had had his practice reduced: "His practice had been reduced to the ill and the poor, Jews only, the ones who had not had the money or foresight to leave" (9). His grandfather was a hero of the World War. We might recall Martin Gilbert's words:

> The fanning of popular resentment and physical attack was not only against wealthy Jews, or those who had supported the democratic parties, or the Communists. It was an assault upon every Jew in Germany: an attempt to turn all German Jewry into an outcast, fit only for persecution, harassment and expulsion. The Jew would be driven from every profession, and then from the life of the nation. On 1 May 1934 Der Sturmer gave vent to this all-embracing hatred in

a special fourteen-page issue by reviving the medieval "blood libel" accusation against the Jews of using Christian blood in the baking of their Passover bread, and in other "Judaic" rituals. (Gilbert 42-43)

As Hilberg has argued convincingly in *The Destruction of the Jews,* "The Germans controlled the Jewish leadership, and that leadership, in turn, controlled the Jewish community. . . . Truly the Jewish communal organization had become a self-destructive machine" (125). Gradually, we see the noose tighten as the Nuremberg laws are imposed. Gilbert wrote of the Nuremberg laws:

> The Nuremberg Laws made it clear that the Jews were to be allowed no further part in German life: no equality under the law; no further citizenship; no chance of slipping back into the mainstream of German life in which for several generations they had been an integral part, but from which, for two and a half years, they had been gradually cut off.
>
> Following Nuremberg, each move against the Jews could be made with the backing of legal segregation; and such moves began at once. Only a week after Nuremberg Laws were announced, news reached the outside world that Jews had been forbidden access to any holiday resort in Bavaria. (Gilbert 48)

Dorf calls upon Dr. Weiss, who had been his own family doctor, to intimidate him because Dr. Weiss has treated an Aryan.

As the subtitle, "A Novel of Survival and Triumph," indicates, the teleology of Green's *Holocaust* is humanistic. Weiss, the hero, learns that being human has to do with caring for his fellows without regard to wealth or class. While Weiss came from a prosperous family, he has learned that he does not need much: "We lived like wandering ghosts, worse than gypsies. Perhaps it explains why I have adapted so well to life on the kibbutz. In my years of wandering I learned how little a man needs to get by" (243). In the last chapter he agrees to take 40 Greek children of Jewish ancestry to Palestine. Seeing them playing in a field in Theresienstadt, he goes to kick the ball with them: "When I retrieved the ball and came back to the shaven-headed kids, they already knew my name. They clung to my legs, grabbed my hand, and one of them kissed me" (408). He has learned to fight for his country from his partisan experience: "I still have difficulty with Hebrew. But I am no longer a European. Israel is my country. I fought for her liberty in 1947, and I will fight again, and again, and whenever I am asked to. In my days as a partisan in the Ukraine, I learned that it is better to die with a gun in one's hand than to submit to the murderer" (2).

Dorf is a villain of Green's invention; he is propelled by his wife's ambition; like Marlow's Kurtz, he can convince himself to believe anything. Encouraged by his wife, Dorf, a young, amoral, careerist lawyer, ties his kite to Heydrich's tail and flourishes until Heydrich's assassination. At first he resents vandalism, but later he will kill a Jew in cold blood. As Germany is falling, he alone wants to publicize the Holocaust: "We must make clear to the world that we stand between civilization and the Jewish plot to destroy our world, to pollute the race, to dominate us. We, *we* alone, have been men enough to accept their challenge. Why hide it? Why keep it a secret? Why invent excuses?" (381). For a resistant reader, the creation of Dorf as the inventor of Zyklon B almost relieves the real Heydrich and Eichmann of responsibility. Dorf's Uncle Kurt is the good German, the engineer and road builder who tries to save Jews. He is an alternative father figure to Dorf, who recalls, "Kurt's eyes were at that moment the eyes of my father. The look in them was precisely the look he fixed upon me when I had lied, or done something dishonorable. I was such an obedient dutiful child that these occasions were rare indeed. . . . I am committing no sins. I am being obedient, following the rules, laws and destiny of the nation, of our leaders" (200).

The foregoing is an example of pop psychology and embarrassingly silly rationalizations that attempt to explain motivation. But perhaps Green's inarticulate characters show us a serious problem of Holocaust fiction—namely, how does an author dramatize the obsessive and the heinous that transcend comprehensible motive and articulation? Perhaps realism cannot comfortably enter the Holocaust world *because* it relies on naturalizing and domesticating emotions and attitudes of the perpetrators—and the victims—that are inexplicable.

For the Holocaust introduces new dimensions of horror and hate. Ezrahi notes that other modernists understood that the nature of violence changed:

The shift is from violence as a passionate crime of the self to automated, socially enforced, and diffuse violence as the general backdrop for human endeavor. Holocaust literature appears in this context as the culmination of a well-advanced literary process. And if the new literary forms come not only to reflect but in some sense to anticipate current events, Kafka is the writer whose fiction so fully expressed the logic of modern technology, mechanized sadism, and bureaucratic depersonalization that Auschwitz appears almost as the realization of the fantastic world blueprinted in *The Penal Colony*. Still, the next stage, even in the literary history of violence, seems to test or transgress the boundaries of the admissible in art. (*By Words Alone* 5)

World War I had introduced the escalation in wartime technology and the cost of that technology. Were it not for the transportation system, the Germans could not have exacted their price on Jews. As Green stresses, the SS commandeered the trains from the war effort for the final solution, even after the war turned against the Germans. Green dramatizes what Raul Hilberg in *The Destruction of the Jews* makes clear, namely that the destruction of the Jews became a German obsession and took precedence over the war effort:

The war economy lost the aggregate value of those products which two or three million workers in Germany and in the occupied countries could produce in two or three years. This loss was total because the destruction process had removed the Jewish labor force without replacement from going concerns. This does not imply that in individual plants or warehouses Jews were not replaced; it does mean that in the total production picture the loss of Jewish labor could never be made up. (646)

Rudi Weiss has much to say about the Jews that is patronizing to those who had little choice, and repeats stereotypes that do not speak to the complexity of the circumstances that faced European Jews: "My uncle agreed that they should think of fighting back. But how? What sense did it make? Jews spent most of their time arguing with each other—Orthodox against nonbelievers, Zionists against non-Zionists,

Communists against Socialists. Name an internal dispute, and you'd find it" (179). Rudi wants Helena to learn passionate resistance: "She would also have to learn to hate, to want revenge, to realize that there was no way out for us except to run, to hide, and to try to fight. I would have to tell her worse things, too. That we would have to be ready to die, but to die in a brave and resisting way. I was sick of people placidly lining up, making excuses to themselves, following orders, and going to their death" (201). Later Rudi writes of the partisan Jews under the leader, Uncle Sasha: "The atmosphere in the family camp always seemed to me dreamlike, enshrouded in mists. People talked quietly, if at all. There was none of the noisy chatter, the gossiping, the arguing so characteristic of Jewish communities. These people had been witnesses to dreadful crimes against their families and friends; they had no time for argument among themselves, for trivia." (238). For Rudi, Sasha's camp anticipates the vitality of his current life in Kibbutz Agam and the Israelis' fierce sense of purpose.

Green's documentary novel and teledrama do not always, by our contemporary standards, have a sufficiently sophisticated grammar of historical cause and effect. Perhaps he tries to do more than is possible; as Barbara Foley puts it, "Green's encyclopedic survey has the effect of circumscribing and totalizing an experience that surely defies such facile treatment" (Foley 354). Yet when we see the teleplay, we realize that the novel may well be rescued by the visual. For the novel was written from the teleplay and emphasizes the visual; thus when Helena dies, Rudi writes: "I stopped and kneeled over her. Her face was calm, pale. There was no agony on it. The bullets had entered her back and killed her instantly. She lay there, looking tinier than ever, more beautiful, and I buried my face on her breast" (374).

If there is an effective symbol in Green's novel, it is the Bechstein piano that belonged to the Weiss family and is eventually expropriated for Dorf's family. Rudi Weiss recalls: "I see that damned piano as symbolizing an anchor, a deadweight that kept us in Germany, gave us a false sense of security. Some years ago, here at Kibbutz Agam, a Czech professor of languages confessed to me that he too had owned a fine piano in Prague—a Weber. He and his wife had always had the feeling that no possible harm could come to people who owned grand pianos" (101-102).

The assimilated German Jews believe that their culture protects them. Dorf finds in the piano the pictures of the Weiss family at the time of Inga Helms's wedding to Rudi Weiss's brother, Karl, on August 8, 1935. Green's novel dramatizes how that prewar world of comfort and poised confidence went up in smoke. Yet, finally, it proposes too simple an explanation for the Shoah by reducing it to a conflict between the aspirations of the Weiss family and the disruptive agency of the SS villain Dorf.

CHAPTER SEVEN

BEYOND THE CAMPS: KOSINSKI'S *THE PAINTED BIRD*

DISCOVERY
I have found God
In the sulphurous darkness of absolute negation.

An endless brick wall, close-packed and blank
Are his eyes.

I hear his mindless inscrutable voice in
Shapeless silence.

When my brothers walk through gas-chambers of
Auschwitz
I know his sanctuary

In their boots blithely kicking the screaming infant
Helpless to evil

Far beyond frontiers of man's imagining and foot-
ball games
Of judgement-making.

The total absence of love is God
Whose presence

No clearer moments of rapture could stamp in the
Grain of my heart.

Yet his wings of meaning beat impotently patient
Against the opaque

Of my racked
Rejection. I wait in the dense air of living

for the lightning

conductor

of death

—Hilda Schiff
From *Holocaust Poetry*,
ed. Hilda Schiff, p. 193.

At least one of [Kosinski's] works, *The Painted Bird*, seems
likely to stand. Odd in every respect—its expansion of
experience into a surreal inner theater, its construction
with help from editors and translators, its lack of dialogue, and its existence at the shadowy border between
fiction and personal statement—it remains a major aesthetic response to the Holocaust and a provocative
documentation of the complex and reverberative consequences of violence and evil.

—James Park Sloan, *Jerzy Kosinski*, 450.

I

We need to seek a definition of Holocaust fictions that extends beyond
camp and ghetto sites, and includes terrifying war narratives of the
Polish zeitgeist in the war years. Jerzy Kosinski's *The Painted Bird* (1965)
is such a text, but it is also an example of how the murkiness of the war
allowed kinds of self-invention. Kosinski's *The Painted Bird* is a novel in
which the protagonist is a child separated from his parents during World
War II. But the boy is not identified as a Jew, and his ethnicity is left
ambiguous. Indeed, although the boy is sent to the country in 1939, the
time period is not fully grounded by the narrator's consciousness of the

period's history; thus the dark-featured boy is as much the timeless victim of Polish xenophobia as a victim of prejudice in a particular time.

The title of *The Painted Bird* is taken from the custom of peasants who painted birds and then released them to rejoin the flock which, seeing them as aliens, killed them. The speaker sees himself as one who has been painted by experience and therefore cannot rejoin his flock:

> When a sufficient number of birds gathered above our heads, Lekh would give me a sign to release the prisoner. It would soar, happy and free, a spot of rainbow against the backdrop of clouds, and then plunge into the waiting brown flock. For an instant the birds were confounded. The painted bird circled from one end of the flock to the other, vainly trying to convince its kin that it was one of them. But, dazzled by its brilliant colors, they flew around it unconvinced. The painted bird would be forced farther and farther away as it zealously tried to enter the ranks of the flock. We saw soon afterwards how one bird after another would peel off in a fierce attack. Shortly the many-hued shape lost its place in the sky and dropped to the ground. (*The Painted Bird* 44)

More than that, the title implies that those who are "painted" as Jews, Gypsies—or as communists or *other*—are ostracized by the dominant group. When the speaker is finally reunited with his parents, the boy feels ambivalent: "I looked at the tearful face of the woman who was my mother, at the trembling hands of the man who was my father, uncertain whether they should stroke my hair or pat my shoulder, and some inner force restrained me and forbade me to fly off. I suddenly felt like Lekh's painted bird, which some unknown force was pulling toward his kind" (*The Painted Bird* 206).

The text is a kind of bildungsroman manqué; it traces the boy's maturation, but it is a maturation to disillusionment and finally, if not nihilism, cynicism. One *topos* in Holocaust fiction is the conversion experience, although at times it is a *counterconversion* away from faith and humanist values. Schwarz-Bart, for example, writes about a conversion from orthodox belief to loss of faith and agnosticism. But sometimes a reconversion takes place, a commitment to life (Goetzel-Leviathan) or to the Zionist concept of Israel (Gerald Green). But even in these cases the world of the concentration camp survives as trauma. One never leaves that world behind. Other recurring *topoi* include hunger, the death machinery, the sense that past experience is a dream and yet paradoxically lives, the missed opportunity to avoid deportation, the trauma of separation from family, and the replication of socioeconomic structures and hierarchies within the camps.

Not only did Kosinski create imaginary worlds in his novels, but his novels played a crucial role in creating his character and personality. Thus we read *The Painted Bird* with a double optics: on one hand, immersed in the world of his text, and on the other, aware that his life was often a performance, a text he created—what Sloan calls Kosinski's "myth of omnipotence by which he had managed to survive childhood" (Sloan 439). In America, Kosinski passed himself off as a non-Jewish Pole, and even after accepting his Jewishness, he was defensive about the behavior of the Poles. As Sloan writes,

> Beyond the denial of his father and his Jewish heritage was a displacement of feeling itself. Psychoanalytic studies of Holocaust survivors have described the condition of alexithymia, a regression in the form taken by emotions, which makes the affects useless in the processing of information. Psychoanalysts regard this condition as accounting in part for the high level of psychosomatic illness and drug addiction, as well as "numb marriages," among Holocaust survivors. Such individuals have a greatly diminished capacity for love—for romantic or other emotional attachment in the ordinary sense. They have sometimes been described by Freudian analysts as having "as if" personalities; their whole lives, and especially the romantic side of life, consist of going through the motions—*as if* they were actually living their experiences. (168)

It is difficult for us to separate Kosinski's opportunism from his narrator's trauma. Because we know of his self-invention, we reread, aware of the ontology of the novel but also aware that Kosinski illustrates Wallace Stevens's lines in "Tea at the Palaz of Hoon:" "I was the world in which I walked, and what I saw/or heard or felt came not but from myself;/And there I found myself more truly and more strange."

In *The Painted Bird*, the boy, separated from his middle-class moorings, re-creates himself. Kosinski's ultimate fiction was himself. Yet, is this not true of a wide range of historical figures, including Benjamin Disraeli? Thomas Mann writes in *A Sketch of My Life* about the process of writing *Death in Venice*: "Originally the tale was to be brief and modest. But things or whatever better word there may be for the conception *organic* have a will of their own, and shape themselves accordingly. . . . The truth is that every piece of work is a realization, fragmentary but complete in itself, of our individuality; and this kind of realization is the sole and painful way we have of getting the particular experience—no wonder, then, that the process is attended by surprises" (43-4).

Kosinski was born in Lodz, Poland in 1933, of a Jewish father who changed his name from Lewinkopf to Kosinski, a very common Polish name. Kosinski sold his book as an autobiographical account, but it clearly is a work of fiction. It was republished in a paperback edition with a cover illustration of Hieronymous Bosch's *Monster With a Basket* from his *The Last Judgment* in Vienna's Academy of Fine Arts. The issue of whether Kosinski actually wrote *The Painted Bird* has been alive for some time. Kosinski had originally written the book in Polish. According to James Park Sloan, George Reaves worked on the manuscript (316). As Sloan writes: "Several editors and translators participated as 'consultants' on the English text of *The Painted Bird*" (Sloan 198). Peter Skinner did a good deal of revising, and, according to Sloan, "From the beginning [Skinner] was struck by false notes in the manuscript, unidiomatic usages that suggested that the text might have been translated or generated with the use of dictionaries" (205).

I have some doubts as to whether we quite believe in the naive voice of the child and whether we do not at times hear behind it the artistry of the older creator. But that is separate from the issue of who composed the text, or whether his reliance on personal editors discredits his authorship. I am more interested in Kosinski's self-invention and whether his fiction of self is related to Holocaust memory. Kosinski is the ultimate painted bird, honored and decorated with awards and then, at least from his vantage point, vilified by others who want to ostracize him from the flock. For no sooner was he was forced from the flock by an exposé in the *Village Voice* than he completed the transformation of himself into victim by killing himself.

While Kosinski first proposed the book as nonfiction, based on his experience, the editors also had qualms about its obsession with sadomasochistic violence and the possibility of obscenity charges. As early as 1973, when Kosinski was a candidate for the presidency of PEN, concerns were voiced on the degree to which he had relied on others in writing the book.

In response to issues his novel raised, Kosinski wrote *Notes of the Author on The Painted Bird*, which was appended to the German edition and later self-published as a 19-page booklet in 1965 by Scientia-Factum. In his pamphlet, he acknowledges that "to say that *The Painted Bird* is nonfiction may be convenient for classification, but it is not easily justified." Seven years later, he repeats the exact words in an interview. According to Sloan:

> The bizarrely incantatory quality of this near-verbatim repetition makes a certain sense if one grasps the psychological pressures attendant to producing it. Like a man destined to undergo a lengthy and wearying interrogation, Kosinski has arrived at a precise formula for representing his actions, and he clings to it with the resolve that arises from fear that the slightest deviation from the script will lead the whole story to unravel. It's called getting the story straight. If he feared that questions concerning *The Painted Bird*'s facticity were going to come up in other and more threatening contexts, he was not mistaken. (Sloan 218)

Kosinski argues that the modern literary use of language,

> is contrapuntal, employed to lay bare the significant area which exists between language and action, and to highlight the gulf between them. This gulf also seems to be the focal point of modern art. But in *The Painted Bird* the situation is taken further; in the attempt to recall the primitive, the symbols are sought more pertinently and immediately than through the superficial process of speech and dialogue. In addition, the sense of alienation is heightened by depriving the characters of the ability to communicate freely. Observation is a silent process; without the means of participation, the silent one must observe. Perhaps this silence is

also a metaphor for dissociation from the community and from something greater. This feeling of alienation floats on the surface of the work and manifests the author's awareness, perhaps unconscious, of his break with the wholeness of self. (Quoted in Langer, *The Holocaust and the Literary Imagination* 169)

It is surprising how Kosinski's commentary has shaped criticism of the novel. Thus for Langer, a sympathetic critic, Kosinski's "pertinent exposition of fantastic intentions . . . prompted in part by the accusations of Polish critics that he was defaming the national character" is a contribution to "an aesthetics of atrocity" (*The Holocaust and the Literary Imagination* 168).

From 1982, when the *Village Voice* challenged Kosinski's account of himself, to 1991, when he committed suicide, his life had been in a downward spiral. Like the scholar Paul de Man, Kosinski reinvented himself when he came from Europe. In his last novel, *The Hermit of 69 Street*, he defends Chaim Rumkowski, the dictator of the Lodz ghetto, who is the source subject of Leslie Epstein's *King of the Jews*. Sloan comments:

For Kosinski, it was essential to come to grips with Lodz, where he spent his adolescence, where his relatives died or were consigned to death camps, and where he would have certainly perished had his family not gone to Sandomierz and Dabrowa. In the figure of Rumkowski, the question of how to comport oneself under extreme circumstances was brought into high focus. Rumkowski chose one alternative—collaborating to save as many as he could for as long as he could—in keeping with Jewish celebration of the ultimate value of life. Yet he could be criticized for not emulating the Jews of the Warsaw Ghetto who fought to the death under Mordecai Anieliewicz, as well as for the possibility of venal self-interest. In *Hermit* Kosinski laid out the case for Rumkowski, as he would in lectures and appearances before Jewish audiences, quoting at length from Rumkowski's speech of September 4, 1942, asking mothers to give up their children.

What lay behind Kosinski's tenacious defense of Rumkowski? Not a fighter himself, despite the rhetoric of his novels, he needed a model of extreme *choice* in the effort to survive. Rumkowski exemplified man caught in a web of *chance,* in a *blind date* with fate shared by *Poles and Jews,* who looked frankly and realistically at his situation, taking what was, in his terms, the only possible action. In doing so, he reconfirmed the model of behavior in that crisis with which Kosinski was most intimately aware—the actions taken by [his father] Moses Lewinkopf. (Sloan 409-410)

Like Levi and Borowski, Kosinski wrestled with feelings of emptiness and worthlessness, characteristics we see in many of our authors and their characters, including Spiegelman's self-dramatization.

We might close this section with Sloan's assessment of Kosinski:

As a writer, he was clearly not the stylist he was initially credited as being—the surfaces of his books owed too much to others—but neither was he the pure fraud that facile and incompletely informed criticism made him out to be. He was, if nothing else, a great storyteller, whose stories at their best seemed to have mythic resonances. In the age of oral storytelling he would have been recognized as indisputably great. Forced to compose in a foreign language, however, he had difficulty putting his stories into final form. . . . Essentially without a political view, he managed to politicize attacks on his career and his character. When in difficulty, he had a genius for persuading powerful supporters that their interests and their honor lay in defending him. Like all great charlatans, he laid bare the flaws and conceits of those he defrauded, but he also gave good value. In the end no one was so badly damaged by the con as himself. (Sloan 448-449)

II

The first chapter of *The Painted Bird* begins with an italicized third person preface:

In the first weeks of World War II, in the fall of 1939, a six-year-old boy from a large city in Eastern Europe was sent by his parents, like thousands of other children, to the shelter of a distant village. . . . In sending their child away the parents believed that it was the best means of assuring his survival through the

war. Because of the prewar anti-Nazi activities of the child's father, they
themselves had to go into hiding to avoid forced labor in Germany or imprisonment
in a concentration camp. They wanted to save the child from these dangers and
hoped they would eventually be reunited. (Kosinski 1)

But at this point the young boy's voice takes over, and he identifies himself not as a Jew although he speaks of having dark features. "Olive-skinned, dark-haired, and black eyed," the boy is taken for both Gypsy and Jew. He gradually loses his cultured childhood and learns from the peasants that in a grim, Hardyesque universe, only the fittest survive. The self dissolves into fragments, and the only continuity other than the voice is the varied assaults on his physical and psychic being. The novel is often a disguised version of a weird sadomasochistic narrative like *The Story of O*.

The presumably retrospective narrator draws upon his memories of his experience from the ages of six to twelve. Jim Shepard has written:

> In his preface to "What Maisie Knew," Henry James reminds us that "Small children have many more perceptions than they have terms to translate them; their vision is at any moment much richer, their apprehension even constantly stronger, than . . . their at all producible vocabulary." In other words, their feelings can be complex even when their language is not. The writer, James was suggesting, might with certain sleight of hand grant fictional children a language that honors these intuitions, this inner life. (This strategy is also attractive because it enacts the children's helplessness while returning to them their dignity). (Shepard 9)

From a retrospective point of view, Kosinski dramatizes the complexity of a child's feelings between the ages of six and twelve as the child tests and discards a variety of ethical perspectives. But the words and feelings cannot always be separated from the older speaker. A version of Henry James's third-person omniscient voice—or of free indirect discourse— might be more effective than Kosinski's first person because it does not pretend to speak for the young child, only to render his feelings.

Kosinski's narrator strives to establish himself as a kind of prodigy of memory:

The world seemed to be pretty much the same everywhere, and even though people differed from one another, just as animals and trees did, one should know fairly well what they looked like after seeing them for years. I had lived only seven years, but I remembered a lot of things. When I closed my eyes, many details came back still more vividly. Who knows, perhaps without his eyes the plowboy would start seeing an entirely new, more fascinating world. . . . I made a promise to myself to remember everything I saw; if someone should pluck out my eyes, then I would retain the memory of all that I had seen for as long as I lived. (*The Painted Bird* 35)

Of course, no one can remember all he saw, but it is characteristic of Holocaust narratives—or other survivor narratives, like American Civil War memoirs and diaries—to situate oneself at the outset as a survivor and explain one's credentials. Kosinski's novel raises a number of ethical issues. One is whether passing off a fictional document as autobiography is unethical, particularly when Kosinski cross-dresses his younger self as a dark-featured outsider rather than specifically as a Jew. To be sure, novels have passed themselves off as autobiography since Defoe in *Moll Flanders,* and the use of illuminating distortion is a common technique, but universalizing the particular Jewish Holocaust experience is problematic and, to many Jews and non-Jews, objectionable. Another ethical issue disappears—that of exaggerating the extent of his supposed abuse for the sake of its rhetorical effect—once Kosinski abandons the claim that his work is autobiographical rather than fictional.

The narrator at times crosses over into the culture that abuses him and becomes part of it. He learns the suspicion and folk culture of the peasants. Later he is exposed to Christianity and Marxism. Yet, as Ezrahi notes,

in spite of the verisimilitude of event and situation established in the first-person narrative, the novel lacks a plausible existential center and takes on the dimensions of a folk or fairy tale. The boy is never named (the author himself, in notes to the German translation of the novel, refers to him as "the Boy"; even in a universe in which characters exchange names and forge identities so frequently, such complete anonymity is rare), and he soon relinquishes as useless whatever biography he had. (*By Words Alone* 153)

We recall that Conrad's *Heart of Darkness* challenged the idea of Social Darwinists that humans may be evolving to higher forms in part by showing how so-called civilized man abused and exploited so-called primitive cultures. Here the peasants lord over Jews and Gypsies, even while behaving barbarously themselves. Holocaust narratives often include the return of the chastened, experienced self to the original world along the lines of Gulliver or Marlow returning from a voyage. But even more than these literary antecedents, Holocaust narrators—who of course have returned not from imaginary voyages but from real ones—usually cannot build a bridge back to the world of their pre-Holocaust selves.

Has it, indeed, been noticed how Kosinski may have had in mind Conrad's characterization of Marlow in *Heart of Darkness*? For Marlow, Conrad's retrospective teller, descends into a world of horror, confronts experiences that challenge his humanistic beliefs, and finally, after resistance to returning to a world in which he no longer feels comfortable, reintegrates himself into the world he once left. When Marlow realizes that terms like "enemies" and "criminals" are applied indiscriminately to natives, he becomes disillusioned with his position as "emissary of light" assigned by European culture. Similarly, Kosinski shows European pretensions to civilization to be a sham in the face of the abuse of an innocent boy, a boy who becomes "enemy" and "criminal" because he is different. As Langer notes,

> Thus, all intellectual and moral considerations suddenly appear trivial when Garbos suspends the boy from leather straps attached to two large hooks embedded in the ceiling of a small room, and locks him in with the ferocious dog Judas. Man faces beast, mirror images of each other, as life is transformed into a contest between physical cruelty and physical endurance; and if the boy survives, it is not a triumph of the human spirit over bestial will, but a simple conditioning of the muscles of the boy's arms and legs (which he withdraws from the dog's reach whenever it snaps), so that he can sustain the stretched position for many hours without

falling. In a painful parody of the crucifixion, the human creature comes to resemble the side of beef in the Francis Bacon painting, a figure that may once have been a man but which no previous training in humanistic values can help us now to identify. (*The Holocaust and the Literary Imagination* 180)

While Kosinski felt ties to Joseph Conrad and to Bruno Schulz, Sloan notes that Kosinski had problems in written English:

> Kosinski did well enough in spoken English, to be sure; his accent and his occasional Slavicisms were charming. But writing was a different matter. He was, quite simply, no Conrad. In written English, the omission of articles or the clustering of modifiers did not strike readers as charming; instead, it made the writer appear ignorant, half-educated, even stupid. Conrad wrote like an angel but could not make himself understood when he opened his mouth; with Kosinski, it was exactly the other way around. Which might not have been such a handicap had not Kosinski been a writer by profession. (174)

The speaker tells a narrative of his suffering an astonishing variety of continued abuse and exploitation by peasants. As Langer writes,

> For the peasants are surrounded by the menace of the unknown, and the rituals they engage in to propitiate it, together with the crude or brutal methods they use, bare reality to its most natural layers and present vicariously, as if in a dream, though with the concretest of imagery, the unimaginable cruelties of the Holocaust translated into universally potent metaphors. . . . Though *The Painted Bird* is hardly a tract designed to reduce the number of such potential victims, it is very much concerned with dramatizing the "trauma of daily life" so as to produce a shock of recognition quite other than the one Melville had in mind. Episodes like the gouging out of the eyes seek to induce a sense of complicity with the extremity of cruelty and suffering in modern experience, from which history (with its customary distinctions between "then" and "now"), conspiring with the reader's reluctance to acknowledge

such possibilities, unconsciously insulates us. The art of atrocity is the incarnation of such possibilities through language and metaphor. (*The Holocaust and the Literary Imagination* 172, 175-6)

Gradually every remnant of the human values of love, reason, sympathy, and decency disappear from the speaker's world.

The narrator is a young child who not only never identifies himself as a Jew, but speaks once of going to Catholic church with his parents and presumably believing in a teleology reflecting God's loving presence:

> My parents always went to church on Sundays, and sometimes even took me and my nurse. Was it possible that God's wrath was reserved only for people with black hair and eyes, who were called Gypsies? Why did my father, whom I still remembered well, have fair hair and blue eyes, while my mother was dark? What was the difference between a Gypsy and a Jew, since both were dusky and both were destined for the same end? (*The Painted Bird* 85)

At one point he tests the possibilities of prayer: "I was ready to start a new life. I had all that was needed and gloried in the knowledge that the days of punishment and humiliation would soon be past. Until now I had been a small bug that anyone might squash. From now on the humble bug would be an unapproachable bull" (*The Painted Bird* 112).

Whether or not persecution has roots in Kosinski's paranoid fantasy, the novel stands as a historical allegory for victimization of the innocent. He has lived the terror of persecution; he is the perpetual outsider, hated for his difference and otherness. As Ezrahi puts it:

> Precisely, then, because the tainted hero of Kosinski's novel is a child, he taps the most primary sources of fear and terror that have been out of bounds in most of the literature of the Holocaust. In the notes to the German edition of *The Painted Bird*, Kosinski acknowledges that the "essence" of his novel is "hate" and that the world of *The Painted Bird* is the world of elementary symbol, "simple keys to the European culture of the mid-twentieth century." The child, who in Jungian terms represents the "collective unconscious" of

mankind, dramatizes in the crudest, most penetrating way the bestiality of the age. *(By Words Alone* 156)

The narrator recalls how he had adopted but finally rejected Gavrilla's Marxist perspective: "In the Soviet world a man was rated according to others' opinion of him, not according to his own. Only the group, which they called 'the collective,' was qualified to determine a man's worth and importance. The group decided what could make him more useful and what could reduce his usefulness to others. He himself became the composite of everything others said about him" *(The Painted Bird* 173).

Gradually, the speaker comes to be awed by the Germans' power to make explosives:

> If it was true that the Germans were capable of such inven-
> tions, and also that they were determined to clear the world of all
> swarthy, dark-eyed, long-nosed, black-haired people, then my
> chances of survival were obviously poor. Sooner or later I would fall
> into their hands again, and I might not be as lucky as in the past. . . .
>   I dozed off visualizing the inventions I would like to make. For
> example, a fuse for the human body which, when lighted, would
> change old skin for new and alter the color of the eyes and hair.
> *(The Painted Bird* 80)

In a moment of dramatic irony, he plays the devil's advocate and embraces a Manichean view that the devil has defeated the forces of good. He becomes convinced that the persecuting and efficient Germans are the Devil's disciples:

> A man who had sold out to the Evil Ones would remain in their
> power all his life. From time to time he would have to demonstrate
> an increasing number of misdeeds. . . . But hatreds of large groups
> of people must have been the most valuable of all. I could barely
> imagine the prize earned by the person who managed to inculcate
> in all blond, blue-eyed people a long-lasting hatred of dark ones.
>   I also began to understand the extraordinary success of the
> Germans. . . . They preferred attacking other tribes and taking
> crops from them. The Germans probably were noticed then by the

Evil Ones. Eager to do harm, they agreed to sell out wholesale to them. That is why they were endowed with all their splendid abilities and talents. That is why they could impose all their refined methods of wrongdoing on others. Success was a vicious circle: the more harm they inflicted, the more secret powers they secured for evil. The more diabolical powers they had, the more evil they could achieve (*The Painted Bird* 136-137)

The young narrator is a naive, almost anaesthetized witness to the trains taking Holocaust victims to their death as well as to the xenophobic, ignorant Polish peasants finding refuge in the blood libel that Christ was killed by Jews; note the irony of Kosinski's "thoughtfully" to describe how the peasants listened to the "strange tales" of the death trains:

Then a new kind of train appeared on the line. Living people were jammed in locked cattle cars. Some of the men who worked at the station brought news to the village. These trains carried Jews and Gypsies, who had been captured and sentenced to death. In each car there were two hundred of them stacked like cornstalks, arms raised to take up less space. Old and young, men, women, and children, even babies. Some of the peasants from the neighboring village were temporarily employed on the construction of a concentration camp and brought back strange tales. They told us that after leaving the train the Jews were sorted into different groups, then stripped naked and deprived of all their possessions. Their hair was cut off, apparently for use in mattresses. The Germans also looked at their teeth, and if there were any gold ones they were immediately pulled out. The gas chambers and ovens could not cope with the great supply of people; many of those killed by gas were not burned but simply buried in pits around the camp.

The peasants listened to these stories thoughtfully. They said the Lord's punishment had finally reached the Jews. They had deserved it long ago, ever since they crucified Christ. God never forgot. If He had overlooked the sins of the Jews so far, He had not forgiven them. Now the Lord was using the Germans as His instrument of justice. The Jews were to be denied the privilege of a natural death. They had to perish by fire, suffering, the torments of hell here on earth. They were being justly punished for the shameful crimes of their ancestors, for refuting the only True Faith, for mercilessly killing Christian babies and drinking their blood. (*The Painted Bird* 84-5)

The speaker stresses how the Polish peasants were not only heartless but complicit in the atrocities and how they willingly accept the principles of Nazi Genocide. We recall Lanzmann's *Shoah*.

In Kosinski's imagined ontology neither nature nor industrialization are on the side of humans:

I recalled the trains carrying people to the gas chambers and crematories. The men who had ordered and organized all that probably enjoyed a similar feeling of complete power over their uncomprehending victims. They also controlled the fate of millions of people whose names, faces, and occupations were unknown to them, but whom they could either let live or turn to fine soot flying in the wind. All they had to do was issue orders and in countless towns and villages trained squads of troops and police would start rounding up people for ghettos and death camps. They had the power to decide whether the points of thousands of railroad spurs would be switched to tracks leading to life or to death.

To be capable of deciding the fate of many people whom one did not even know was a magnificent sensation. I was not sure whether the pleasure depended only on the knowledge of the power one had, or on its use. (*The Painted Bird* 200)

Kosinski's narrator eloquently captures the horrible juxtaposition of the rhythms of nature and the death trains: "The symphony of the forest was broken only by the puffing of a locomotive, the rattle of cars, the grinding of the brakes. People stood still, looking toward the tracks. The birds grew silent, the owl drew deeper into his hole, draping his gray cloak about himself with dignity. The hare stood up, raising his long ears high, and then, reassured, resumed his leaps" (*The Painted Bird* 88).

The boy's insouciant juxtaposition between nature and the ominous train is not only effective, but the cacophony of his juxtaposition is underlined by the indifference and cynicism of the peasants: "After each train had passed I saw whole battalions of ghosts with evil, vengeful faces coming into the world. The peasants said the smoke from the crematories went straight to heaven, laying a soft carpet at God's feet, without even soiling them. I wondered whether so many Jews were necessary to compensate God for the killing of His son. Perhaps the world would soon become one vast incinerator for burning people. Had not the priest said that all were doomed to perish, to go 'from ashes to ashes'"? (*The Painted Bird* 89).

Nature, including mankind, is often predatory, as when the boy arranges for the carpenter to fall into the rat pit: "The man completely disappeared, and the sea of rats churned even more violently. The moving rumps of the rats became stained with brownish red blood. The animals now fought for access to the body—panting, twitching their tails, their teeth gleaming under their half-open snouts, their eyes reflecting the daylight as if they were the beads of a rosary. . . . Suddenly the shifting sea of rats parted and slowly, unhurrying, with the stroke of a swimmer, a bony hand with bony spread-eagled fingers rose, followed by the man's entire arm" (*The Painted Bird* 55).

As the persecution of the Jews gradually intrudes into his consciousness, Kosinski's narrator becomes more and more aware that he lives in an amoral, indifferent cosmos—the "remorseless process" of Conrad's world. As Ezrahi writes:

> It is significant that, although the Jews appear, quite literally, on the periphery of the world through which the Boy wanders, the manner of their appearance provides the missing link in his education. The trains themselves represent the technology of death which is the hallmark of the Nazi system, and the machines of torture and murder that have been perfected by "civilized" humanity in concentration camps are far more efficient than the crude instruments of torture improvised by the unlettered peasants a few miles away. Ultimately, then, although the Boy has served his apprenticeship among the peasants, it is the demonic control, the premeditated savagery and sadism of the Nazis which appear as the superior method, and when the Boy collaborates in his act of revenge, it is by mass murder, and it is effected through the use of technology. (*By Words Alone* 158)

Ironically, when his friend takes his revenge on those that abuse the speaker, it is by controlling the trains:

> The Boy, whose looks mark him for the same destination as that of the Jews, watches silently and a few times even presses himself between the rails and allows the trains to go over him, symbolizing his own narrow escape. And he learns the lesson well and efficiently. Determined never to find himself in a train filled with the victims, he becomes an accomplice to a derailment of a train filled with other victims—innocent, market-bound peasants—and this incident closes the cycle by which, as Kosinski says, the oppressed becomes the oppressor. (*By Words Alone* 158)

It is as if the boy were trying to get a hand on the very technology that was destroying Europe.

III

The cumulative atrocities climax in the young speaker's being thrown into an outhouse depository, making him mute. As Lawrence Langer writes:

> The inexpressible quality of the experience for which Kosinski— perhaps paradoxically—finds verbal and metaphorical equivalents, is symbolically extended to the victim, who henceforth appears as the incarnation of silence: the ordeal of immersion has deprived him of his voice and turned him into a mute. Thus his last civilizing link with human reality is severed and he is condemned—at least for the time being—to a life of gathering *impressions*, as if the habit of seeking to *express* reality blurred the sensibilities and obscured one's conscious awareness of the atrocities men suffered in *l'univers concentrationnaire*. In losing the power of speech, the boy-narrator is forced to focus on what Kosinski calls "motivated action," thus reinforcing the fictional strategy adopted by the novelist himself from the beginning, that of discarding the oblique method of implying action through dialogue and drawing the reader into the physical substance of reality, the immediate act, as if the words used to describe it were illusory veils that disintegrated upon touch.

Like the boy, the reader is sucked into the manure pit of experience with the explicit intention of inducing in him an imaginative access to the same nausea which literally overwhelms the boy in the novel. Such a strategy penetrates the intellectual facade of the reader as spectator and reaches the organs and nerve ends of his being, dissipating aesthetic "distance" and creating a reader *engagé*, a direct emotional participant in the experience of atrocity. (*The Holocaust and the Literary Imagination* 181-182)

Deprived of language, the boy identifies with the tree stumps:

From the black earth that the sun never reached stuck out the trunks of trees cut down long ago. These stumps were now cripples unable to clothe their stunted mutilated bodies. They stood single and alone. Hunched and squat, they lacked the force to reach up toward the light and air. No power could change their condition; their sap would never rise up into limbs or foliage. Large knotholes low on their boles were like dead eyes staring eternally with unseeing pupils at the waving crests of their living brethren. They would never be torn or tossed by the winds but would rot slowly, the broken victims of the dampness and decay of the forest floor. (*The Painted Bird* 126)

The phantasmagoric language reflects the nightmare world of the Holocaust; the image of mutilation extends the effect of the sadistic actions performed on the boy's body or psyche. Yet his resilience is in juxtaposition to these wasteland images. As Langer writes,

The central (and longest) episode in *The Painted Bird* dramatizes this un-Darwinian descent of man from the pedestal of civilization into the mire of brutish endurance, for at its end the boy has lost his last link with his human heritage—the power of speech. For Darwin, biology and man's capacity to adapt to his environment gradually differentiated him from his animal ancestors; in Kosinski, history, as an expression of the ambitions of the Third Reich, sanctions cruelties that are as generic to human nature as the charity which once was idealized into its fundamental attribute. (*The Holocaust and the Literary Imagination* 178)

The most effective passages are those like the foregoing, in which Kosinski develops sustained analogies with nature. The phantasmagoric images owe something to Kafka and perhaps Schulz's *Street of Crocodiles*. It is often the language of metaphor. Kosinski writes of a world in which man devolves into beast. In fact, had the boy suffered the physical torture he describes, he would have been long dead; nor can one quite believe in the incredible sadism of the Polish peasants to a young child, as when Garbos puts up hooks to hang the boy while his vicious dog Judas stands below, waiting for the child to fall. In fact, this book is full of acts of mindless torture, and its overdeterminacy not merely of violence but perversion and sadism at times short-circuits a sympathetic reading. One feature we note is that Kosinski enjoys describing sexual excess beyond the need of his text—as when he depicts the Kalmuks' raping and pillaging with pornographic zeal:

> Some other soldiers were raping from the front and from the back two young girls, passing them from one man to the next, forcing them to perform strange movements. When the girls resisted, they were flogged and kicked. . . . The drunken Kalmuks, more and more aroused, became frenzied. Some of the Kalmuks copulated with each other, then competed in raping women in odd ways: two or three men to one girl, several men in rapid succession. . . . Other feats followed. Helpless women were passed from one trotting horse to another. One of the Kalmuks tried to couple with a mare; others aroused a stallion and tried to push a girl under it, holding her up by her legs. (*The Painted Bird* 159, 160)

Does not Kosinski admire revenge for its own sake, as when Mitka kills some village peasants—after his friends have been killed in their village—without learning whether he has killed the perpetrators or the innocents? Later the speaker and the friend who feigns muteness, the "silent one," do the same when they use a train switch to cause a murderous accident, and then learn that they have failed to punish the man who beat the speaker: "The familiar shape of the stand was there, with its jugs of milk and cream, bricks of butter wrapped in cloth, some fruit. From behind them, as in a puppet show, popped up the head of the man who had knocked out my teeth and pushed me into a barrel" (*The Painted Bird* 203).

The boy himself has turned into a predatory creature of the night, more comfortable in a world of intrigue, animality, and license:

> All cats are the same in the dark, says the proverb. But it certainly did not apply to people. With them it was just the opposite. During the day they were all alike, running in their well-defined ways. . . . I was soon familiar with the night city. I knew quiet lanes where girls younger than myself solicited men older than my father. . . . I found an inconspicuous house from which young men took piles of leaflets to post on government buildings, posters which the militiamen and soldiers tore down in rage. I saw the militia organize a manhunt and I saw some men killing a soldier. In daytime the world was at peace. The war continued at night. (*The Painted Bird* 210)

Finally he regains his voice in response to the need to answer the telephone:

> I held the receiver to my ear, listening to his impatient words; somewhere at the other end of the wire there was someone, perhaps a man like myself, who wanted to talk with me . . . I had an overpowering desire to speak. . .
>
> I opened my mouth and strained. Sounds crawled up my throat. Tense and concentrated I started to arrange them into syllables and words. I distinctly heard them jumping out of me one after another, like peas from a split pod. I put the receiver aside, hardly believing it possible. I began to recite to myself words and sentences, snatches of Mitka's songs. The voice lost in a faraway village church had found me again and filled the whole room. I spoke loudly and incessantly like the peasants and then like the city folk, as fast as I could, enraptured by the sounds that were heavy with meaning, as wet snow is heavy with water, confirming to myself again and again and again that speech was now mine and that it did not intend to escape through the door which opened onto the balcony. (*The Painted Bird* 213)

Ironically he returns to himself by means of the technology used to destroy Europe, even as he returns to civilization. Kosinski's closing words remind us that speech is crucial to our sense of self. We might think of Conrad, another Pole writing in English who, although despairing of communicating in his letters, continued writing and dramatized the efficacy of communication in texts such as *Heart of Darkness* by showing how one member of an audience is deeply moved to retell Marlow's tale of self-discovery from his perspective. The boy's regaining speech could be a trope for the recent outpouring of Holocaust studies, an outpouring that can only be called the return of the repressed. For decades many Jewish intellectuals tiptoed around this subject only to discover that it is not only their subject but the subject of the end of the twentieth century. Does this have to do with the aging of the last witnesses, the aging of scholars who need to come to terms with their ethnic heritage as they approach death, or a sense that the year 2000 requires summation and definition—or all of the above?

CHAPTER EIGHT

THE ONTOLOGICAL PROBLEMS OF DOCUFICTION: WILLIAM STYRON'S SOPHIE'S CHOICE

FROM IN THE MIDST OF LIFE
After the end of the world
after death
I found myself in the midst of life
creating myself
building life
people animals landscapes

this is a table I said
this is a table
there is bread and a knife on the table
knife serves to cut bread
people nourished by bread

man must be loved
I learnt by night by day
what must one love
I would reply man

. . . .

—Tadeusz Różewicz
(Translated by Adam Czerniawski)

> Sophie, with an inanity poised on her tongue and choked
> with fear, was about to attempt a reply when the doctor
> said, "You may keep one of your children."
> *"Bitte?"* said Sophie.
> "You may keep one of your children," he repeated. "The
> other one will have to go. Which one will you keep?"
> "You mean, I have to choose?"
> "You're a Polack, not a Yid. That gives you a privilege—a
> choice."
> Her thought processes dwindled, ceased. Then she felt
> her legs crumple. "I can't choose! I can't choose!" She
> began to scream. Oh, how she recalled her own screams!
> Tormented angels never screeched so loudly above hell's
> pandemonium. *"Ich kann nicht wählen!"* she screamed.
>   —William Styron, *Sophie's Choice*, 483

I

Let us begin with a comment that James E. Young in "Holocaust
Documentary Fiction: The Novelist as Eyewitness" made on "documentary fictions" of the Holocaust:

> [B]y mixing actual events with completely fictional characters, a
> writer simultaneously relieves himself of an obligation to historical
> accuracy (invoking poetic license), even as he imbues his fiction
> with the historical authority of real events. By inviting this ambigu-
> ity, the author of documentary fiction would thus move the reader
> with the pathos created in the rhetoric of historically authentic
> characters, even as he suggests the possibility that both his events
> and those in the world are fictional. (Lang 201-2)

But, we shall ask, does the ontology of *Sophie's Choice* work? Does the
pressure of fact and history cry out and overwhelm the fictive ontology?
Young continues:

> Several other questions arise at this point. First, why is the writer of
> Holocaust fiction so forcefully compelled to assert the factual basis

underlying his work? That is, why is it so important for [some] novelists to establish an authoritative link between their fictions and the Holocaust experiences they represent? Second, to what extent are this literature's dramatic interests, and its supposed documentary interests, served in such claims to historical authority? And how does the perception of authority in the Holocaust novel affect the way readers approach and respond to Holocaust fiction? That is, can Holocaust documentary fiction ever really document events, or will it always fictionalize them? . . . The difference between fictional and nonfictional "documentary narratives" of the Holocaust may not be between degrees of actual evidential authority, but between the ontological sources of this sense of authority: one is retrieved and one is constructed wholly within the text as part of the text's fiction. As it was for the diaries and memoirs, the operative trope underpinning the documentary character of Holocaust fiction is the rhetorical principle of testimony or witness, not its actuality. (Lang 202, 212)

Styron's *Sophie's Choice* (1976) is a medley of genres: *kunstlerroman* (a novel about an artist's development), romance, and Holocaust story. We need to ask whether the sections about the Holocaust are more effective for their intrusions into a novel about America in 1947. Or is this a powerful if somewhat oblique look at how a survivor is shaped by the Holocaust? By 1976, the Holocaust had become something of a familiar subject although it remained for Gerald Green's *Holocaust* a few years later to put it visually into the popular imagination with his teleplay series.

Styron's semi-autobiographical Conradian narrator, Stingo, is a veteran of World War II, an aspiring young, southern writer living in Brooklyn who becomes close friends with Nathan, a brilliant but emotionally disturbed and drug-addicted Jew, and Nathan's lover, Sophie. Sophie is a Polish refugee and camp survivor, who, in a series of monologues to Stingo gradually reveals her complicated past. Thus the novel has two narrators, Stingo and Sophie; the latter's narrative is framed by Stingo, who falls in love with Sophie. After she has initiated him into adult sexuality, she returns to Nathan and they are found together in a double suicide.

Like Nick Carroway, Stingo tells the story retrospectively, very much aware of what he has learned. Conscious of writing in the American tradition, and indeed of immodest efforts to write as heir to Melville, he echoes *Moby-Dick*'s opening, "Call me Ishmael:" "Call me Stingo, which was the nickname I was known by in those days, if I was called anything at all" (4). Stingo is Ishmael, obsessed not with Captain Ahab's quest for the whale but with the quest of his demonic and psychotic double, Nathan, for Sophie's love.

Styron uneasily combines the verisimilitude of documentary— including numerous references to those who wrote about the Holo-caust—with the fictional lives of Nathan, Sophie, and Stingo. Notwith-standing the narrative conventions that pretend to give the novel a documentary character, readers are well aware that they are reading a work of fiction. Stingo's tale is about events that took place in 1947, but he tells his audience that it was not until 1967 that he began to think of his book, and even "the preparation I went through at that time required that I torture myself by absorbing as much as I could find of the literature of *l'univers concentrationnaire*. And in reading George Steiner, I experienced the shock of recognition" (216).

The older narrator is trying to write the Great American Novel, a historical novel that addresses the horrors of the twentieth century even while dramatizing the growth of consciousness of the representative Southern voice growing up in the North and thus recalling the American tragedy of the Civil War. But readers can see that the American Civil War and Holocaust as interchangeable contiguous metonymies that represent one another is a farfetched and insensitive comparison. And we tire of Stingo's ingenuous political lectures: "Real evil, the suffocating evil of Auschwitz—gloomy, monotonous, barren, boring—was perpe-trated almost exclusively by civilians. . . . [I]n modern times most of the mischief ascribed to the military has been wrought with the advice and consent of civil authority" (151). At times the speaker's polemics objectionably universalize the Holocaust, particularly in view of his own romanticizing the Poles as victims of the same magnitude as the Jews and his use of the word "torture" to describe his *own act of reading* about the Holocaust (216).

Like the governess in James's *The Turn of the Screw*, Sophie is a riddle, and we cannot always know how her psyche and memory distort events.

Sophie's disingenuousness struggles with her *desire to tell*, to reveal her story. Like Stingo, we are blocked by Sophie's evasions. Sophie's choice—her *selection* of her male child as the one who will live and her daughter as the one who will die—is Conradian. Sophie, like Jim, has a need—a compulsion—to tell, to explain, to extenuate and, finally, to understand; thus she reveals to Stingo her darkest secrets. The title refers most obviously to a grotesque choice she had to make between saving her son and saving her daughter at an Auschwitz selection. But the choices she makes are a continuing focus of the story, including her choice to leave the younger Stingo for the destructive and psychotic Nathan, who has already abused her. As Kurtz is for Marlow, the manic-depressive Nathan is the nightmare of her choice. Discourse dominates the story as she wanders back and forth over the same terrain; and the same is true for Stingo, who strays far and wide in his narration. In his first encounter with Sophie and Nathan he learns that they are the couple upstairs who make his ceiling shake from their sexual activities. For both, telling is the agon and that, as we have seen, is a recurring *topos* that Holocaust fiction draws from modernism.

As in James, Conrad, and Fitzgerald, Styron creates for Sophie a narrative that is a kind of client-centered therapy in which we become—along with Stingo—the audience of her dramatic monologue and listen to her probing for positional assurance if not truth. When reading we need, like a client-centered therapist, to discover what the truth is, if we can, and recognize the contradictions in her narration. We need to make our own narrative as we listen to her unfold the layers of her memory.

Styron's narrator recalls Marlow's meditative tales, for Stingo's experience and response is the center. He himself is not always a perceptive teller. Stingo is a Marlovian listener, a surrogate for us, but also, like Marlow, an engaged character trying to define himself and his values as well as to recapture the romanticism of his younger self. Just as Marlow's inquiry into Kurtz and Jim becomes an inquiry into his values, Stingo's effort to understand Nathan and Sophie becomes the catalyst for his own epistemological and semiological quest to understand himself and why he writes. Yet Stingo's prolixity interferes with his efficacy as a narrator. His tiresome tales of sexual initiation suggest a less than hilarious version of an older Holden Caufield, for Salinger's figure seems to have been a catalyst in Stingo's creation as an innocent alone in the big city. Styron-Stingo's obligatory narration of his Heminwayesque drinking binges become tedious, too. Stingo's meditations on the spiritual turmoil of the doctor who forces Sophie to choose between her children are unconvincing: "I have always assumed that when he encountered Sophie, Dr. Jemand von Niemand was undergoing the crisis of his life: cracking apart like bamboo, disintegrating at the very moment that he was reaching out for spiritual salvation. . . . [H]e had rejected Christianity while still outwardly professing faith in God" (485-486). But is Stingo, who has a spiritual bent, describing the doctor's crisis of belief or his own?

How reliable is Sophie? Is it possible that she is not any more reliable than the unstable Nathan who invents his past and present, who claims to be a Harvard graduate and an important scientist for a pharmaceutical company? Is Nathan's exposure a psychotic warning to the reader about narrative unreliability? It is not until page 484 of the novel that she reveals the truth about her children. Her story changes each time she revisits the past. Styron's narrator emphasizes how historical circumstances connive with the individual psyche to shape human behavior: "But now it again becomes necessary to mention that Sophie was not quite straightforward in her recital of past events, even granted that it was her intention to present a very abbreviated account. I would learn this later, when she confessed to me that she left out many crucial facts in the story she told Nathan" (146).

Sophie's Choice focuses on the relationship between memory and narrative, a relationship central to our study. Sophie's narrative of the war years is a model of refracted memory; her narrative is very much shaped by who the audience is, Nathan or Stingo. For Sophie, as for Bulstrode in *Middlemarch*, the past is a harrowing present. Like Jim in Conrad's *Lord Jim* after his jump from the *Patna*, she is enclosed by a wall of facts that shape her action. When Nathan loses control with Sophie, we recall how in the Conrad novel Marlow lost control with Jewel on Patusan and how Gentleman Brown scored a direct verbal hit on Jim: "Did the same anti-Semitism for which Poland has gained such world-wide renown—did a similar anti-Semitism guide your own destiny, help you along, *protect* you, in a manner of speaking, so that you became one of the minuscule handful of people who lived while *the millions died?*" (209).

There are many things, she learns, that she cannot tell Nathan. For example, after Nathan says, "I despise homosexuals," she cannot tell him that she slept with Wanda, but she *can* tell her confidante Stingo, whom she imagines as an empathetic audience. Moreover, Nathan is capable of torturing her with accusations of collaboration. After he becomes violent with her in Connecticut, Sophie begins to drown her sorrows in alcohol. That her narrative to the psychotic Nathan is shaped by her fear of his abusive personality is a radical version of how audience expectations shape narratives. Indeed, his intimidating power is part of his appeal to her, in much the same way that she had been magnetized by her father. Sophie had aided her father, a law professor in Poland, a vicious anti-Semite and author of a book entitled *Poland's Jewish Problem*, who wanted to send Jews to Madagascar: "The Professor . . . was a charter adherent of a blazingly reactionary political faction known as the National Democratic party. . . . One of his major themes was 'superfluous Jews,' and he scribbled away at length about the matter of 'population transfer' and 'expatriation'" (239-240). Her father, ironically, is arrested and killed by the Nazis. (The narrator's father, a decent, humane Southern gentleman, is depicted as a striking contrast to Sophie's father.) She justifies her sexual interest in Professor Durfield, a Nazi functionary she met while serving as her father's secretary, by her husband's lack of sexual interest: "You may as well know now, Stingo, about another lie I told you weeks ago. I really had no love for Kazik either at the time, I had no more love for my husband than for a stone-faced stranger I had never seen before in my life. Such an abundance of lies I have given you, Stingo!" (245). Now we understand that Sophie's *choice* includes not only whether at any moment to narrate the truth as she knows it, but also how much of the truth to narrate. Yet she is not in control of her telling, and her own trauma shapes not only her efforts to recapture the truth and the concomitant repression and sublimation, but also her conscious lies and evasions.

Nathan is her other self: the Jew who has been trying to rescue her from her own history *and* whom she has been unsuccessfully trying to insulate from her *history*—beginning with her father, her husband, and continuing with Josef, who garroted those who betrayed Jews, Wanda, his fellow partisan, and Höss. But, we ask, how could her father make her be his factotum? Yet, in what becomes a characteristic way of making decisions, she lets the choice be made for her. Sophie made the choice to follow her father at 16—perhaps in a foreshadowing of later magnetic attraction to powerful men like Höss and Nathan and the Professor Durfield, even Josef and Wanda, "two selfless, courageous people whose allegiance to humanity and their fellow Poles and concern for the hunted Jews were a repudiation of all that her father had stood for" (372).

Rereading, we realize that Sophie is traumatized into passivity after her terrible choice, but we cannot be sure that this passivity does not precede her choice. Sophie plays the role of amanuensis to her father, Höss, and, in an odd way, Nathan and even Stingo. For all of them, she becomes an alter ego, a secret sharer. How do we know whether Sophie was simply seducing commandant Höss at Auschwitz at the behest of the partisan resistance *or* if she was doing it for herself? She tells Stingo both versions. She uses her father's anti-Semitic pamphlet to insinuate herself into Höss's good graces with the idea that she will seduce him and he will let her son, her lone surviving child, be part of *Lebensborn*, which Stingo, in his role of Holocaust historian, explains is a eugenics program of breeding members of the "New Order" supplemented "by the organized kidnapping in the occupied lands of racially 'suitable' children" (302).

Sophie's guilt makes her believe she is drawn to "badness," and that belief shapes her telling. Sublimated anger drives her telling. After speaking of how she begged Höss, the narrator observes: "Sophie halted, gazing again for long moments into that past which seemed now so totally, so irresistibly to have captured her" (285). Rereading, we understand more fully the pain and guilt that shapes her telling: "But such a terrible place was this Auschwitz, Stingo, terrible beyond all belief. . . . [I]f what the people done was not so noble, or even was like animals, then you have to understand it, hating it maybe but pitying it at the same time, because you knew how easy it was for you to act like an animal too" (286).

A recurring *topos* in Holocaust narratives is that with power comes the power to name and the power of language; for Sophie, first her father, then Höss can say to her what he wishes without any sense of propriety: "Sophie kept her eyes shut as the flow of his weird Nazi grammar, with its outlandishly overheated images and clumps of succulent Teutonic word-bloat, moved its way up through the tributaries of her mind, nearly drowning her reason" (281). And she allows Nathan to appropriate the same linguistic power. But Nathan has the power of words, of naming, over her and possibly over Stingo, who is also magnetized by Nathan and, although he may not realize it, sexually attracted to him. Nathan's paranoia finds a target in Stingo's Southern-ness. Notice how he attacks Stingo's novel-in-progress with malicious verbal energy: "You have a pretty snappy talent in the traditional Southern mode. . . . But that old Negro woman in the beginning of the book. . . . It would be funny—the travesty of a Negro—if it weren't so *despicable*. You may be writing the first Southern comic book" (208). That Styron asks us to think of Southerners as victims of prejudice in a Holocaust novel will seem limp to some readers, especially Jews who have lost families in the Shoah. Moreover, we notice that within Styron's novel it is Jews—including Nathan—who are at times stereotyped if not travestied.

Does not Stingo finally have the power of naming, of defining the grammar of Sophie's and Nathan's pysche when he tells and reshapes their tale? That the younger Stingo is self-conscious about writing his novel—not what became *Sophie's Choice* but *Inheritance of the Night*—gives further emphasis to the importance of language: "I hugged Sophie softly and thought of my book; a thrill of pride and contentment went through me when I considered the honest workmanship I had so far put into the story. . . . Would I be able to summon the passion, the insight to portray this young suicide? Could I make it all seem *real?*" (449). Stingo is writing of a suicide in his novel-in-progress, at the very same time Sophie is making a suicidal decision to return to Nathan and her death.

II

We need ask whether a Jewish reader responds differently to Styron than does a non-Jewish reader, even a non-Jewish Southern reader. Styron's older voice is conscious of building on a prior tradition of Holocaust writing: "Thus the jaded reader surfeited with our century's perdurable feast of atrocities will be spared here a detailed chronicle of the killings, gassings, beatings, tortures, criminal medical experiments, slow deprivations, excremental outrages, screaming madnesses and other entries into the historical account which have already been made by Tadeusz Borowski, Jean-François Steiner, Olga Lengyel, Eugen Kogon, André Schwarz-Bart, Elie Wiesel and Bruno Bettelheim, to name but a few of the most eloquent who have tried to limn the totally infernal in their heart's blood. . . . A survivor, Elie Wiesel, has written: 'Novelists made free use of [the Holocaust] in their work. . . . In so doing they cheapened [it], drained it of its substance'" (218). At times, the narrator is doing what he says he will not do, that is, *draining* the Holocaust of its substance by using it as contextual rather than essential role. While Styron often eloquently *imagines* the Holocaust, his claim that Sophie's tortures were equal to those of Jews is a dubious claim that cannot be measured. In the above passage the narrator's tone is patronizing, if not fey.

When discussing the ethics of Holocaust narratives we need to consider how sensitive the author is to the feelings of his audience, how he renders history. Does Styron forget that the Jews were the primary victims and minimize their suffering while focusing on the culture of those Poles who, while at times victims, joined in the worst excesses? What about the inclusion of extensive anti-Semitic speeches and the rendering of Jewish stereotypes in America? At times, to a Jewish reader at least, we feel Styron's moral blindness in both Sophie's behavior and Stingo's attitudes. With Stingo's focus on Poland as "a beautiful, heart-wrenching, soul-split country" resembling the American South, the Jews as victims of genocide become at times a lost subject. Jewish and other sensitive readers may feel that the lives of by far the largest group of Holocaust victims should not be consigned to background anonymity while the suffering of Poles are foregrounded. Certainly a far greater percentage of Poles survived than Jews.

Styron is not beyond insensitivity if not anti-Semitism; nor perhaps is Styron totally without Jewish stereotypes. Take Sophie's drunken outburst of anti-Semitism: "Oh, it was so very Jewish of Nathan to do that—he wasn't giving me his love, he was *buying* me with it, like all Jews. No wonder the Jews were so hated in Europe. . . . God, how I hate them! . . . All my childhood, all my life I really hated Jews. They deserved it, this hate. I *hate* them, dirty Jewish *cochons!*" (353). The narrator is not above joining in the chorus of anti-Semitism: "This nasty discharge vexed me, even though I thought I understood its source. . . .

I found myself brooding blackly on my recent robbery. And Morris Fink. *Fink!* That fucking little hebe, I thought, trying vainly to belch" (353). Stingo is conscious in Brooklyn of living with Jews as when he goes to meet the stereotypical Leslie Lapidus: "My childish fancy suggested that they blew a shofar, whose rude untamed notes echoed through a place of abiding gloom where there was a rotting old Ark and a pile of scrolls. Bent kosher women, faces covered, wore hair shirts and loudly sobbed. . . . Spectral and bony phylacteries flapped through the murk like prehistoric birds, and everywhere were the rabbis in skullcaps moaning in a guttural tongue as they went about their savage rites—circumcising goats, burning oxen, disemboweling newborn lambs" (162-163). But while Styron may be trying to reveal Stingo's parochialism and insularity, to the resistant reader humor based on Jewish facial stereotypes is *especially* tasteless in a novel in which the Holocaust plays a large role.

Surely one cannot always apply the word "sensitivity" to Styron's attitudes to Jews. For example, Stingo's justification for the Professor's pamphlet leaves much to be desired and, indeed, reveals something of his underlying prejudice: "The piece had been written from the particular viewpoint of Polish culture" by a man who was not really a "quisling" or "collaborator" (249). Sophie herself comes to hate her father *not* for his racial ideas but for *using* her as his instrument: "It was at last coming clear to me that this man, this father, this man which give me breath and flesh have no more feeling for me than a servant, some peasant or slave, and now with not a word of thanks"(246).

At times it seems not only as if the younger Stingo replicates Sophie's—and the Nazis'—obsession with Jews, but so does the retrospective older Styron-Stingo who is telling the story. One Jewish character, Morris Fink, hypothesizes that Nathan is a golem, and we think that about Hoss and Sophie's father—and Hitler?; as he puts it: "He's been invented, that's what, like Frankenstein, see, only he's been invented by a rabbi. He's made out of clay or some kind of shit like that, only he looks like a human. Anyway, you can't control him. I mean, sometimes he acts normal, just like a normal human. But deep down he's a runaway fuckin' *monster.* That's a golem" (60). But with Styron we understand—even if Stingo does not—that fictional characters are the ultimate aesthetic golems; as Styron knows, the artist as God can create them in any way he wishes. For has he not created a fictional version of the story of a young artist's growth that owes a good deal to Joyce's *A Portrait of the Artist As a Young Man*? Is Stingo not like the rabbi creating a golem through language in his novel? Within a novel's imagined ontology, fictional characters often get out of control; but, unlike golem, they can be destroyed as Styron destroys Nathan and Sophie. Indeed, he not only destroys his younger self, Stingo, who loses his name, but as Styron finishes his novel, he leaves his former self sealed in a fictive world. Yet, finally, we as resistant readers understand that unlike Holocaust realist writers such as Hersey and Green, Styron does not have the historical perspective foregrounded, and the merging of particular and general does not quite work because he does not provide an objective view of events with a grammar of historical cause and effect.

Styron's often compelling but lengthy novel ends with an attempt at eloquence and profundity which has also a bathetic, somewhat tedious note; his narrator, who is no longer known as Stingo, discusses passages from his journal, including the journal entry: *"Some day I will understand Auschwitz."*

> This was a brave statement but innocently absurd. No one will ever understand Auschwitz. What I might have set down with more accuracy would have been: *Someday I will write about Sophie's life and death, and thereby help demonstrate how absolute evil is never extinguished from the world.* Auschwitz itself remains inexplicable. The most profound statement yet made about Auschwitz was not a statement at all, but a response.
>
> The query: "At Auschwitz, tell me, where was God?"
> And the answer: "Where was man?" (513)

The narrator continues on a note of Christian humanism that seems to undermine the novel's intensity and be at odds with both the story of Nathan and Sophie's fatal love affair and the historic tale of man's inhumanity to man: "The second line I have resurrected from the void may be a little too facile, but I have kept it. *Let your love flow out on all living things*" (513). Yet, to be fair to Styron, Stingo expresses some skepticism: "For did not Auschwitz effectively block the flow of that titanic love, like some fatal embolism in the bloodstream of mankind? Or alter the nature of love entirely. . . " (514). Throughout the novel, the wordiness of

Stingo's monologues is ironized by the devastating silence of the Holocaust, of Auschwitz, if not Nathan and Sophie's death—and the final pages illustrate this. We might close with a comment of Barbara Foley's: "Those narrative forms—both factual and fictive—that rely upon an informing teleology, generally prove inadequate to the task of encompassing the full significance of Holocaust experience" (Foley 353).

CHAPTER NINE

KENEALLY'S AND SPIELBERG'S *SCHINDLER'S LIST*: REALISTIC NOVEL INTO EPIC FILM

I

There is a paradoxical Jewish saying, "Only the dead can forgive." What is the purpose of discussing major imaginative texts about the Holocaust? For one thing, it brings to the forefront the works that have given a human dimension to the Holocaust by focusing on the fabric of lived experience; for another, it transforms that lived experience into universal terms that reach out to an audience for understanding and empathy half a century later. Moreover, historical perspectives can not only be enriched but actually presented by individual acts of imagination and memory. We all make use of the process of using stories to give the chaos of life form and shading. Stories are attempts to impress and dominate our emotions and are ways of facing painful truths. We use language to understand ourselves, but also to escape and evade ourselves. Even as our narrative weaves together empty space in our current lives and our personal history, they reveal the psyche of us tellers.

Thomas Keneally's *Schindler's List* is a third-person story that seeks, as Keneally puts it in his Author's Note, "To use the texture and devices of a novel . . . while [avoiding] all fiction" (10). It is a popular novel, without the aesthetic self-consciousness of our other texts, excepting perhaps *The War from Within.* As his narrator-surrogate tells us in the prologue, "this is the story of the pragmatic triumph of good over evil, a triumph in eminently measurable, statistical, unsubtle terms" (14). At times the narrator-surrogate has reconstructed conversations based on memory of survivors whom he has interviewed. Of course, the distance in years makes this different from a first-person historical memoir such as *Night.* The use in the 1993 edition of photographs from Yad Vashem and Leopold Pfefferberg, one of the Jews Schindler saved, not only bridges the gap between film and book, but gives the story some further journalistic authenticity.

What distinguishes Keneally's *Schindler's List* from our other novels is that it is by a non-Jew and its central character is a non-Jew. It is worthwhile to compare the Jewish perspective of Spielberg's film of the novel and the perspective of Keneally, who is not Jewish but empathetic toward his protagonist and the survivors. Keneally somewhat confuses two traditions: that of the Just Men and that of the Righteous Gentile. The Legend of the Just Men is the basis of Schwarz-Bart's novel, *The Last of the Just,* which we will examine in the next chapter; as Keneally explains it: "There is the Talmudic legend of the *Hasidei Ummot Ha-olam,* the Righteous of the Nations, of whom there are said to be—at any point in the world's history—thirty-six. Stern [Schindler's Jewish business manager and confidante] did not believe literally in the mystical number, but the legend was psychologically true for him, and he believed it a decent and wise course to try to make of Schindler a living and breathing sanctuary" (*Schindler's List* 68). The tradition of the Righteous Gentile is, Keneally writes, "a peculiarly Israeli honor based on an ancient tribal assumption that in the mass of Gentiles, the God of Israel would always provide a leavening of just men" (394). In 1961 "[Schindler] was declared a Righteous Person," but that is not the same as a Just Man (394). Keneally writes as if Schindler were a Just Man, a man who feels the suffering of all mankind, a simple Jewish soul who acts out of instinct and feeling, and whose position is mysteriously designated by God. For Keneally, Schindler's living for a time by the Talmudic "verse" (but is the Talmud commentary in verse form?) "He who saves a single life saves the world entire" (368) is enough to make him a Just Man.

It is as if not only Schindler but the narrator—by bearing witness—were contending for a place among the Righteous Gentiles. In his prologue, Keneally's narrator is aware that to write of virtue is difficult, particularly of a virtuous man who has large faults: "[A]lthough Herr Schindler's merit is well documented, it is a feature of his ambiguity that he worked within or, at least, on the strength of a corrupt and savage scheme, one that filled Europe with camps of varying but consistent inhumanity and created a submerged, unspoken-of nation of prisoners" (14). Yet Schindler is a heavy drinking, narcissistic womanizer with a keen sense of self- interest for making his economic way. His is a story of metamorphosis into a fully empathic human who feels for the plight of the Jews and acts nobly and bravely on his feelings. Schindler begins as if he *enjoys* the gamble of offering bribes for workers who would staff his enamel factory, while seeing if he has the legerdemain to protect his workers from persecution. Yet his moral antennae awaken to the inhumanity of a world of cattle cars hauling human cargo: "But what his curtness covered was dismay at those crowds at Prokocim who, for want of a blue sticker, stood waiting for the new and decisive symbol of their status, the cattle car, to be hauled by heavy engine across their range of vision. Now, the cattle cars told them, we are all beasts together" (125). Gradually he begins to think of himself as one with the Jews with whom he is working and often living: "We'll have to wait a little longer for our freedom" (269).

The Prologue makes us aware of the novelist's power to present. The novel relies on references to the crystallizing Prologue, a drunken dinner party Goeth gave in autumn 1943 at which Schindler promises to save Helen Hirsch: "He murmured encouragement. He'd see her again. He'd try to get her out. Out? she asked. Out of the villa, he explained; into my factory, he said. Surely you have heard of my factory. I have an enamelware factory" (29). We see Oskar characteristically bribing Nazi officers—in this case Bosch, who is absent from the film—Goeth bragging about abusing "Lena" (Helen Hirsch) without his superior officer Scherner intervening, Pfefferberg and Lisiek scrubbing the bathtub a few days before Lisiek is shot, and the whores of the German officers. Schindler, who wouldn't take a whore from Amon Goeth, visits Helen in the kitchen for the first time and explains to her: "He won't kill you, because he enjoys you too much, my dear Helen. He enjoys you so much he won't even let you wear the Star" (28). That personal touch and interest—those human concerns—effectively open the novel.

It is the prologue, one suspects, that gave Spielberg the idea that the book could be dramatized cinematically. From the outset, the novel's narrator does not hide that Schindler will help Jews, but rather anticipates it. Keneally reminds us of his retrospective point of view—one that contains full knowledge of the complete narrative—after giving details of the Nazi killing mechanism: "To write these things now is to state the commonplaces of history. But to find them out in 1942, to have them break upon you from a June sky, was to suffer a fundamental shock, a derangement in that area of the brain in which stable ideas about humankind and its possibilities are kept" (137).

In an odd way Schindler is drawn to Commandant Goeth—the name "Goeth" perhaps a play on "Goethe" without the final "e": "[T]he revulsion Herr Schindler felt was of a piquant kind, an ancient, exultant sense of abomination—of the same sort as, in a medieval painting, the just show for the damned. An emotion, that is, which stung Oskar rather than unmanned him" (15). Is the naiveté and awkwardness of the odd and quaint "unmanned" intentional? At the novel's opening party we see how Schindler inevitably compromises himself: "He felt the nausea that goes with being used, and at the same time a sensation close to joy" (20).

In the novel, Amon arrives to clear the ghetto; from that point on, the rule of law ceases to exist. The Jews realize that nothing will protect them and that there are no rules or self-regulating structures. Of the killing of Diana Reiter, a Jewish architectural engineer supervising the construction of the barracks who opined that the foundation was not properly excavated, the narrator remarks in terms that stress the breakdown of all pretenses to justice: "As for Hujar [the NCO who shot Miss Reiter] and his colleagues, they knew now that instantaneous execution was to be the permitted style of Płaszów" (169). In the film Amon is still a shadowy double of Schindler, but now he shares that role with Stern who becomes Schindler's conscience. Early on Stern—rendered in indirect discourse—sees Schindler as possibility, as "sanctuary," as "just Goy" (46). (We should note the heavy-handed offensiveness of Keneally's use of the term "just Goy.") After Stern quotes the aforementioned Talmudic "verse"—"He who saves the life of one man saves the entire world"—and Schindler responds, "Of course, of course," Stern "rightly or wrongly, always believed that it was at that moment that he had dropped the right seed in the furrow" (48). Schindler may have already given compensation to the Nussbaum family—though it is "not possible to prove," according to the narrator—whom he displaced when he was given their apartment, compensation that enabled them to escape to Yugoslavia. He also tells Stern of the coming pogrom: "His leaking of the news to Stern, far more than the unconfirmed Nussbaum story, goes some way toward proving his case" (57).

Keneally, we realize from the outset, is not a phrasemaker in the vein of Conrad or Joyce. The narrator doesn't explore as fully as he might the Conradian suggestion that Goeth was Schindler's darker self, a secret sharer like the murderous Leggatt is to the Captain, like Kurtz to Marlow, or Jim to Marlow and Brierly: "Oskar had the characteristic salesman's gift of treating men he abhorred as if they were spiritual brothers, and it would deceive the Herr Commandant so completely that Amon would always believe Oskar a friend. . . . Oskar despised Goeth in the simplest and most passionate terms. His contempt would grow without limit, and his career would dramatically demonstrate it. Just the same, the reflection can hardly be avoided that Amon was Oskar's dark brother, was the berserk and fanatic executioner Oskar might, by some unhappy reversal of his appetites, have become" (170-171). In listening to Amon, is Oskar not fascinated and captivated by a man free of ethical constraints? Does Schindler need to spend so much time drinking with this psychotic scoundrel or is there an attraction to Goeth, his darker self? We think of how Conrad's Marlow is drawn to those with soft spots and places of decay.

While Keneally's narrator is sympathetic to the Jews from the outset, he misses some important implications of the story he tells. In rendering Schindler's final speech, does Keneally realize how Germanic is Schindler's stress on "order"—repeated "twice"—and "discipline" (terms resonant of Nazi proclamations) and how Schindler's words are for this reason out of touch with the Jewish sensibility of those who had survived, including the women who had spent some weeks in Auschwitz? "After six years of the cruel murder of human beings, victims are being mourned, and Europe is now trying to return to peace and order. I would like to turn to you for unconditional order and discipline—to all of you who together with me have worried through many hard years— in order that you can live through the present and within a few days go back to your destroyed and plundered homes, looking for survivors from your families. You will thus prevent panic, whose results cannot be foreseen" (369). When the narrator presents Schindler's *apologia* for the Germans, we need remember that his speech is in front of Nazi soldiers on the eve of liberation and that he is protecting his Jews: "The fact that millions among you, your parents, children, and brothers, have been liquidated has been disapproved by thousands of Germans, and even today there are millions of them who do not know the extent of these horrors" (370). But do we take umbrage when Keneally writes of a former Nazi, "if anyone had earned the right to make that defense and have it listened to with—at least—tolerance, it was surely Herr Oskar Schindler" (374). As resistant readers, we know that Schindler may be engaging in some self-justification and suspect that he may have willfully or naively missed what has happened. Has, we might ask, Keneally shown us the degree to which the Germans—wearing SS uniforms, or guarding concentration camps, or shepherding people to the gas chambers—were complicit?

Drawing upon the oral testimony of survivors, Keneally establishes the verisimilitude of his story. He moves from a close knowledge of the characters' motives to historical and geographic perspectives. The narrator establishes a relatively intimate relationship with the audience. Writing of Oskar—his appellation for Schindler—and his relationship with his father, the narrator comments in the colloquial terms of sharing with his audience a private confidence: "It is a sweet thing to outstrip a father whom you haven't forgiven." He implies his familiarity with the geography of Cracow and Schindler's factory: "Some of the floor space in the building on the left as you emerged from the lobby into the interior of the factory was occupied by present production" (72). Occasionally he looks forward to later historical events: "When the Russians came from the east, that wood with its population of victims would fall to them before living and half-dying Płaszów" (223).

Keneally dramatizes how, from the outset of Hitler's arrival in Poland, the Jews wanted to believe in an alternative ontology, a safe haven from the materiality of history's engulfing chaos. They believe they are indispensable: "Stern and Ginter considered at that stage, that a Jew who had an economic value in a precocious empire hungry for skilled workers was safe from worse things" (89). The pathos of the optative dominates each of our texts; desperately, the Jews recreate sustaining fictions to protect their psyches. Within the novel, the Jews in summer 1941 originally accept the ghetto as a small "but permanent realm" in a way that suggests Appelfeld's *Badenheim 1939:* "There had been a post office; there had even been ghetto postage stamps. There had been a ghetto newspaper, even though it contained little else than edicts from the Wawel and Pomorska Street. . . . It had seemed for a brief time that schooling would proceed here in formal classrooms, that orchestras would gather and regularly perform, that Jewish life would be communicated like a benign organism along the streets, from artisan to artisan, from scholar to scholar" (116-117).

As Jews do to Trumpelman in Epstein's *King of the Jews,* the desperate Jews begin to totemize Schindler into a miracle worker if not a messianic figure. As the Jews' plight worsens, his stature grows: "Oskar had become a minor god of deliverance, double-faced—in the Greek manner—as any small god; endowed with all the human vices; many-handed; subtly powerful; capable of bringing gratuitous but secure salvation" (232). Paradoxically, he replaces the rabbis as the man to whom they look for wisdom: "But if rabbis came, they remained only a few days on their way to Auschwitz—not long enough for people requiring the rites of *kiddushin* and *nissuin* to locate them and ask them, before they stepped into the furnace, for a final exercise of their priesthood" (246-247).

In the book the narrator traces Schindler's awakening, but even in 1942 he emphasizes his naiveté: "He still hoped, in a way that was almost childlike and to which history would pay no regard, that the fall of the evil king would not bear away that legitimacy—that in the new era he would go on being Hans Schindler's successful boy from Zwittau" (137). Yet the magic qualities of Schindler are emphasized within the novel. His verbal legerdemain—accompanied by lavish bribes—creates the impossible. Lusin, a character not in the film, believes in his magic. Schindler exorcises the imminent threat of German guards killing his prisoners when he produces bread for a Sabbath at Brinnlitz. The narrator writes: "But that Saturday bread was truly celebrated more in terms of the magic of the event, of the wonder-working" (362).

Keneally's narrator is amazed at the Nazi stupidity of diverting, "in the midst of a desperate battle," human and technological resources from the European war to what he calls an "extermination" that has not a military or economic meaning but only "a psychological" meaning (148). Does

Keneally fully understand that the war against the Jews was the *principle* campaign of the National Socialists? Does he not realize that ingrained hatred of Jews motivates the Germans and that an entire country had to be infected with the virus of fanaticism for the Holocaust to succeed?

Keneally admires the courage of those who try to save themselves *without* sacrificing their fellows. One of Keneally's continuing themes— one that we will encounter in the excoriating analysis of the Judenrat in Epstein and Spiegelman—is the collaboration of a minority of Jews in the hopes they can save themselves; they extend to its logical conclusion the belief that Jews will somehow survive: "But the situation would settle; the race would survive by petitioning, by buying off the authori- ties—it was the old method, it had been working since the Roman Empire, it would work again. In the end the civil authorities needed Jews, especially in a nation where they were one in every eleven" (45). (Once again we feel more than a nuance of insensitivity in Keneally's reductive summary of what he imagines to be one aspect of the Jewish psyche and of his assumption that Jews think of purchasing their rights to live as humans).

Yet the principle collaborators—those who know too much—finally become victims, too. The Judenrat and the Jewish police think their positions confer privilege. Does Keneally fuly realize the self-serving quality of Poldek Pfefferberg's rationalizations for joining the Judenrat? "He believed he understood its purpose—that it was not only to ensure rational behavior inside the walls but also to achieve that correct degree of grudging tribal obedience which, in the history of European Jewry, has tended to ensure that the oppressors will go away more quickly, will become forgetful so that, in the interstices of their forgetfulness, life may again become feasible" (97). Isn't he rather gentle on Poldek, who is something of an operator—what Vladek, Art's father in *Maus*, calls a *Kombinator?*

Let us look at the previous passage to examine the narrator's tone. What the narrator lacks is a Jewish sensibility, an awareness of the role of religion and faith, of the Jewish myth that each pogrom is an iteration of the destruction of the Temple and/or of the Pharaoh's torments in Egypt. In the foregoing passage, the irony is weak and lacks the felt empathy of someone who knows the culture he writes about. As our discussion of Hersey's *The Wall* made clear, Gentiles successfully can dramatize Jewish perspectives. Whatever Keneally's intentions, his narrator is sometimes using a blunt instrument to examine the Jewish history and culture. For example, in the following anecdote, does he understand the mixture of shtetl fatalism, hope, and the acceptance that lives are a plot written in God's book?

> "Where's the electric fence?" Clara asked the woman. To her distraught mind, it was a reasonable question to ask, and Clara had no doubt that the friend, if she had any sisterly feeling, would point the exact way to the wires. The answer the woman gave Clara was just as crazed, but it was one that had a fixed point of view, a balance, a perversely sane core.
> "Don't kill yourself on the fence, Clara," the woman urged her. "If you do that, you'll never know what happened to you."
> It has always been the most powerful of answers to give to the intending suicide. Kill yourself and you'll never find out how the plot ends. (321)

Does not his comment conflate the mixture of fatalism and hope that is so much part of the unassimilated part of the Eastern Jewish community? What I am questioning is whether Keneally's story has a sensibility commensurate with his obvious sympathy with the Jews, and whether his failure to grasp fully the nuances of his story is an aesthetic or moral issue. My argument is that the aesthetic and the moral in fiction are inextricably related. I want to be clear that I don't believe that only Jews can write effectively about Jews anymore than I believe men are disqualified from writing effectively about women or whites about blacks—or, in both cases, vice versa. I am asking the question because I feel Keneally's text is heavy-handed and reductive, and want to know why when I first read it—before seeing Spielberg's magnificent film—I found the novel merely a good read.

II

Spielberg has converted the novel into a moving black-and-white film that gives the viewer a sense of a newsreel or documentary. He has tightened the wordy historical novel into what Daniel Fogel has called a "historical fable, a fable about choosing goodness and heroism" (315).

If the film is based on the novel, it is also a mythopoeic fable of the Holocaust, using as its source extant images, many of which are in the consciousness of educated people. Thus *Schindler's List* is not only about the Holocaust but about an established visual lexicon of extant and preceding Holocaust images. Spielberg's use of red to illuminate the well-dressed young girl in the scene in which the ghetto is destroyed and again when her remains are exhumed stresses *Schindler's List* as an illuminating distortion and emphasizes its fictionality. The little girl in red alludes to a striking visual image in Wiesel's *Night,* in which his sister Tzipora, a well-groomed girl of seven with "a red coat over her arm," is driven from her home (17).

The book gives background and context to the film. When we reread—or read for the first time—the book after seeing the film, we realize that Keneally describes some characters in detail who are not specified in the film. In the book, the narrator tries to maintain a double optics including the dramatization of Schindler's awakening and a retrospective perspective. We learn that Julian Scherner is the *oberscharführer* who commands respect within the Nazi hierarchy, and whom Schindler bribes, and that Julius Madritch is the man Schindler visits to convince him to help buy Jews. The novel's narrator shows us how Schindler's marriage iterates that of his father, whom he has hated for a long time, and shows him to be appalled by the Nazis earlier than he is in the film.

The film opens with the Jews arriving in Cracow. The early visualization of Schindler as a dandy, a decadent, a refugee from the Vienna cabaret world, wearing a Nazi pin, makes his conversion all the more striking. The opening scene presents him as an exotic, a master of legerdemain, a confidence man who ingratiates himself with the Nazis: "Why, that's Oskar Schindler." As David Thomson writes, "We are accomplices in his nerve and the film's itemization of his magic. The silk suit, the swaggering tie, the cuff-links, the gold Nazi pin, the bank-notes that appear in his hand beneath the waiter's nose" (45). And does not Schindler perform the same kind of magic with his factory, his list, and the relocation? Schindler is an actor, a man who wears the motley of modernism but who, for a brief time, does achieve a coherent self.

What Keneally, the novelist, does is give a rich fabric of detailed experience for us to imagine, while Spielberg, the film director, visualizes select details while omitting others. Spielberg's film depends on heightening a few major scenes at the expense of the chronological novel, which at times reads almost like the narrator's diary: the liquidation of the Cracow ghetto, the selection at the Płaszów camp, the making of the list, the transportation of the men to Brinnlitz, the women sent by error to Auschwitz and their rescue, and Schindler's departure from Brinnlitz at war's end. While the novel's narrator continues the Schindler story beyond the end of the war, the film reduces his postwar story to a few sentences of rolling text. In the novel, Schindler is arrested three times—not, as in the film, only once.

The film takes the narrator's words and gives them to characters. Such is the case when Amon Goeth speaks of the erasure of Jewish history. In the book, the narrator comments: "Everyone wanted to be here today, for today was history. There had been for more than seven centuries a Jewish Cracow, and by this evening—or at least by tomorrow—those seven centuries would have become a rumor, and Cracow would be *judenrein* (clean of Jews)" (174). The book gives the impetus to Spielberg's emphasis on Schindler as magician. Take the response to Schindler of Lucia, a character absent from the film: "Since she knew friends vanished, she feared his friendship; she wanted him to continue to be a presence, a magical parent. . . . Many of the Emalia prisoners felt the same" (204).

Certainly Spielberg made clear in interviews and in his commitment to sponsorship of the oral history Holocaust survivor project that he made the film out of a deep emotional need to declare his heritage. Spielberg is ethically committed less to the details of story than to a historical epic. As in his 1998 war epic *Saving Private Ryan*, every detail serves a thematic purpose. Spielberg's film of *Schindler's List* often visualizes without identifying characters; thus while the novel identifies Danka Dresner as the girl who is hidden while her mother is denied a place, the film does not. Spielberg's narrator is principally the omniscient camera, although on occasion he provides textual inserts rather than voice-overs. His role is that of community conscience, urging the contemporary psyche to witness with him the Shoah. Much of what he dramatizes is within the ken of Schindler's optics. During the *Aktion*, the camera shows us from Schindler's vantage point the small girl in red—the only use of color before the final scene in Israel—purposefully moving through the streets alone. But when she climbs the stairs in search of a hiding place, we are outside Schindler's optics. He later uses red to show her body exhumed with the rest of the Płaszów corpses. As Jews come out of hiding after the *Aktion,* the camera shows Nazi troops lying in wait as if they were hunting prey. After the German troops spray buildings with bullets, we see piles of corpses. Even as we watch a film *depending* on technological ingenuity, we understand that the then advanced technology was the instrument of the Jews' demise. The soldiers use stethoscopes to locate where people are hiding. While Schindler would use modest industrial procedures to make enamel mess kits in his factory as a way of protecting Jews, the Germans use their technology to arrange efficient transport, imprisonment, gassing, and body burning for vast human extermination. That guns and cigarette lighters do fail is Spielberg's reminder that technology will not triumph over the human spirit, for within his teleology, finally, the Germans do fail.

The film depends on brilliantly rendered visual moments. We might think of the concluding scenes: Stern shaking Schindler's hands as the latter leaves the Brinnlitz factory that has provided refuge for the Jews, reversing the past narrative, the Jews now *helping* Schindler; and the survivors, accompanied by actors who played the parts of the actual people, visiting Schindler's grave. Thus, it is inevitable that the film becomes an illuminating distortion of the novel. In a sense, when we read we all become directors and imagine visualization; but, in another sense, at least some readers resist and even resent visualization and have cognitive experiences that are more intellectual, introverted, and meditative than visual.

Stern crystallizes in the film more than in the book the Jewish ability to survive by means of cunning and courage. Stern represents Schindler's upright double in the film, the moral counterweight to Amon Goeth. Schindler is frequently alone with one or the other in dark scenes to stress how they are both shadowy doppelgängers. As Fogel notes, "Spielberg takes several of Keneally's characters and collapses them into the figure of Itzhak Stern" (315). Stern becomes more central in the movie, while another aide, Bankier, disappears. Spielberg combines Bankier and Pemper with Stern; it is Bankier, not Stern, who is rescued from the cattle cars. Stern refuses to acknowledge Schindler's toast or thank you, just as Schindler hates to be thanked. Stern is rectitude personified. Stern becomes not only Schindler's financial accountant but his moral accountant. After Schindler transfers his anger and rejects the idea, proposed by the Pearlman daughter, of saving her elderly parents, it is Stern who by means of disapproving facial expression becomes his conscience. He is the Jew who is linked to the rabbinical tradition of righteous people, the pure *Tsadikim*. He is the ethical figure who is juxtaposed to the collaborators—Goldberg and his fellow opportunists—whom we first see as black marketeers in the Catholic church.

The film collapses the novel's two *Aktions* against the Jews into one. In that *Aktion* it is through Schindler's eyes that the camera shows, in the longest scene, the destruction of the ghetto. We see the terror of the liquidation: the frightened Jews trembling in the dark, one family's jewels hidden in bread that is swallowed by all family members, other families uprooted and herded like animals, names being read as Germans arrive at apartments, the SS's arrogant tossing of a Rabbi's prayer book, Poldek Pfefferberg escaping into the sewers, Stern unable to find papers, Jewish doctors mercy-injecting their patients with lethal medications to spare their being shot in their sickbeds.

While Keneally focuses on the chronology of events, the tick-tock of passing time, Spielberg uses a biblical style, highlighting major episodes at length and reducing other episodes to nothing. Erich Auerbach writes:

> The Homeric poems present a definite complex of events whose boundaries in space and time are clearly delimited. . . . The Old Testament, on the other hand, presents universal history: it begins with the beginning of time, with the creation of the world, and will end with the Last Days, the fulfilling of the Covenant, with which the world will come to an end. Everything else that happens in the world can only be conceived as an element in this sequence. . . . As a composition, the Old Testament is incomparably less unified than the Homeric poems, it is more obviously pieced together—but the various components all belong to one concept of universal history and its interpretation. (13-14)

Just as for Auerbach the unity of each biblical episode depends in part on its place in this universal history, so in Spielberg crystallizing episodes—drawn from the *topoi* of past Holocaust narratives—relate to the mythopoeic narrative of the Holocaust that he wishes to present. If for Auerbach events are seen retrospectively in terms of a perspective informed by full knowledge of a history stretching from Genesis to the Apocalypse, for Spielberg those events seen retrospectively stretch from the rise of Hitler to the current State of Israel. If for Auerbach the fragmentary, discrete presentation of events within the Bible depended upon interpretation in terms of a teleology, so too for Spielberg a teleology is present in the survival and flourishing of the offspring of Schindler's Jews, themselves metonymies for the Jewish State.

Spielberg carefully focuses on a panorama of recurring *topoi*—*topoi* drawn from the lexicon of prior Holocaust texts—that crystallize Holocaust narrative. Spielberg wants to etch in our psyches indelible images of the Shoah. He also wants to show that the relentless Nazi logic of reducing humans to anonymous numbers had a grotesque teleology. As the ghetto is formed, we see the beginning of the homogenizing process that reduces individual Jews to a collective noun, *Jews*, and the physical displacement, on March 20, 1941, of wealthy Jews, who carefully take their mezuzahs (the ritualistic scroll Jews attach to their doorpost). The camera shows us Schindler taking over one of the wealthy Jewish family's homes, while the family moves to a small apartment already inhabited by less sophisticated Jews with whom they have in common only their Jewish identity. As the wealthy Jews depart, the camera shows a little girl throwing dirt, spitefully shouting out repeatedly, "Goodbye Jews"; when we view the film a second time, we think of how the camera focuses later on children as victims. We see the gathering power of the Judenrat and Jewish policeman, visually represented by the conniving Goldberg. The camera shows Nazi sadism in the form of the shooting of a one-armed man who is unable to shovel snow; it lingers upon the sorting of Jewish possessions—suitcases, shoes, gold teeth—from those already sent to the death camps. We see Amon Goeth's arrival and the subsequent arbitrary shooting of the female Jewish construction engineer who expresses an opinion. Before the destruction of the Cracow ghetto, we hear Goeth's speech about erasing six centuries of Jewish history, "They are now a rumor. They never happened." The camera shows us how, before a "selection," the women prick their fingers to get blood to rub on their faces to give them color. These images give way to the horror of Jews transported in boxcars, summary executions, and the Auschwitz gas chambers.

Spielberg develops Keneally's tale to focus on scenes in Schindler's moral education. The scene switches to the bacchanalia at Goeth's house—recalling Keneally's prologue—with Schindler there. Keneally dramatizes Schindler's rejection of Goeth's values for Stern's. Before departing as his accountant, Stern informs Schindler about fees and payoffs. Schindler impatiently yells: "It gives me a headache," and gives Stern valuables. But despite Schindler's insouciance, he is growing in moral responsibility. After Stern says, "Don't let things fall apart, good luck," he returns to camp; the camera ironically focuses on the sign *"Arbeit macht frei."* During the bacchanalia, Schindler visits Helen Hirsch, who tells him how Amon beats her for such transgressions as throwing out bones he wanted to keep for his dogs. Touched, Schindler tells her: "I know you are suffering." When Helen talks about how a woman has been shot arbitrarily and how Goeth's wrath is unpredictable, Schindler realizes with us that Goeth represents the arbitrariness of persecution in a world where chaos and serendipity rule. Yet as viewers we understand that Spielberg has created biblical time in which everything is related to a retrospective view of history from a contemporary vantage point of knowing the miraculous survival story of these particular Jews. Schindler's surviving Jews include both the rabbi whose life is spared because of a pure accident of a broken gun and the boy who saves a group of accused chicken thieves by pointing to a man who has been already shot as the thief and is rewarded by being summoned by Schindler as an "essential worker."

In the film Schindler is a mysterious figure whose motives are not always clear. He is, like Epstein's Trumpelman, a confidence man who believes in his own performances. He is uncomfortable with gratitude, yet always likes to be the center of attention. He is competing with his father. He knows that the key to his success is the war. Gourevitch has complained of the film that "few characters emerge with any individuality. . . . Schindler's decency is presented as kind of enigmatic equivalent to Goeth's barbarity" (50). But in part, we do see in the film an awakening of Schindler's consciousness and see how his humanity takes over from the profit motive; we see how human ties and commitment to community begin to matter. As the factory is closing down, Stern and Schindler look at each other; it seems as if one is going to Auschwitz and the other is going home. Stern finally drinks with him. Symbolically Stern acknowledges Schindler as a fellow anti-Nazi. After Schindler has learned the camp and his labor are being evacuated, he tells Stern, "Some day this is going to end. . . . I am going home." We then see him alone in his apartment in the dark, a woman in his bed, listening to a recording by Billie Holiday while surrounded by money. We hear her sing "God Bless the Child," which includes such lines as "Yes, the strong get more, while the weak ones fade." He has an epiphany, we know, because in the next scene he visits Amon and asks for *his people,* and tells him: "I want my people. It's good for me. . . . It's good for the army." Amon's response: "What is one worth to you?" What was missing for him, Schindler learns, what differentiates "between success and failure" is war, and he is right—for not only his business success but his *moral* success does depend on war.

Schindler's legerdemain extends to inventing himself. Schindler wants to be known as someone who "did something extraordinary"—and by the end he really has. He knows that the key to his success *is* the war. As the film progresses, Spielberg creates a structure of affects for his viewers, urging us to see the transformation of Schindler's moral stature. Originally he is a schemer and profiteer interested in making his fortune. He appears in church among black marketers; with Poldeck Pfefferberg's help we see him delivering exotic foodstuffs and liquor as gifts to ingratiate himself with the Germans. He will provide "panache" and "presentation" to restart an enamel factory in exchange for money from two wealthy Jews, whom he will repay in enamelware. He tells them, "Money is not still money." Originally he had hired Jews because they were cheap labor. Yet when he wants ten healthy women, he tests prospective Jewish women employees at typing but hires them according to their beauty, and then he makes love to them.

Let us examine how Spielberg's narrative is organized to reshape our view of Schindler. Even though we know he is a sensualist and womanizer, he refuses to see the young Pearlman woman, who looks shabby, but when she dresses up and wears lipstick, he welcomes her. She begs: ""They say no one dies here. Your factory is a haven. . . . Please bring [my parents] here." After she leaves, he bursts out to Stern, "Send them away; it's not a factory!" But often Schindler *says* "no," and *does* yes. Stern is his conscience, and Schindler, pondering the ethics of rejecting

Ms. Pearlman's request, remarks: "War brings out bad." (In this scene, Stern is hovering over the very typewriter on which he later types the list of those who will be evacuated to Brinnlitz.) After Stern tells Schindler how Amon killed 25 men arbitrarily, Schindler asks, "What do you want me to do?" We see Goldberg (in the film, as in the novel, a member of the Jewish police, but in the film at times also Schindler's factotum) calling the three Pearlmans' names and then bringing them to the factory. After the Pearlmans arrive, Spielberg switches back to Schindler's instructions to bring them to the factory; this is an example of the film's visual "discourse"—or narrative ordering—controlling and giving shape to story.

Narrative in film is a function of the camera. Spielberg zooms in with his lens to highlight faces in the darkness in the crowd scenes and rescues these faces from anonymity. Within a gloomy, dark, grainy background, he suddenly casts light on faces as if he were recalling Rembrandt's portraits of fully realized humans rather than victims. In the Płaszów forced labor camp, we see men and women separated by barbed wire and, because they are forbidden to speak to one another, communicating by whistle not as if they were signaling to fellow humans but as if they were calling their dogs. Spielberg reinforces his narrative with subtly chosen sequences of images. For example, the smoke from the opening Shabbat candles is first iterated in Schindler's cigarette smoke and the factory smoke, but gradually the smoke foreshadows the exhuming and burning of corpses when Płaszów is evacuated. In April 1944, Schindler sees ashes on his car from the 10,000 incinerated bodies of Płaszów. Finally, when the film turns to the Auschwitz inferno, the smoke gushes from the Auschwitz crematoriums, the destination of most of the Jews whom Schindler does not save.

Contrary to Philip Gourevitch's reading, many of the Jews are heroic in their desire to survive and to protect their families. Gourevitch complains that the Jews are not "allowed to say something about their own plight" (52). But is not the film's point that while they are reduced to silence by domination and enslavement, the intervention of Schindler enables a small group to endure, survive, and recapture their humanity? In the novel, the narrator traces the process from ghetto to labor camp to extermination. At first Jews, more than in the film, welcome the ghetto:

> But perhaps the ghetto was the bottom, the point at which it was possible to take organized thought. . . . Yet it also consecrated the Jews to their own specialness, to a richness of shared scholarship, to songs and Zionist talk, elbow to elbow, in coffeehouses rich in ideas if not in cream. Evil rumors emanated from the ghettos of Lodz and Warsaw, but the Podgórze ghetto as planned was more generous with space, for if you superimposed it on a map of the Centrum, you found that the ghetto was in area about half the size of the Old City—by no means enough space, but not quite strangulation. (85-86)

What these passages describe is a epistemology, an optics of hope in the face of disconfirming events. For events continue to limit, to restrict, to imprison, and, finally, condemn to death.

Reflecting his own desire to recuperate the past, Spielberg nostalgically makes us aware of European Jewish culture. More than the novel, the film accentuates Jewish customs and family tradition. At the Cracow factory we see a beautifully improvised Jewish wedding. The novel opens with *Shabbat* candles. At Brinnlitz, after Schindler approaches the rabbi and tells him it is Friday, a small group celebrates the Sabbath and we see the candles that echo the film's opening scene. After Schindler's Jews learn of the war's end, the Brinnlitz survivors take part in a *Kaddish* service for those who have died. Finally, the film ends with the moving scene of the actors accompanying survivors as they place stones on Schindler's grave.

Yes, at times Spielberg's images of the Jews are naive, relatively passive, and devoted more to the Jewish family culture than to the rituals of the religiously observant. The aforementioned Friday service at the Czech factory seems to have a limited number of participants and to be celebrated at Schindler's initiative. Unlike the Germans, the Jews are abstemious in drink. If at times the Jews are more materialistic then spiritual, as when they swallow their jewels with their children before the liquidation of the ghetto, most of Spielberg's portrait camera shots stress their humanity, decency, gentleness, and courage in the face of terror.

After the Cracow ghetto is liquidated, the Jews are moved to a forced labor camp at Płaszów, ten kilometers from the center of Cracow, on a site that was once a Jewish cemetery. Spielberg dramatizes and

visualizes the *topos* of selection. We hear an announcement that everyone alive should come to selection. The selection principle for Amon is
who can work. Schindler dramatizes the grotesque irony of Amon,
shirtless, being physically examined and found overweight, while we see
emaciated Jews running naked through mud. While the women who are
not chosen celebrate their having not been selected, we see kids waving
happily, leaving as a song is played and they are led to trucks,
presumably for transport away to death camps. Their innocent marching
to the trucks ironically anticipates the film's final scene when the
Schindler Jews symbolically march across Europe to Israel. When the
women discover that their children are being tricked into getting on
trucks as if they were going picnicking, they throw themselves at the
guards in an effort to rescue their children from the Nazi guards.
Spielberg's special focus on children works effectively; he alternates
shots of unsuspecting children readied for transport, with shots of
children hiding—some in excrement beneath primitive toilets.

Spielberg focuses on the powerlessness of Schindler. After the
selection, Schindler arrives to observe the transports presided over by
Amon. While he sweats in the hot sun, he is moved by hands reaching
out of the cattle cars, one offering jewels. Humoring Amon and laughing
while Stern (always in his business suit) looks on, Schindler hoses Jews
himself before getting others to help. Amon tells him it is cruel to raise
false hopes and he and the other Nazis laugh, but Schindler arranges for
them to get water when the train stops. Yet even if he saves some Jews
for another day by quenching their thirst, we understand the pathos of
Schindler's intervention.

The motif of the list, typed in black and white, recurs throughout the
film. Finally the power of the word rescues a few fortunate souls. The film
opens after the Germans defeat the Poles in 1939; we see lines of desks at
which functionaries, probably Jews, are making of lists of Jews forced to
relocate from the country to the city. Spielberg shows the names being
typed just as they will be later. In a way, the photographing of German
officers at the nightclub—with Schindler—is an ironic documentation of a
list of new German arrivals to Cracow. While the photographs document
how officers stuff themselves with food and drink, one says, "Jews always
weather the storm," and another says ominously, "Not this time." Soon lists
of *names* give way to simple *numbers* of victims.

In a film where the visual is predominant, it is paradoxically the Word—both written and spoken—that decides who lives and who dies. In the midst of the bacchanalia at Goeth's house, Spielberg's camera switches to the Judenrat drawing up lists. Schindler meets Stern there. We see names being called on March 20, 1941, the date when all Jews must enter the ghetto; this, too, anticipates Schindler's list of those who will accompany him to Brinnlitz. We see Jews, looking sad, streaming across bridges in large numbers. When Stern advises workers on how to get papers as "essential workers" for Schindler's factory, we see the beginnings of the seminal list. With Schindler and his paramour looking on, we see the Judenrat preparing lists for a selection. As if to show the limitations of any Jew, the camera shows Stern—who himself had seemed something of a magician in getting people work cards—on a list of people being deported. But Schindler—*flaneur*, chameleonic character, impresario, and hero—exerts pressure to get him taken off. Schindler has the wits to stop the train; when he initials a list to get Stern off, a German says "it makes no difference . . . just paperwork."

Perhaps by 1993 a Holocaust film may preserve and visualize the horrors of the Shoah in a way that was impossible in 1945. Perhaps a film now can examine sadistic psychosis in complex ways as when the film raises the possibility of Goeth's leniency only to have it dashed. I am thinking of the memorable scene in which Schindler teaches Goeth about the concept of pardon by reference to the generosity of Roman emperors. Like Conrad's Kurtz—who, as the darker self who commits atrocities in the name of exterminating the brutes, is to Marlow as Goeth is to Schindler—the narcissistic and megalomaniacal Goeth has no restraints in the gratification of his lusts once he is outside civilized sanctions. No sooner does Goeth assume the role of benevolent despot and pretend he is emperor than he shoots Lisiak—the boy he has pardoned after his bungling in the stables—because Lisiak cannot remove the stain from Goeth's bathtub. The camera shows Stern— Schindler's conscience and moral double—walking nearby, and we see two missed shots going to either side of the boy. As we see Stern shift his body weight before the third shot kills the boy, the camera shifts to Helen Hirsch doing Goeth's nails; we realize that her life is under continuous threat even though Schindler assures her that Goeth will not shoot her because it pleases him to alternately flirt with and abuse her.

Nothing gives us a better sense of the psychosis of Goeth and the collective and arbitrary notion of justice that makes the social psychosis of the Holocaust possible. Goeth represents random and senseless killing: "He has no set rules." Within the film, he represents violence for its own sake. At times, Spielberg's Holocaust images are generic crystallizing images borrowed from prior texts and films that become a reservoir of intertextual resources. In a way, Spielberg's film depends on evoking memories from our past knowledge of Holocaust texts— including many in this study such as Wiesel's *Night*, Hersey's *The Wall*, Levi's *Survival in Auschwitz*—even while providing in his graphic images vital vignettes for those whose prior reading does not include either Keneally's novel or major Holocaust narratives. For example, the story of Helen Hirsch recalls *Sophie's Choice*, where Sophie is a house servant to the camp commandant. To be sure, Spielberg is recalling how Keneally's narrator's alludes to *Sophie's Choice*: "In planet Auschwitz, where the Schindler women moved as warily, as full of dread as any space travelers, Rudolf Höss ruled as founder, builder, presiding genius. Readers of William Styron's novel *Sophie's Choice* encountered him as the master of Sophie—a very different sort of master than Amon was to Helen Hirsch; a more detached, mannerly, and sane man; yet still the unflagging priest of that cannibal province" (317).

The juxtaposition of parallel scenes is a crucial Spielberg technique. At times he segues into two or three parallel thematic incidents that pertain to his two major figures and seem to be going on almost simultaneously; of course we realize that neither Schindler nor Goeth can be in two places at the same time. For example, we have Goeth and Schindler in their roles of heavy drinkers and womanizers. Thus we see the juxtaposition of Goeth's abusive behavior to Helen Hirsch with both a Jewish wedding and Schindler at a nightclub flirting with a singer. Goeth visits Helen Hirsch while she is wearing a sheer nightgown—an odd garment to be wearing, we think, considering her knowledge of Goeth's compulsive lust—that shows her nipples. Spielberg's camera juxtaposes Schindler's seduction by a nightclub singer with Goeth touching Helen. Goeth is torn between wanting to touch her and demonizing her. Echoing Shylock, he asks, "Has not a Jew eyes?," but he recoils from kissing her and physically beats her for supposedly seducing him. The scene crystallizes the often bizarre attraction that Jewish women held for Nazis—including the sometime Nazi, Schindler. As Amon almost kisses Helen, the camera immediately shifts to Schindler kissing a singer (who is not Jewish). Then, no sooner do we see the traditional glass broken at a Jewish wedding than we see Amon tearing apart his basement in a violent rage after he decides not to molest Helen.

Continuing the focus on heterosexual relations in a bizarre world marked by arbitrary racial distinctions, the scene shifts to Schindler's birthday celebration; he is presented with a birthday cake by his grateful Jewish workers, and he kisses a somewhat unwilling Jewish girl. For this trespass, Schindler is arrested for violating racial and resettlement laws. Fixated by Helen Hirsch, Amon, Schindler's darker self, speaks for *himself* when he says: "[Jews] cast spells on him [Schindler]." When Amon offers a gratuity, he is told by a senior German officer from the film's first scene: "[Jews] don't have a future."

Finally Schindler's list of workers for Brinnlitz is the single antidote to selection. That Schindler has thrown his lot in with Jews shows that his moral education is complete. When Stern begins typing the list in black and white on a typewriter, we see Schindler approaching Germans who refuse to help him before we return to Stern's typing the list. Schindler orders Stern to include "all the children" connected with the factory on the list. As Schindler says a name, Stern types it. The camera shows Schindler delivering money, even as the typing of the list goes on. Clearly, the word has never been more powerful, for names represent life: "How many?" he asks; Stern responds, "Six hundred." He tries unsuccessfully to get financial support from the German Julius Madritsch, who had been generous in the past but who now refuses. The camera juxtaposes a close-up of Stern's face with that of Julius Madritsch. Stern suddenly realizes that Schindler is *buying* the Jews from Goeth: "The list is an absolute good. It is life." When he holds up the list, do we not think of Moses holding up the tablets—the written list of the Ten Commandments that he received from God and brought down from Mount Sinai? Continuing to expand Schindler's stature in the final third of the film, Spielberg emphasizes Schindler's legerdemain and magic, as when he gambles with Amon for Helen and wins her in a game of twenty-one. As we hear the list of names called, the camera focuses on each face; the last one is that of Helen Hirsch. In the novel, we recall, Goldberg is a scoundrel who sells places on the list and includes other pernicious and despicable Judenrat collaborators. Spielberg, we might note, is not as hard as Keneally is on Goldberg—who in the film is more a comic figure—or, indeed, as are most of our authors on the Judenrat; in the film's early scenes, the Judenrat functionaries are seen as helpless appointees.

For Spielberg, the Shoah culminates in Auschwitz; for Keneally, Auschwitz is within his story as an important tributary to Schindler's story. Spielberg uses Keneally's episode of the transport train mistakenly taking the Schindler women to Auschwitz, but he expands on the novel's Auschwitz pages so as to make the graphic Auschwitz scenes central to his film epic. The last section of the film begins by crystallizing the Auschwitz experience and showing us the experience suffered by so many others outside of the tiny group of fortunate Schindler Jews. Recalling the motif of a list as text with overwhelming consequences, Schindler's women are sent in error to Auschwitz because of "a paper-work mistake." We first hear the story of Auschwitz from a young woman, a story that anticipates these later Auschwitz images. As the Schindler women's train approaches Auschwitz, a little child puts his hand in a cutting motion across his throat to signal danger. (Spielberg is referring perhaps to Lanzmann's *Shoah* where Poles take great credit for giving this fruitless warning.) We see Schindler's Jewish women in camp having their hair cut and stripping under the eyes of Nazi guards; the camera graphically depicts their anxiety in the "delousing" area as, in a state of terror, they await the gas. As the shower heads release water instead of gas, we see the women's pathetic exaltation and better understand the pure sadism of the Nazi torture system.

The Schindler women return to their barracks, and we see smoke and falling ash. The camera shows us ashes that look like snowflakes, and we recall the ashes on Schindler's car when the Germans burned dead bodies at Płaszów. We see another selection: "How old are you, mother?" to which a woman answers by hopefully proclaiming, "We are Schindler Jews." The camera switches to Schindler talking to the camp Commandant. Even the Commandant's eyes are shaded; as if he were lurking in dark shadows, only his mouth is lighted. Schindler puts diamonds on the Commandant's table: "In coming months, we shall need portable wealth, " to which the Commandant responds as he takes them, "I am not comfortable with them on the table. . . . I'll cut you three hundred units from the new shipment." Schindler: "I want these." The Commandant: "You shouldn't get hung up on names. It creates paperwork." Then we see another *list* of women being read by an Auschwitz official. But even as the Schindler women are being loaded to leave Auschwitz, the armed German guards take some of their children and struggle to restrain their screaming mothers. Schindler intervenes, taking hold of the girl in glasses based on the Dressner girl in the novel: "These fingers polish the insides of forty-five-millimeter shell cases."

In the film, Schindler gives up his womanizing. He not only returns to the Catholic Church, but assures his wife, "No doorman or maitre d' will ever mistake you again." (In the book he still frolics with women.) Now living with him, his wife works in the factory clinic. The factory produces nothing, but Schindler maintains the factory. "Brinnlitz maintained its prisoners' lives by a series of stunts so rapid that they were nearly magical. To tell the strict truth though, Brinnlitz, both as a prison and as a manufacturing enterprise, was itself, of its nature and in a literal sense, the one sustained, dazzling, integral confidence trick" (340). In the film when Stern tells him that there is rumor that he has recalibrated machines to produce bad shells, Schindler responds: "We'll buy shells and pass them off as ours."

Schindler's characteristic *chutzpah* becomes almost magical, as if it were a biblical figure who can create miracles and suspend history. Not only does he, in the aforementioned scene, get a train *out of Auschwitz* by claiming the women are "essential workers," but he sustains the Brinnlitz factory for seven months by his legerdemain—although he makes no shells and runs out of money. When Schindler speaks to the Nazis at his factory, he intimidates them: "If you shoot without cause, you go to prison, I get paid. . . . Guards are no longer allowed on the factory floor without my permission." When the announcement of unconditional surrender on radio is heard, Schindler calls the German guards to the factory and speaks to them together with his workers: "Tomorrow you'll begin the process of looking for survivors. In most cases you won't find them. We survived. Think of yourselves. Thank Stern. I am a criminal. At five after midnight I shall flee." To the guards, he says: "You can dispose of these people, or you can return to your families as men, not murderers." The guards' leaving after his eloquent speech testifies once again to Schindler's charisma and the power of his personality. Isn't this another Schindler miracle?

After the Germans surrender, Spielberg wonderfully juxtaposes moments of silence with the mourner's Kaddish; we see gold taken willingly from a grateful worker's mouth and a gold ring being made. Then the camera switches to Schindler's wife packing for their imminent departure. The workers take him to his car, and he gives orders to distribute cloth, vodka, and cigarettes. The rabbi presents him with an explanatory letter for his potential captors, and Stern presents him with the gold ring—an ironic reminder of his original gold Nazi pin—that says "Whoever saves one life saves the world"; after Schindler drops it and picks it up, he is deeply moved: "I could have gotten more out. If I made more. I threw away so much," to which Stern responds: "There will be generations for what you did." Not fully rational, Schindler claims his car could have bought ten more Jews; even his Nazi pin would have saved one. For the first time, he collapses in tears, and the Schindler Jews come forward to hug him. Schindler and his wife get into the car—we see Schindler's face in the dark—and he leaves Brinnlitz driven by a single prisoner in stripes.

It is worth noting how Spielberg changes the conclusion to emphasize Schindler's humanity and narrow the distance between viewer and character. While in the film, Schindler dramatically breaks down as he leaves, in the book, we recall, he puts the ring on his finger after making his final speech. The speech is taken down in shorthand for posterity, perhaps to create a text on which he could base his plea for leniency. In the book, a group of eight volunteer prisoners accompany him, and he departs in prison clothes. Indeed, in the book we are told that to prevent his departure, "Someone, frightened by the idea of Oskar's departure, had cut the wiring [under the hood of his Mercedes]" (375).

One of the film's great mythopoeic moments is when a Russian soldier arrives to find the Schindler Jews sleeping on the ground, and, articulating generations of the Jews' plight as marginalized denizens of Europe, says, "Don't go East, they hate you there. Don't go West," before asking "Isn't there a town over there?" (While he is identified in the novel but not the film as a Jew, we assume from the mixture of insouciance, worldliness, and cynicism in the aforementioned words that he is a Jew.) As Schindler's Jews start walking forward, they become erect, resolute, proud, and attractive; we realize that the "town" is Israel, the Zionist homeland of the Hebrew song "Jerusalem the Golden" that we are hearing.

As they walk, we see the man who gave gold from his teeth for the ring; we see new faces, rather than the expected faces such as Stern or the rabbi, as if to stress the anonymity of those walking. Spielberg switches to Amon being hanged in Cracow; his last words are "Heil Hitler." He had, we are told by the written text that appears on the screen as a kind of epilogue, been in a sanitarium. After we see Amon's hanging, the camera switches to the scene in which Schindler's Jews put stones on his grave to commemorate his death. In the closing scene in Israel, in color rather than black and white, we see the aging Mrs. Schindler, although we know that the Schindler marriage broke up. She is a kind of metonymy for the missing Schindler. From the film's continuing written epilogue we learn that Schindler failed at his marriage and business and that in 1958 he became one of the Righteous Gentiles. We see the "Schindler Jews" gathered together; each of the Schindler Jews whose stories we have seen is accompanied by the actor playing his or her part. We learn from the text on the screen that there are 6,000 heirs of Schindler Jews, 2,000 more than all the Jews left in Poland.

The stones that we see at the end of Schindler's List are the paving of a road made from Jewish gravestones in the Płaszów labor camp, the campsite that had been a Jewish cemetery. Made from Jewish graves, they are a moving visual elegy that evokes the world now dead, but alive in Israel's collective memory. We recall the Prologue of Keneally's novel: "When level with the Administration Building, the Adler moved onto a prison road paved with Jewish gravestones. The campsite had been till two years before a Jewish cemetery. Commandant Goeth, who claimed to be a poet, had used in the construction of his camp whatever metaphors were to hand. This metaphor of shattered gravestones ran the length of the camp, splitting it in two, but did not extend eastward to the villa occupied by Commandant Goeth himself" (16). Are the gravestones not Spielberg's final image, etched indelibly on our memories of the destruction of the rich Jewish culture of Europe? In a sense, this image of the shattered cultural history of

European Jewry serves as an epilogue not only to his film—a film that brings together the *topos* of prior Holocaust texts—but to my study of Holocaust narratives.

PART THREE

MYTH, PARABLE, AND FABLE

CHAPTER TEN

SCHWARZ-BART'S MYTHOPOEIC AND HISTORICAL HUMANISM: *THE LAST OF THE JUST*

André Schwarz-Bart's *The Last of the Just* (1959), unlike our other novels, places the Holocaust within a diachronic history. The narrator traces the history of a Lamed-Vovnick back to the Middle Ages. He speaks as if he were a rabbi reciting a Jewish legend: "Rivers of blood have flowed, columns of smoke have obscured the sky, but surviving all these dooms, the tradition has remained inviolate down to our own time. According to it, the world reposes upon thirty-six Just Men, the Lamed-Vov, indistinguishable from simple mortals; often they are unaware of their station. But if just one of them were lacking, the sufferings of mankind would poison even the souls of the newborn, and humanity would suffocate with a single cry. For the Lamed-Vov are the hearts of the world multiplied, and into them, as into one receptacle, pour all our griefs" (4-5). The Just Man feels more intensely and compassionately than other men. As the Just Man Mordecai tells his wife Judith, "[H]e himself doesn't know, isn't aware that his heart is bleeding away. He knows it is simply life passing through him" (57).

Recalling the way the Bible intermingles the pedestrian and the sublime moments when God's majesty and lessons to humankind are revealed, the novel intermingles the colloquial with moments of height-ened significance in terms of the teleology of the Hasidic legend: "Our eyes register the light of dead stars. A biography of my friend Ernie could easily be set in the second quarter of the twentieth century, but the true history of Ernie Levy begins much earlier, toward the year 1000 of our era, in the old Anglican city of York. More precisely, on March 11, 1185" (3). One Lamed-Vov will always be a descendent of Rabbi Yom Tov Levy who suffered "solitary agony" by killing his followers as they awaited slaughter. But we should note the ambiguity of such martyrdom—the reenacting of a Massada temperament, which has an aspect of passivity. And passivity recurs in the legends of Just Men throughout the text, even when childhood play—acting out of anti-Semitic cultural assumptions that Jews crucified Christ—results in the violent punishment of Ernie Levy, the last of the line of Levy Just Men who eventually goes to the gas chamber as a "Christ-killer." Indeed the legend is always held at an ironic distance as a discursive formation, a hypothesis that does not quite work as a necessary and sufficient explanation of what happened to Jews in Europe through the second millennium. While our other novels in this study establish a certain normalcy to Jewish life prior to the worst days of the Nazis, albeit one on which pogroms and prejudice proleptically punctuate the coming of the Holocaust, Schwarz-Bart writes a history of recurring atrocities all over Europe.

Schwarz-Bart writes in a European tradition that sees events in terms of their historical context. In his *Mimesis: The Representation of Reality in Western Literature*, Erich Auerbach uses what he called "historical relativism" to examine how history is a synchronic and diachronic process that shapes individual behavior and community values. Like Vico, whom he admires, Auerbach perceives history as a dramatic and dialectic process; for Auerbach, however, unlike Vico, history is not shaped by immutable laws extrinsic to history's unfolding. Like Auerbach, Schwarz-Bart prefers an inductive method in which he and his characters interpret from their own understanding rather than a deductive historiography that relies on applying *a priori* categories to historical events. Schwarz-Bart dramatizes a grim pattern of repetition in the form of virulent anti-Semitism, and he locates this pattern at every cultural stage and in every country of Europe.

As the novel moves toward the present, Schwarz-Bart seems to replace the historiography of chronicle with the nominalism and specifics of the realistic novel. But Schwarz-Bart is less interested in realism than in rendering the significance of events in terms of the cultural context in which they took place. What interests him is the complex response of individuals to crucial events that have confusing explanations and multiple implications and the intersection of individual experiences with the maelstrom of history. Thus he sustains his study of character in terms of their emotional and psychological response to events. As his novel unfolds, Schwarz-Bart displaces myth with history, Platonic stress on immutable laws with Aristotelian focus on the specifics of dramatic action, and panoptic visions with the fabric of individual experience and feeling.

Schwarz-Bart's novel begins with the legend of the Just Men, and traces the history of a family of Lamed Vovnicks named Levy culminating with the story of the man his narrator calls "my friend" Ernie Levy. Until Ernie's grandfather, Mordecai, the family chronicle is a historical prologue. After witnessing, in the years of the Russian Revolution and the world war, the killing of his three brothers in a pogrom at the hands of the Cossacks at Zemycock where the Levys had lived for generations, Benjamin, the only surviving son, goes to Germany, where he encounters the Depression. The history of the Levys is intermingled with twentieth-century history, including the migration of Russian and Polish Jews to the west. When the novel reaches the second quarter of the twentieth century, it begins ominously to look forward, not only by emphasizing rail transport, as when Benjamin moves from Berlin to Stillenstadt, but also in the narrator's comments: "Later, it required old age and, above all, the approach of violent death in the concentration camp to make Benjamin decide to express his love to his wife" (124). Juxtaposed to the Jews' desire to retain family and private life are the inexorable forces of history that they cannot contain and that are overwhelming them. After the aforementioned violence towards Ernie, based on the Jews' supposed responsibilities for Christ's crucifixion, the narrator comments, "[T]he act of aggression against Ernie took its place in the series of anti-Semitic acts that announced Hitler's rise to power" (140). After Hitler comes to power, the narrator at the end of chapter three ironically writes: "It was the year 1933 after the coming of Jesus, the beautiful herald of impossible love" (140). Chapter four opens with the Jew's anxious and pervasive fear of violence that dominates the life

of Jews in Germany in the face of anti-Semitic demonstrations and the
continuous threat of violence.

In chapter one Schwarz-Bart tries to re-create the language of
unsophisticated Polish Jewish peasants. Schwarz-Bart's narrative voice
renders the conflict between psyche and God without interior monologues. The Just Men are often simple folk, such as Chaim Levy, who
writes simple tales for children, and his idiot son Brother Beast, who has
moments of cruelty. The Just Man appellation mysteriously descends on
a Levi.

Ernie, the last of the Just Men, is a witness to major events of the
Holocaust in Poland, Germany, and France, and ends up in the gas
chambers of Auschwitz. As the novel moves into the twentieth
century, the language of realism replaces the parabolic language of
legend; Ernie remains a character, like Woolf's Orlando, who chame-
leonlike changes identity in response to history and circumstances
even while retaining his capacity to feel with extraordinary intensity
and compassion. At times, especially towards the denouement, the
narrator renders Ernie's feelings in prophetic terms and biblical
rhythms, while at other times the narrator maintains a diachronic and
synchronic historical sense: "The Germans reached such perfection in
Vernichtungswissenschaft—the science of massacre, the art of extermination—that for a majority of the condemned the ultimate revelation
came only in the gas chambers" (351).

The Just Man, as Ernie's grandfather Mordecai puts it, "senses all the
evil rampant on earth, and he takes it into his heart!" (174). The
patriarch Mordecai passes on compassion to him; Ernie is "admitted to
the banal yet extraordinary world of the soul and sniffing out its secret
miseries, trusted blindly to that small, ridiculous key that the patriarch
had passed on to him—compassion" (177). Something in Ernie's soul
finds fighting back anathema. Silent defiance—passive-aggressive
behavior—is something else as when he refuses to sing for the Nazi
teacher Herr Geek. When he is attacked by schoolboys he finds no
reference "to any such phantasmagoria in the Legend of the Just Men"
(233). Yet he does fight back when they try to undress him and "feel[s]
hate for the first time" (236). He is called a "dog" and lashes out, biting
his oppressors. But he cannot live with the discovery of his own
animality: "The beast in his heart was roaring so horribly that he was

afraid he would die on the spot" (236). He then feels the emptiness of despair and moves toward suicide. After he feels annihilated he begins to kill insects obsessively, beginning with a ladybug, and—in a parody of the Germans' megalomania and moral cannibalism—to eat his kill: "How could he have pretended to those heights, to the even greater heights of the Just Man—he, a puny, rapacious insect; he, crawling on a heavy, enormous belly swarming with its insect nourishment . . . ? *I was not a Just Man, I was nothing*" (242). In 1934 he seems to have committed suicide as a child—at a time when the ironic narrator tells us "hundreds and hundreds of little German-Jewish schoolboys came up for their examinations in suicide, and hundreds of them passed" (255)—in response to humiliation of the Jews, only to be reborn into another life. The narrator makes clear that the first death of Ernie is part of the hundreds of childhood suicides in 1934: "So the first death of Ernie Levy takes its place among the statistics beside hundreds of similar (though more irrevocable) deaths" (255).

Yet Ernie has another life to live. As the narrator moves from Poland to Germany to France, Ernie is a specific individual and an allegorized *Every Jew*. After learning upon his return from the front that his plan to save his family by enlistment did not work, he cultivates the life of the body and lives in sensual gratification; he savors "a bestiality that was aboriginal and therefore his own" (294): "Certain people (whose testimony we cannot trust absolutely) claim to have noticed that *the fatter the late Ernie Levy's paunch grew, the thinner grew his face.* And his companions accused him of chewing stiffly, even sadly" (290).

Ernie perceives the horror of the Holocaust in metaphysical terms; although he remains and must remain as a Just Man, a simple soul, it is the narrator who renders Ernie's perceptions. He learns that "the soul is the slave of life," and that the metaphysical is a function of the physical: "Hell, Ernie discovered in the infirmary, the real Hell, is simply the vision of a hell, nothing more than that, and to struggle in Hell, he came to understand as he watched the fights break out around the garbage cans that served them as cooking pots, is to play the Devil's game" (352).

Notwithstanding their humanity, a troubling aspect of the Just Men to a contemporary reader is their passivity and acceptance. While Schwarz-Bart's novel takes a more complex view of the Lamed-Vov than is usually noticed, and one that dramatizes in its plot a more inclusive and passionate view of the Holocaust than the narrator's occasionally steep and icy historical perspective, one wishes at times for a narrator who might be more critical of the Jewish acceptance of an inevitable cycle of persecution and deprivation and less willing to place Ernie's fate within that cycle.

Let us turn to the denouement. Ernie, as Just Man, comes into his own when he responds to the misery of others; in small ways he brings comfort. His presence is a catalyst for returning others to their humanity; a man from whom Ernie seeks a gift for Golda—after he finds her emaciated, deformed and miserable in the camp—teaches him: "'It's very important to give'—he hesitated, his smile widened—'when you have nothing'" (357).

Schwarz-Bart's novel graphically anticipates the relentless documentation of Lanzmann's *Shoah*. Ernie is caught up in the efficiency of the Nazi transport system, a system that the narrator demonizes as a monstrous prehistoric creature: "Ernie, arching up on his elbows, again discovered—without believing it—the fantastic darkness of the freight car, which seemed to be rolling by itself in a clacking of wheels and axles, delivered up companionless to the locomotive, an antediluvian beast breathing fire, dragging to its lair the hundred or so bodies stretched out on the jolting floor" (361-362). Schwarz-Bart's narrator renders the graphic horror of the transport system, the ravages of dysentery and excrement on the trains—"a gaseous ring of decomposing entrails" (367)—and the stacks of corpses.

Ernie's wedding dream sustains him, but finally on the train to the death camp, he can no longer dream. The Holocaust reduces humans, climate, machines to an interchangeable level: winds become voices become dust become children become cement slabs become promenade: "Gusts of wind like human voices raised black dust from the slag gravel that carpeted the camp. There were only a few children in front of the dormitory for the 'normal' prisoners, running around on the cement slab with their mufflers flapping; the slab was the internees' authorized promenade" (354). Does not this rhetorical process anticipate the metamorphoses of men into ashes? Words lose their nominalistic distinction, their specifying and distinguishing function. When "the apocalyptic beast visits the Jews to destroy them," the beast is the materiality of evil that renders irrelevant the moral capacity of language:

"When the fourth night fell on the chaos of tangled bodies—a Polish night squatting on their smashed souls like some fantastic beast against which some of the adults were still struggling, blowing on their hands of rubbing frostbitten limbs—no complaint, no protest, no lament issued from the children's half open mouths" (366).

In Lanzmann's epic *Shoah*, we recall that the survivor Abraham Bomba had insisted that *dreaming* kept him and others alive. On the transport train, Ernie encourages children to believe that they are *dreaming* rather than actually living their terror: "'All this,' Ernie said—the children were hanging on his words—'is because you believe in this train and everything that's happening, and they don't really exist'" (363). Ernie offers the hope of the kingdom of Israel even though he *knows* the truth. Finally his voice is still; he can no longer speak; drained of words, he weeps blood, "And wiping off the tears of blood that furrowed his cheeks, he turned away from the girl to hide from her the death of the Jewish people, which was written clearly, he knew, in the flesh of his face" (369). Throughout Ernie has been associated with blood; for Ilse, his German girl friend: "The Jewish boy's eyes were like two black cherries set into the white flesh of his cheeks; she thought that if she bit lightly at them, delicate red juice would flow, the delectable blood of cherries" (215).

The camp itself is another descent into the circles of hell. The reversal of roles in which, when a Jew trips while disembarking from the train, a German shouts to his savage *dog*, [before the terrified eyes of the motionless group] '*Man, destroy that dog!*'" (368) underlines the Nazis' willed metamorphosis of Jews into animals, others, objects, ashes: "Ernie realized that they were no longer driven by hate but were going through the motions with the remote sympathy one feels for a dog, even when beating him" (368). By denigrating Jews as dogs, the Nazis have deprived Jews of their identity, their very selves; they not only use a technology that transports and gasses Jews, but they also create a linguistic system—a grammar—in which words and sentences have been deprived of their meaning and redefined in a new grotesque lexicon. As we have seen in Levi, this attack upon language is another way that the Nazis attacked the minds and dignity of their victims.

We need to ask whether Ernie is a hero or a submissive, self-deluded Jew. He leaves unoccupied France for occupied Paris and seeks out the Paris association of old Zemyock; when he sees Golda in Dancy, "He had no intention of glorifying himself, of separating himself from the humble procession of the Jewish people" (314); yet he feels cut off from God: "In spite of all his efforts he had not once been able to reach the person of God. There was an unbreachable wall between them, a wall of Jewish lamentations, rising all the way to heaven" (315). Does he not believe that "the Jewish heart must break a thousand times for the greater good of all peoples. *That* is why we were chosen, didn't you know"(324)? Do we not as resistant readers find his passivity, his turn-the-other-cheek responses, frustrating? Do we not prefer to read of the resistance of Hersey's ghetto fighters and Jews fighting with Partisans in the woods? Ernie feels infinite guilt and pity: "'Look now, my God, the oppressed weep and there is no one to console them! They are naked to the violence of their oppressors, and there is no one to console them!' And while Golda's tears flowed silently, he discovered that the dead which were already dead were happier than the living which were yet alive" (326). But he feels rather than acts, and suffers in his soul; indeed his action is *his suffering*. Finally, even though he had not been selected to be gassed, he chooses death rather than life when he goes with Golda. As he walked through the gates, "It seemed to him that an eternal silence was closing down upon the Jewish breed marching to slaughter—that no heir, no memory would supervene to prolong the silent parade of victims, no faithful dog would shudder, no bell would toll. Only the stars would remain, gliding through a cold sky" (372). Even in the gas chambers, he tries to provide comfort, shouting "with all the gentleness and all the strength of his soul, 'Breathe deeply, my lambs, and quickly!'" (373).

From the outset the narrator often speaks with bitter irony about the Jews: "But unable to resign themselves to those sinks of iniquity, the factories—where the Sabbath was not respected, and where one could not observe in their plenitude and magnificence, as at home, the six hundred and thirteen commandments of the Law—they died of hunger, piously" (34). The narrator gradually emerges from the anonymity of objectivity and focuses on Ernie; yet as he recounts the gruesome horrors of the destruction of the European Jews, his focus is on the dialogue between Ernie, his modern Job, and the ineluctable web of history. He begins some sections of chapter six, entitled "The Dog," with dates: "On November 6, 1938," "On November 11, 1938" (262, 271). The narrator alternately widens and narrows his lens, moving from a hawklike to a microscopic perspective to capture the Holocaust. Thus he satirizes Mordecai's—Ernest's grandfather's—view that everything happens according to God's plan, and stresses the way hope turns to dust. He recalls a ship of Jewish children sunk by the British as the ship approached Palestine. He recalls how Ernie enlists in the French army to give his family a French identity and to protect them, he thinks naively, from the camps. By taking on the voice of an historian gathering the record of the unspeakable, while recovering evidence from the scant sources that remain, the narrator gives specificity to the anonymous and rescues the human from the statistical.

If the narrator empathetically feels the terrible burden of his tale, isn't it because he is—perhaps—a Just Man? He begins the last section of chapter eight, the book's final section, when Ernie is transported and gassed, with "I am so weary that my pen can no longer write" (370). After Ernie's death at Auschwitz the narrator returns to the obsequies of the opening epigraph and provides a Mourner's Kaddish for the anonymous millions:

> And so it was for millions, who turned from *Luftmenschen* into *Luft*. I shall not translate. So this story will not finish with some tomb to be visited in memoriam. For the smoke that rises from crematoriums obeys physical laws like any other: the particles come together and disperse according to the wind that propels them. . . .
>
> And praised. *Auschwitz.* Be. *Maidanek.* The Lord. *Treblinka.* And praised. *Buchenwald.* Be. *Mauthausen.* The Lord. *Belzec.* And praised. *Sobibor.* Be. *Chelmno.* The Lord. *Ponary.* And praised. *Theresienstadt.* Be. *Warsaw.* The Lord. *Vilna.* And praised. *Skarzysko.* Be. *Bergen-Belsen.* The Lord. *Janow.* And praised. *Dora.* Be. *Neuengamme.* The Lord. *Pustkow.* And praised. . . .

> Yes, at times one's heart could break in sorrow. But often too, preferably in the evening, I can't help thinking that Ernie Levy, dead six million times, is still alive somewhere, I don't know where. . . . Yesterday, as I stood in the street trembling in despair, rooted

to the spot, a drop of pity fell from above upon my face. But there was no breeze in the air, no cloud in the sky. . . . There was only a presence. (374)

We recall that Ernie has died before from suicide and has been miraculously reborn. This not only stresses his allegorical identity but suggests that the gas chambers might not be the end of his soul. That the soul survives in the narrator demonstrates that the human remnant of European Jewry has survived to tell its tale. Has not its very telling in 1959, the year of the novel's publication, affirmed its rebirth?

CHAPTER ELEVEN

AHARON APPELFELD'S PARABLES

I

Aharon Appelfeld was born in Romania in Jadova, Bukovina on February 16, 1932. As a nine-year-old he escaped from the Transnistria camp and hid in the forests until the Russian army took him along as they marched west. He recalls how he was educated in an assimilated home that valued German culture: "I grew up in an assimilated Jewish home where German was treasured. German was considered not only a language but also a culture, and the attitude toward German culture was virtually religious. All around us lived masses of Jews who spoke Yiddish, but in our house Yiddish was absolutely forbidden. I grew up with the feeling that anything Jewish was blemished. From my earliest childhood my gaze was directed at the beauty of non-Jews. They were blond and tall and behaved naturally. They were cultured, and when they didn't behave in a cultured fashion, at least they behaved naturally" (*Beyond Despair* 77). Only in Israel, to which he emigrated after the Holocaust, did Appelfeld become interested in the spiritual aspect of Judaism.

Clearly Appelfeld has his own work in mind when he writes in an essay entitled "After the Holocaust": "There was a need for some kind of unmediated relation, simple and straightforward, to those horrible events in order to speak about them in artistic terms" (Lang 91). During the war, Appelfeld claims that Jews erased and repressed their past because it was too painful: "Memory was our enemy" (quoted in Boxer 6). After the war for him it was nature—"contact with the trees in the forest, with the moist earth, the straw"—that restored his memory; restoration of memory was "like reattaching something to your body organs which were cut off" (quoted in Boxer 6).

The childlike simplicity of his tales reflects his view that children best understand the immediacy but not the importance of the events they observe. An escapee from the camps who spent two years wandering around the forest without his parents, Appelfeld writes in part from the perspective of one of the children who survived: "Ultimately the children did not absorb the full horror, only that portion of it which children could take in. Children lack a sense of chronology, of comparison with the past" ("After the Holocaust," in Lang 90). We might understand the perspective in *Badenheim 1939* (1980) as that of an innocent child gradually experiencing what is puzzling and disillusioning. And are not the *Maus* books in the same vein? And the poems and drawings of the children transported to the camps, an exhibit of which I saw in 1995 in Prague, show how children reduce events to their essentials. Their geometric forms, thick lines, and intrusive shapes speak for the children's anxiety, dread, and experience of the unspeakable.

In "After the Holocaust," Appelfeld remarks, "The closer death came to us, the greater was our refusal to admit its existence. . . . Everyone held onto his little hopes—mostly trivial matters" (Lang 85). Badenheim speaks to the banality of life in a bath resort as the Holocaust—in the form of the Sanitary Police—begins to intrude, makes inroads, establishes its dominance, and finally overwhelms the residents and visitors. In a sense Badenheim is Jewish Europe and the visitors are the agents of death. Appelfeld's characters live, he implies, like all of us, an illusion; the oasis of a resort that builds a wall against the exigencies of life is a reason for vacation—for vacating our daytime, routinized selves. Like *Maus*, Appelfeld's parable suggests Kafka's parables. Indeed, Appelfeld has acknowledged his deep debt to Kafka and what he calls Kafka's "courage of the absurd":

> I discovered Kafka here in Israel during the 1950s and as a
> writer he was close to me from my first contact. He spoke to me
> in my mother tongue, German, not the German of the Germans
> but the German of the Hapsburg Empire, of Vienna, Prague, and

Czernowicz, with its special tone, which by the way, the Jews worked hard to create.

To my surprise he spoke to me not only in my mother tongue, but also in another language which I knew intimately, the language of the absurd. I knew what he was talking about. It wasn't a secret language for me and I didn't need any explications. I had come from the camps and the forests, from a world that embodied the absurd, and nothing in that world was foreign to me. What was surprising was this: How could a man who had never been there know so much, in precise detail, about that world?

Other surprising discoveries followed: the marvel of his objective style, his preference for action over interpretation, his clarity and precision, the broad, comprehensive view laden with humor and irony. And, as if that weren't enough, another discovery showed me that behind the mask of placelessness and homelessness in his work stood a Jewish man, like me, from a half-assimilated family, whose Jewish values had lost their content, and whose inner space was barren and haunted. (*Beyond Despair* 63)

With its seeming lack of entailment between sentences and discontinuity of narrative elements that deflate plot expectations and cinematic zoom lens, the beginning of *Badenheim 1939* suggests Kafka's "The Hunter Gracchus." The detached matter-of-fact voice with which the speaker presents the inconceivable and the careful tracing of the transformation of the Badenheim population—both hosts and guests—into prisoners not only suggest *Metamorphosis* and Hasidic tales, but anticipates Spiegelman's *Maus*. Appelfeld's exaggerations—his illuminating distortions and cartoon imagination—suggest the paintings of such German and Austrian Expressionists as Otto Dix, George Grosz, Egon Schiele, and Gustav Klimt.

Appelfeld chose to write in Hebrew, the language he learned after arriving in Israel: "I learned Hebrew by dint of much effort. It is a difficult language, severe and ascetic. Its ancient basis is the proverb from the *Mishna*: 'Silence is a fence for wisdom.' The Hebrew language taught me how to think, to be sparing with words, not to use too many adjectives, not to intervene too much, and not to interpret." (*Beyond Despair* 71-72). He began to write about the Holocaust when few in

Israel wanted to hear about the subject: "[F]or a large number of Israeli Zionists," as Michael André Bernstein notes, "the entire experience of Diaspora Jewry, and even more so the Shoah, was a source of profound national embarrassment" (*Foregone Conclusions* 56).

Appelfeld wrote as a Jewish and Zionist writer in a country often resistant to being reminded of the Holocaust. Indeed, why, we might ask, does Appelfeld choose 35 chapters for *Badenheim 1939*? Thirty-six is the number of the Lamed-Vov, the Just Men, and his writing a book that is one chapter short may refer to Schwarz-Bart's *The Last of the Just*. At the very least, the brief, even terse chapters call attention to the missing figure from a time of faith, namely the figure of the Lamed-Vov, who can feel the suffering as the Jews are transformed from citizens to prisoners. Or is the ironic narrator—or perhaps the reader who knows what the inhabitants of Badenheim cannot know about what will happen to them and the Jews of Europe—supposed to be that figure, the thirty-sixth Lamed Vov who transcends the thirty-five chapters?

Appelfeld's Badenheim is a resort for emancipated Austrian Jews of some means, Jews who have long forgotten their Eastern European roots. Remember that in 1939 the *Anschluss* had already taken place, but Appelfeld is reticent about the historical context. While the Hebrew title, *Badenhaym 'Ir Nofesh* translates as *Badenheim, Holiday Resort* and has no date, the reader understands that he is referring to the quiescence of Austrian Jews in the 1930s until after the German annexation of Austria in 1938. As Philip Roth remarks to Appelfeld in a piece entitled "A Conversation with Philip Roth" that is reprinted in *Beyond Despair*, "Your reticence as a historian, when combined with the historical perspective of a knowing reader, accounts for the peculiar impact your work has— for the power that emanates from stories that are told through such very modest means. Also, dehistoricizing the events and blurring the background, you probably approximate the disorientation felt by people who were unaware that they were on the brink of a cataclysm" (*Beyond Despair* 65). Badenheim is not merely a place where comfortable Jews take their vacation, but a state of mind, a state of moral indolence. Like another tale of moral illness, Mann's *Death in Venice*, which it surely recalls, *Badenheim 1939* begins in spring and ends in fall. Like Mann's Venice there is something dissolute in Badenheim; Badenheim is infected by moral illness: "There was a secret intoxication in the air.

Respectable businessmen did not bring their wives here, but anyone who had breathed the air and been infected could not keep away" (21).

Appelfeld does not dramatize the violence of the perpetrators in his novels. We see only minor functionaries rather than SS savagery. Yet, as Michael André Bernstein has noted, Appelfeld blurs the two quite separate periods before and after the *Anschluss*: "The two principal epochs, although chronologically close, are quite different moments, both historically and chronologically; collapsing them makes utterly unbelievable the consciousness of Appelfeld's characters, because it endows them with expectations and reactions completely inappropriate to their new circumstances" (*Foregone Conclusions* 65). But perhaps this is Appelfeld's point—namely that Jews need to be vigilant and suspect of particular historical circumstances that make assimilation seem feasible. Bernstein criticizes Appelfeld's "lack of penetration into the lived moral world" of his characters (*Foregone Conclusions* 67). But is Bernstein forgetting that in allegory and parable the consciousness of characters takes a back seat to the lessons the author wishes to inculcate? The ironic discrepancy between our knowledge of what is happening and the characters' obliviousness is the point of the novel. Yet we need to take seriously Bernstein's concern that Appelfeld's disdain for the Austrian Jews' self-immersion, assimilation, and collaboration in their destruction reinforces the view of those who blame the victims. As Bernstein puts it, "Beneath the melancholy of its coolly appalled tone, the deeper irony of a work like *Badenheim 1939* is that while it finds a new idiom in which to narrate the margins of catastrophe, it also finds itself entrapped in the very explanations it deems unacceptable as soon as they are spelled out more clearly" (*Foregone Conclusions* 71-72).

Mann's Venice is infected with cholera victims; the city refuses to acknowledge the epidemic and the ill refuse to recognize their plight. From the German perspective, Badenheim is infected with Jews who refuse to recognize that they are victims, but the city is willing to act on its diagnosis. The ironically named Sanitation Department—Appelfeld's euphemism for the Nazis—has the hygienic responsibility of addressing the illness. Just as in *Death in Venice*, in which Venice was a solution to Aschenbach's problem of repression and self-control, Poland becomes the alternative to the constricting and increasingly controlled life that the Jews of Badenheim lead as they become imprisoned and oppressed by the Sanitation Department. The Sanitation Department puts up barbed wire and turns the resort into a concentration camp. In the guise of sending the Jews to Poland, the Department sends them to death camps.

Appelfeld's text does not provide the expected historical context in *Badenheim 1939*. In the Roth interview, he notes: "Historical explanations have been alien to me ever since I became aware of myself as an artist. And the Jewish experience in the Second World War was not 'historical.' We came into contact with archaic mythical forces, a kind of dark subconscious the meaning of which we did not know, nor do we know it to this day" (*Beyond Despair* 66). He wants to write alternatives to chronological histories and Holocaust testimonies: "If you read the many collections of testimony written about the Holocaust, you will immediately see that they are actually repressions, meant to put events in proper chronological order. They are neither introspection nor anything resembling introspection, but rather the careful weaving together of many external facts in order to veil the inner truth. The survivor himself was the first, in the weakness of his own hand and in the denial of his own experiences, to create the strange plural voice of the memoirist, which is nothing but externalization upon externalization, so that what is within will never be revealed" (*Beyond Despair* 14).

Thus his texts are his parabolic response to those of whom he speaks of enveloping the Holocaust "in a kind of mystical aura, intangible, which must be discussed as a kind of experience that cannot be expressed in words, but rather in prolonged silence" ("After the Holocaust," Lang 90-91). He is influenced by the caricatures and illuminating distortions of Sholem Aleichem and others in the Yiddish folk tradition for the serious purpose of revealing how underlying the apparent worldliness of Badenheim denizens is the innocence and naivete of the *shtetls* that leaves the Jews unequipped for the Nazis of the Sanitation Department.

The Badenheim Jews, especially the guests, are not a pleasant lot. From the major who had fought in World War I and shoots himself rather than register, to the conductor whose parents had converted to Christianity, many want to be emancipated from their Jewishness, want to forget their heritage and antecedents. Another man claims not to know if his forefathers were Jewish and is puzzled when everything is taken away from him and he is taken to Badenheim. Yet even those who deny their Jewishness have to register, including those who think themselves as Austrian Jews superior to *Ostjuden*.

It is as if Badenheim *were* a shtetl, but each Jew *thinks* it is a resort where some Jews live and others visit. We might recall Appelfeld's words from *Beyond Despair*: "Rather clear childhood memories underlie *Badenheim 1939*. Every summer we, like all other petite-bourgeois families, would set out for a resort. Every summer we tried to find a restful place, where people didn't gossip in the corridors, didn't confess to one another in corners, didn't interfere with you, and, of course, didn't speak Yiddish. But every summer, as though we were being spited, we were once again surrounded by Jews, and that left a bad taste in my parents' mouths, and no small amount of anger. . . . Assimilated Jews built a structure of humanistic values and looked out on the world from it. . . . In Badenheim I tried to combine sights from my childhood with sights of the Holocaust" (*Beyond Despair* 70-71).

As Badenheim is turned into a camp, "the descendants of old Badenheim families" arrive: "The curse of the town had pursued them all these years and now it had finally caught up with them" (129). We realize that every vestige of religion has been absent until, of all things, an old rabbi appears—or rather reappears; he had officiated in "the local synagogue—or to tell the truth, the old-age home" (125). Historically, we recall that in the 1930s as the Jews become isolated and less assimilated in Germany and Austria, Jewish life thrived for a time. Emancipated Jews metamorphose into their repressed forebears. Jews begin to learn Yiddish; Samitzky begins to walk with a stoop and teach others the Yiddish that he, more easily than the others, recalls. As they lose their food and lodging—"Everything had been taken from them; it was like a bad dream"—they invent the world into which they are going (122). As the guests long for an alternative to their living hell, they imbue Poland with the same optative vision that had brought them to Badenheim. Poland now becomes the alternative space for which they long. Are they not re-creating a shtetl or victim mentality? Ironically, deportation to the East becomes their fantasy of hope and their internal metaphor for vacation. *Elsewhere* becomes *other*, an alternative to the closing circle.

Holocaust fictions and memoirs remind us that Jews did not disbelieve the way secular Jews today do. Mysticism, interwoven into the day-to-day experience of European Jewry, plays a role not only in *Badenheim 1939* but in such diverse texts as Wiesel's *Night*, Spiegelman's *Maus* books, Epstein's *King of the Jews*, Schwarz-Bart's *The Last of the Just* and Keneally's *Schindler's List*. All six authors give credence to other forms of narrative—dreams, nightmares, hallucinations, fantasies, self-serving distortions—that were alternatives to the bizarre positivism, the bogus Nazi reason and logic that created the teleology of the Final Solution and kept the Jews from understanding it. Perhaps, these authors imply, Jewish faith and imagination interfered with their logic and prevented them from seeing what was happening to them. Wiesel, trained in the cabbala, responds to the supposedly mad Madame Schlacter's proleptic dream: "Fire! Fire! . . . Jews, listen to me! I can see a fire! There are huge flames! It is a furnace! . . . Look at the fire! Flames, flames everywhere" (23). The element of mysticism that was part of European Jewry is present in Vladek Spiegelman's belief that the Torah-reading *Parshas Truma* signifies good luck for him (*Maus I. 57*).

Yet, even while recalling this lost world of faith, Appelfeld demurs from using it as an explanation for the Holocaust: "There is a tendency to speak of the Holocaust in mystical terms, to link the events to the incomprehensible, the mysterious, the insane, and the meaningless" ("After the Holocaust" 92), and he strongly objects to this tendency. Nevertheless, Trude, the wife of the pharmacist Martin in *Badenheim 1939*, possesses foresight in the prophetic tradition of seers: "Haunted by a hidden fear," her delirious dreams are more on the mark than the intellectual machinations and rationalizations of the other citizens and guests (17); her husband Martin's fear that "he was becoming infected by her hallucinations" is a fear of *knowing* (17). Among other things, *Badenheim 1939* is about a dialectical debate about optics, between ways of seeing and ways of knowing, between reason and imagination and mysticism and reality; once Martin registers Trude and himself with the Sanitation Department, once their freedom is surrendered, her hallucinations cease as if her imagination were incarcerated (79). Trude's prophetic vision recalls the beadle in the first chapter of Wiesel's *Night*: "The whole world . . . was poisoned and diseased" (9). She sees Frau Zauberblit's dead brother walking beside her.

Paradoxically, the Jews cooperate completely with their deportation, always relying on their version of reason and logic that sees a silver lining in every act of limitation and deprivation. Theirs is an optics of hope for a people who put the best face on things even while complaining. Thus, according to Frau Zauberblit, "there was nothing like [the Sanitation Department] for order and beauty" (36). Often Appelfeld takes an ironic stance towards the strain of apocalypticism and messianism that sustained some Jews during the Holocaust. When "four filthy freight cars" arrive to supposedly take them to Poland but quite clearly to death camps, Dr. Pappenheim closes the novel by remarking: "If the coaches are so dirty it must mean that we have not far to go" (175). It is as if the voice were mocking the limited powers of deduction in a nightmare world where the perverse logic of the oppressors render irrelevant the apparently reasonable logic of the victims. In their innocence, the Jews have convinced themselves once again of their coming redemption, albeit a secularized version for some: "the sky opened and light broke out of the heavens. The valley in all its glory and the hills scattered about filled with abundance, and even the trembling, leafless trees standing wretchedly at the edge of the station seemed to breathe a sigh of relief," as if the Day of Judgment had arrived and the Messiah would arrive (174). Who, we might ask, is the mysterious Peter on the last page walking "as if on an illuminated tray"? Is it the headwaiter? Is it a Christian offer of hope that proves a chimera? A reminder of the story that Peter denied Christ three times before the cock crew?

Just as Kafka's narrator adopts Gregor Samsa's perspective to depict his feelings when he awakes as a giant cockroach, Appelfeld's ingenuous narrator sees the intrusions of the Sanitation Department from the perspective of the self-indulgent Jews; self-deluded and unaware of what is really going on, they are metamorphosed from guests into prisoners and prepared for the death camps without having a clue as to their actual fate. The inability of the Jews to perceive the obvious is bitterly satirized, even while Appelfeld understands that we cannot deal with the obvious when it is so bizarre as to be incomprehensible: "The inspectors of the Sanitation Department . . . took measurements, put up fences, and planted flags. Porters unloaded rolls of barbed wire, cement pillars, and all kinds of appliances suggestive of preparations for a public celebration" (23). Or: "Estrangement, suspicion, and mistrust began to invade the town. But the people were

still preoccupied with their own affairs—the guests with their pleasures and the townspeople with their troubles" (31).

Trapped in systems of thought that used to work, the Jews have
great faith in laws and procedures: "Every committee had a board of
appeals, that was a well-known fact. No committee could simply do as
it pleased. There was a question of procedure, after all. And if the lower
courts made a mistake, then the higher courts were always there to
remedy it" (123). In *The Retreat* (1982) and *The Iron Tracks* (1991; trans.
1998), Appelfeld shows how compulsive faith in routine sustains the
illusion of normalcy.

Appelfeld crystallizes a phenomenon we see in all of our novels.
The Jews of Badenheim assume that they live in a structured world of
sense, logic, and meaning, and of course, we understand to our horror
that they do, but it is not the benevolent world of their expectations.
Ironically, as their words cease to matter to others and they are the
victims of arbitrary rules that are left unexplained, their words become
the reality to which they cling, much as children at play often take part
in an imaginative play world of their own making: "Old arguments and
forgotten conversations and slips of the tongue—nothing seemed to
disappear. They were all still there, clear as the day they were uttered"
(115-116).

Pappenheim is a Jewish Candide; speaking of the Sanitation
Department's registering of Jews, he writes: "I should say . . . that the
Sanitation Department wants to boast of its important guests and is thus
writing their names down in its Golden Book" (34). Dr. Pappenheim is
an impresario who arranges entertainment for guests. He is a self-
deluded charlatan—it is not at all clear what earns him the title of
"doctor"—who believes his own rubbish; to the aged whores, he says:
"There's room in our kingdom for all the Jews and for everyone who
wants to be a Jew too. Ours is a vast kingdom" (62). He is a kind of
Judenrat official, but what about the Sanitation Department? After all,
who else but Jews live in Badenheim? Are we to infer that they are the
Judenrat organizing the ghetto and the eventual deportations? Is it clear
whether they are Nazis or Jews or a mixture? Appelfeld, like many of the
authors we have been considering, including Keneally and Spiegelman,
is fascinated with the Jewish police and Jewish council, for they live on
a moral borderland, empowered to collaborate even while convincing

themselves that they can save their own lives, their families—and, in some cases, others.

II

Appelfeld's *The Age of Wonders* (1978) is divided into two parts. The first part begins before the boy's twelfth birthday in the late 1930s and the second part takes place in 1965. Each part revolves around a handful of crystallizing events, encounters with the outside world— often in the form of odd personalities—that have historical and personal significance. The first part is narrated by a precocious young man who observes the gradual effects of anti-Semitism on his family until they are deported; his father is a well-known Austrian writer who disdains the Jewish bourgeoisie and prides himself on being an Austrian. Even more than *Badenheim 1939*, *The Age of Wonders* is a scathing satire of Jews who would ignore their heritage and disdain their less sophisticated fellows. The encroaching shadows—a recurring image—toll the days of Jewish presence in Austria coming to an end, even as they place the boy in a kind of Jewish half-life. Gradually, in Part One, Appelfeld peels away the layers of pretense and self-delusion that enwrap the nameless boy's family. He reveals a world where objects—as in the strange cosmos of Bruno Schulz— have as much vitality as people. Recall the summer before the first train ride when, as a boy, he became aware of anti-Semitism: "Abandoned objects had lain scattered on the deserted banks, and the people too had seemed forsaken in the silence. There were lots of fish, small and plump, peeping up from the riverbed in mute despair. They swam slowly and bitterly, with a restlessness that infected me too" (3-4).

The second part, told by an omniscient narrator, examines the man—his name now revealed as Bruno (could Appelfeld have had Bruno Schulz in mind even though he disclaims Schulz as a major influence?)—returning home from Jerusalem many years later for a visit to the Austrian village of his birth. It is 1965, and he finds only vestigial remnants of the Jewish community and the world he had known. Book One does not have a separate title (nor do the chapter headings), but Book Two is entitled, "Many Years Later When Everything Was Over";

"everything" includes the Holocaust and, he fears, perhaps his childless marriage. Our gloss to Book Two might be Appelfeld's own words: "Most Holocaust survivors are burdened with a feeling of guilt. Since that feeling is not clear, since it is undefined, it has assumed various guises over the years. Along with the guilt feeling, in parallel with it, if you will, there is also a desire for atonement. If the guilt were clear, the expressions of atonement could also be formulated with a certain clarity. But since the feeling of guilt has remained in a deep hollow of mystery, the expressions of atonement have also failed to find a clear outlet" (*Beyond Despair* 50-51).

The Age of Wonders, like the later *The Iron Tracks* (1991), is about the irrational hope on the part of the protagonists that revisiting the past might undo it. *The Iron Tracks*, Appelfeld's most recently translated novel, is a characteristic Appelfeld fable. The first-person narrator, Erwin Siegelbaum, buys and resells Jewish books and ritual objects that have survived the Holocaust. Siegelbaum's father had been an anti-Semitic communist who was responsible for organizing Ruthenian peasants and burning the property of Jewish merchants living in Ruthenia. Like the title figure in *The Immortal Bartfuss* (1983; trans. 1988), Siegelbaum is emotionally anaesthetized by his experience during the war. He has been living on trains and in inns since the end of the Second World War. Recalling Dostoevsky's underground man, he is obsessed with killing Colonel Nachtigal, who is responsible for killing his parents in a concentration camp. After endless delay, he fulfills his task, but his closing words are hardly triumphant: "I had done everything out of compulsion, and always too late" (*The Iron Tracks* 218). In 32 spare chapters, Appelfeld presents small villages in postwar Europe, notably Austria and Ruthenia, where only a few remnants of Jewish life survive. For 41 years, Siegelbaum's life has been composed of the routines of the traveling salesman: buffets, alcohol, one-night stands. He is the quintessence of the wandering Jew, iterating the *tracks* of a culture that has virtually disappeared. Gila Ramras-Rauch has written of Siegelbaum: "He maintains a yearly cycle, like the reading of the Torah, in weekly portions, and he has 22 stations, parallel to the letters in the Hebrew alphabet. He returns compulsively to a forlorn train station where, during the war, after three days in a sealed car, the people inside were deserted by the Germans" (190.) We think of Gregor Samsa, who turns into an insect because, caught up in a routine that drives him to depression and to alienation from his fellow humans, he loses all self-regard and no longer thinks and feels like a living person.

When in *The Age of Wonders* Bruno returns, it is as if he were inanimate and the objects around him were alive: "Despite the mist he saw that the shutters were open in Lauffer's shop and one cabinet was illuminated by electric light. It caught his eye. Strange, he reflected, objects survive longer; they are passive. Otherwise how could they withstand such changes? Could it be said, perhaps, that they lacked sensitivity?" (258-259). Bruno is in danger of repeating not only his father's marital history but also his father's discomfort with Jewish merchants and religious Jews: "To come home and sit next to a solid little Jew wearing a black skullcap whose whole being proclaimed self-satisfaction, grossness, and ugliness—in the worst of his dreams he could not have imagined such a thing possible. . . . Only when he got off the train and was standing on the platform did the Jewish salesman become real again: a giant insect spreading his limbs out in front of him" (178, 180). Like his father did in the late 1930s, he begins to drink a lot and to feel sorry for himself. Does not the name Bruno recall Bruno Schulz's bizarre first-person speaker who attributes life to inanimate objects and often iterates the life of his father?

For Appelfeld, the transportation system represents the ability of the Nazis to control and organize the Jews. Appelfeld uses the train in the opening and closing chapters of each part to frame a novel in which the transport system becomes the ultimate horror. Rereading, one feels the effectiveness of the proleptic opening sentence of Book One: "Many years ago Mother and I took the night train home from the quiet, little-known retreat where we had spent the summer" (3); they take first-class accommodations, then later they are pariahs even in third class. Book One ominously concludes: "By the next day we were on the cattle train hurtling south" (174). In chapter one, the Jews are mysteriously ordered to register and a pattern of isolation, of identification as Other begins: "Due to the special circumstances, the security forces requested all foreign passengers and all Austrian passengers who were not Christians by birth to register at the office that had just been opened in the sawmill." In the very next sentence Appelfeld's narrator's use of the passive voice ironically distances the human agency of those who are beginning to make fateful decisions about their victims: "Passengers were requested to bring their passports, identity cards, or any other identifying documents with them" (10). After the Jews register, the headwaiter becomes a "sentry posted . . . to keep order" and anticipates the "trooper" who herds them into cattle cars at the end of Book One (17). This registration begins a process that culminates in the last scene of Book One when before transport they are herded into a temple and locked in for the night.

Book Two of *The Age of Wonders* begins with Bruno's arrival by train and ends with his departure: "His eyes focused vacantly on the blinking railway signal, waiting for the brass plate to fall and the whistle of the engine to pierce the air" (270). We recall Appelfeld's words in *Beyond Despair* about the desire of his generation to amputate memory: "For many years the members of my generation were concerned with the . . . suppression of memory. It was impossible to live after the Holocaust except by silencing memory. Memory became your enemy. . . . People learned how to live without memory the way one learns to live without a limb of one's body" (*Beyond Despair* ix).

The first chapter of *The Age of Wonders* is an awakening; the boy knows after the registration humiliation and the vacation without his father that "nothing would ever be the same again" (17). From the outset the young boy, who is narrating, observes that his parents' marriage is in the process of falling apart. "Father was completely absorbed in his literary triumphs. Drunk with success, he spent his time traveling to Prague and Vienna and back again. But his successes brought us no joy. A bitter tenseness engulfed the house; it was as if we were dust to the steamroller of his success" (5). It is as if something mechanistic and polluted has the family in its grip. The Father is a self-hating Jew who leads the chorus of voices stereotyping the Jews and whose views are rendered with bitter irony: "Believe me, Judaism has nothing to offer you, or me either. It simply doesn't exist. But for the anti-Semites it would have vanished long ago" (103). When his writing is attacked, his father loses confidence and wallows in self-pity. His father becomes mentally ill when pilloried in print by a fellow Jew. His antidote to the collapse of the culture to which he has given his life and the illusion that he is an Austrian, not a Jew ("Jewish sentimentality is no good for Art" [53]), is self-hatred, which takes the form of drunkenness, financial irresponsibility, promiscuity, and disgust with his own work as a writer: "He was locked in struggle with some enemy that I, at any rate, had not met" (28). Rereading, and aware of Book Two, we think, "not yet."

Appelfeld's mode is allegory and his techniques often include the cartoon and grotesque. In *The Age of Wonders*, as in *Badenheim 1939*, Appelfeld uses a kind of fable structure to show how well-to-do and successful assimilated Jews are anesthetized not only to the gathering storm but to their own Jewishness, as he puts it in *Beyond Despair*: "The twenties and thirties saw a great drive towards assimilation. Mass emigration, communism, and inner collapse undermined Eastern European Judaism and threatened to bring it down. Assimilation was everywhere. True, great communities, ancient and deeply rooted ones, still maintained the traditional forms, but more through inertia than inner strength. That was the final, difficult stage in the transition from tribal, religious unity to modern petite bourgeoisie" (*Beyond Despair* 4).

That the narrator's father's favorite writer is Kafka alerts us to the nonrealistic and parabolic structure of *The Age of Wonders*. When his father learns of the registration of Jewish passengers, with Kafkaesque logic worthy of Gregor Samsa, the supposedly rational secular father attributes problems to the mysteries brought by Eastern Jews: "When mother told him about the strange night train that had stopped to have its Jewish passengers registered, he denounced the bureaucracy at first, but immediately added that ever since the *Ostjuden* had arrived things had gone haywire. They must have brought evil spirits with them" (24). And the secular son cannot put the concept of evil spirits behind him in either part. Appelfeld has written in *Beyond Despair*: "People will never forget the astounded expressions of the German and Austrian Jews, most of them assimilated for generations, who were exiled to the ghettos in the East. There they encountered, to their astonishment, the ghetto Jews, Yiddish Jews, whom they had attempted to ignore for so many years" (*Beyond Despair* 10).

Among other things, the first part of *The Age of Wonders* is a *bildungsroman*, the story of a boy growing up in grotesque circumstances. Nature itself is etched on the teller's memory as discordant, a disruption of expected patterns. Recurring references to mysterious "secrets" emphasize the discrepancy between a young narrator's innocence and the incomprehensible undoing of his world. At least in the first English translation by Dalya Bilu, it is not altogether clear that he and his mother have been literally or figuratively expelled from their vacation retreat: "I knew that new waters had come into the river, that we had been expelled, without anyone having had to say, 'Go'" (6). The boy feels our "silent, secret decay," which seems to be that of the family but is, of course, of the position of Jews in Austria (7). His explanation about why he and his mother left their summer house takes us from a realistic to an allegorical mode: "New, wild waters came down from the mountains and mixed everything up" (8). The disruption of his birthday party is proleptic of more serious disruptions by the authorities: "Father, who couldn't stand this sweetness, said nothing. Perhaps it was Mother's desperation that silenced him, her stricken attempts to gather a few crumbs of attention. What's happened? her face asked again. Nothing, it seemed. Only a fleeting, impalpable stillness as the people stopped talking and sank into the flowing vacuity of the music" (33). In chapter one the raucous woman, who insists on the humanity of the Jews, is a grotesque figure from German expressionism, a cartoon who penetrates and exposes the pretensions of her fellow travelers, and owes something to the influence of such figures as Lyonel Feininger, Otto Dix, Egon Schiele, Gustav Klimt, and George Grosz.

Appelfeld's chapters are often pithy vignettes, almost visual sketches frozen in time as if they were a series of paintings, only partially tied together by chronology. The narrator watches his personal and historical moorings drift away as if he were anesthetized or were watching a film. Of the narrator, Gila Ramras-Rauch writes:

A mixture of sadness and doom engulfs the boy as he watches the coming apart of his parents' marriage, reflecting the disintegration of his extended family and the eventual demise of his community in the small provincial town of Bukovina. This attitude of wary observation is by no means unique to him. Indeed, one might say it is typical of the Jew in general, and it is matched by a corresponding sense of being observed. That is, the Jew leads his life with a constant awareness of the observing eye of the outer world and tries to interpret the intention of the gentile framework within which he lives. (143)

The boy's air of detachment is a facade for deep pain, and we see the result of that pain in Book Two where Bruno not only has difficulty with intimacy and with engaging external experience, but is oddly inarticulate.

Appelfeld invokes the ominous invisible hand that in the *Book of Daniel* wrote "Mene mene tekel upharsin" ("numbered, numbered, divided, conquered") as a rebuke to Belshazzar while he was drinking vessels plundered by his grandfather, Nebuchadnezzar, from the holy temple: "[A] hand that had invaded the room from outside, spreading its fingers out imploringly as if to say, 'Pull one vein out of me and I'll be cured'" (26). If the young boy cannot become our Daniel foretelling the end of the Nazis, the omniscient narrator of Part Two can. But in Part One the aforementioned hand cannot be cured by pulling a vein and the Jews' days are numbered, and indeed they are already divided, Jew against Jew.

In *The Age of Wonders*, Appelfeld follows Mann in *The Magic Mountain* and *Death in Venice* and Kafka in *The Metamorphosis* in using illness as an important metaphorical pattern for moral and social disease; the sickly boy in a wheelchair on the train is a proleptic figure in chapter 1, the last sentence of which binds him to the boy: "But above all the steady gaze of the boy: as if it had been nailed to my forehead" (23). Shadows, illness, aging, death, promiscuity, madness (his mother's insane sister Theresa and her embrace of Catholicism dominate chapter 3), hysteria, and debauchery are in every chapter and seem to penetrate every page. For example, the boy describes the train ride from Baden in terms that focus on his Aunt Theresa's physical and emotional illness: "But above all I remember this journey, our mad flight through the night with Mother's younger sister, Theresa, whose face, in the middle of our holiday, had suddenly been overshadowed by a secret passion, pale and consuming, that gradually had spread until it covered her neck. For several days she had said nothing, as if fallen into a waking sleep. And when she came to, sharp wrinkles had appeared in her cheeks. Her pursed mouth had muttered words I did not understand. But one thing I knew: this was no longer the place for her" (56).

Debauchery is a form of moral illness in Appelfeld. Another metaphor is sexual lust and abandon as if in the frenzy of the cultural collapse, people inevitably turn to loveless sex; very much as in *Death in Venice*, sex becomes feverish, frenzied, and linked to moral illness. When Charlotte, the actress—who anticipates Lotte in *The Retreat*—is dismissed from the theater because she is a Jew, her drunken anger highlights a debauched party that ends with the boy again feeling an unspoken tie to another kind of outcast, the Jew as pariah. "Suddenly I sensed Charlotte's drunk little face and her lost look directed, trembling, at my forehead, and my father's hand, as if it were touching me, not her" (38).

III

The Retreat (1982) begins in 1937; like *Badenheim 1939* and *The Age of Wonders*, it begins with the turning point to the Holocaust catastrophe— the dotted line where from a retrospective view, Appelfeld's narrator can see the inevitability of catastrophe. *The Retreat* takes place in a mountain home for aging Jews called the Institute for Advanced Studies. The "institute" is an allegory for a concentration camp, where the underlying cynical concept of "Arbeit Macht Frei" rules.

Appelfeld is indebted to Mann's sanitarium in *The Magic Mountain* where people come to die. Poignantly, the retreat's organizer and leader Balaban—a kind of Trumpelman figure—is a Jew who teaches the Jews to blame themselves and to undergo a physical regimen that will make them into Austrians; they are also supposed to lose their accents. Balaban, originally a Polish Jew and a "horse trader" who arrived in Austria and embraced Austrian customs had planned, as a commercial venture, a sanitarium for aging Jews. But "Balaban took note of his mistake and learned his lesson. A year later he brought out a different prospectus in a different color, with no mention of the shameful dietary detail and, above all, with an entirely different program: horseback riding, swimming, seasonal hunting, organized hikes and what he called assimilation into the countryside. This proposal was well received by all. Balaban promised that within a short space of time he would painlessly eradicate embarrassing Jewish gestures and ugly accents. No one would have to be ashamed any more" (62). At the retreat, as in the concentration camps, the Jews stand in line at the hatch to get their food in tin bowls and mugs. "The cook took the two bowls and placed in each a potato in its skin, a piece of fish, and a slice of beetroot. . . . The meal was coming to an end. A few people stood by the long sink and washed their dishes. The sight reminded Lotte of the yard of an army camp, but she immediately realized her mistake. These people were no longer young, well-dressed, their movements too were restrained and subdued, and showed consideration for each other's privacy" (54, 55-56). Gradually conditions get worse and the Jews are freezing, huddled in blankets.

These are in fact Jews who have been discarded by their anti-Semitic employers and their heartless families; under the leadership of Balaban, the Jews are supposed to retrain and lose their Jewish qualities before returning. But of course they do not return, and they die at the retreat. The Jews who gather at the retreat have lost their Jewish identity and in fact regard other Jews in stereotypical terms. Each Jew thinks that he or she is somehow different than other Jews. Of Lotte, the actress who has lost her job because she is Jewish, the narrator writes, "From her youth she had felt an aversion for all things Jewish. Jewish actors and writers counted for nothing in her eyes" (9). The retreat contains Jews ashamed of their Jewishness, deracinated outsiders who have tried to assimilate but are now cast out by Austrian culture as the Nazis come to power.

At first some inhabitants "went back to town changed and full of health" (63). Gradually the denizens abandon this plan and turn the center into an old age home—a place where no work is done because nothing is to be done and where they huddle in the hall and play cards. Balaban's followers, such as Lang who follows his physical regimen after the others have abandoned it, become acolytes of this confidence man, a figure anticipated by Leslie Epstein's Trumpelman in *King of the Jews*: "But of our own free will and in full possession of our senses we decided that for the good of us all we must change our former way of life, eradicate our defects for once and for all" (91). Rauch expresses the views that the Jews need be transformed: "Once a man realizes that his body is weak and ugly, his nerves destroyed, his soul corrupt, that he bears within him a decayed inheritance, in short, that he is sick and, what is worse, that he is passing his sickness on to his children, what can he desire more deeply than reform? . . . If only the Jews knew how to drink, to relax, they would surely be different—stronger, braver, perhaps even more honest. But the Jews are rodents: not for nothing does the world regard them as animals of the rodent species. I myself, madam, what was I all those years, but a rodent? Balaban, in the simplicity of his heart, understood it better than we did" (103-105).

While the Jews gradually let activity and organization give way to sloth and hopelessness, eventually after Balaban's death, they—in the face of beatings and hunger—pull themselves together as a *Jewish* community. Despairing, the aging Jews finally become a community that takes care of itself and no longer depends on the Austrians for approval: "The pain was cruel, the shame terrible, but Herbert got up every morning and went out to endure his suffering. The provisions he brought back were scant, but nevertheless their meager meals were eaten in tranquillity" (164).

Appelfeld's parables, as we have been noting, rely heavily on exaggeration, fantasy, and illuminating distortion. In *The Retreat*, he again relies on the carnivalesque and grotesque rather than the realistic. He tells his tale in simple sentences befitting a parable, but with excruciating irony and anger—anger at the Jews for self-delusion and even more so at the Austrians for tormenting them. Appelfeld's novels have the discontinuity of dreams, especially nightmares; his characters, like Spiegelman's, are cartoons. His characters are inarticulate, unself-conscious and unaware of anything beyond their immediate lives. As Ramras Rauch notes:

> [Appelfeld's] characters are fragmented and dislocated, though his fiction is not. He does not violate the rules of traditional syntax. Terms such as *meaninglessness, abyss,* and *void,* often used by postmodern writers, become the daily, often unexpressed experience of his characters. The unarticulated self bears an unspoken sense of horror. It is the very absence of the direct depiction of the Holocaust experience and its omnipresence that conveys the sense of horror. The human being as a "torn fabric" is depicted in highly metaphorical language, and that gives his fiction its power. The frequent omission of casual relationships between events, the technique of juxtaposition rather than comprehensible continuity, and the depiction of an almost "flat" character devoid of particular characterizations tie him to postmodern techniques. (18-19)

As in *Badenheim 1939*, doom and foreboding are on every page. The parabolic structure, the short, taut chapters, the apparent logic disguising foolishness and quixoticism all give the novel's story an eerie inevitability: "And thus the days crept by. Exercise, someone would remember. Why aren't I exercising? Isn't that what I came here for? I left a flourishing shop, business connections, customers and friends. Instead of exercising, breathing fresh air into my lungs, I spend my time playing poker. Isn't that a crime!" (75).

Appelfeld is again targeting the Judenrat system of complicity: Jews who police themselves become oppressors to please their persecutors. Balaban has internalized Austrian values and organized the Jews to improve themselves through their own efforts. Appelfeld depicts self-hatred, the internalization of prejudiced perspectives, as one of the reasons for the concentration camps. The characters are traumatized, abandoned, castigated, deprived of a sense of self. Ironically, the camps are organized by Jews, for Jews, but the purpose is to isolate them from society until they transform themselves into idealized Austrian peasants at home with nature. In fact, the Austrians are louts who move at the outset from harassing the Jews from their social and economic positions to, by the end, beating the Jews. Lotte's daughter is married to an Austrian who beats her regularly.

Appelfeld tells and retells his stories from a survivor's perspective. He examines the past from the perspective of a Zionist now living in Israel. Writing from an Israeli perspective, Appelfeld insists that Jews must have pride in their culture and not try to be what others expect. In a way *The Retreat* shows the need for a Jewish state and culture in which Jews will live, proud of who they are. Appelfeld's point is that if a people are regarded as inferior and different by an alien culture, they may start believing it.

In *The Retreat*, once again Appelfeld's target is assimilated Austrian Jews who patronize Eastern Jews. Jews who have forgotten their traditions and heritage are now rejected by their own assimilated families; families, Appelfeld implies, had once been the cornerstone of Jewish life. One of the unpleasant aspects of his book is the way he casts blame on the victims. To be sure the narrator of *The Retreat* identifies himself at the end as one of the institutes' "inmates": "Outside it was warm and pleasant. It was possible to sit on the slopes and look around and reflect: Not far from here busy cities exist, trams drive back and forth, people get up early to go to work, a clerk opens his counter, a maid takes off her shoes so as not to enter the house with mud from the countryside. One detail after the other, as if filtered through a fine sieve. One thing was clear: these things no longer belonged to us" (163). But cumulatively this self-hatred becomes irritating to the reader, a kind of rhetorical bullying. Appelfeld expects us to be repelled by anti-Semitic nonsense—ostracized Jews establishing an institute where they are desperately trying to undo their Jewishness—but the very iteration becomes overdetermined and makes us wonder why he engages in this excessive iteration of anti-Semitic stereotypes. Doesn't the iteration of anti-Semitic stereotypes partly reinscribe the very prejudices that he would mock?

We might conclude our discussion of Appelfeld with words with which Philip Roth summarizes Appelfeld's work in his interview with the writer: "Indeed, all that Appelfeld is not adds up to what he is, and that is a dislocated writer, a deported writer, a dispossessed and uprooted writer. . . . His sensibility—marked almost at birth by the solitary wanderings of a little bourgeois boy through an ominous nowhere—appears to have spontaneously generated a style of sparing specificity, of out-of-time progression and thwarted narrative drives, that is an uncanny prose realization of the displaced mentality. As unique as the subject is a voice that originates in a wounded consciousness pitched somewhere between amnesia and memory, and that situates the fiction it narrates midway between parable and history" (*Beyond Despair* 61).

CHAPTER TWELVE

ILLUMINATING DISTORTION AND HISTORICAL CARTOON: LESLIE EPSTEIN'S *KING OF THE JEWS*

PIGTAIL
When all the women in the transport
had their heads shaved
four workmen with brooms made of birch
twigs
swept up
and gathered up the hair

Behind clean glass
the stiff hair lies
of those suffocated in gas chambers
there are pins and side combs
in this hair

The hair is not shot through with light
is not parted by the breeze
is not touched by any hand
or rain or lips

In huge chests
clouds of dry hair
of those suffocated
and a faded plait
a pigtail with a ribbon
pulled at school
by naughty boys.

The Museum, Auschwitz, 1948
—Tadeusz Różewicz
(Translated by Adam Czerniawski)

Leslie Epstein's *King of the Jews* (1979) at first seems a traditional novel. Carefully structured, it is a terrifying examination of the Judenrat in an imaginary ghetto, modeled on Lodz. We might begin our discussion of Epstein's novel by recalling Raul Hilberg's scathing indictment of the Judenrat:

> The Jewish councils, in the exercise of their historic function, continued until the end to make desperate attempts to alleviate suffering and to stop the mass dying in the ghettos. But at the same time, the councils responded to German demands with automatic compliance and invoked German authority to compel the community's obedience. . . . As time passed by, the Jewish councils became increasingly impotent in their efforts to cope with the welfare portion of their task, but made themselves felt all the more in their implementation of Nazi decrees. (146)

Epstein's major character, Trumpelman, is based on Rumkowski, the head of the Judenrat at Lodz, and a figure whom Kosinski tenaciously and quixotically defended. When the 1989 film *Lodz Ghetto* appeared, it became an important companion piece to Epstein's novel, and perhaps should be seen first. In the film, Jerzy Kosinski is the "voice-over" that speaks Rumkowski's words; given his own novel, *The Painted Bird*, about a young Holocaust victim, perhaps we should say Kosinski cross-dresses as Rumkowski. The film shows how Rumkowski deludes himself and the Jews into thinking that if they become indispensable workers for the

German war machine, they will avoid the fate of other Jewish communities in Poland. (It is worth noting that in his authoritative study of the same Judenrat, Isaiah Trunk, whose view of some Judenrat is far more tolerant than Hilberg's, has nothing good to say about what he calls the "Rumkowski regime" [Trunk 542]). Rumkowski somewhat narcissistically assumes a position of grandeur as the "Eldest"; the ghetto citizens pathetically fantasize that he can somehow save them. While the Lodz ghetto lasts the longest, it is annihilated in July 1944, and of 200,000, only 800 remain in hiding until the war ends. At the German behest, Rumkowski presides over the gradual destruction of the ghetto, even agreeing to let all children under ten and the elderly be deported; the film strongly suggests that he knows that their fate is extermination. In the film, based on witnesses and diaries, he self-justifyingly proclaims, "I am a servant of the Authorities." He keeps promising what he calls peace—"Work camps are your passports to peace"—and is seemingly oblivious to the hunger, starvation, cold, illness, and death that is omnipresent in the ghetto. By imposing harsh discipline on the inhabitants and using violence against his political enemies, he becomes a kind of parody of Hitler. Jewish policeman are bribed with larger food rations to carry out German atrocities. Finally Rumkowski cannot save even his own family, and he voluntarily boards the train to Auschwitz with those closest to him.

Epstein reminds us of the parallel by having his unnamed town include a "Rumkowski Monument" and a "Rumkowski Geyser." More than any of the narratives in our study, *King of the Jews* examines the complicity of the Jews in their own destruction. Organized in eleven chapters, the novel is about the attrition of a significant Jewish community. In chapter eleven—a number signifying renewal—the surviving orphans take the ship *Urania* to New York. One might say that the novel is organized in ten chapters of equal length and a coda in which two of the orphans, the now blind Kipnis and the once fragile Lipiczany, voyage to the United States. But in contrast to *Schindler's List*, the novel leaves us not with a sense of renewal, but of loss and waste. For Trumpelman, the self-proclaimed King of the Jews, is a self-serving fraud and his schemes only postpone the inevitable.

The novel is a scathing satire of the idea that if only the Jews had handed over a few Jews many more would have been saved, an idea that dominates the Judenrat—as it did the Lodz Judenrat under Rumkowski—and even shapes the way Lipsky, Trumpelman's enemy and failed assassin, is betrayed by his followers. Trumpelman's collaboration gradually turns him into a stage villain, as when he comments on the joint hanging of his two rivals, the police chief of the Jews, Rievesaltes (a ruthless gangster), and Lipsky, his Marxist opponent: "These pipsqueaks know the Elder has got back his strength" (*King of the Jews* 308). Yet although Trumpelman is revealed as a scoundrel, the novel asks us to consider whether death postponed, even if only for some months, justifies compromise. To this question, Epstein's novel does not answer a resounding "No," whatever his intent. For in the 200 survivors within Epstein's novel (rather than the actual 800 Lodz survivors), is there not—as *Schindler's List* reminds us—the promise of future generations?

Epstein examines the role of the Judenrat—the Jews appointed by the Nazis to govern the ghetto. The Judenrat is placed in the position of the moral crossing guards and corrupted by that responsibility. Gradually, the Judenrat, led by Trumpelman, makes a series of moral compromises until they become complicit with their persecutors. The Judenrat lives on the borderland between the culture of the Others and the ghetto. In the guise of preserving life they preserve their own comforts. But the Judenrat in this novel saves no one. Nomberg the Rabbi speaks of shooting Jews on a widespread basis during the general strike.

Epstein's narrative strategy is to have his narrator observe Trumpelman as a mysterious phenomenon—usually with journalistic objectivity but at times with wonder—and on relatively infrequent occasions, to have the narrator record his words. But the narrator never reveals Trumpelman's psyche through interior monologue or indirect discourse. Trumpelman, leader of the Judenrat, is a confidence man, arriving in "our town" in 1918-1919 as a "doctor" without a medical degree who relies on quack remedies as well as sweet candies posing as magic elixirs. He has been an insurance salesman who misappropriates premiums, depends on gangsters to intimidate customers by means of mysterious fires, and finally absconds with the premium money and another man's wife, only to reappear some years later to cure an epidemic in a Jewish orphanage. After the insurance fraud Trumpelman disappears, but reappears, as the narrator explains, two years later: "And so our history changed. Or else—this is a thought that sometimes comes to us who are still living—

it did not change, and everything that happened was destined to be. In that case the reappearance of Trumpelman did not affect the way our lives were twisted, like rags, one jot" (23).

The novel opens with the narrative voice positioning himself: "In the winter of 1918-1919, on a day when the wind was blowing, I. C. Trumpelman arrived in our town. He was wearing a brown overcoat and a brown hat and had a large suitcase in either hand" (11). The narrator addresses his audience as "Ladies and gentleman" as if he were making a presentation, trying to explain how the Jews were taken in by this man who had at first "true, genuine feeling" for children: "All too soon the whole town, or at least the Jews in it, tens of thousands of people, would call to him, would cry out to him, by that very name [Chaim]. We all became his children" (16). At other times he addresses his audience less formally: "Have you ever seen a big, furry dog coming out of the water?" (225). The narrator himself becomes something of a chameleonic trickster engaging his audience from diverse perspectives; by presenting the narrator in this way, while stressing the terrible conditions of the ghetto, Epstein wins sympathy for Trumpleman and keeps him on the moral borderland as long as possible.

The narrator provides the camera by which we can imagine the past. He interweaves images of trains and fires. When the Jews begin to burn parts of their houses as fuel, he says: "The entire Ghetto, with its chimneys smoking and smoking, was like a train rushing down an empty track, toward nowhere, while all the time the fireman chops up his boxcars for fuel" (76-77). During the fire from which Trumpelman drags Einhorn, the narrator writes: "Sparks like so many human souls flew into the blackened sky" (81). The recurring image of fire—of Jews going up the chimney as Spiegelman's Vladek graphically and bitterly recalls—is another grim *topos* that ties our diverse texts together from *Night* to *Maus* and gives the Holocaust metaphor its visual and visionary aspect.

In *Modernity and the Holocaust,* Zygmunt Bauman argues that the "lesson of the Holocaust is the facility with which most people, put into a situation that does not contain a good choice. . . . argue themselves away from the issue of moral duty . . . adopting instead the precepts of rational interest and self-preservation" (206). But he is speaking of the Germans, collaborators, and bystanders, not the victims. Yet we can fully understand how much more difficult ethical behavior is for those asked to make terrible choices and to risk their lives and their families' lives. Epstein examines the diverse ethical responses of the Jews and is especially ironic about those members of the Judenrat who, in the name of saving their community, pursued self-interest. In some ways Trumpelman's magnetism to the desperate Jews parodies the German attraction to Hitler. Isaiah Chaim—I. C. (we recall how *I* in the Greek alphabet stands for *J*, thus ironically suggesting the initial of Jesus)—Trumpelman, head of the council of Elders, becomes the outlet of the Jews' hopes as the circle of death closes in. (Chaim—which, ironically, means "life" in Hebrew—was Rumkowski's middle name.) The desperately trapped ghettoites believe he alone can save them and call him "Messiah" (168, 338). Early on in his leadership in the ghetto, he wins their confidence through a series of events, culminating in his rescuing a child from a fire: "The Jews began to say, in so many words: *Nothing can happen to our Elder. Bullets bounce off him. So nothing will happen to us, either*" (82). As President of the Judenrat, he is totemized in the early ghetto days of summer, 1940 into a messianic figure: "There was a special relationship between the Elder and *his* Jews. It was democratic, like Roosevelt in America, and at the same time it was royal. Just to be near him was considered good fortune, good luck" (124; emphasis mine). He is particularly cherished by children.

As the narrator shows, the Jews' capacity for self-delusion seems infinite: "Hope! What a thing it is! Like a worm! Cut it and cut it and cut it! Still it won't die!" (280). Madagascar exists as a pathetic utopian alternative to which Jews cling, even as deportations and starvation decimate the ghetto. Listening to *Aida*, Trumpelman muses: "What was the famous opera about? He hardly knew. Ethiopians. Elephants. Something about the river Nile? Was Madagascar, he wondered, such a land? Would Jews sing songs there to each other?" (170). Even the Lipskyites, who abandon their leader to survive, are driven by Marxist rhetoric and a fantasy of life in the Soviet Union under Stalin. Kipnis argues that "'Lipsky is our Commander, but above Lipsky, above all the generals and admirals, there is only one leader: the Man of Steel!' The boy wheeled. He pointed to the portrait, pasted to the wall, of the man with the mustache, the smoking pipe" (304).

Trumpelman's theory is that if he makes "his" Jews indispensable to the Others—sometimes ironically called "the Men of Valor," or "the

Blond Ones" but never "the Nazis"—by making their uniforms better and faster, they will spare them. Rereading, we realize that the image of a little gosling who follows the first thing he sees at birth applies not only to the Germans following Hitler, but also to the Jews: "Peasants, mimicking calls, have always led ducks to the water and sheep to the slaughterhouse. What is new, a contribution of our own times, is that the same can be done to a man" (41). Charismatic magnetism turns humans into lemmings. Ironically it is the orphans who, under his direct charge, play a leading role in the resistance against Trumpelman. His organization of the ghetto is an extension of the organization of the Hatters' orphanage. He regards the Jews as his children and himself as the parent, the Elder, who knows what is best for them. Of course the Holocaust flames consume "his" Jews just as it consumes all other categories of Jews.

Yet we understand a relationship between his abusive behavior in slapping the Jews—even, on one occasion, pouring out their soup—and the Germans physically manhandling him (116, 141). We see that he is a performer, a trickster, a weaver of the most improbable tales, who, like Hitler, elicits the fanatic belief of others; that Hitler is referred comically and fearfully to as "Horowitz" by the Jews, as if they needed to domesticate him to a human identity, establishes a metonymical link between Trumpelman and Hitler as charismatic, self-serving demagogues. The Germans help Trumpelman establish his credentials as a powerful figure by staging scenes such as his closing the house of pleasure and, at another time, pretending that the Jews will be shipped to Madagascar.

Gradually Trumpelman makes greater and greater compromises with the Nazis as he once had with the gangsters in the ghetto. Finally he is concerned only with saving himself and his privileged quality of life. And the same can be said of the rest of the Judenrat whose only concern becomes their own welfare and who rationalize taking part in selections of other Jews by thinking that they are saving those they do not select. One cannot be sure whether Trumpelman believes his fantastic stories about his life as a medicine man among American Indians; he seems to be taken in by his own megalomania and, from a psychological point of view, becomes increasingly psychotic. His deception becomes self-deception. Like Hitler, he wants complete control; he gives the Judenrat members suicide pills that turn out to be only sleeping pills. No sooner do Judenrat members think they have committed suicide to avoid putting together a list of deportees than he awakens them.

Epstein uses illuminating distortions to show how the process of isolating, depriving, and decimating a community changes the very essence of human behavior. Trumpelman wears a black cape with gold trim as if he were a magician (248). Having nothing else to believe, the Jews desperately need to believe in him no matter how bogus his words or outrageous his behavior. Does Trumpelman stage his wedding to an aging cabaret singer—who is little more than a self-serving whore who sells herself to the highest bidder—to give hope to the Jews, or does he really believe, as he says, that "The Elder and the Elder's wife will give birth to a line of kings" (132)? Does he know that the gift of Madagascar as a Jewish refuge is a hoax? The narrator shows that no matter how hard the Jews try to preserve their way of life, living in the ghetto is and must be a function of the Others and their edict. Indeed, Trumpelman begins more and more to mirror Hitler. That he has his own Elite Guards— different from the Jewish police—recalls the privileged position of the SS. His speeches become that of a raving demagogue; his only goal is to preserve his own power. He issues money with his picture on it, money to be distributed in exchange for Jewish jewels, crystal, and porcelain. Instead of taking bribes from the child smugglers, the Jewish police are given a bounty for capturing the children. To obtain a son after his wife miscarried, Trumpelman puts the boy's mother, Madame Gumbiner, on an early list of deportees. He has the Russian Taradash shot because he thinks it is Czerniakow, the son of the former leader of the Warsaw ghetto, coming to take over.

Epstein is comically parodying the Western imaginative tradition which the Nazis' compulsive linearity sought to destroy. Perhaps he is despairing that this tradition did little to foster a humane, tolerant response to fellow humans. As in Shakespeare's tragedies, the natural world responds to heinous human acts. Indeed the Hatter orphans, whose lives he had once saved, enact a mock *Macbeth* to show how Trumpelman and his wife have let egotism and ambition take hold of their passions and undermine their ethics. Thus at the hanging of his enemies, as a photograph is being taken of the ranting Trumpelman gloating, "a cloud, a big one, churning and foaming, had come down like a whirlwind and hid the Elder, along with his two bitter enemies, from view" (309). Abused by the Germans and lacking his cape, Trumpelman gathers the children to watch the sun spread the same kind of stuff that his candy dispensed: "There, on the horizon, the real sun was leaking something. Red stuff, like jam, came out of it and spread over the nearby sky" (120). It is as if Trumpelman can command the elements, although we as readers understand the "red stuff" as proleptic of spilled Jewish blood.

More than the other Holocaust narratives under discussion, the culture of the victims mirrors the culture of the exploiters. Epstein praises Appelfeld for

> the clear demonstration that the worst that evil can do is to make its victims resemble the victimizers. That takes not only courage but imagination, a special grace, a psychic confidence, what Coleridge called a suspension of disbelief—that is, of one's preconceived notions, prejudices, even one's worldliness; a suspension, in brief, of that power of repression which allows the reader to keep his own unconscious unavailable to himself, disconnected from the vision of the author, and permits him to say, like a "Good German" or an indifferent Pole: *none of that has anything to do with me*. ("Writing about the Holocaust," Lang 268).

Trumpelman's own passion for power becomes his sole motivation. After he becomes obsessed with establishing a line of kings—he even has his own taster, Nigel Lipiczany—and plotting to destroy his rivals, the aforementioned performance of *Macbeth* stresses the parallels between Trumpelman and his wife and the Macbeths. The more Trumpelman becomes a Nazi puppet, the more he becomes deranged and obsessed by power.

Epstein uses comic perspectives to emphasize the ludicrous quality of the Jews' pathetic powerlessness and desperate efforts to save themselves. In a valuable essay entitled "Holocaust *Laughter?*" Terrence Des Pres has discussed the carnival aspect of the novel, yet I do not laugh (Lang 219-33). Is it because I know that Epstein has culled real events in the ghettos from his sources or that as a rereader, I know the participants in some of the farcical events are all dead, or that I realize the comedy derives from desperate deprivation sadistically inflicted by the occupiers? It is like watching a man deprived of his wheel chair trying to walk on his knees. Is that comic? Do we nervously laugh because we fear that we might have been one of the victims or, worse, because we fear that we might have been among those who did not take part in resistance and ghetto uprisings? Des Pres has stressed that the Jews live in the world of Bakhtinian carnival, but as we reread, what we know about the death camps and the transport system subverts carnival as surely as the ghetto carnival is meant to subvert the dominant culture. Perhaps in Brueghel's paintings, to quote Des Pres, "the antimimetic order cancels, for a time, official reality" ("Holocaust *Laughter?*," Lang 227), but can this happen in a novel where the teleology of obliterating a culture, a people, dominates? Finally, the irony is at the expense of carnival, humor, play. Can we really agree that "carnival excess frees the citizens of Suburb Balut from bondage to an order of death" ("Holocaust *Laughter?*" Lang 227)? Each effort of carnival ends in a further deterioration of life, so that reality reinscribes itself.

I am not sure I share the laughter that Des Pres finds in the martyrdom of Klapholtz, the artist whose mural of the French flag and the "enormous" lettering of "VIVE LA FRANCE!" disrupts the wedding (*King of the Jews* 134):

> On Wesola Street passersby stopped and stared. The rickshaw drivers made their customers get out of the rickshaws, and they too fell in line. The caravan swept by the shed of the crystal sorters, and those workers, mostly old women, came outside and joined the throng. They tramped straight up the thoroughfare. There was not a soldier or policeman in sight. The ground shook. The buildings seemed to tremble. At Brzeszinska the comb-and-cork shop emptied out. Brush makers lined the sidewalk, waving strips of paper like flags. The demonstration grew and grew. What a spectacle it was. A procession of resolute Jews! They seemed to themselves to consist of an irresistible force. The world, which had been snatched from them, would be seized once again. What could they not do?
>
> The broken body of Klapholtz, draped over the wooden staves of the leading wagon, rocked back and forth. His arms and legs and

the head on his neck seemed full of energy. Someone ran up and attached a flower to his trousers. He was their martyr, their hero. Ladies and gentlemen, what other artist—not even Victor Hugo, not Michelangelo—has moved men so greatly, or filled them with the conviction that they could change the course of their lives?

So began the first day of the Five Day General Strike. (*King of the Jews* 149)

Were I to share in a laugh, would I not become a collaborator? That Epstein's visual exaggerations recall the illuminating distortions of cartoons, posters, and banners may be why Des Pres thinks of laughter. We might think of the flat surface—the resolution of foreground and background—as well as the bold colors and heightened details at the expense of realism that we associate with political posters or indeed the father of modern poster art, Henri Toulouse-Lautrec. Perhaps Epstein is influenced by cinema cartoons of his own American youth with one-dimensional stage villains, stereotypical characters (the "Blond Ones," the "Men of Valor," the "Others," the "Totenkopfers"), and the cosmological response to human problems. He finds comic names for the rabbis—Pshiskher, Wolf-Kitzes, Kornischoner—who engage in abstract and foolish talmudic debate about how to respond to the demand for names to be deported. The Judenrat, too, have cartoon names; Philosoff, Popover, Bagman, Mordechai Kleen, Schpitalnik, and Urinstein. They decide to take cyanide—provided by the wily Trumpelman—only to discover they have swallowed sleeping pills. Epstein often abandons realism for fantasy, surrealism, and nightmare. The Jews call the leader of the Others *Horowitz*, not Hitler, as if eschewing Hitler's name would deny his presence.

In fact the Jews are essentialists who believe in the spoken and written word, and who are seduced and cajoled by the desire to believe that the Others *and* Trumpelman speak the truth. As if he were presenting a magic show or vaudeville act, the narrator addresses us as "Ladies and gentlemen." Trumpelman is both a realistic character and the ghettoites' nightmare of self-serving complicity whose apparent death is followed by his miraculous reappearance in another guise. Even at the end we cannot be sure he has died, although at the time of writing, he would have been over 100.

We find ourselves seduced by the possibility of laughter, but what we are witnessing deflects laughter. To domesticate the Holocaust is to become like Trumpelman. There is more poignancy than comedy in Klapholtz's followers investing the funeral procession—their transport system (a parody of the German trains)—with meaning: "He was their martyr, their hero." Epstein's creation of Klapholtz may have been based on Yitzhak Wittenburg, the community commander of partisans in Vilna who was turned over by his followers to Jacob Gens, whose role as collaborating leader of the Vilna ghetto had much in common with that of Rumkowski's. But what we need to stress is that this apotheosis of Klapholtz parodies how the desperate Jews totemize Trumpelman into a potential *übermensch*, how their constructs are the source of their psychic needs. It also parodies the process of mythmaking that creates martyrs and heroes, including Hitler's inspiring followers with the conviction that they could change the course of their lives if they attended to his words.

Epstein's techniques include implying that the point of view is that of a survivor, ironic structural echoes, hyperbole, illuminating distortion, and metaphoricity. As he puts it in his essay, "Writing About the Holocaust": "Imagination, the reordering of experience, the emphasis upon emotion, the recombining and splitting and turning upside down and inside out of events, so that—to use examples from my own work—a river from Warsaw should run through Lodz, the horses which froze in Finland should have their manes crystallized in Poland, and that babies whose birth was outlawed in Vilna should nonetheless howl in the ghetto of the Balut: all this of course is anathema to the historian" (Lang 264).

The narrator is a witness, a member of the ghetto who somehow survived to tell the tale of the complete destruction of the vibrant and prosperous Jewish community. One of the 200 who are still living, he desperately wants to understand what happened to him and the community. Indeed, at a distance of years, the narrator mocks the propensity for Jewish ethical questioning of retaliatory violence when he raises the question of the moral position of the partisans. Recalling how Einhorn had cracked the head of a Polish taxi driver and had taken his car, the narrator winkingly remarks: "Now, more than three decades later, we can stop and ask, *was this right or wrong?*" (323), only to add: "At the time, however, no one gave it a thought" (323). He seems to be sympathetic and knowledgeable about the resistance led by Lipsky, although he doesn't identify himself as one of them. Since he knows about Nigel's journey of discovery outside the ghetto, when Nigel learned about the gassing or carbon monoxide poisoning in buses, he could be Nigel. He is knowledgeable about Jewish tradition. Des Pres notes, "the narrator's voice promotes a wonderful civility, a sweet insistence on decorum in a world where decorum sounds out of place and quaint" ("Holocaust *Laughter?*" Lang 222). He is trying to find a discourse by which what happens can be made comprehensible to those outside the ghetto.

Epstein wants us to consider how we retrospective readers occupy a similar moral position, protected by circumstances from experiencing in our lives what the ghetto, the camps, and the concomitant need for self-preservation were really like. He has his narrator address us as "Ladies and gentlemen" as a way of stressing our immunity from the world he describes, a world in which Jews were regarded not as "Ladies and gentlemen" but as vermin—a world in which for a Jew to die in bed, as people once died, was unique: "Centuries before, in another geological age, the age of reptiles, of fishes, people used to perish on account of diseases. . . . In modern times that happened to only one in a hundred thousand" (286). For, as Epstein wants us to realize, the Holocaust years he is describing in his bizarre illuminating distortion—a distortion that mimes the unthinkable and illogical quality of the events themselves— bear no relationship to anything preceding or succeeding them.

PART FOUR

FANTASY

CHAPTER THIRTEEN

THE COMIC GROTESQUE OF SPIEGELMAN'S *MAUS*

THE SURVIVOR

I am twenty-four
led to slaughter
I survived.

The following are empty synonyms:
man and beast
love and hate
friend and foe
darkness and light.

The way of killing men and beasts is the same
I've seen it:
truckfuls of chopped-up men
who will not be saved.

Ideas are mere words:
virtue and crime
truth and lies
beauty and ugliness
courage and cowardice.

Virtue and crime weigh the same
I've seen it:

in a man who was both
criminal and virtuous.

I seek a teacher and a master
may he restore my sight hearing and speech
may he again name objects and ideas
may he separate darkness from light.

I am twenty-four
led to slaughter
I survived.

                    Tadeusz Różewicz
        (Translated by Adam Czerniawski)

By using cartoon figures to present the Shoah, Spiegelman creates in his *Maus* books a wildly inventive bibliocosm that invites us to look on the major *topoi* of the Shoah from a radically innovative formal perspective. Mice are Spiegelman's vehicles for exploring the twentieth century history of Europe from 1935 to 1945 and his own history as a survivor's son from 1948, the year of his birth. As we read volume one we become accustomed to a world in which the Jews, depicted as mice, live among Poles—who are depicted as pigs but are seldom seen except in a barely sketched background in one frame of the first chapter of volume one, a chapter that concerns private life leading up to his father's marriage on February 14, 1937.

Depicting the Jews as mice emphasizes their position as *Others*, consigned to live apart in their mouse holes. As Spiegelman depicts the mice in bed or at dinner, we become accustomed to them as illuminating distortions who speak as humans. As Arlene Fish Wilner writes, "The most obvious disjunction is, of course, between the escapism usually associated with cartoon panels and the horrific realism of the subject" (171). Gradually we accept that these mice with human features— except for tails, usually hidden by clothes—think, feel, and love as if they were humans. For they are! They retain the humanity of which the Germans—who labeled them "vermin" and sought to exterminate them—wished to deprive them. As Marianne Hirsch has noted, "Maus sounds like mouse but its German spelling echoes visually the recurring Nazi command, 'Juden Raus' ("Jews out"—come out or get out) as well as the first three letters of "Auschwitz," a word that itself has become an icon of the Holocaust" (11). The last syllable, "rat," of the often collaborationist and betraying Judenrat also suggests the more benign term "mouse." Perhaps the absence of tails at first tellingly indicates that the metamorphosis is progressive; until we see swastikas on cats, there are no mice tails. The pictures and words combine for a subtle psychology of character worthy of a modern novel. Unlike the mice in Disney cartoons who are buffeted by disaster and come back to life again and again, we soon realize that these mice stay dead.

At the top of the acknowledgment and copyright page of volume two, following a double title page, is a quotation from a newspaper article that appeared in Pomerania, Germany, in the mid-thirties: "Mickey Mouse is the most miserable ideal ever revealed. . . . Healthy emotions tell every independent young man and every honorable youth that the dirty and filth-covered vermin, the greatest bacteria carrier in the animal kingdom, cannot be the ideal type of animal. . . . Away with Jewish brutalization of the people! Down with Mickey Mouse! Wear the Swastika Cross!" (II. 4). Clearly, in addition to the obvious metaphor that the Nazis as cats toyed with the Jews as powerless mice, this linkage of mice and Jews from Nazi propaganda was one source of Spiegelman's inspiration. As Thomas Doherty has noted:

> The cartoon medium possesses a graphic quality well-suited to a confrontation with Nazism and the Holocaust. . . . The medium is bound up with the ideology of Nazism and the artist's critique of it. Spiegelman's artistic style and animating purpose are shaped by the two graphic media whose images make up the visual memory of the twelve-year Reich—cartoons and cinema. Both arts are intimately linked to the aesthetic vision and historical legacy of Nazism. From this perspective, cartoons become not just an appropriate medium to render the Holocaust but a peculiarly apt response to a genocidal vision. (71-72)

Even as Spiegelman's characters see themselves as human, we see them as mice and cats within an imagined world in which different nationalities are presented as different animals. Spiegelman's black-and-white frames, his lack of nominalistic detail in facial expressions and shapes, and the sparseness of dialogue paradoxically invite the experienced reader to fill in details by drawing upon his or her own experience of the Holocaust while presenting the crystallizing themes in lucid and graphic form to those who are less aware of history, whether because of age or knowledge. As Joseph Witek writes, "Spiegelman performs subtle wonders of characterization and expression using only two dots for eyes and two lines for eyebrows. . . . The more open and spare panels of Maus allow one's eye to flow smoothly from scene to scene" (106). Spiegelman varies his style from the understated style that matches his father's rather understated, anesthetized tone to the expressionist hyperbole and manic energy of the insert entitled "Prisoner on the Hell Planet: A Case History" (I.100-103), which depicts a younger Spiegelman in a mental hospital after his mother dies and shows him wearing the striped uniform of concentration camp inmates.

Not only are the characters in the insert humans, but the insert includes a photograph of Art and his mother on vacation in 1958. The occasional photographs not only reconnect the figures to our human world but deliberately call attention to the creative intelligence behind the metaphoricity of the mouse trope. In volume two Art includes photographic inserts of his brother Richieu (in the dedication) and, at the end, of his father in the striped camp uniform. As Marianne Hirsch has written, "Taken together, the three photographs in Maus I and Maus II reassemble a family violently fractured and destroyed by the shoah; they include at different times, in different places, all the Spiegelmans—Art and his mother, Art's brother, and finally Vladek. Distributed over the space of the two volumes, these three photographs tell their own narrative of loss, mourning, and desire, one that inflects obliquely, both supports and undercuts the story of Maus itself" (Hirsch 16). Yet Spiegelman stresses that the picture of Vladek—taken after his release when he had returned to physical health—is staged in a souvenir shop in front of a curtain, and is, like his own cartoons, an illuminating distortion, a performance.

In their use of comic-book forms, the Maus books are experimental, postmodern, and radical. Why do the characters wearing animal masks move us? We might think at first that the mice masks would remove the characters from our empathy and sympathy. Yet as fellow humans in a cartoon universe rather than a category of their own, the characters wearing mice masks but having recognizable human experience within a history which we recognize become paradoxically all too human and engage our sympathies. After all, have we not seen presidents and kings in cartoons?

Buffeted about by a history that we cannot control and that often repels us, do we at times not feel like the cartoon Jews in Spiegelman's tale? Why does the carnivalesque nature of cartoon reality, the implied mockery of hegemonic pretension, successfully realize the Holocaust in such diverse works as Appelfeld's *Badenheim 1939* and Epstein's *King of the Jews* as well as *Maus*? Yet, when laughing, do we not feel empathetic with the victims and slightly complicit with the perpetrators? Do we not as readers—and especially those of us who are Jewish readers—occupy a moral borderland in which we are the crossing guards, the *Judenrat*? Finally, are not the *Maus* books effective in part because they upset us in their form as well as content?

In *Maus: A Survivor's Tale, I: My Father Bleeds History*, the narrator-cartoonist responds to his father's comment about personal relationships—"It has nothing to do with Hitler, with the Holocaust"—with the reassurance: "But Pop—It's great material. It makes everything more *real*—more human" (I.23). His father reluctantly probes the past, and when he does, he prefers to focus at first on his personal life—his sexual conquests and his more comfortable periods—in part because in reclaiming his history he is reclaiming his own homeland: *his story*. Sem Dresden has insightfully commented about how Spiegelman's indirection intensifies representation of reality:

> Thus, *Maus: A Survivor's Tale* at first sight produces precisely the opposite of what was previously called figurative narration. But in this way the narrator achieves a different kind of parable and resemblance: he makes his point in the figures he draws, and he speaks, as is customary in comic strips, in simple words. The indirectness is that whereas everybody, from childhood on, knows that a fable does not refer to existing reality, here that relation is precisely emphasized. . . .
>
> . . . In the numerous (subtle) drawings, the Jews are presented as real mice of small stature, and the SS men, by contrast, often as big menacing animals nonetheless invariably confined within a small frame. Consequently, the whole leaps into sharp relief as in a miniature. And as for humor, I hardly dare say it, but humor is not completely absent. When the father mouse recounts that he thought it dangerous to go out into the street with his wife because she had a markedly Jewish and therefore conspicuous appearance, the problem

arises of how to show that in a mouse. Spiegelman draws a mouse without a tail. . . . This is startling, maybe even rather amusing, but clearly and above all frightening. It is possible that many will find this kind of representation insupportable, but in my opinion they would be wrong: a form of indirection and estrangement is created that, far from making one lose sight of the inexorable reality, makes it all the more strongly felt. (*Persecution, Extermination, Literature,* 45-46)

Kafka's *Metamorphosis* and the processes of metamorphosis and metaphoricity underlie *Maus*. The characters gradually devolve not simply into mice but into creatures primarily concerned with their own self-preservation and sometimes that of their spouses and children. If people are treated as insects, Kafka implies, they become insects in their own minds. As a Jew, Kafka understood the psychology of cultural diminishment. Like Kafka, who takes his metaphor, "an exploited man is like an insect," to its logical conclusion—that is, an exploited man *is* an insect, Spiegelman plays with the metaphor that weak men are mice. Spiegelman surely has read not only Kafka but also Wiesel's *Night* in which the Jews are called swine ("you, lazy swine" [17]) and dogs ("You'll all be shot, like dogs")—with the results that, in a classic response to verbal abuse, the Jews begin to feel that they are no longer human.

Let us turn to Spiegelman's graphics. The blood-red title of the first and originally only volume of *Maus* (1986) is repeated at the bottom in the extended title, *A Survivor's Tale: My Father Bleeds History;* the red title is above the black Nazi insignia in the midst of which is a picture of a white cat. Upon second glance, we see that the black section over the cat is the rest of the cat's head (including the second ear) and that the cat bears a strong resemblance to Hitler. Spiegelman's Nazi insignia looks like cartoon versions of arms and legs harassing the two bewildered mice huddled below—mice with much more human features and human dress than the cat—representing his frightened father and terrorized and cowering mother. The cat and the black Nazi insignia, the swastika, are enclosed within a white circle—a cosmos, a globe—into which the blue mice and their faint greyish purple shadows intrude. The large title letters figuratively drip blood onto the circle below; that the "S" of Maus within the white circle contains the right angle of the swastika implies the effect of the German cat on the mice. As Thomas Doherty notes,

The pivotal inspiration for Spiegelman's cat and mouse gamble was the visual stereotypes of Third Reich symbology, the hackwork from the mephistoes at Goebbel's Reichsministry and Julius Streicher's venomous weekly *Der Sturmer*—the anti-Semitic broadsheets and editorial cartoons depicting Jews as hook-nosed, beady-eyed *Untermenschen*, creatures whose ferret faces and rodent snouts marked them as human vermin. . . . It is film that generated the iconic image of anti-Semitism under the Third Reich. . . . From subhumans to nonhumans, the Jews are linked with vermin, to be eradicated, like plague bearers, from the Fatherland. (74)

On the back cover of volume one, two mice—Spiegelman's surrogate self, lying on the floor, ubiquitous cigarette dangling from his mouth in front of his father sitting in an armchair—are superimposed on a map of Poland and its surrounding countries during World War II. On the map are marked major places in the story, while within this larger map, inserted on the right, is a second map, a street map of Rego Park where his father lives, complete with a small drawing of his house at the bottom; at the top of this second map is marked the Alexander's department store where his father buys a new coat. As if to emphasize how the past remains a harrowing part of the present, the street map is framed in the blood red of the title and of the bottom area of the cover page. The juxtaposition of scale—a few blocks of Rego Park and much of Eastern Europe—reminds us that history is composed of a concatenation of life stories and that Rego Park and other parts of New York became the reservoir, along with Israel, of the remnants of European Jewry that survived.

The second volume (1991)—the first chapter of which is called "Mauschwitz"—has the same cartoon at the top, but instead of foregrounding the two helpless mice, Spiegelman foregrounds six identical mice. The mice are enclosed by barbed wire, three pronounced strands of which seem to go through the page, only to meet outside the page and outside our field of vision as if to emphasize their helplessness. The mice wear concentration camp uniforms to show how the camps tried to deprive them of their individuality. The largest mouse on the left is cut off by the blood red of the side binding. Two of the mice are up against the barbed wire, two in the next row, the fifth behind, and the sixth is still further receding in the distance. The blood-red title "*Maus*" is exactly the same as in volume one. The title at the bottom is preceded by a large number "II"; on the top of two lines within the camp cartoon is the generic title of both volumes: "A Survivor's Tale;" underneath in the red border is the rest of the title of volume two: "And Here My Troubles Began." When we open the book, we see that the six mice on the cover in concentration camp uniform are the foremost of an endless series of receding mice in concentration camp garb, all with similar expressions but smaller as the eye moves upward. Is not Spiegelman perhaps questioning the traditional receding perspective that has dominated Western art since the Renaissance and, by implication, of the Eurocentric standards that inflicted such pain as the Holocaust? We recall that on the inside cover of volume one, the Jews in the ghetto—even while depicted as mice and wearing the homogenizing badge of the Jewish star—were strongly differentiated, while here they are homogeneous.

Maus is about memory—the terrifying historical past humanized in Vladek's memory and the troubled and painful personal recollections in both Vladek's narrative until his death in 1982 and in Art's story. The suggestive relationship between the two somewhat homophonic terms—Maus and memory—echoes throughout. Terence Des Pres has remarked: "It appears, moreover, that Spiegelman manages this double story only so long as the fairy-tale element intervenes; he requires a comic shield against knowledge too starkly hideous and weighted with guilt to face apart from laughter's mitigation. . . . It seems clear that the cat-and-mouse fable, together with its comic book format, work in a Brechtian manner to alienate, provoke, and compel new attention to an old story" ("Holocaust *Laughter?*" 228-229).

In the *Maus* books, the narrator-cartoonist is as much the subject as the father. Indeed, just as in Conrad's *Heart of Darkness*, in which Marlow's quest to discover the meaning of Kurtz's experience becomes an inquiry into the meaning of his own life, so Spiegelman's persona, Art, is learning about himself while examining his father's experience. He is looking for the appropriate semiotics with which to understand not only the Holocaust, but his own relationship to his father as the child of a survivor.

After these worst of times, the war ends; his father is reunited with his mother and Art is born in 1948. The subtitle of II, "And Here My

Troubles Began," refers to his father's comment "Here, in Dachau, my troubles began;" *troubles*, we soon realize, refer not only to typhus that led, at least in Vladek's own mind, to diabetes and his failing health, but also to the son's sense of his heritage of guilt and neurosis. Thus, "my troubles" refers to Art's own emotionally scarred life. As he puts it at the beginning of the second book—after his first book has been a stunning success and brought him great acclaim: "I mean, I can't even make sense out of my relationship with my father. . . . How am I supposed to make any sense out of Auschwitz? . . . Of the Holocaust?" (II.14). As his father's son, he is imbued with the Holocaust; one of his childhood fantasy games—recalling *Sophie's Choice*—is to decide "which of my parents I'd let the Nazis take to the ovens if I could only save one of them. . . . Usually I saved my mother" (II.14). Born after the Holocaust and the reuniting of his parents, he wonders whether he would have gotten along with the brother who died during the Holocaust. Art calls him "my ghost-brother" because his brother's "large, blurry" photo-graph—presumably the one in the dedication to volume two—hung in his parents' bedroom rather than his own (II.15). His words belie his statement that he didn't feel guilt about replacing that brother: "The photo never threw tantrums or got in any kind of trouble. . . . It was an ideal kid, and I was a pain in the ass. I couldn't compete" (II.15).

While his father—to cite the subtitle on the title page of volume one—"bleeds history," the son *bleeds art*. Put another way, Vladek's history (*his story*) fathers Art; as he admits to Francoise, his self-controlled and sympathetic non-Jewish wife, "One reason I became an artist was that he thought it was impractical—just a waste of time. . . . It was an area in which I wouldn't have to compete with him" (I.97). The *Maus* books, particularly in the more self-reflexive and at times self-immersed volume two, dramatize an oedipal struggle with his father for his mother's love. Even while we compassionately respond to the son's traumatic writer's block and neurosis and see how it is the result of his upbringing, even as we realize his memories are as real as his father's, we also are aware of the distinction between, on one hand, the Holocaust circumstances shaping the father and, on the other, suburban life shaping the son in Rego Park. When during his reminiscences his father loses his narrative line—often by complaining about his second wife, Mala—the son becomes the father of his own father and scolds him and cajoles him back to his testimony. While the father recalls acting intuitively to save his life during the Holocaust, Art is paralytically self-conscious about his ability to create. At the beginning of the second book, he self-abasingly remarks to his wife: "I feel so inadequate trying to reconstruct a reality that was worse than my darkest dreams. . . . There's so much I'll never be able to understand or visualize. I mean, reality is too complex for comics. . . . So much has to be left out or distorted" (II.16).

Let us examine volume one more closely. Preceding its two-page prologue dated 1958 is a page containing acknowledgments—and a quote from Hitler: "The Jews are undoubtedly a race, but they are not human." In the prologue, dated "Rego Park, N.Y. c. 1958," father and son are depicted with mouse heads and tails. The son had been roller skating. The opening frame shows children on roller skates with mouse heads and tails; a pipe-smoking, two-legged figure with a dog face—later we understand dogs as Americans—looks on as he mows his lawn. When young Art falls while skating, his friends leave him and he goes home crying. His father cynically says: "If you lock them together in a room with no food for a week. . . . *then* you could see what it is, friends!" (I. 6). Rereading, we recall the passage in which he tells Anja, his wife—and Art's mother: "Don't worry about friends. Believe me, they don't worry about you. They just worry about getting a bigger share of your food" (II.56). On the title page following the prologue, along with the "Contents," is an almost full-page picture of an elegant figure dressed in black with the mouse head but without the mouse tail; he is dancing with a shorter, high-heeled, floral-dressed and bejeweled mouse who lacks a tail. Underneath is an ominous shape on which they dance, a shape that could be a shadow, implying the encroaching and unforeseen historical events that will obliterate their lives.

Opening with Artie—the father's diminutive for "Art"—visiting his father Vladek, chapter one of volume one is ironically called "The Sheik" because his father remembers that as a boy he was told that he looked like Rudolph Valentino. We do not see much of his facial features; the son is compulsively smoking and the father wears spectacles. By first humanizing Vladek, Spiegelman prepares the reader to respond to his father as an individual when later he becomes a victim of persecution. And his father continues to father Art, the narrator, in the present, and to father him as an oppressive presence still caught, as we all are, in our historical circumstances. Vladek says pointedly to his son, who always is compulsively smoking in his presence during the interviews and on most other occasions: "Because I never smoked—I had cigarettes to trade for food" (II. 54).

During the scenes that dramatize the complex father-son relationship informing the interviews that are the source of the *Maus* books, Art's obsessive behavior—including his obsession with his mother's death—mirrors his father's in ways he does not always see. Is not his compulsive smoking a kind of parody of his father's repetition compulsion that takes the form of repeating locutions and *saving* everything? As a child Art had dreams of "men coming into our class and dragging all us Jewish kids away" and fantasies of "Zyklon B coming out of the showers" (II.16). Does not his own abrupt manner—including his rudeness to Mala when he tells her how terrible her coffee is—recall his father's bullying rudeness? In spite of himself, does he not show symptoms of the same kind of self-absorption and dependence on his wife that we see in Vladek?

To return to the graphics of *Maus*, on the back of volume two is a 1944 map of Auschwitz and an Auschwitz II (Birkenau) map that features a foregrounded "Gas Chamber and Crematorium II" from which exits a huge column of black smoke; the column, three inches in height, blots a good deal of the map and suggests the sharp angles of the Nazi insignia; here the insert at the left, labeled New York—larger than the Rego Park insert of volume one's back page but much smaller in scale— is again framed in red and is of the New York area including the Catskills vacation area, where volume two opens, and Rego Park.

That Art captures his father's spoken testimony on a tape recorder is, like the photographs, part of the documentary nature of *Maus*; we realize that the cartoons, along with the photographs, his father's oral testimony, and his own narrative to the psychiatrist, are Spiegelman's way of presenting a complicated, multifaceted view of his father's and his own life. Except for the striking title, the cover pages, and the introductory material, much of the time words take precedence over images as we become accustomed to Spiegelman's basic trope of the Jews as mice. Yet, as we read, we never forget the images. At crucial moments the visual images of the drawings dominate the verbal text.

One such moment is the overpowering segment in *Maus I* from the 1972 underground comic *Prisoner on the Hell Planet.* The cartoonist-narrator, obviously a surrogate for Spiegelman, depicts himself in clothing that suggests his father's concentration camp uniform. The aforementioned photographic insertion, which he shows us at the close of volume two, emphasizes how the son has transferred the position of victim to himself. Dressing in concentration camp garb, Art has transformed his psyche into an imprisoning camp. Just as his father Vladek's liberation is only partial, so the creation of *Maus*—among other things, a desperate kind of self-therapy—does not free Art from his past. Clearly he conflates his terrifying memory of the state mental hospital—he, like his mother, has been institutionalized—with his father's memory of the concentration camp. This is a visual example of how Art's trauma finds external confirmation for his own inner chaos. The focus is his mother's suicide in 1968, and his feeling that she "committed the perfect crime," leaving him imprisoned in his own guilt: "You *murdered* me, mommy, and you left me here to take the rap!!!" (I. 103). The last word of volume one is Art's muttering "Murderer" to himself as an accusation of his father for destroying his mother's diaries, which he takes as metonymy for the father's not taking care of his fragile mother and driving her to suicide by his unreasonable demands (I.159).

The narrator's depiction of himself dressed in the garb of the prison camps comes right after he presents, as part of his father's reminiscence, an *Aktion* in which the Jews of Sosnowiec are held and separated in two groups, one that may go home and one that is to be deported. During the Sosnowiec selection, Vladek's own father, who had been spared, willingly goes on the side with the deportees to protect his daughter (Vladek's sister) who has been, with her four children, "selected" for the "bad side"—and "those on the bad side," Vladek recalls, "never came anymore home" (I.91). When we see Vladek display at the end of the second book the photos of all those he has lost, and recapitulate in our minds what he has gone through, including the loss of his parents, we are more forgiving of Vladek's obsessive and self-indulgent behavior.

Another example of the strong preeminence of the visual is the way that Art presents himself in 1987: After the success of *Maus I* and five years after the death of his father in 1982, the cartoonist-narrator feels very small and depicts himself as metamorphosing in stages into a tiny infantile child mouse ("I want—I want—my Mommy!" [II. 42]); he retains that size when he visits his psychiatrist. In his insecurity after the publishing triumph of volume one, Art the narrator (Spiegelman's surrogate) doubts himself and feels not like a Jew, but like a person posing as a Jew. In the scene in which he is a dwarf mouse in the psychiatrist's office, both he and the psychiatrist wear masks. We might recall the deft visual rendering of the Beckett-like dialogue between the psychiatrist—himself a Czech Jew and survivor of Terezin and Auschwitz—when he depicts himself as a little mouse boy of about three in a big chair. His miniature version of his mouse self exclaims: "Samuel Beckett once said: 'Every word is like an unnecessary stain on silence and nothingness'" (II.45). Following a humorous frame in which the two smoke in self-absorbed silence, in the next frame Art looks up and says: "On the other hand, he SAID it" (II.45). When the psychiatrist, perhaps not fully grasping Art's point, responds: "He was right. Maybe you can include it in your book," Art gloomily retreats: "My book? Hah! What book?? Some part of me doesn't want to draw or think about Auschwitz. I can't visualize it clearly, and I can't BEGIN to imagine what it felt like" (II.46).

Finally, the visual often dominates when characters are visualized not as humans with animal heads but as wearing the masks of the animals. By showing profiles, Spiegelman can show the mouse mask (II. 45). He stresses that the very *mouseness* of the Jews—which was a condition of how others saw them—has been internalized at times into the psyches of the survivors and their families. Interestingly, when he is with his father within his imagined mouse ontology, the narrator always depicts himself as a mouse, not the human figure who periodically wears a mouse mask at those times when he feels diminished.

The Jews are systematically deprived of their humanity until they become toys for the German cats. *Maus* begins when Spiegelman's father is making his way in the world, marrying comfortably, and living a life in which private concerns dominate. But his life—*his story*—is invaded and overwhelmed by history. Spiegelman has a double focus: (1) his father's increasingly grim retrospective personal narrative of the wartime years; and (2) his often humorous but poignant present relationship with his caring but intrusive father.

Spiegelman reminds us that his father's memory shapes all his behavior. Thus without asking, Vladek throws out his son's old coat and gives him the used jacket he had been wearing but has just replaced. Vladek sometimes substitutes his caring for people with an obsession with objects, but isn't that (we realize even if Art does not) a function of the losses—wife, child, dignity, self—he has suffered? There is some truth in the testimony of Mala, Vladek's second wife with whom he is always quarreling (as if she were responsible for his first wife's history), that "He's more attached to things than to people!" (II. 93)—perhaps, we realize, because when one loses both people and things, one discovers losing things is easier.

The metaphoricity—should we say *metaferocity?*—of mice not only keeps his father's Holocaust story at a distance with which the narrator can cope but holds at bay his own narrative of guilt and pain, too. Spiegelman's words and drawings reinscribe this memory. In the fourth section of volume one, "The Noose Tightens," we read of a world of relocations, public hangings, Jewish police, deportations, and, finally, Auschwitz.

The title page of chapter two, volume one, ironically entitled "The Honeymoon," shows small well-dressed mice attending to a three-sectioned swastika flag that emerges from a building on the left and overshadows them. Even as Vladek becomes prosperous, his wife has a nervous breakdown and needs to go to a sanitarium; as they travel to Czechoslovakia they see a swastika flag and they learn of a pogrom in Germany. The elegant dancing scene described above anticipates their visit to a sanitarium—"one of the most expensive and beautiful in the world"—that suggests Appelfeld's Badenheim resort and Mann's sanitarium in *The Magic Mountain* (I.32). For as they discover when they return to Poland three months later, the rest of Europe is devolving into a nightmare for Jews.

Another aspect of the mouse analogy is that to survive the victims at times become like mice hoarding their crumbs. We watch how communities unravel and self-preservation becomes by necessity the only focus. We see how the terrible tension between self-survival and guilt hovers over impossible moral choices. Vladek criticizes those who operate only in their self interest—he calls such a person a "Kombinator," "a schemer . . . a crook" (I. 116). But Vladek himself has something of that reputation and knows how to look after himself as when he gives his father-in-law, whose house has become the residence of the entire family after the Nazis seize family property, only half of what he makes while pretending to give him all (I. 77).

Vladek's physical and emotional journey recapitulates the *topoi* of the Holocaust narrative: the rise of the Nazis and its effects on Jews, the deprivation of property and human and legal rights, the isolation and marginalization, the physical beatings, the ghettos, concentration camps, starvation and debilitating illness, torture, gas chambers and chimneys, and finally, a liberation with burdens of nightmare and guilt. Vladek, the father figure in *Maus*, has been historically shaped and carries the invisible internal tattoos of his exodus.

Maus has important parallels to *The Odyssey*. *Maus* is a postmodern yet humanistic response to the way Jews survived by Odyssean wiliness, compromise, and courage even while passionately feeling the pain of loss. The figure of the son in *Maus* is a retelling of Telemachus's search—and that of Joyce's Stephen Dedalus—for a father as well as of Odysseus's search for a home. As Odysseus, Vladek is trying to return home, but in the absence of his first wife, who has committed suicide, he cannot find that home with his second wife. Doesn't Spiegelman's humanization of his father's postwar diurnal life—of the father's obsessive, frugal collecting, his painful domestic life, and his poignant comic defenses—recall Joyce's Bloom? Perhaps we can say that Spiegelman, the postmodernist, actualizes in his narrative the darkest impulses in the modernist James Joyce's *Ulysses*: the hanging of an innocent hero, Bloom, prior to the trial in the epic-romance telling in "Cyclops"; the metaphorical crucifixion of Bloom at the end of "Cyclops" by Bloom's acquaintances; and the obsession on the part of the Irish with making distinctions between Jews and others. Is not Spiegelman obsessed with *difference* as a function of what he has learned from his father about the historical difference imposed on his father and fellow Jews?

I ask myself why I—who rarely even read *Doonesbury*, wouldn't think of reading any other comics, and never had much interest in comics or cartoons—am so fascinated and enthralled by *Maus*. What is so compelling and why do I continually reread it? As Terence Des Pres has written, "In Spiegelman's book, laughter is used to dispel and to embrace, a kind of comic ambiguity that diffuses hostility, on the one hand, and on the

other prompts charity towards those who suffered, those who remember, and also those who might simply wish to know" ("Holocaust
Laughter?" 232).

Much of Holocaust narrative is quite conservative and traditional.
Authors reflexively return to expected narrative forms as if they were
necessary strategies for the solemnity and high seriousness required by
the subject matter. As Des Pres remarks, "In its homage to fact, high
seriousness is governed by a compulsion to reproduce, by the need to
create a convincing likeness that never quite succeeds, never feels
complete, just as earnestness feels inadequate to best intentions" ("Holocaust *Laughter?*" 219). Ironically but understandably, many of our authors
revert at times to the very polemical and pontificating stance of the
world in which the Holocaust took place, a world in which Nazi
language and forms dominated and deprived them of space for playful
and innovative kinds of discourse. The paradox is that perhaps at this
distance of years the Holocaust may be better grasped within the human
ken of understanding rather than when isolated as a sacred event apart
from human history. Just as Picasso captures the horrors of war in the
abstractions and distortions of *Guernica,* so Spiegelman's comic imagination seizes upon the potential of cartoons to emphasize the terrifying
ludicrousness of Nazi behavior. He allows us to laugh at human foibles.
Rather than look at these mice from a steep and icy peak, our dominant
emotion is to see our human commonality with them.

CHAPTER FOURTEEN

CYNTHIA OZICK'S FABLES:
"THE SHAWL" AND "ROSA"

I

While we have been careful to differentiate between memoirs and documentary fiction posing as memoirs, and realistic novels and fables, Holocaust narratives have become a genre of their own with their own *topoi*, archetypes and patterns of continuity and disruption. Holocaust narratives draw upon history and recast it in narrative form. But history often depends on the lived experience of individuals; just as Holocaust narratives—diaries, memoirs, meditative essays such as Levi's *The Periodic Table*—create a fictional order, so do Holocaust fictions depend often on actual events, or at least the verisimilitude of such. Thus, Sidra DeKoven Ezrahi remarks "'[T]he distorted image of the human form which the artist might present as but a mirror of nature transformed can hardly be contained within the traditional perimeters of mimetic art, because, although Holocaust literature is a reflection of recent history, it cannot draw upon the timeless archetypes of human experience and human behavior which can render unlived events familiar through the medium of the imagination" (*By Words Alone* 2-3). As an "exception" to traditional mimesis, Ezrahi continues, "the representation of the Holocaust in art is, essentially, an oscillation and a struggle between continuity and discontinuity with the cultural as well as the historical past" (3-4).

Ozick's volume *The Shawl* (1989), composed of two stories that originally appeared in *The New Yorker*, partakes of fable and realism; "Rosa" (1983) is more realistic than the earlier story "The Shawl" (1980) but retains the qualities of fable. By the 1980s, Ozick may have felt that the realistic tradition in Holocaust fiction had somewhat played itself out, and Ozick is influenced by the parables and folktales of the Yiddish and rabbinic tradition of Isaac Bashevis Singer and Franz Kafka and perhaps the magic realism of South American writers like Gabriel García Márquez.

Ozick is an observant Jew and a Zionist. The two stories that comprise *The Shawl*, "The Shawl" and "Rosa," embody two aspects of Holocaust fiction: life within the horrors of the camps and the death marches, and the retrospective view of those events by a survivor whose life has been shaped for decades by the horrors of those events. The relationship between the two stories shows how memory imbues the present with a corrosive energy. In a sense, the structure mirrors the younger Vladek's position in the Holocaust and the older Vladek's position in the American present in *Maus*. And the narrator of *The Shawl* stories is a version of Art. Even though the narrator is an omniscient third-person voice, Ozick's fiction uses what James Young has called the "rhetorical principle of testimony":

> If this "rhetoric of fact" is intended to provide an unusually compelling reading experience, merely to move the reader, then Adorno's objections to "Holocaust art" retain a certain validity. For in this case, the authors would indeed be wringing pleasure from the naked pain of the victims. If, on the other hand, these works only want to refrain from conferring an essential fictionality on actual historical events, then we might take into account both the legitimate impulse to document events *and* the manner in which "real past events" are inevitably fictionalized by any narrative that gives them form. (*Writing and Rewriting the Holocaust* 57)

Neil Davison writes: "Many of us would readily admit, however, that we 'feel' zeitgeist through fiction as much as we gain knowledge of event through documentation; moreover, while we may recognize the particular ideology shaping a narrative, we nonetheless gain perspective on culture and process through alternating our reading between fictive and historical works" (294).

In the first, much shorter story, "The Shawl"—its 2,000 words took up two pages when it appeared in *The New Yorker* in 1980—Rosa's focus is entirely on her abortive effort to save her daughter Magda who is fifteen months old and starving. Ozick's genius is to capture the tiny eye in the storm of history, to render a victim's pain at the moment of crisis. Holocaust literature often works best when rendering the nominalistic fabric of experience from the perspective of someone acted upon by events beyond her control. As Andrew Gordon notes, "Ozick manages to avoid the common pitfalls of Holocaust fiction: on the one hand, she does not sentimentalize, but on the other, she does not numb the reader with a succession of horrifying events" (1). That she never uses the word "Jew, " "Nazi," or "concentration" paradoxically increases the story's impact. The story's focus is on a woman protecting her baby; the reader must make sense of what is happening—if it were a death march, as it at first seems, why the electrified fence unless they stop at a camp along the way?—and must give the tale historical context and setting. The story itself is a kind of skeleton, a miniature of the Holocaust. The story's lack of sentimentality gives it its power. Rosa knows she can't protect the baby, yet she is obsessed with trying; for her, Magda and the shawl become interchangeable.

Rosa's perceptions are a mixture of stark realism and fantasy; she fears that someone will eat Magda. Her obsession with cannibalism is an apt metaphor for the Nazis devouring life and a metonymy for a world in which human life has been reduced to a struggle for survival. Almost delirious, Rosa knows Magda is about to die and fears that someone will steal her, perhaps—such is the power of hunger in the death camp—to "eat her" (6): "[S]he should have been dead already, but she had been buried away deep inside the magic shawl, mistaken there for the shivering mound of Rosa's breasts. . . . Magda was mute. She never cried. Rosa hid her in the barracks, under the shawl, but she knew that one day someone would inform" (5-6). When Magda is exposed to the eyes of the camp guard, she is thrown to her death.

Ozick shows how the instinct for motherhood is all that remains; Rosa's adolescent niece Stella, the third party in their group march, thinks only of herself. To stay warm Stella takes the protecting shawl in which Rosa hides Magda, whom she is nursing. Once Rosa is stripped of the shawl, it is too late. She hears voices in the electrically charged fence. She sees Magda thrown against the fence by the steel helmets: "All at once Magda was swimming through the air. . . . She only stood, because if she ran they would shoot, and if she tried to pick up the sticks of Magda's body they would shoot, and if she let the wolf's screech ascending now through the ladder of her skeleton break out, they would shoot; so she took Magda's shawl and filled her own mouth with it, stuffed it in and stuffed it in . . ." (9-10). In a moment of desperate hope, she holds up the shawl to catch Magda's attention, but the guard is described in the powerful visual metonymy of a helmet above a shoulder, moving away from her, and Magda has become materialized as a creature. Rosa cannot run to her dead daughter lest she be shot. She hears "steel voices" and perceives Magda as a "butterfly touching a silver vine" (9-10). The powerful metaphoric passage of the butterfly, equated in Greek mythology with soul, is an appropriate image for Magda, but she is also "feathered"; her "pencil legs" are stressed. These images are juxtaposed to the steel, the metal hardness of the captors and their equipment. Rosa must suppress her instinctive "wolf's screech ascending through the ladder of her skeleton"; learning from Magda, she finds sustenance in a piece of cloth and nourishes herself on the taste of Magda's saliva. Indeed, oddly, the baby nourishes the mother; Rosa's quiet keeps Rosa and Stella alive. Is not her submission to her fate a grotesque version of the story of Abraham and Isaac? Rosa has been forced to offer her child to please a extrinsic power. Magda's suckling on the blanket is a grotesque parody of the expected scene of the nurturing mother saving the child. Rosa perceives in metaphors that intensify the grim sense of lifelessness and reinforce the claustrophobic quality of the situation. The phantasmagoric perceptions reflect her physical and psychological debilitation.

"The Shawl" is a play on the Hebrew term *Shoah* or *Sho'ah,* which literally means "desolation." As Davison notes, "Since the late 1960s the term has often been adopted to replace the word 'Holocaust' in naming the Nazi attempt at a genocide of the Jews. Those who employ the term believe that both the overuse of the word Holocaust, as well as its Greek etymology, rendered it both ineffectual and even insulting to the memory of those Jews and others who perished as a result of the Nazi regime. The 1985 premiere of Claude Lanzmann's documentary film, *Shoah*, did much to popularize this use of the term" (291). Yet for Rosa and even Stella and Magda the shawl is a pedestrian object transformed into a totem or fetish, a way of creating meaning in a time of terror. And the shawl recalls, too, the Jewish prayer shawl that honors the sacredness of life—here in the face of the Germans' efforts to destroy the Jewish people. Ozick wrote to Susanne Klingenstein, "The Shawl is *about*—no, is symbolically, the Nazi murders" (Klingenstein, 172). In "The Shawl" and "Rosa" we readers share in the morally confused universe of the characters, and we see the world through their obsessed and turbulent perspectives even as we try to make sense of it.

The shawl represents a tradition of Jewish life disrupted and destroyed: on a personal level, it represents the continuity of Jewish family life, protective warmth that bonds mother and daughter, but it always suggests the prayer shawl, the tallis worn by orthodox Jewish men at prayer; "The Shawl" opens in fragments to render Stella's feelings in basic, instinctive terms—as inchoate particulars of incomprehensible experience—as if to stress how human life has been so reduced to a struggle to survive that speech is no longer the province of the tortured: "How they walked on the roads together, Rosa with Magda curled up between sore breasts, Magda wound up in the shawl. Sometimes Stella carried Magda. But she was jealous of Magda. A thin girl of fourteen, too small, with thin breasts of her own, Stella wanted to be wrapped in a shawl, hidden away, asleep, rocked by the march, a baby, a round infant in arms. Magda took Rosa's nipple. . . . There was not enough milk" (3). We are in a world virtually deprived of dialogue. The only word is Stella's accusation "Aryan" (5)—which may, we learn in "Rosa," have some validity—and her excuse "I was cold" (6). Stella, Rosa believes, envies the protection that the shawl affords and the sparse food that Rosa's nipple promises but does not provide. Almost as if she were already deprived of life as she is deprived of sound, Magda is called the "shawl bundle" (4) and sucks on the shawl because Rosa's breasts are dry: "Magda's eyes were always clear and tearless. She watched like a tiger. She guarded her shawl. No one could touch it; only Rosa could touch it. Stella was not allowed. The shawl was Magda's own baby, her pet, her little sister. She tangled herself up in it and sucked on one of the corners when she wanted to be very still.

Then Stella took the shawl away and made Magda die. Afterward Stella said: 'I was cold.'" (6) . The parabolic nature of the story is emphasized by its surrealistic metaphors: "The weight of Rosa was becoming less and less; Rosa and Stella were slowly turning into air" (6). Yet paradoxical, these fantasy images are all the more compelling as a way to represent the horror: "Magda flopped onward with her little pencil legs scribbling this way and that, in search of the shawl; the pencils faltered at the barracks opening, where the light began" (7). Rereading, we see it as if Magda's pencils had written the text of Rosa's life.

The use of nonhuman images to describe humans stresses the dehumanizing quality of the camps. Looking into Magda's face through a gap in the shawl, Rosa sees "a squirrel in a nest" (4). As if an animal, Stella is described twice as "ravenous" (1, 5). Rosa is reduced to an animal protecting her young. Her sacrifice and love give a human touch to her feelings. Magda makes her first sound after the shawl is lost; she howls in the square in the roll-call area:

> "Maaaa—"
> It was the first noise Magda had ever sent out from her throat since the drying up of Rosa's nipples.
> "Maaaa . . . aaa!" (7-8)

Magda's instinctive cry contrasts with the omniscient narrator's elaborate prose about the lice and the rats and with her own prior silence.

The brevity of the story intensifies its claustrophobic nature. The reader is in a world where the usual patterns of thought—and life—are absent. Humans are reduced to silence, living with excrement, threatened with annihilation—this is the ontology of "The Shawl." Ozick's narrator creates an ontology in which the child's death is inevitable. How brilliant and powerful is the distinction between life and death, between expansion and reduction: "In the barracks they spoke of 'flowers,' of 'rain': excrement, thick turd-braids, and the slow stinking maroon waterfall that slunk down from the upper bunks, the stink mixed with a bitter fatty floating smoke that greased Rosa's skin" (8-9). "Flowers" and "rain" have become euphemisms for human excrement and waste. The world has constricted to an electric fence enclosing "lamenting voices" (9).

II

If "The Shawl," the first story, is a parable, a kind of grim magic realism, of the cultural rape by the Nazis of the Jews, of the gradual degradation resulting from deprivation, "Rosa," the sequel, is a tale of madness in contemporary America—but madness induced by Rosa's searing memories. "Rosa" owes much to magic realism, in which the protaganist's fantasies, dreams, and hallucinations become a living part of the imagined ontology. The deprivations and pressures of Rosa's situation have skewed her imagination; hers is a world of fantasy and the grotesque. The shawl—a metonymy for the memory of Magda—haunts Rosa as Holocaust memories haunt survivors.

"Rosa" is a story about Florida retirement for a woman who has nothing to retire *to*. It is also a story about how traumatic memory feeds obsessions and fixations. The reader immediately realizes that there is a relationship between the Rosa of "The Shawl" and this Rosa, an old woman living in squalor and filth in Miami. We are told that she writes "her daughter Magda" in "excellent literary Polish" (14). We wonder if Magda survived, but soon learn that she did not.

The narrator's words continually recall "The Shawl," and mirror Rosa's fixation on the Holocaust. She is 58 and has smashed her New York City store, as if she could reverse how the Nazis smashed Magda. "Rosa" opens with a startling sentence climaxing in an act of destruction: "Rosa Lublin, a madwoman and a scavenger, gave up her store—she smashed it up herself—and moved to Miami" (13). Her memory feeds her violent resistance: "The power to smash her own. A kind of suicide. She had murdered her store with her own hands" (46). As Rosa's baby has been smashed, as if she were an object, so she reenacts that destructive act. From the opening sentence, it is as if the narrator wants to recall the camps—and yet remind us of the difference. The text conceals as it reveals; the narrator first gives us Rosa's perspective, but relies on the reader to see an alternative one.

Rosa is consumed by hate and anger. Rosa lives in the shtetl of her own memories. Now in "Rosa" she hates her niece Stella, who had taken

Magda's shawl, and her fantasy of cannibalism echoes the earlier story. We recall how Rosa, disoriented by the death march, suspected Stella of wanting to eat Magda. Her "cannibal dreams" about Stella recall her premonition that Stella would devour Magda before Stella steals her shawl (15). Since Stella is now nearly 50, which means almost 36 years have passed, we know that "Rosa" takes place in about 1980.

Miami has become a "paradise" to survivors who escaped the camps. It has become a Jewish ghetto, a hyperbolic world recalling memories of pre-Holocaust Europe. Restaurants woo prospective diners with "Remembrances of New York and the paradise of your maternal kitchen" (29). When Rosa surveys the cafeteria, we think of Appelfeld's "The Retreat," in which a convalescent home was a metaphor for the ghetto: "Everyone had canes, dowager's humps, acrylic teeth, shoes cut out for bunions. Everyone wore an open collar showing mottled skin, ferocious clavicles, the wrinkled foundations of wasted breasts" ("Rosa" 24). She prides herself on her "aristocratic sensibility" and yet in Miami she lives in squalor, eating odds and ends, sleeping on filthy sheets. She sees herself in a mirror: "The reflection of a ragged old bird with worn feathers. Skinny, a stork. Her dress was missing a button, but maybe the belt buckle covered this shame" (23-4). She sees herself as an old woman: "If she moved even a little, an odor would fly up: urine, salt, old woman's fatigue" (24). In part because of her own complicity, she is now part of a different ghetto, the self-enclosed camp of the old. The scars of the events of "The Shawl" are always with her.

Time has stopped for Rosa. She gives her name as "Lublin, Rose" as if she were still filling out forms. Rosa's trauma lives every day as a continuing presence, "still quivering" arrow, as Eliot says of Bulstrode's past in *Middlemarch*. As Freud has written, "It must be explained that we are able to postulate the principle of a repetition-compulsion in the unconscious mind, based upon instinctual activity and probably inherent in the very nature of the instincts—a principle powerful enough to overrule the pleasure-principle, lending to certain aspects of the mind their daemonic character, and still very clearly expressed in the tendencies of small children; a principle, too, which is responsible for a part of the course taken by the analysis of neurotic patients. Taken in all, the foregoing prepares us for the discovery that whatever reminds us of this inner repetition-compulsion is perceived as uncanny" (quoted in Hertz's

"Freud and the Sandman," in Harari, *Textual Strategies* 300-301). Neil Hertz in "Freud and the Sandman" remarks: "repetition becomes 'visible' when it is colored or tinged by something being repeated, which itself functions like vivid or heightened language, lending a kind of rhetorical consistency to what is otherwise quite literally unspeakable. Whatever it is that is repeated—an obsessive ritual, perhaps, or a bit of acting-out in relation to one's analyst—will, then, feel most compellingly uncanny when it is seen as *merely* coloring, that is, when it comes to seem most gratuitously rhetorical" ("Freud and the Sandman," *Textual Strategies* 301).

Rosa's life is defined by Magda's death. Rosa repeats Magda's death every day in her fantasies, in her fixations, obsessions, and compulsions. Rosa lives in anger; "thieves," she believes, took her life. Rosa wants to live in the lost paradisiacal space of 39 years earlier, before her nightmare began. Her memory resists and distorts actual events. Rosa has asked for Magda's shawl to be sent by Stella: "Magda's shawl! Magda's swaddling cloth. Magda's shroud" (31). Rosa has a repetition compulsion. Several times, she reiterates "My Warsaw isn't your Warsaw" (19) and "Thieves took it." But more important the camps have left her with a special language and epistemology.

Like Appelfeld's Austrian Jews, Rosa considers herself superior to the other Jews. Like Spiegelman's father, Vladek, she needs to see herself as *different* and better. In Levi and Borowski, we saw the human need for differentiation in the camps, to distinguish between Jews and Poles, Greek Jews and Italian Jews, etc. Rosa had been taught mock Yiddish; the revelation of Madelaine Albright reminds us, as Zbigniew Brzezinski puts it, "of the symbiosis and interpretation between Jewish and non-Jewish populations in central Europe" (Erlanger, *The New York Times*, Feb. 5, 1997, 87). As we saw, Appelfeld's assimilated Jews patronized Eastern Jews. In the Gentile world, Yiddish was a sign that Jews couldn't speak a real language; to Eastern Jews, Yiddish *is* the voice of the Jew.

Words are the tools by which Rosa reconstructs life. She carries on a correspondence with Magda, to whom she writes at least daily, and she idealizes the world she left. She feels the most anger at being deprived of *her* Polishness, her language, her culture. As she repeats her love of her daughter and hatred of Stella in hyperbolic terms, she continuously repeats her superiority, as a member of a prominent Jewish Warsaw family, to lower-class Jews. Writing in Polish is for her a way of escaping her present pain: "To Retrieve, to reprieve. . . .To lie" (44). And what, we readers ask, *is* the lie? That Magda perished? Who, we ask, is the father? Was Rosa in a brothel?

Rosa's husband was in fact the son of a converted Jew married to a Gentile; but Rosa had been raped by a German (43). Rosa is still imprisoned by the long ago events, and her behavior parodies and repeats them. Can the reader be sure of the truth? Rosa's words are her own. How do *we* know? Rosa was engaged to the son of a converted Jewish woman who married a gentile, but how do we know that Magda's father was not the German who raped her? Yet Rosa can't lock out the truth: "My child, perished. Perished" (44). Past terrors inform the present. As if Rosa no longer has a coherent self, her fragmented perceptions recall "The Shawl."

Ozick shows us that the pain of Holocaust survivors is reinforced by the Holocaust industry, epitomized by Dr. Tree. She destroys Tree's letter in the fire that suggests the camps and resonates with memories of Magda's death: "Big flakes of cinder lay in the sink: black foliage, Stella's black will. Rosa turned on the faucet and the cinders spiraled down and away. . . . The world is full of fire! Everything, everything is on fire! Florida is burning!" (39).

Ozick's text dramatizes the dialogue in Holocaust studies about which language is appropriate: Yiddish, Polish, Hebrew. Rosa prefers to retain her pre-war identity before time stopped. "'I read only Polish,' she told Persky. 'I don't like to read in English. For literature you need a mother tongue'" (57). We think of *The Wall* in which Hersey dramatizes not only the distinction between the Westernized Jews and those who come from Eastern European shtetls but the conflict within characters between a self shaped within a Western enlightenment epistemology and value system, and a self dependent on intuition, family, and community culture.

Rosa's concluding letter to Magda, who is addressed, among other things, as "my paradise," revives her snobbery and arrogance. Through language Rosa insists on separating herself from the other Jews. The ghettos anticipate the worse horrors in the camps. In her post-Holocaust life, Rosa herself does learn "to organize" her necessities—*organize*, we recall, is the ghetto word for getting necessary food and clothing to survive (as in "organizing" a pair of shoes)—but she can't organize her mind.

Rosa's life revolves around the loss of Magda; so resistant is she to reality that she creates the ˇfiction that Magda lives, and is a doctor married to a doctor. She is partly aware that Magda is a fantasy, but only partly. In a letter she writes to Magda, she invents the past, and consigns Stella to dementia. Rosa's father, she recalls, is a nobleman and her own mother wanted to convert to Catholicism. Her words in the letter iterate her feelings in "The Shawl": "I'm saving you" (42).

Repetition compulsion—obsessive fascination with her own misery—shapes her every perception. Rosa becomes fixated on her lost underpants as if they were a metonymy for the shawl or Magda, as if she would somehow undo her plight by finding her pants, which represent her sexuality. She sets off on a pathetic odyssey to find her underpants: "Rosa walked; she saw everything, but as if out of invention, out of imagination; she was unconnected to anything" (47). Irrationally, she searches for her pants where she has never been. She gets locked into a gay beach area at night and thinks of being "locked behind barbed wire!" (49). The reference points for every perception are the overwhelming memories of the past. As if a witness who must speak, she challenges a hotel manager: "'Only Nazis catch innocent people behind barbed wire'" (51).

She recapitulates her past in every act as if it were embedded in her skin like the tattooed numbers of camp survivors: "They had trapped her, nearly caught her; but she knew how to escape. Speak up, yell. The same way she saved Stella, when they were pressing to take her on the boat to Palestine. She had no fear of Jews; sometimes she had—it came from her mother, her father—a certain contempt" (52). What she has lost, we realize, is her life, not her underpants: anticipating *Maus*, she imagines herself as a small insignificant animal, a rodent: "Nobility turned into a small dun rodent. . . . Lost. lost. nowhere" (53). Her *overactive* imagination compares Persky, the man who wishes to flirt with her, with an out-of-fashion button seeking a matching button. He is an optimist, but she would deflate him with a splash of her cynicism: "The life after is now. The life before is our *real* life, at home, where we was born. . . . Before is a dream. After is a joke. Only during stays. And to call it a life is a lie'" (58). Again, we think of *Maus*, where the anthropomorphized mouse figures are subservient to cats. Recalling her mother's fascination with virgin and child, she sees herself as "a Madonna" (59).

Rosa's language is polluted by the past. Ozick, like Spiegelman, uses black humor to render the survivor's pain; notice Rosa's response to his advances: "I'm not your button, Persky! I'm nobody's button, not even if they got barbed wire everywhere!" (61). Juxtaposed with the shawl as the image of suffering nostalgia is the image of buttons—representing present involvement in the world—and the underpants, representing the potential for future sexuality. Despite Rosa's longing for the symbolic shawl, buttons and underpants represent the real. While we cannot be sure if Persky is not partly a confidence man, Persky, unlike Stella, can deal with America and make it work. Yet, because Rosa has no husband, and Persky's wife, if he can be believed, is hospitalized for mental illness, their dialogue on buttons has a Beckett-like quality of miscomprehension and Ozick expects us to see the grotesque humor in their dialogue:

"Speaking of buttons, I'll go and push the elevator button. Tomorrow I'll come back."

"Barbed wire! You took my laundry, you think I don't know that? Look in your dirty pockets, you thief Persky!" (61)

Her mind is haunted by the past, the living Stella still cold-hearted and ironic, and the dead butterfly, Magda. Rosa cannot imagine her daughter without thinking of herself; it is a kind of desperate narcissism, if not infantile regression, caused by the trauma. Rosa remembers that Magda might be part-German: "The other strain was ghostly, even dangerous. It was as if the peril hummed out from the filaments of Magda's hair, those narrow bright wires" (65-66). The filaments suggest again Rosa's obsession with the electric fence.

Notice the unity of time: Persky rings the next morning after she discovers her underwear in her room. She has connected her phone and retrieved the shawl. When she does open the shawl box, the shawl becomes an effigy of Magda, but "For some reason it did not instantly restore Magda, as usually happened, a vivid thwack of restoration like an electric jolt" (62). Like so many of Rosa's phrases, "electric jolt" is a grim echo of "The Shawl." Electric wires suggest the camp fence against which Magda was electrocuted, and also the modern industrial world that engenders such horrors, including the tram running through the Warsaw ghetto. The electric wire of the tram running right through the ghetto in the letter becomes a metonymy for the electric fence on which Magda was thrown.

Survivors invent their own reality, and Rosa's existence is one in which the past is a living, harrowing present. Survival for Rosa means to breathe in a world of psychological imprisonment; yet, we are aware that she is alive, has human experiences, including the possibility of Persky, that she loves and hates and is part of the living world she disdains. Her mind re-creates the telephone (an extension of the electric fence) as a pathetic metonymy for Magda, but Persky offers her an alternative—the hope of transforming her life. The very announcement of Persky's visit seems to offer the promise of exorcising the memory of Magda: "The shawled telephone, a little grimy silent god, so long comatose—now, like Magda, animated at will, ardent with its cry. . . . Magda was not there. Shy, she ran from Persky. Magda was away" (70). When Rosa runs from Persky, who represents life, is she exorcising Magda, who represents death? Is the ringing phone a metonymy for a potentially vital and enriching alternative to her obsession with Magda? Or is she still locked in her repetition compulsion within the electrified barbed wire of her memory?

CHAPTER FIFTEEN

BRUNO SCHULZ'S NIGHTMARE IN *THE STREET OF CROCODILES* AND *SANATORIUM UNDER THE SIGN OF THE HOURGLASS* AND CYNTHIA OZICK'S RESPONSE IN *THE MESSIAH OF STOCKHOLM*

I

Among the Holocaust narratives is a subgenre that implies rather than addresses the Holocaust. Indeed, as we have noted, Kosinski's *The Painted Bird* is about a kind of xenophobia that is not Holocaust-specific and the dark boy victim could be a gypsy or a European of different ancestry than the Poles. Bruce Chatwin's *Utz* is about a Jewish collector of Meissen porcelain who sustains his collection through the Holocaust, although it is not clear why the authorities let him do this. Schulz's two collections, *The Street of Crocodiles* (originally published in 1934 under the title *Cinnamon Shops* without the later story "The Comet") and *Sanatorium under the Sign of the Hourglass* (originally published in 1937) are not Holocaust books. Yet they have a strange anticipatory intelligence. In light of what we know of history—and of Schulz's own life—we read his books differently. What Stephen Holden wrote about a recent Hungarian film is appropriate to the Eastern European phantasmagoria in *The Street of Crocodiles* and *Sanatorium under the Sign of the Hourglass*: "What if what we call our past is just a dream, and life is really a process of waking up to a different and harsher reality than anything we've been prepared to experience? The fear that life may only be a collection of memories and symbols that we willfully organize into a coherent narrative, the anxiety that what we call 'home' may only be an illusion, permeates Attila Janisch's 1997 film, 'The Long Twilight'" (Holden). It is as if in the 1930s Schulz intuitively understood the moral illness hanging over Europe, and subsequent events brought grotesque life to his feverish imagination. Among other things, Bruno Schulz's *The Street of Crocodiles* is an elegy for a way of life that disappeared. As Michael Kandel writes,

> These were Schulz's people, the people of Drogobych, at one time the Klondike of Galicia when oil was struck near the city and prosperity entered it and destroyed the old patriarchal way of life, bringing false values, bogus Americanization, and new ways of making a quick fortune—when the white spaces of an old map of the city were transformed into a new district, when the Street of Crocodiles became its center, peopled with a race of rattleheaded men and women of easy morals. The old dignity of the cinnamon shops, with their aroma of spices and distant countries, changed into something brash, second-rate, questionable, slightly suspect. (Introduction, *Street of Crocodiles* 11)

Schulz's books are fantasies in the tradition of Bosch, Ensor, and Kafka. If anything, *Sanatorium* has less of a plot then the first. If ever a book were about itself, a work of self-conscious reflexivity, pure textuality, it is this one. In *Sanatorium under the Sign of the Hourglass* anything is possible, for the rules of nature do not apply. Schulz's fictional surrogate turns up in a variety of fictional personae from a child to an old age pensioner. Perhaps in the title story he too is dead like his father. Humans take flight and metamorphose. Take the old-age pensioner who has turned into a child before being blown away by wind and finally disappearing: "'Boys, help, help!' I shouted, already suspended in the air. I could still see their outstretched arms and their shouting, open mouths, but the next moment, I turned a somersault and ascended in a magnificent parabola. I was flying high above the roofs. Breathless I saw in my mind's eye how my schoolmates raised their arms, and called out to the instructor: 'Please, sir, please, Simon has been swept away!'" (*Sanatorium* 170). After he is thought dead, his father turns into a crab and is boiled by his family for dinner. But being too fastidious to eat him, they put the dishes of seasoned crab in the sitting room: "One morning, we found the plate empty. One leg lay on the edge of the dish, in some congealed tomato sauce and aspic that bore the traces of his escape. Although boiled and shedding his legs on the way, with his remaining strength he had dragged himself somewhere to begin a homeless wandering, and we never saw him again" (*Sanatorium* 178)

The world is a kind of bibliocosm, a book that expands and contracts at will. As author, Schulz becomes God who can create in his book at will. The Authentic Book "unfolds while being read, its boundaries open to all currents and fluctuations. . . . This is the phenomenon of imagination and vicarious being. An event may be small and insignificant in its origin, and yet, when drawn close to one's eye, it may open in its center an infinite and radiant perspective because a higher order of being is trying to express itself in it and irradiates it violently" (*Sanatorium* 12-13).

The Book is a postulate, a site of infinite possibilities. The narrator begins by rejecting his father's view that "The Book is a myth in which we believe when we are young, but which we cease to take seriously as we get older" (*Sanatorium* 3). The *Book* is a controlling metaphor; it stands for energy and imaginative and creative action. It is a verb as well as a noun: "And the process of sleeping is, in fact, one great story, divided into chapters and sections, into parts distributed among sleepers. When one of them stops and grows silent, another takes up his cue so that the story can proceed in broad, epic zigzags while they all lie in the separate rooms of that house, motionless and inert like poppy seed within the partitions of a large, dried-up poppy" (*Sanatorium* 156). Just as Schulz's *Sanatorium* is complemented by his drawings, so is the imagined Book: "The drawings were full of cruelty, pitfalls, and aggression. . . . Fierce and rapacious, I would, with lightning bites, savage the creation that tried to escape from under my crayon. And that crayon only left the paper when the now dead and immobile corpse displayed its colorful and fantastic anatomy on the page, like a plant in a herbal" (*Sanatorium* 17). *Maus* may owe a debt to Schulz's integration of text and drawings in *Sanatorium*.

One might ask just how much Schulz's Jewishness—from which he was apparently alienated—has to do with the production of these weird, claustrophobic fantasies about idiosyncratic, obsessive figures—most notably Joseph and his father—who cannot function in daily life. Retrospectively do we see them as symptoms of a diseased culture? When the Germans arrive, did Schulz know how to take care of himself, or did he retreat into his aesthetic, narcissistic world, oblivious to the threats around him?

Along with Huysman and Wilde, Schulz has a kinship with the decadent tradition in Europe. He thumbs his nose at nature and, at times, its limitations. His point is that any drawings, any book—an old catalogue, even a stamp collection—may open the imagination of the reader-observer: "Can a stamp album serve as a textbook of psychology? What a naive question! A stamp album is a universal book, a compendium of knowledge about everything human. Naturally, only by allusion, implication, and hint. You need some perspicacity, some courage of the heart, some imagination in order to find the fiery thread that runs through the pages of the book" (*Sanatorium* 48). Nature and time defy our expectations. Rather than imitating reality, *texts* create reality: thus, the narrator writes of Eddie the cripple: "Every now and then he rises from the table and runs round the room, his hands in his windswept hair, and as he circles thus, he occasionally climbs a wall, flies along the wallpaper like a large gnat blindly hitting the arabesques of design, and descends again to the floor to continue his inspired circling" (*Sanatorium* 155).

Schulz's concept of the sanatorium anticipates Appelfeld's *The Retreat* and *Badenheim 1939*. It is the city of the dead, a city that replaces his city, Drogobych. (We think of how the dead occupy coterminous space with the living in Kafka's "The Hunter Gracchus.") Bizarre events occur. A telescope metamorphoses into paper and expands until it is large enough to ride: "Like a large black caterpillar, the telescope crept into the lighted shop—an enormous paper arthropod with two imitation headlights on the front. The customers clustered together, retreating before this blind paper dragon; the shop assistants flung open the door to the street, and I rode slowly in my paper car amid rows of onlookers, who followed with scandalized eyes my truly outrageous exit" (*Sanatorium* 124). It seems as if the narrator's father can be in two places at once: "How do I reconcile all this? Has Father been sitting in the restaurant, driven there by an unhealthy greed, or has he been lying in bed feeling very ill? Are there two fathers? Nothing of the kind. The problem is the quick decomposition of time no longer watched with incessant vigilance" (*Sanatorium* 127). He and his father sleep on the same bed; a kind of bizarre incestuous fantasy unless— and even if—they are both dead: "Time put back—it sounded good, but what does it come to in reality? Does anyone here get time at its full value, a true time, time cut off from a fresh bolt of cloth, smelling of newness and dye? Quite the contrary. It is used-up time, worn out by other people, a shabby time full of holes, like a sieve" (*Sanatorium* 131). He leaves, finally, and becomes a vagabond railway man.

We realize that the world of the Jews of Drogobych, a provincial city in Galicia, a province in Southeastern Poland, had disappeared. Schulz, a former teacher of drawing at the local high school, was among about 150 inhabitants of Drobobycz killed on November 19, 1942, in an *Aktion* carried out by local sections of the SS and the Gestapo.

Schulz's themes are: (1) the power of imagination to make one's own world, no matter what the circumstances, and (2) the fragility of diurnal human life, not only in terms of survival but in our assumptions about day-to-day sanity. Sudden disruptions of order, uprisings in dreams, radical changes of behavior, unsuspected flights of fantasy, even lunacy are the stuff of man in his stories. Imagination, fantasy, phantasmagoric landscapes are what his father uses to counter the monotony and boredom of the daily world. Words like "indifference" and "monotony" recur (*Street of Crocodiles* 142, 159).

Schulz is deeply indebted to Kafka and Mann. In the section entitled "Birds" in *The Street of Crocodiles*, his father is transformed into a bird:

> One day, during spring cleaning, Adela suddenly appeared in Father's bird kingdom. Stopping in the doorway, she wrung her hands at the fetid smell that filled the room, the heaps of droppings covering the floor, the tables, and the chairs. Without hesitation, she flung open a window and, with the help of a long broom, she prodded the whole mass of birds into life. A fiendish cloud of feathers and wings arose screaming, and Adela, like a furious maenad protected by the whirlwind of her thyrsus, danced the dance of

destruction. My father, waving his arms in panic, tried to lift himself into the air with his feathered flock. (*Street of Crocodiles* 50)

It is as if Kafka's *Metamorphosis* were Schulz's inspiration:

My father at the time no longer possessed that power of resistance which protects healthy people from the fascination of loathing. Instead of fighting against the terrible attraction of that fascination, my father, a prey to madness, became completely subjected to it. The fatal consequences were quick to follow. Soon, the first suspicious symptoms appeared, filling us with fear and sadness. Father's behavior changed. His madness, the euphoria of his excitement wore off. In his gestures and expressions signs of a bad conscience began to show. He took to avoiding us. He hid, for days on end, in corners, in wardrobes, under the eiderdowns. I saw him sometimes looking pensively at his own hands, examining the consistency of skin and nails, on which black spots began to appear like the scales of a cockroach. (*Street of Crocodiles* 14-15)

If matter can be transformed, why can't humans become other kinds of matter, too? In *Street of Crocodiles*, the narrator recalls how his father imagined tailor's dummies as if they were golems—legendary creatures brought to life by magical powers. From our vantage point, it is as if Hitler were a diabolic version of his father's fantasy, a golem created by the bizarre imagination: "He was fascinated by doubtful and problematic forms, like the ectoplasm of a medium, by pseudomatter, the cataleptic emanations of the brain which in some instances spread from the mouth of the person in a trance over the whole table, filled the whole room, a floating, rarefied tissue, an astral dough, on the borderline between body and soul" (*Street of Crocodiles* 69). Recalling his father's "Treatise on Tailors' Dummies *or* the Second Book of Genesis," he shows an affinity for his father's delusions and fantasies:

"Figures in a waxwork museum," he began, "even fair-ground parodies of dummies, must not be treated lightly. Matter never makes jokes: it is always full of the tragically serious. Who dares to think that you can play with matter, that you can shape it for a joke, that the joke will not be built in, will not eat into it like fate, like destiny? Can you imagine the pain, the dull imprisoned suffering, hewn into the matter of that dummy which does not know why it must be what it is, why it must remain in that forcibly imposed form which is no more than a parody. (*Street of Crocodiles* 64)

The Holocaust makes real the nightmares of Schulz's father. For the inconceivable does occur on a daily basis. We see that paranoia is redefined as knowing all the facts. Schulz draws upon and mocks rabbinic traditions in which every conceivable subject was debated.

References to the shofar and especially the golem underline the Jewish context. His father is like a talmudic shtetl scholar living in a hermetic world separate from the events of the world. Yet, in his bizarre view of the dummy persecuted, we get a sense of the psychosis of the father as *isolato*—and of the son, too, as *isolato* who perhaps fears that his self-created book, his dummy, will be mocked and the creator persecuted.

Schulz's speaker's vision of Pan recalls Aschenbach's encounters, in Mann's *Death in Venice*, with the various Dionysian figures:

It was the face of a tramp or a drunkard. A tuft of filthy hair bristled over his broad forehead, rounded like a stone washed by a stream. . . . His dark eyes bored into me with the fixedness of supreme despair or of suffering. He both looked at me and did not, he saw me and did not see. . . .

And suddenly on those taut features there slowly spread a terrible grimace. The grimace intensified, taking in the previous madness and tension, swelling, becoming broader and broader, until it broke into a roaring, hoarse shout of laughter.

Deeply shaken, I saw how, still roaring with laughter, he slowly lifted himself up from his crouching position and, hunched like a gorilla, his hands in the torn pockets of his ragged trousers, began to run, cutting in great leaps and bounds through the rustling tinfoil of the burs—a Pan without a pipe, retreating in flight to his familiar haunts. (*Street of Crocodiles* 80)

But this ominous figure is lying in wait for Europe. And Schulz's speaker, especially in *The Street of Crocodiles*, is a kind of Apollonian figure, withdrawn from the world of passion into an aesthetic realm. Yet, paradoxically, Schulz's speaker also lives in the Dionysian world of fantasy, the one he creates for his father. Schulz has an eye for the bizarre and bestial in human life—the Dionysian, the impulse for terrifying disruption of an ordered, rational life. As Jerzy Ficowski puts it,

> When Schulz's popularity as a writer threatened his privacy and solitude, his creative work began to slacken, and more and more frequently he fell into barren and agonizing states of depression. He spoke and wrote to his friends many times of the blessings of seclusion, seeing it as absolutely essential for his art, although at the same time he was painfully aware of his isolation. In reply to a letter, he wrote to one of his acquaintances: "You overrate the benefits of my Drogobych existence. What I lack here too, even here, is silence, my own musical silence, the tranquil pendulum subject only to its own gravitation, having a clear line of movement, not troubled by any foreign influence. This substantial silence—positive, full—is itself almost art. (Introduction, *Street of Crocodiles* 21-22)

He writes of his father's psychotic imagination which transforms reality into fantasy and grotesque, a world that recalls the world of Bosch, Brueghel, and Ensor. We also see a strong debt to the distortions and exaggerations of German expressionism, too, including the work of Nolde, Kirchner, and Heckel. Yet, ironically, the Holocaust transformed his father's psychotic and paranoid visions into reality. Of course, Schulz's narrative voice, his surrogate, not only shares a bizarre imagination with his father, but objectifies his own fantasies and hallucinations in the dramatization of his father. One guesses that he is writing as much about himself as his father. We realize how his father's seemingly paranoid fears are finally realized by later historical events. His father is something of a demagogue, a version of a Nietzschean *Übermensch*, a Hitler manqué who creates reality to his own will: "It was not because there was no grain of truth in Father's discoveries. But truth is not a decisive factor for the success of an idea" (*Street of Crocodiles* 152). He remarks of his father's philosophical lectures: "It is worth noting how, in contact with that strange man, all things reverted, as it were, to the roots of their existence, rebuilt their outward appearance anew from their metaphysical core, returned to the primary idea, in order to betray it at some point and to turn into the doubtful, risky and equivocal regions which we shall call for short the Regions of the Great Heresy" (*Street of Crocodiles* 58).

The story "Cinammon Shops" is about the power of the imagination of the speaker, a young boy, who is sent home from a family theatre outing to get his father's wallet. The fantasies are triggered by anger and anxiety:

> It is exceedingly thoughtless to send a young boy out on an urgent and important errand into a night like that, because in its semiobscurity the streets multiply, becoming confused and interchanged. There open up, deep inside a city, reflected streets, streets which are doubles, make-believe streets. One's imagination, bewitched and misled, creates illusory maps of the apparently familiar districts, maps in which the streets have their proper places and usual names but are provided with new and fictitious configurations by the inexhaustible inventiveness of the night. (*Street of Crocodiles* 88)

That the boy has been living with a father who has become a frightening presence in his life is reflected in his surreal description:

> His face and head became overgrown with a wild and recalcitrant shock of gray hair, bristling in irregular tufts and spikes, shooting out from warts, from his eyebrows, from the openings of his nostrils and giving him the appearance of an old ill-tempered fox.
>
> His sense of smell and his hearing sharpened extraordinarily and one could see from the expression of his tense silent face that through the intermediary of these two senses he remained in permanent contact with the unseen world of mouseholes, dark corners, chimney vents, and dusty spaces under the floor. (*Street of Crocodiles* 85)

Finally, in a version of the Cinderella story, the boy imagines himself on a magic ride on a riderless horse, a ride that takes him from the stifling world of today into a fantasy world in which all things are possible:

At last we stopped. I got out of the cab. The horse was panting, hanging its head. I hugged its head to my breast and saw that there were tears in its large eyes. I noticed a round black wound on its belly. "Why did not you tell me?" I whispered crying. "My dearest, I did it for you," the horse said and became very small, like a wooden toy. I left him and felt wonderfully light and happy. I was debating whether to wait for the small local train which passed through here or to walk back to the city. I began to walk down a steep path, winding like a serpent amidst the forest; at first in a light, elastic step; later, passing into a brisk, happy run which became gradually faster, until it resembled a gliding descent on skis. I could regulate my speed at will and change course by light movements of my body. (*Street of Crocodiles* 96-97)

We realize that the narrator's father's bizarre imagination is a metonymy for his own; moreover, the boy, living like his father in a fantasy, is a version of the author who frees himself in the ontology of his fictions from the claustrophobic world of Drogobych. Yet the boy's fantasies have a gentleness, a utopian and idealistic frailty that his father's visions lack.

When Schulz writes of the fantasy of the Great Season in "The Tale of the Great Season" we realize that Hitler had already come to power in 1934. We see a striking parallel in the coming of the "vast night" following the "plague of dust," as if Schulz had written an allegory of the transformation in the life of Jews:

And while the children's games became increasingly noisier and more complicated, while the city's flushes darkened into purple, the whole world suddenly began to wilt and blacken and exude an uncertain dusk which contaminated everything. Treacherous and poisonous, the plague of dusk spread, passed from one object to another, and everything it touched became black and rotten and scattered into dust. People fled before it in silent panic, but the disease always caught up with them and spread in a dark rash on their foreheads. Their faces disappeared under large, shapeless spots. They continued on their way, now featureless, without eyes, shedding as they walked one mask after another, so that the dusk became filled with the discarded larvae dropped in their flight. Then a black, rotting bark began to cover everything in large putrid scabs of darkness. And while down below everything disintegrated and changed into nothingness in that silent panic of quick dissolution, above there grew and endured the alarum of sunset, vibrating with the tinkling of a million tiny bells set in motion by the rise of a million unseen larks flying together into the enormous silvery infinite. Then suddenly night came—a vast night, growing vaster from the pressure of great gusts of wind. In its multiple labyrinths nests of brightness were hewn: the shops—large colored lanterns— filled with goods and the bustle of customers. Through the bright glass of these lanterns the noisy and strangely ceremonial rites of autumn shopping could be observed. (*Street of Crocodiles* 129-130)

In terms of plot and character, not much happens, but the accretion of language—"contamination," "poisonous," and "treacherous"—creates an ominous effect. The ghetto life was marked by a kind of group manic depression, in which intermittent and frantic quest for pleasure interrupted the tedium, grimness, and desperation of daily life.

In this tale the speaker identifies "the fathers of the city" as members of the Great Synhedrion (*Street of Crocodiles*, 135), who, we realize, soon will become the Jewish councils and Judenrat. Schulz could almost be describing life in the ghetto: "The dense crowd sailed in darkness, in loud confusion, with the shuffle of a thousand feet, in the chatter of a thousand mouths—a disorderly, entangled migration proceeding along the arteries of the autumnal city. Thus flowed that river, full of noise, of dark looks, of sly winks, intersected by conversations, chopped up by laughter, an enormous babel of gossip, tumult, and chatter" (*Street of Crocodiles* 130). The speaker imagines his father as an Old Testament prophet: "When my father, horrified by the hideousness of sin, merged his angry gestures with the awe-inspiring landscape, the carefree worshipers of Baal below him gave themselves up to unbridled mirth. An epidemic of laughter took hold of the mob" (*Street of Crocodiles* 134). In reductive psychoanalytic diagnostic terms, the father is a psychotic who has totally lost his grip on reality. But he is also a prefiguration of learned Jews who found refuge in a hermetic world while the flames of European conflagration gathered.

The comet in the tale of that name is an allegory of a grotesque apocalyptic moment, when assumptions and expectations are turned upside down. Is the comet a possible metonymy for Hitler's coming to power? According to Schulz's narrator, the comet causes not only a breakdown of social conventions and quotidian habits, but mass hysteria:

> Lost in the infinite, we had almost forsaken the earthly globe under our feet; we were disoriented, losing our bearings, . . . emigrants from an abandoned globe, plundering the immense antheap of stars. . . . After short, incoherent days, partly spent in sleeping, the nights opened up like an enormous, populated motherland. Crowds filled the streets. . . . The stairs broke under the weight of thousands, at all the upper floor windows little figures appeared, matchstick people jumping over the rails in a moon-struck fervor, making living chains, like ants, living structures and columns—one astride another's shoulders—flowing down from windows to the platforms of squares lit by the glare of burning tar barrels. . . .
>
> Again the sky opened above us with its vastness strewn with stellar dust. In that sky, at an early hour of each night appeared that fatal comet, hanging aslant, at the apex of its parabola, aiming unerringly at the earth and swallowing many miles per second. All eyes were directed at him, while he, shining metallically, oblong in shape, slightly brighter in his protuberant middle, performed his daily work with mathematical precision. How difficult it was to believe that that small worm, innocently glowing among the innumerable swarms of stars, was the fiery finger from Belshazzar's feast, writing on the blackboard of the sky the perdition of our globe. But every child knew by heart the fatal formula expressed in the logarithm of a multiple integer, from which our inescapable destruction would result. What was there to save us? (*Street of Crocodiles*, 154-155, 157)

Note how the comet is described in apocalyptic terms in the third-person singular; the "he" and "him" is a "small worm" whose words—in a parody of the Book of Daniel—write a prophecy of "our inescapable destruction." Schulz renders the ominous feelings of social disruption—

"we were disoriented, losing our bearing," "emigrants from the abandoned globe"—in metaphorical terms that capture the uncertainty and
moral laxity of people living under circumstances they cannot control.
Surely Schulz was aware of various solutions to the Jewish problem that
were proposed, like mass emigration—actually deportations to a place
such as Madagascar. If there is a dominant motif in *The Street of
Crocodiles*—even in the English title—it is anxiety, nervousness, fear of
the unknown, and a concomitant desperate desire to know and control.

Schulz is writing at a time when industrialism still is associated with
promise; yet he seems skeptical about modernist improvements that
have little effect on the inner life that his introspective, private self
values. When discussing the advent of electrical gadgets, Schulz anticipates the triumph of technology in the German system of mass
destruction: "It was the age of electricity and mechanics and a whole
swarm of inventions was showered on the world by the resourcefulness
of human genius. In middle-class homes cigar sets appeared equipped
with an electric lighter: you pressed a switch and a sheaf of electric
sparks lit a wick soaked in gasoline. The inventions gave rise to
exaggerated hopes. . . . In every house electric bells were installed.
Domestic life stood under the sign of galvanism" (*Street of Crocodiles* 142-
143). His view of riders of velocipedes reminds us of the modernist
fascination—seen in Picasso, Mann, Stevens, and Joyce—with such
popular culture figures as circus performers, clowns, magicians, and
street singers. Of cyclists, he writes: "Man was entering under false
pretenses the sphere of incredible facilities, acquired too cheaply, below
cost price, almost for nothing, and the disproportion between outlay
and gain, the obvious fraud on nature, the excessive payment for a trick
of genius, had to be offset by self-parody" (*Street of Crocodiles* 144).

The reversal of daily life, the dehumanization and transformation of
men to creatures—as in the aforementioned story "Birds"—is a strange
prolepsis of the Holocaust. Schulz writes as an outsider and *isolato* who
imagines the delusions of other outsiders, principally his father. He
writes of the disruption of daily routines—the kind of disruption of time
that turmoil and displacement did create in Jews who experienced
mindless violence and deportation: "Time, begets sometimes other
years, different, prodigal years which—like a sixth, smallest toe—grow
a thirteenth freak month. . . . There are people who liken these days to

an apocrypha, put secretly between the chapters of the great book of the year; to palimpsests, covertly included between its pages; to those white, unprinted sheets on which eyes, replete with reading and the remembered shapes of words, can imagine colors and pictures" (*Street of Crocodiles* 125, 126). As Jerzy Ficowski writes, "Schulzian time—his mythic time—obedient and submissive to man, offers artistic recompense for the profaned time of everyday life, which relentlessly subordinates all things to itself and carries events and people off in a current of evanescence. Schulz introduces a subjective, psychological time and then gives it substance, objectivity, by subjecting the course of occurrences to its laws" (Introduction, *Street of Crocodiles* 18).

Given his strange, discontinuous images, his encyclopedic pastiches, his meditative riffs, his absence of a traditional plot, characters, or dramatized narrator, Schulz more than our other writers belongs to postmodernism. Schulz finds refuge from pain in an aesthetic world, as do Spiegelman and Epstein. Do not Holocaust writers such as Spiegelman, Epstein, and Schwarz-Bart, draw upon this grotesque and hyperbolic tradition? Did these writers know Kafka and Schulz? Perhaps we see the influence of Schulz's grotesque cartoons in Spiegelman's *Maus* and Epstein's visionary moments in *King of the Jews*.

II

I close with a novel by Cynthia Ozick based on the fantasy that a son of Bruno Schulz, author of *The Street of Crocodiles* and *Sanatorium Under the Sign of the Hourglass*, survived. Her response is a trope for how we read Holocaust fiction, trying desperately to discover not only the essential facts of an experience that eludes us but more importantly to learn what it felt like to be a victim, a survivor, or a survivor's child. *The Messiah of Stockholm* (1987) depends on a dialogue with Schulz's fiction. Ozick's novel uses the conceit that Schulz had a son who lived and made his way to Stockholm. Prior to her title page is Schulz's self-portrait. Ozick creates a character who tries unsuccessfully to capture a lost world. She has dedicated her novel to Philip Roth who excavated Schulz from literary archaeology and edited the "Writers from the Other Europe" series in which Schulz's two books were published. After she had reviewed *The Street of Crocodiles*, Roth sent her two original Schulz drawings. According to Russell E. Brown, the idea came to her during a 1984 visit to Stockholm when a rumor circulated that a lost novel, entitled *The Messiah*, putatively written by Schulz had been found there.

A Swedish journalist, Lars Andemening, believes obsessively in a heritage that, it turns out, he has invented: "His name was his own fabrication. . . . [H]e was the son of a murdered man, a man shot down in the streets over forty years ago, in Poland, while the son was still in the mother's womb. . . . [T]his father of his was a legend, a dream; or, more exactly, an errant seed thrown back by a corpse. Lars had never learned his mother's name, but his father had become his craze (*The Messiah of Stockholm* 4). The self-invented son, too, is an *isolato*, a strange man more at home with fixations and obsessions than human inter-course. Like his father and grandfather, he too lives in the imagined ontology of his head. Ozick may be playing with Stephen Dedalus's famous contention in *Ulysses* that paternity is a legal fiction. Adopting Schulz as her artistic father, Ozick invokes his phantasmagoric style.

Ozick is no doubt thinking of such anonymous victims as Lars Andemening when she writes:

> But the lost lives of the slaughtered and the maimed lives of the survivors are something else. The Holocaust happened *to* its victims. It did not happen *in* them. The victims were not the participants. The event swept over them, but they were separate from it. That is why they are "sanctified"—because they did not perform evil. Even as they were herded into the sealed and gaseous tomb, they were being separated from its meaning. . . . The people for whom the Holocaust "happened" were the people who made it happen. The perpetrators *are* the Holocaust; the victims stand apart. In this distinct sense, I would deny that the Holocaust belongs to the Jews. It belongs to the history and culture of the oppressors; it is theirs. It is German universities and churches that should be holding Holocaust conferences. And no Jew need or ought to be present. ("Roundtable Discussion," Lang 284)

Schulz was murdered on the streets by the Nazis during an *aktion* in 1942. Ozick's book is a search for the essence of a writer, even as Lars's search is for his father and for his father's missing novel, *The Messiah*. Both quests crystallize the relationship between memory and narrative that is my subject, and they explore the question of whether we can recuperate the past. Is Lars's effort to return to a life—a life that never was anything but a figment of his imagination—a trope for the evanescent fictionality of the hope that we can recapture the past? He illustrates that memory is narrative, and that memory is always part fiction. Yet when he gives up his quest for purity, he descends to mediocrity as if it were the dream after all that had value. The search for *The Messiah* is really the search for the "authentic Book," the original book in the opening chapter of *Sanatorium under the Sign of the Hourglass*: "The Book is a postulate. . . . a goal" (*Sanatorium* 3). Does Ozick reach the imagination of Schulz, or does she dramatize the impossibility of doing so? Is she finally like Lars, part of the everyday world, limited by time and nature? When Lars abandons his obsessive-compulsive behavior and his imaginative power, he is able to function in this world. Art requires compromises with life. Ozick, one might say, offers Aristotelianism to Schulz's Platonism; Lars converts from the latter to the former.

While the Holocaust hovers over the novel, it is elusive. By reincarnating Schulz in her novel, Ozick, like Lars, has become "a scholar of loss." But can Ozick, anymore than Lars, recapture the lost past? Is this a world that must elude us? Is the ethical question, "How can we do justice to that period?" best answered by: "We can respect it in memory but we cannot recreate it or metamorphose it without desecrating it?" Is Ozick finally aligning herself with Adorno? If words create their own cosmos, their own bibliocosm, how can we recapture the past? For Lars, his father's eye becomes a metonymy for his origin: "An eye. A human eye: his own; and then not his own. His father's murdered eye" (*Messiah of Stockholm* 8). The eye is a kind of reincarnation of his father, and the focus of his obsession. Ozick has captured the style of the father to describe the putative son. Within the novel, Lars's obsession takes on reality when the supposed sister—a child of Bruno and a 15-year-old model—turns up with the manuscript of Schulz's missing novel, *The Messiah*.

The *Messiah of Stockholm* is also a detective story in which Lars seeks out the truth of the claim that his father's lost book has been discovered. While there is an important retrospective between pages 13 and 49, the actual story takes place within a very brief time.

Lars's mind is immersed in the phantasmagoric world of his father's prose; take, for example, the echo of the conclusion to Schulz's "The Old Age Pensioner," a story in *Sanatorium under the Sign of the Hourglass* in which the old man is blown away by the wind: "Lars saw, or almost saw, his father's body, not at all a skeleton—an incandescent apparition billowing with light, puffed out, the light stretching his father's skin to palest transparency. This balloon-father, shedding luminosity, light falling in sheets from his swollen body, drifted into the white flux and merged with it. First a blur, then a smudge, than a blankness: above the Academy's roof now there was only the shower of snow-hyphens brightly descending" (*The Messiah of Stockholm* 49). The drawing facing the title page recalls how Bruno Schulz was both writer and artist. In free indirect discourse, Ozick renders Lars's mind: "The drawings were unearthly enough on their own—dwarfish, askew, psychological, symbolical. Abnormal. The drawings, what were they? Frozen panic" (*The Messiah of Stockholm* 39). When he thinks of his father drawing a dog in a business suit, we recall a drawing in Schulz's *Sanatorium Under the Sign of the Hourglass* illustrating a dog in human shape. To mock Lars's self-invention, the charlatan Eklund invents a sister who is a kind of mirror image of Lars himself: "In this very bag, the one in her hand (it was light enough, it wasn't a big tome), lay the work of a genius who happened—she wasn't going to be shy about this, she wouldn't hide *his* light under a bushel!—who happened to be her own father. Dead. Murdered. A victim, long ago, but immortal. And she was the daughter. *Here I am!*" (*The Messiah of Stockholm* 55). Schulz's point is that reality and nature are arbitrary, and that we are limited by time and logic. Ozick plays with these notions, but really can't escape time and logic or undermine the linearity of plot. Yet she would subscribe to Schulz's view of writing: "This is the phenomenon of imagination and vicarious being. An event may be small and insignificant in its origin, and yet, when drawn close to one's eye, it may open in its center an infinite and radiant perspective because a higher order of being is trying to express itself in it and irradiates it violently" (*Sanatorium* 13).

Ozick may have found the source for a journey backward into a prior time in the bizarre visit of Joseph, the dutiful son and speaker to the sanatorium in the title story of *Sanatorium under the Sign of the Hourglass.*

When he tries to visit his father, he finds himself in the City of the Dead, but a city that replicates the living city, Drogobych: "Time put back—it sounded good, but what does it come to in reality? Does anyone here get time at its full value, a true time, time cut off from a fresh bolt of cloth, smelling of newness and dye? Quite the contrary. It is used-up time, worn out by other people, a shabby time full of holes, like a sieve (*Sanatorium* 131).

Lars attempts to escape time and the limitations of body by re-creating his father and merging with him. Ozick quotes a supposed letter from Schulz to another Polish writer: *"Dear Witold . . . These are the mass instincts that eclipse within us a clarity of judgment, reintroducing the archaic and barbaric epistemologies, the arsenal of atavistic and bankrupt logic. . . . You side with inferiority"* (*The Messiah of Stockholm* 48). What her novel shows is that there is no exit from the claustrophobic world of logic, as there is no exit from history. Despite Schulz's phantasmagoria he is gunned down in a "wild action," the victim of a pogrom.

Not only Lars but Ozick herself takes as a point of departure a quote from *Street of Crocodiles*, which is one of her novel's epigraphs:

> My father never tired of glorifying this extraordinary element—matter.
>
> "There is no dead matter," he taught us, "lifelessness is only a disguise behind which hide unknown forms of life. The range of these forms is infinite and their shades and nuances limitless. The Demiurge was in possession of important and interesting creative recipes. Thanks to them, he created a multiplicity of species which renew themselves by their own devices. No one knows whether these recipes will ever be reconstructed. But this is unnecessary, because even if the classical methods of creation should prove inaccessible for evermore, there still remain some illegal methods, an infinity of heretical and criminal methods."

While Ozick's prose resonates with Schulz's, does she not finally show how the metamorphosis of matter is impossible? The only "criminal method" is the forgery of Schulz's text; but if it isn't a forgery, then Lars has destroyed the original by turning it into ashes.

Lars's efforts to invade the past and create himself in the context of history is an ethical question; so too is the apparent forgery of *The Messiah* discovered by Dr. Eklund and his probable daughter. A Polish orphan—or so he has been told, Lars has invented a father. His father has been reborn in his body, he believes or would like to believe. Lars is a self-appointed Messiah announcing the Good News of his father's literary achievement. Like Lars, Eklund would be a midwife for a lost culture, but is Eklund a fraud? Is Ozick ironic about the attempt to overcome the passage of time and re-create a lost culture? It is worth noting that the novel is about power. Eklund manipulates Heidi and his daughter. Knowing is power. Writing is power. When Lars joins the reviewing culture, he begins to put behind him his mole-like existence.

The Polish refugees of Stockholm, with mysterious Jewish roots, become an image of his own displacement. Lars is 42, and Schulz died in 1942 at the age of 50. Lars, like his fictional father, has retreated into a phantasmagoric world of fantasy and nightmare. Indeed, Schulz himself had been obsessed with his own father in *The Street of Crocodiles* and, as for Lars, his father had represented a personal and historical past. For Schulz understanding his father's bizarre behavior and mind was a parable for understanding himself, just as Lars uses his fictional father to understand himself. Similarly Schulz is conceived as Ozick's fictional double—as a dramatization of what might happened to her had she lived in Central Europe in Hitler's years. If Schulz creates the Authentic Book in *Sanatorium*, Ozick is his self-appointed heir. She is an assimilated Jew, like Schulz, struggling within her own identity.

When we meet Lars, he has lost his wife and child and been oddly reborn as a recluse, as if his development was arrested like that of Schulz's narrator in Joseph. He has: "the face of a foetus; it was as if he was waiting for his dead father to find him, and was determined to remain recognizable" (*Messiah of Stockholm* 6). Lars is a minor book reviewer for a Stockholm newspaper; his focus is Central Europe. The Kafkaesque drabness of his life, recalling Gregor Samsa's, contrasts with his rich fantasy life. Ozick has him recall Schulz's phrase: "*Reality is as thin as paper and betrays with all its cracks its imitative character*" (*The Messiah of Stockholm* 59). His real life is in imagining that of another, his supposed father. Note the novel's other epigraph:

Jag är stjärnan som speglar sig i dig.

. . .

Din själ är mitt hem. Jag har inget annat.

I am the star that mirrors itself in you.

. . .

Your soul is my home. I have no other.

—Pär Lagerkvist, *Aftonland*
Translated by W. H. Auden and Leif Sjöberg

He has cast off his family and developed a simple routine; he reads obsessively, takes a nap, awakes to write his review. Living as the acolyte of the man he thinks is his father, Lars becomes obsessed with the bizarre imagination of both Schulz and Schulz's father.

A strange woman plays the role of Adela, the putative sister named after the family servant who attends to the bizarre psychotic father in *The Street of Crocodiles*. Lars notices a resemblance between her and Dr. Eklund and realizes they are father and daughter. Eklund is the supposed husband of Heidi, the bookstore owner who keeps producing tantalizing Polish documents. Heidi, the aged bookstore owner in whom Lars confided for four years, has entrapped him in his fantasies. Heidi is a confidence woman who sets him up; she is also a double, insisting on facts and logic. Lars thinks Heidi's knowledge of concentration camps comes from her own experience. As if she were Faust and he Mephistopheles, they search for the full story of Schulz's life. In an effort to learn about his life in Drobobycz, Heidi finds letters and they study photographs. Schulz had turned his back on his Jewish origin but that origin is the cause of his death.

When Eklund finally appears with the manuscript of Schulz's lost novel, *The Messiah*, Lars is most skeptical. The possible transformation of matter is Schulz's theme, and it is echoed by Eklund when he reveals how he has transformed his identity from "Alter Eckstein to Olle Eklund" (120). Heidi and Eklund try to seduce Lars with money to announce the discovery of *The Messiah*, but he won't bite. Before he burns the manuscript, he had surrendered the father myth: "Lars had no father. No father ever again. He was giving his father up—to the probabilities, if not to the facts. There were no facts. Beyond the shooting there was nothing at all" (*The Messiah of Stockholm* 94). Ozick chooses to begin chapter 13 with the revelation of the burning. Burning is a trope within the entire novel, and is linked metonymically to Heidi and Eklund. Heidi proleptically plays with matches the way Conrad does with the knife that Mrs. Verloc uses to kill her husband in *The Secret Agent*: "Dr. Eklund's matches—the same smothered crash of spark after spark, every match in concert with every other, all designed to light a recalcitrant fire in the great man's pipe" (118).

Lars believes Eklund perpetuates a fraud by inventing the lost novel for him as reviewer to bring to the world's attention. But the spell had been broken when Ecklund kicked Adela to the floor, and she ran out with the putative manuscript: "He bent to it, and, bending, grieved over the afterimage of Adela's hair bundled like feathers at his feet. Dead bird. He had kicked her down: his father's daughter. His sister, his sister. He saw then that the white patch was a page of *The Messiah*, overlooked in the battle and left behind. He snatched it up with the knowledge that his right hand would burst like a grenade at the touch of the sheet. He was ready to lose his right hand for the sake of an errant paragraph out of *The Messiah*" (*The Messiah of Stockholm* 86-87). Interestingly, the father in *The Street of Crocodiles* is obsessed with birds and had invented a bird kingdom—which was dispersed by Adela in Schulz's chapter in *The Street of Crocodiles* entitled "Birds."

Just as Schulz was an ambiguous figure within Jewish culture, separated from the German-speaking Austrian Jews and the Orthodox practices of the Hasidism, so Lars separates himself from to the Swedish culture. Lars, like his father, lives—until he burns the treasured manuscript he has been seeking—in a world of childhood fantasy where reality and dream blur. Once he breaks the magic, he becomes part of the world he disdained, and he moves into a larger and comfortable apartment. His talismanic quilt—note the homophonic play on *guilt*—is abandoned "heaped on the leather chair with its cracked leg, in the angle of the hallway" (*The Messiah of Stockholm* 140). But when Adela, "a madonna of contempt," returns to visit with her own son and, tells him that he destroyed the real *Messiah*, neither he nor the reader can be absolutely sure that she is not telling the truth (*The Messiah of Stockholm* 140).

The putative *Messiah*—"the Risen Messiah"—echoes Schulz's obsessive style. Transmigration is the theme—humans to idols to book to a bird, climaxing in the following passage: "It was a birth. The Messiah had given birth to a bird, and the moment the bird flew living out of the relentlessly wheeling contrivance that had been the Messiah, the thing—or organism—collapsed with the noise of vast crashings and crushings, cardboard like stone, cotton like bone, granite petal on brazen postulate: degraded and humiliated" (*The Messiah of Stockholm* 69, 111).

We recall Schulz's own description of the "authentic book": "Let's return to the Authentic. We have never forsaken it. And here we must stress a strange characteristic of the script, which by now no doubt has become clear to the reader: it unfolds while being read, its boundaries open to all currents and fluctuations" (*Messiah of Stockholm* 12). Lars's coming to terms with *The Messiah* reiterates the eccentric process of reading *The Street of Crocodiles* or *Sanatorium Under the Sign of the Hourglass. The Messiah* is *the book*, what is hoped for and what gives birth to infinite possibilities, indeed, to Lars's ability to act and write. It is the "foetal ape" within him that finally dies, as it must, before he can be reborn as an ordinary fellow (*The Messiah of Stockholm* 102).

Is not Ozick implying that Lars's obsessive quest for *The Messiah* and the truth about the man he believes is his father, like Schulz's quest for the authentic, mirrors our own quest for the essential truth about the past and especially the virtual extermination of Jewish Europe? While the attempt is necessary for our survival and deserving of our effort, can we ever fully imagine what life was like then? Yes, memory distorts, words fail, facts elude us, fictions fall short. Yet do we not join Ozick in affirming that creating narrative in memoirs, diaries, and fiction is our best hope for understanding the Holocaust?

WORKS CITED AND DISCUSSED

Appelfeld, Aharon. "After the Holocaust." In *Writing and the Holocaust*. Ed. Berel Lang. New York: Holmes & Meier, 1988, 83-92.

———. *The Age of Wonders*. Trans. Dalya Bilu Boston: David R. Godine, 1981.

———. *Badenheim 1939*. New York: Pocket Books, 1980.

———. *Beyond Despair: Three Lectures and a Conversation with Philip Roth*. Trans. Jeffrey M. Green. New York: Fromm International, 1994.

———. *The Iron Tracks*, Trans. Jeffrey M. Green. New York: Schoken Books, 1998.

———. *The Retreat*. Trans. Dalya Bilu. New York: Dutton, 1984.

Auerbach, Erich. *Mimesis: The Representation of Reality in Western Literature*. Trans. William Trask. 1946; Princeton. Princeton University Press, 1953.

Bauman, Zygmunt. *Modernity and the Holocaust*. Ithaca, N.Y.: Cornell University Press, 1989.

Bernstein, Michael André. *Foregone Conclusions: Against Apocalyptic History*. Berkeley: University of California Press, 1994.

———. "Lasting Injury: Competing Interpretations of the Nazi Genocide and the Passionate Insistence on Its Uniqueness." *TLS*, March 7, 1997, #4901, 3.

Bettelheim, Bruno. *Freud's Vienna and Other Essays*. New York: Vintage, 1991.

———. *The Informed Heart: Autonomy in a Mass Age*. New York: Free Press, 1960.

———. *Surviving and Other Essays*. 1952; New York: Vintage, 1980.

Borowski, Tadeusz. *This Way for the Gas, Ladies and Gentlemen*. Intro. by Jan Kott. New York: Penguin, 1976.

Boxer, Sarah. "Giving Memory Its Due in an Age of License." *The New York Times*, October 28, 1998, E6.

Brenner, Rachel Fedman. "Writing Against Herself: Anne Frank's Self-Portrait as a Young Artist." *Modern Judaism* 16:2 (1996), 105-134.

Brown, Russell E. *Myths and Relatives: Seven Essays on Bruno Schulz.* München: Verlag Otto Sagner, 1991.

Clifford, James. *The Predicament of Culture: Twentieth-Century Ethnography, Literature, and Art.* Cambridge, MA: Harvard University Press, 1988.

Cohen, Roger. "France Confronts its Jews, and Itself." *The New York Times Week in Review,* October 19, 1997, 1.

Conrad, Joseph. *The Portable Conrad.* Ed. Morton Dauwen Zabel. New York: Viking, 1969.

Davison, Neil. "Inside the *Shoah*: Narrative, Documentation and Schwarz-Bart's *The Last of the Just.*" *Clio*: 24:3, 292-322.

Dawidowicz, Lucy. *The War Against the Jews, 1933–1945.* 1975; New York: Bantam, 1986.

Déak, Istvan. "Memories of Hell." *NYR* 44:11, June 26, 1997, 38-43.

Des Pres, Terence. "Holocaust *Laughter?*" In *Writing and the Holocaust.* Ed. Berel Lang. New York: Holmes & Meier, 1988, 216-33.

————. *The Survivor: An Anatomy of Life in the Death Camps.* New York: Oxford University Press, 1970.

Doherty, Thomas. "Art Spiegelman's *Maus*: Graphic Art and the Holocaust." *American Literature* 68:1 (March 1996), 69-84.

Dresden, Sem. *Persecution, Extermination, Literature.* Trans. Henry G. Schoax. Toronto: University of Toronto Press, 1995.

Epstein, Leslie. *King of the Jews.* New York: Summit Books, 1979.

————. "Writing about the Holocaust." In *Writing and the Holocaust.* Ed. Berel Lang. New York: Holmes & Meier, 1988, 261-70.

Erlanger, Steven. "Albright Grateful for Her Parents' 'Painful Choices.'" *The New York Times,* February 5, 1997, A8.

Ezrahi, Sidra DeKoven. *By Words Alone: The Holocaust in Literature.* Chicago: University of Chicago Press, 1980.

————. "Considering the Apocalypse: Is the Writing on the Wall Only Graffiti?" In *Writing and the Holocaust.* Ed. Berel Lang. New York: Holmes & Meier, 1988, 216-33.

Fiedler, Leslie. *Love and Death in the American Novel.* 1960; New York: Stein and Day, 1966.

Fogel, Daniel Mark. "*Schindler's List* in Novel and Film: Exponential Conversion." *Historical Journal of Film, Radio, and Television,*" 14:3, 1994, 315-20.

Foley, Barbara. "Fact, Fiction, Fascism: Testimony and Mimesis in Holocaust Narratives." *Comparative Literature* 34:4 (Fall 1982), 330-360.

Frank, Anne. *The Diary of a Young Girl*. Trans. B. M. Mooyaart. Intro. Eleanor Roosevelt. Garden City, New York: Doubleday, 1952.

The Diary of Anne Frank. Critical Edition prepared by the Netherlands State Institute for War Documentation. Intro. Harry Paape, Gerrold Van Der Stroom and David Barnouw. Ed. David Barnouw and Gerald Van Der Stroom. Translated by Arnold J. Pomerans and B. M. Mooyaart. New York: Doubleday, 1989.

Frank, Michael. "Telling It All to a Friend: Dear Diary . . ." *The New York Times*, May 16, 1997, 1, 14.

Freud, Sigmund. *The Standard Edition of the Complete Psychological Works*. Trans. James Strachey. London: Hogarth, 1953-73, Vol. XVII.

Gilbert, Martin. *The Holocaust: The Jewish Tragedy*. London: Collins, 1986

Gilman, Sander. *Jewish Self-Hatred: Anti-Semitism and the Hidden Language of The Jews*. Baltimore: Johns Hopkins University Press,1980.

———. "To Quote Primo Levi, Redest Keynjiddish, Bist Nit Kejnjid" ("If You Don't Speak Yiddish, You're Not a Jew"). *Prooftexts* 9 (1989), 139-160.

Goetzel-Leviathan, Sophie. *The War from Within*. Ed. Rebecca Fromer. Trans. Goeffrey A. M. Block. Berkeley, CA: Judah L. Magnes Museum; 1987.

Gordon, Andrew. "Cynthia Ozick's 'The Shawl' and 'The Transitional Object.'" *Literature and Psychology* 30:1 and 2 (1994). 1-9.

Gourevitch, Philip. "A Dissent on *Schindler's List*." *Commentary* 97, Feb. 94, 49-54.

Green, Gerald. *Holocaust*. New York: Bantam, 1978.

Harari, Josué, ed. *Textual Strategies*. Ithaca: Cornell University Press, 1979, 296-321.

Hersey, John. *The Wall*. New York: Pocket Books. 1950.

Hertz, Neil. "Freud and the Sandman." In *Textual Strategies* ed. Josue Harari. Ithaca: Cornell University Press, 1979, 296-321.

Hilberg, Raul. *The Destruction of the European Jews*. 1961; New York: New Viewpoints, 1973.

———. "I Was Not There." In *Writing and the Holocaust*, ed. Berel Lang. New York: Holmes & Meier, 1988. 17-25.

Hirsch, Marianne. "Family Pictures: *Maus*, Mourning and Post-Memory." *Discourse* 15:2 (Winter 1992-1993), 3-29.

Holden, Stephen. "An Unsettling Sifting of Truth and Trust." *The New York Times*, January 23, 1998, E10.

Howe, Irving. "Writing and the Holocaust." *The New Republic*, October 27, 1986, 27-39.

In Memory's Kitchen: A Legacy From the Women of Terezin (edited by Cara De Silva translated by Bianca Steiner Brown; foreword by Michael Berenbaum) Northvale, New Jersey: Jason Aronson, 1996.

Keneally, Thomas. *Schindler's List*. New York: Simon & Schuster, 1982.

Kimmelman, Michael. "In The Faces of the Living: Horror in the Dead." *The New York Times*, September 17, 1997, 1, 26.

Klingenstein, Susanne. "Destructive Intimacy: The Shoah between Mother and Daughter in Fictions by Cynthia Ozick, Norma Rose, and Rebecca Goldstein." *Studies in American Jewish Literature* 11:2 (Fall 1992), 162-173.

Kosinski, Jerzy. *Notes of the Author on "The Painted Bird."* New York: Scientia-Factum Inc., 1965.

———. *The Painted Bird*. New York: Houghton Mifflin, 1965.

Kuhiwczak, Piotr. "Beyond Self: A Lesson From the Concentration Camps." *Canadian Review of Comparative Literature/Revue Canadienne de Littérature Comparée* September/septembre 1992, 19:3, 395-405.

Lang, Berel, ed. *Writing and the Holocaust*. New York: Holmes & Meier, 1988.

Langer, Lawrence L. *The Holocaust and the Literary Imagination*. New Haven and London: Yale University Press, 1975.

———. *Holocaust Testimonies: The Ruins of Memory*. New Haven: Yale University Press, 1991.

Levi, Primo. *The Drowned and the Saved*. Trans. Raymond Rosenthal. New York: Summit, 1986.

———. *Moments of Reprieve*. Trans. Ruth Feldman. New York: Summit, 1985.

———. *The Periodic Table*. Trans. by Raymond Rosenthal. 1975; New York: Schocken, 1984.

———. *The Reawakening*. Trans. Stuart Woolf. New York: Summit, 1986.

———. *Survival in Auschwitz: The Nazi Assault on Humanity*. Trans. Stuart Woolf. 1958; New York, Macmillan, 1959.

Levin, Nora. *The Holocaust: The Destruction of European Jewry 1933-1945.* New York: Schocken, 1973

Mancini, Rochelle. "Jewish Cookery, or Borscht Improved." *Congress Monthly* 64.4, July-August 1997, 17-19.

Mann, Thomas. *Death in Venice.* Trans. H. J. Lowe-Porter. New York: Vintage, 1936.

Muller, Melissa. *Anne Frank: The Biography.* Trans. Rita and Robert Kimber. New York: Metropolitan Books/Henry Holt & Company, 1998.

Muschamp, Herbert. "Museum Tells a Tale of Resilience, Tuned to the Key of Life." *The New York Times,* September 15, 1997, 1-2.

————. "Shaping a Monument's Memory." *The New York Times,* April 11, 1993, 1.

New Mahzor, The. Bridgeport: CT. The Prayer Book Press of Media Judaica. 1978.

Ozick, Cynthia. *The Messiah of Stockholm.* New York: Alfred A. Knopf, 1987.

————. "Roundtable Discussion." In *Writing and the Holocaust.* ed. Berel Lang. New York: Holmes & Meier, 1988, 277-84.

————. *The Shawl.* New York: Alfred A. Knopf. 1989.

————. "Who Owns Anne Frank?" *The New Yorker,* October 6, 1997, 76-87.

Patruno, Nicholas. *Understanding Primo Levi.* Columbia: University of South Carolina Press, 1995.

Ramras-Rauch, Gila. *Aharon Appelfeld.* Bloomington: Indiana University Press, 1994.

Ricouer, Paul. "The Model of the Text." *Social Research* 5:1 (Spring 1984), 185-218.

Ringelblum, Emmanuel. *Notes from the Warsaw Ghetto: The Journal of Emmanuel Ringelblum.* Ed. and Trans. Jacob Sloan. New York: Schocken, 1958.

Sanders, David. "John Hersey: War Correspondent into Novelist" In *New Voices in American Studies.* Ed by Ray B. Browne, Donald Winkelman and Allen Hayman. West Lafayette, Indiana Purdue University Studies: West Lafayette, Indiana, 1966, 49-58.

Schiff, Hilda, ed. *Holocaust Poetry.* New York: St. Martin's Press, 1995.

Schulz, Bruno. *Cinammon Shops and Other Stories.* Trans Celina Wieniewska. London: Macgibbon & Kee, 1963.

————. *Sanatorium under the Sign of the Hourglass.* Trans Celina Wieniewska. New York: Walker and Company, 1978.

————. *The Street of Crocodiles.* Trans. Celina Wieniewska. Intro. Jerzy Ficowski. Trans. Michael Kandel. New York: Penguin, 1977.

Schwarz-Bart, André. *The Last of the Just.* New York: Atheneum, 1961.

Seeskin, Kenneth. "Coming to Terms with Failure: A Philosophical Dilemma." In *Writing and the Holocaust.* Ed. Berel Lang. New York: Holmes & Meier, 1988, 110-121.

Seidman, Naomi. "Elie Wiesel and the Scandal Rage." *Jewish Social Studies: History, Culture and Society* 3:1 (Fall 1996), 1-19.

Shepard, Jim. "In the Absence of Language," Review of Deborah Eisenberg's *All Around Atlantis." The New York Times Book Review,* September 21, 1997, 9.

Sloan, James Park. *Jerzy Kosinski.* New York: Dutton, 1996.

Spiegelman, Art. *Maus: A Survivor's Tale.* Volume I: *My Father Bleeds History.* New York: Pantheon, 1986.

————. *Maus: A Survivor's Tale.* Volume II: *And Here My Troubles Began.* New York: Pantheon, 1991.

Styron, William. *Sophie's Choice.* New York: Random House, 1976.

Suleiman, Susan, and Inge Crossman, eds. *The Reader in the Text: Essays on Audience and Interpretation.* Princeton: Princeton University Press, 1980.

Terdiman, Richard. *Present Past: Modernity and the Memory Crisis.* New York: Cornell University Press, 1993.

Thomson, David. "Presenting Enamelware," *Film Comment* 30 (March/April 1994) 44-50.

Todorov, Tzvetan. *Facing the Extreme: Moral Life in the Concentration Camps.* Trans. Arthur Denner and Abigail Pollack. New York: Metropolitan Books/Henry Holt, 1966.

Trunk, Isaiah. *Judenrat: The Jewish Councils in Eastern Europe under Nazi Occupation.* 1972; New York: Bison Books, 1996.

Waaldijk, Berteke. "Reading Anne Frank as a Woman." *Women's Studies International Forum* 16:4 (1993) 327-335.

Whitney, Craig R. "France Amasses Bitter Evidence Five Decades After the Holocaust." *The New York Times,* October 6, 1997, 1.

Wiesel, Elie. *A Jew Today.* Trans. Marion Wiesel. New York: Random House, 1978.

————. *Memoirs: All Rivers Run to the Sea*. New York: Alfred A. Knopf, 1995.

————. *Night*. Trans. Stella Rodney. New York: Bantam, 1960.

Wilner, Arlene Fish. "'Happy, Happy Ever After Story' and History in Art Spiegelman's *Maus*." *Journal of Narrative Technique* 27:2 (Spring 1997), 171-189.

Witek, Joseph. *Comic Books as History: The Narrative Art of Jack Jackson, Art Spiegelman, and Harvey Pekar*. Jackson: University of Mississippi Press, 1989.

Young, James E. "Holocaust Documentary Fiction: The Novelist as Eyewitness." In *Writing and the Holocaust*. Ed. Berel Lang. New York: Holmes & Meier, 1988, 200-215.

————. *Writing and Rewriting the Holocaust: Narrative and the Consequences of Interpretation*. Bloomington: Indiana University Press, 1988.

INDEX

A

Adorno, Theodor, 22, 304, 332
Albright, Madelaine, 311
Aleichem, Sholem, 36, 254
Allegory, 185, 243, 248, 253, 263-264,
    266, 326, 328
American Civil War, 122, 182, 198
Anieliewicz, Mordecai, 179
Anti-Semitism, 6, 31-32, 46-47, 66, 108,
    130, 161-162, 166, 200-204, 240-242,
    259-260, 262, 267, 270, 293
Appelfeld, Aharon, 33, 36-37, 39-40, 42,
    215, 249-270 passim, 279, 291, 300,
    311, 320
    "After the Holocaust," 37, 249-250,
        254, 256
    The Age of Wonders, 259-266 passim
    Badenheim 1939, 40, 42, 215, 249-259
        passim, 263, 266, 268, 291, 300,
        320
    Beyond Despair: Three Lectures and a Con-
        versation with Philip Roth, 250-253,
        255, 260, 262-263, 270
    The Immortal Bartfuss, 260
    The Iron Tracks, 258, 260
        Erwin Siegelbaum, 260
    The Retreat, 42, 258, 266-270 passim,
        310, 320
Appleman-Jurman, Alicia, 115
    Alicia: My Story, 115
Aristotle, 18, 98, 241, 332
Auden, W. H., 336
Auerbach, Erich, 221-222, 240
Auschwitz, 22, 24, 26-29, 31-34, 37, 51,
    59, 61-65, 77, 81-83, 87, 91-94, 96,
    99, 115, 119, 123-124, 129-130, 135-
    141, 166, 170, 173, 198-199, 202,
    206-207, 213, 215, 219, 223-225, 229,
    231-232, 242, 247, 272-273, 288, 295,
    297, 299-300
Autobiography, 39-40, 70, 90, 16, 116,
    177

B

Babi Yar, 90

Bacon, Francis, 184
Bakhtin, M. M., 106, 280
Bauman, Zygmunt, 81, 275
Beckett, Samuel, 299, 314
Bellow, Saul, 17
Belzec, 26, 34, 82, 247
Bennahmias, Daniel, 124-125
Bergen-Belsen, 106, 115, 119, 120, 122-
    123, 247
Bernstein, Michael André, 8, 252-253
Bettelheim, Bruno, 71-73, 113-114, 204
Bible, The, 13-14, 46, 52, 56, 130, 221-
    223, 232, 239, 242, 260, 265, 306,
    327-328
    Book of Daniel, 13-14, 46, 52, 130,
        265, 328
    Book of Job, 246
    Genesis, 152
    Jesus Christ, 68-69, 185, 241
    Old Testament, 56, 221, 306, 327
    The Torah, 57, 256, 260
Bilu, Dalya, 264
Birkenau (Auschwitz II), 32, 59, 61, 81-82,
    124, 129, 138-139, 140, 166, 297
Blake, William, 10
Borchardt, George, 58
Borowski, Tadeusz, 34, 37, 40-41, 79-80,
    109, 129-142 passim, 180, 204, 211
    Farewell to Maria, 129-130
    This Way for the Gas, Ladies and Gentleman,
        40-41, 129-142 passim
        Vorarbeiter Tadeusz, 130-134,
        137-138
    Wherever the Earth, 129
    World of Stone, 129-130
Bosch, Hieronymous, 177, 318, 324
    The Last Judgement, 177
Boudier-Bakker, Ida, 112
Boxer, Sarah, 249-250
Brecht, Bertolt, 294
Brenner, Rachel Fedman, 111, 113-114
Brown, Russell E., 331
Brueghel, Pieter, 280, 324
Brzezinski, Zbigniew, 311
Buchenwald, 60, 63, 66, 166, 247

Buna, 59, 61, 82

C
Cabaret, 29
Cabbala, 49, 59, 69, 256
Camus, Albert, 137
Célan, Paul, 8
Chagall, Marc, 68
Chatwin, Bruce, 317
  Utz, 317
Chelmno ("Kulmhof"), 26, 28-30, 82, 247
Clifford, James, 53
Cohen, Roger, 7
Coleridge, Samuel Taylor, 279
Columbia University, 17
Commentary, 17
Communism, 7, 260, 263
Conrad, Joseph, 46, 58, 75-76, 169, 183-
  184, 189, 194, 197, 199-200, 213,
  228, 294, 337
  Heart of Darkness, 58, 75-76, 169, 183,
    194, 199, 213, 228, 294
  Lord Jim, 199-200, 213
  The Nigger of the "Narcissus," 46
  The Secret Agent, 337
Constructivism, 6
Cornell University, 15-20
Cossack Uprisings, 164, 241
Crusades, 164
Czarist Persecution, 164
Czerniawski, Adam, 2, 151

D
Dachau, 295
Dante, 85-86, 96, 98, 136-137
Darwinism, 183, 191
Davison, Neil, 304, 306
Dawidowicz, Lucy, 54-55, 143
de Gaulle, Charles, 9
de Man, Paul, 179
Déak, Istvan, 10, 12, 34
Deconstruction, 54
Defoe, Daniel, 182
  Moll Flanders, 182
Der Sturmer, 167, 293
Des Pres, Terence, 8, 45, 52, 60, 62, 70-
  71, 279-281, 283, 294, 301-302
Disraeli, Benjamin, 177
Dix, Otto, 251, 264
Documentary Fiction, 41-42, 51, 162,
  171, 196-207 passim, 297, 303
Doherty, Thomas, 289, 292-293
Dora, 247
Dos polyishe yidntum (Polish Jewry), 51
Dostoevsky, Feodor, 114, 260

  Notes from Underground, 114, 260
Dresden, Sem, 11, 13, 38, 40-41, 291-292
Dubner Maggid, 2-3

E
Eichman, Adolph, 163-164, 169
Einaudi, Giulio, 98
Eliot, George (Marian Evans), 200, 310
  Middlemarch, 200, 310
Eliot, T.S., 6, 18, 46-48, 84
  The Wasteland, 84
Enlightenment, The, 54, 108, 151, 312
Ensor, James, 64, 318, 324
Epstein, Leslie, 23, 33-34, 36, 42, 97, 179,
  215-216, 223, 256, 267, 271-283
  passim, 291, 330
  King of the Jews, 23, 33-34, 36, 42, 97,
    179, 215, 223, 256, 267, 271-283
    passim, 291, 330
  Lipsky, 274, 276, 283
  Trumpelman, 215, 233, 266-267,
    272-279, 281-282
Erlanger, Steven, 311
Ethnic Studies, 6
Ezrahi, Sidra DeKoven, 33, 35, 78, 80-81,
  130, 133-135, 141, 143-146, 158-159,
  161-163, 169-170, 182-183, 185-186,
  189-190, 303

F
Farben, I. G., 32
Feninger, Lyonel, 264
Ficowski, Jerzy, 324, 330
Fiedler, Leslie, 17-18
Fitzgerald, F. Scott, 199
Fogel, Daniel Mark, 217, 220
Foley, Barbara, 116, 147-148, 153, 162,
  171, 207
Frank, Anne, 16, 19-22, 35-37, 40, 71-73,
  90, 101-115 passim, 118, 121, 143,
  145-146, 152
  Anne Frank: The Diary of a Young Girl, 20-
    22, 36, 40, 101-115 passim, 143,
    146, 152
  The Diary of Anne Frank (the Critical
    edition), 102-103
Frank, Michael, 104
Frank, Otto, 20-22, 102-103, 109, 112
Frankl, Victor, 13
Freud, Sigmund, 32, 55, 95, 176, 310-311
Fromer, Rebecca, 123
Futurism, 6

G
Garbo, Greta, 109

Gawkowski, Henrik, 28, 32
Gens, Jacob, 282
German Expressionism, 251, 264, 324
Gies, Miep, 102
Gilbert, Martin, 34, 81-82, 101, 114-115, 124, 143, 149-150, 155-156, 159, 165, 167-168
Gilman, Sander, 86, 113
Gleiwitz, 65
Goebbels, Joseph Paul, 293
Goering, Herman, 32
Goethe, Johann Wolfgang, 118
Goetzel-Leviathan, Sophie, 10, 33, 40, 115-125 passim, 175, 210
    The War from Within, 10, 33, 40, 115-125 passim, 210
Goodrich, Frances, 20, 113
Gordon, Andrew, 305
Gourevitch, Philip, 223, 225
Grabow, 30-31
Green, Gerald, 6-7, 33-34, 41, 143, 146, 161-172 passim, 175, 197, 206
    Holocaust, The, 6-7, 33-34, 41, 143, 146, 161-172 passim, 197
        Dorf, Erik, 162-166, 168-169, 171-172
        Weiss, Rudi, 163-172
Grossman, David, 5
    See Under: Love, 5
Grosz, George, 251, 264

H
Habermas, Jürgen, 8
Hackett, Albert, 20, 22, 113
Hardy, Thomas, 18, 181
Hartman, Geoffrey, 18
Hawthorne, Nathaniel, 18
Heckel, Erich, 324
Heine, Heinrich, 76
Hellman, Lillian, 22
Hemingway, Ernest, 200
Hersey, John, 6, 35, 37, 41, 109, 143-159 passim, 162-164, 206, 216, 229, 246, 312
    The Wall, 6, 35, 41, 109, 143-159 passim, 164, 216, 229, 312
        Apt, Rachel, 147, 150-151, 153, 158
        Berson, Dolek, 147, 150-152, 154, 158
        Noach, Levinson, 146-154, 156-157- 158-159
Hertz, Neil, 310-311
Heydrich, Reinhard, 162, 163, 165, 169

Hilberg, Raul, 23-24, 42, 143, 161, 164-165, 168, 170, 272-273
Hill and Wang (publishers), 57-58
Hillesun, Etty, 5, 115
    An Interrupted Life: The Diaries of Etty Hillesun, 5, 115
Himmler, Heinrich, 32
Hirsch, Marianne, 288, 290
Hitler, Adolph, 13, 14, 65, 84, 107, 115, 152, 167, 205, 214, 222, 234, 241, 273, 276-278, 281-282, 291-292, 296, 322, 324, 326, 328, 335
Holden, Stephen, 318
Holinshed, Raphael, 6
Homer, 86, 94, 96, 221, 301
    The Odyssey, 86, 94, 96, 301
    The Iliad, 96
Howe, Irving, 17, 22-23, 34
Hugo, Victor, 281
Huysman, Joris Karl, 320

I
In Memory's Kitchen: A Legacy from the Women of Terezin (edited by Cara De Silva), 122
Iser, Wolfgang, 47
Isherwood, Christopher, 29

J
James, Henry, 181, 198-199
    Turn of the Screw, The, 198
    What Maisie Knew, 181
Janica, Barbara, 26, 31
Janisch, Attila, 318
    "The Long Twilight," 318
Janow, 247
Joyce, James, 84, 91, 206, 213, 301, 329, 331
    Dubliners, 91
    A Portrait of the Artist as a Young Man, 91, 206
    Ulysses, 84, 301, 331
Judenrat, 121, 148, 156-158, 164, 216, 222, 228, 231, 258, 269, 272-274, 276-278, 281, 288, 291, 327
Jung, Carl, 185

K
Kafka, Franz, 36, 64, 170, 192, 250-251, 257, 260-261, 263, 265, 292, 304, 318, 320-322, 330, 335
    "The Hunter Gracchus," 251, 320

Metamorphosis, 251, 257, 260-261, 263, 265, 292, 322, 335
The Penal Colony, 170
Kandel, Michael, 318
Kapos, 63, 65, 70, 78, 94, 130, 135-136, 164
Kazin, Alfred, 17
Keneally, Thomas, 41, 145, 209-235 passim, 256, 258, 273
Schindler's List, 41, 209-235 passim, 256, 273
(see Spielberg for book and film characters)
Kimmelman, Michael, 13
Kirchner, Ernst Ludwig, 324
Klimt, Gustav, 251, 264
Klingenstein, Susanne, 307
Koch, Ilse, 66
Kogon, Eugen, 204
Kolo, 29
Kosinski, Jerzy, 6, 36-37, 39-40, 173-194 passim, 272, 317
The Hermit of 69 Street, 179
Notes of the Author on The Painted Bird, 178
The Painted Bird, 6, 40, 173-194 passim, 272, 317
Kott, Jan, 129-130
Kuhiwczak, Piotr, 129, 132-133

L
Lagerkvist, Par, 335-336
Aftonland, 335-336
Lang, Berel, 80-81, 279, 331
Langer, Lawrence L., 33, 37-38, 80, 82, 87, 91, 95, 114, 116-117, 123, 137, 140-141, 179, 183-185, 190-191
Lanzmann, Claude, 7, 23-33 passim, 87, 188, 231, 244, 245, 307
Shoah, 7, 23-33 passim, 87, 188, 231, 244, 245, 307
Bomba, Abraham, 26, 29, 32, 245
Glazer, Richard, 29, 32
Karski, Jan, 26
Muller, Filip, 28
Oberhauser, Joseph, 25
Piwonski, Jan, 25-27
Podchlebnik, Mordechai, 30
Schalling, Franz, 29-30
Srebnik, Simon, 25, 28, 30, 31
Suchomel, Franz, 26, 28-29
Wirth, Christian, 25-26
Laval, Pierre, 9
Lawrence, D. H., 6
Lengyel, Olga, 204
Leonard, William Ellery, 17

Levi, Primo, 4, 34-38, 40, 65, 75-99 passim, 101, 108-109, 111, 116, 120, 122-123, 129, 136-137, 145, 180, 229, 287-288, 303, 311
"The Canto of Ulysses," 76, 84-86, 98, 136-137
The Drowned and the Saved, 76-78, 84-85, 91, 96-97
Moments of Reprieve, 76, 78-79, 97-98
The Periodic Table, 4, 40, 76, 82-83, 85, 86-91 passim, 98, 303
The Reawakening, 40, 75-76, 84, 91-97 passim, 98-99, 123
Survival at Auschwitz: The Nazi Assault on Humanity, 36, 38, 40, 65, 76-86 passim, 91-92, 96-98, 108, 119, 122, 229
Levin, Meyer, 22
Levin, Nora, 143, 146, 149, 152
Liebe-Schutz, Anne, 21
Life is Beautiful, 3
Lindon, Jerome, 50, 66
Lodz Ghetto, 27-28, 31, 97, 177, 179, 226, 272-275, 282
Lodz Ghetto (film), 273
London, Jack, 82
The Call of the Wild, 82
Luther, Martin, 166-167

M
Magic Realism, 304, 309
Maidanek, 247
Malamud, Bernard, 17
Mancini, Rochelle, 122-123
Jewish Cookery, or Borscht Improved, 122-123
Mann, Thomas, 177, 252-253, 265-266, 300, 321, 323, 329
Death in Venice, 177, 252-253, 265-266, 323
The Magic Mountain, 265-266, 300
A Sketch of My Life, 177
Márquez, Gabriel García, 304
Marx, Karl (Marxism), 182, 186, 274, 276
Massada, 240
Mauriac, François, 10, 51, 56-58, 68-71, 73
Mauthausen, 247
McCarthyism, 17
Melville, Herman, 184, 198
Moby-Dick, 198
Memoir, 34, 38-40, 45-125 passim, 141, 182, 197, 254-255, 303, 338
Mendelev, Dmitri Ivonovich, 88
Michelangelo, 281

Milland, Ray, 109
Milton, John, 10, 18-19
Modernism, 4, 6, 47-48, 65, 169, 178, 199, 218, 301, 329
Muller, Melissa, 109
   Anne Frank: The Biography, 109
Muschamp, Hebert, 13, 53
Mussolini, Benito, 81

N
Naturalism, 158
Nazi Regime, 7, 34, 38, 50, 54, 102, 129, 140, 149, 157-159, 161, 166-167, 181, 188-189, 201-202, 211-216, 218, 220, 222, 224, 227, 230-233, 240, 242, 244-245, 253-254, 256, 258, 261, 265, 267, 274, 277, 279, 288-289, 292, 295, 302, 305-307, 309, 313, 331
Neuengamme, 247
New Criticism, 17-18
New Mahzor, The, 2-3
New York City Museum of Jewish Heritage: A Living Memorial to the Holocaust, 13
New York Times, 13
New Yorker, The, 304-305
Nietzsche, Freidrich, 324
Nolde, Emil, 324
Nuremburg Laws, 89, 166, 168
Nuremburg Trials, 15, 148

O
O'Conner, Flannery, 19
Onég Shabbat Group, 146, 157
O'Neill, Eugene, 89
Oswiecim (Auschwitz), 25
Ozick, Cynthia, 20-21, 102, 109, 303-315 passim, 317, 330-338 passim
   The Messiah of Stockholm, 317, 330-338 passim
      Lars Andemening, 330-338 passim
   "Rosa," 303-315 passim
      Magda, 305-307, 309-315
      Rosa, 305-307, 309-315
      Stella, 305-307, 309-314
   "The Shawl," 303-315 passim
      characters in, *see under* Ozick, Cynthia, "Rosa"
   "Who Owns Anne Frank?," 20-21

P
Pachter, Maria, 122
Papon, Maurice, 8-9

Partisan Review, 17
Patruno, Nicholas, 98
Pawiak Prison, 137
PEN, 178
Petain, Marshal Henry Philippe, 9
Picasso, Pablo, 64, 302, 329
   Guernica, 302
Plato, 117, 241, 332
Ponary, 247
Pope John Paul II, 7
Postmodernism, 6, 47, 268, 290, 301, 330
Pound, Ezra, 6, 18, 46, 48
Psychoanalysis, 53, 55, 70, 78, 176, 327
Pustkow, 247

R
Ramras-Rauch, Gail, 260, 264, 268
Realism, 127-235 passim, 281, 288, 303-305
Reaves, George, 177
Rembrandt, 225
Ricouer, Paul, 47-49
   "The Model of the Text," 47
Ringelblum, Emmanuel, 146, 150-151, 155-157, 159
   Notes from the Warsaw Ghetto: The Journal of Emmanuel Ringelblum, 146, 150-151, 155-157, 159
Roosevelt, Franklin Delano, 155, 276
Roth, Phillip, 17, 252, 254, 270, 330-331
   "Writers from the Other Europe," 330-331
Różewicz, Tadeusz, 1-2, 195, 271-272, 287-288
   "In The Midst of Life," 195
   "Pigtail," 271
   "Posthumous Rehabilitation," 1-2
   "The Survivor," 287-288
Rumkowski, Chaim, 97, 179-180, 272-274, 276, 282
Russian Revolution, 241

S
Sachs, Nellie, 45, 75
   "A Dead Child Speaks," 45
   "O Night of the Weeping Children," 75
Salinger, J. D., 199-200
   Catcher in the Rye, 199-200
Samuel, Maurice, 144
Sanders, David, 148
Schiele, Egon, 251, 264
Schiff, Hilda, 173-174
   "Discovery," 173-174

Schiller, Johann Christoph Freidrich von, 118
Schulz, Bruno, 36, 42, 184, 192, 259, 261, 317-338 passim
  Cinammon Shops and Other Stories, 42, 317, 325
  Sanatorium Under the Sign of the Hourglass, 317-338 passim
  The Street of Crocodiles, 192, 317-338 passim
Schumann, Jacob, 31
Schutz, Anne Liebe, 21
Schwarz, Daniel R., 15-20 passim
Schwarz-Bart, André, 10, 36, 39, 42, 145, 166, 175, 204, 210, 239-248 passim, 252, 256, 330
  The Last of the Just, 10, 36, 42, 166, 210, 239-148 passim, 252, 256
  Levy, Ernie, 240-248
Scientia-Factum, 178
Seeskin, Kenneth, 22
Seidman, Hillel, 146
Seidman, Naomi, 51, 58, 66-67, 69-70, 73
Shakespeare, William, 6, 229, 278-279
  Macbeth, 278-279
  The Merchant of Venice, 229
Shepard, Jim, 181
Siberia, 34
Sighet, 50-51, 64-65
Singer, Issac Bashevis, 304
Sjoberg, Leif, 336
Skarzysko, 247
Skinner, Peter, 177
Sling Blade, 163
Sloan, Jacob, 157, 159
Sloan, James Park, 174, 176-180, 184
Sobibor, 26-27, 29, 34, 82, 166, 247
Sonderkommando, 34, 124
Sorrow and the Pity, The, 7
Spiegelman, Art, 3, 6, 33-34, 36, 39-40, 42, 90, 109, 159, 180, 216, 250-251, 256, 258, 268, 275, 287-302 passim, 304, 311, 313-314, 320, 330
  Maus: A Survivor's Tale. I: My Father Bleeds History, 3, 6, 33-34, 36, 42, 90, 109, 159, 216, 250-251, 256, 275, 287-302 passim, 304, 311, 313, 320, 330
  Maus: A Survivor's Tale. II: And Here My Troubles Began, 90, 250, 256, 287-302 passim
  Spiegelman, Vladek, 109, 216, 256, 275, 290, 294-298, 300-301, 304, 311

Spielberg, Steven, 3, 7, 32-33, 209-235 passim, 274
  Saving Private Ryan, 219
  Schindler's List (film), 3, 7, 32-33, 209-235 passim, 274
    Goeth, Amon, 211-213, 219-220, 222-230, 234
    Schindler, Oskar, 209-235 passim
    Stern, Itzhak, 210, 212-214, 220, 223-228, 230-231, 233-234
Stalin, Josef, 276
Steiner, George, 146, 162, 198
Steiner, Jean-François, 204
Stevens, Wallace, 176, 329
  "Tea at the Palaz of Hoon," 176
Story of O, The, 181
Streicher, Julius, 293
Styron, William, 5, 41, 195-207 passim, 229, 295
  Sophie's Choice, 5, 41, 195-207 passim, 229, 295
    Nathan, 195-207 passim
    Sophie, 195-207 passim, 229
    Stingo, 195-207 passim
Supremetism, 6
Swift, Jonathan, 183
  Gulliver's Travels, 183

T
Talmud, 19, 56, 60, 69, 210, 212, 281, 323
Terdiman, Richard, 11-12
Thersienstadt, 122-123, 166, 168, 247
Thomas, D. M., 5
  The White Hotel, 5
Thomson, David, 218
Thoreau, Henry David, 104
Time Magazine, 153
TLS (Times Literary Supplement), 6
Todorov, Tzvetan, 34, 48
Toulouse-Lauterc, Henri, 281
Treblinka, 26, 28-29, 32, 125, 145, 151, 247
Trudeau, Gary, 301
  Doonesbury, 301
Trunk, Isaiah, 273

U
United Jewish Appeal, 19
United States Memorial Holocaust Museum, 33
Uris, Leon, 5, 146, 162
  Mila 18, 5

V
Van Der Stroom, Gerrold, 103

Vichy government, 9
Vico, Giambattista, 240
Vietnam War, 17
Village Voice, 177, 179
Vilna Ghetto, 25, 247, 282
Voltaire, 114, 258
   Candide, 114, 258

W
Waaldijk, Berteke, 103, 112
Wannsee Conference, 165
Warsaw Ghetto, 16, 27-29, 33, 90, 116,
   119, 143-159 passim, 163, 166, 179,
   226, 247, 278, 282, 311, 314
Warsaw Uprising, 145
Westerbork, 107
Whitney, Craig R., 9-10
Wiesel, Elie, 10, 33-34, 36-40, 45-73
   passim, 101, 108-109, 111, 114, 116,
   145, 152, 204, 210, 218, 229, 256,
   274, 292
   A Jew Today, 53-54
   Memoirs: All Rivers Run to the Sea, 57-58,
     66, 68-69

Night, 10, 33, 36, 38, 40, 45-73 passim,
   108, 114, 116, 152, 210, 218, 229,
   256, 274, 292
Wilde, Oscar, 320
Wilder, Thornton, 89
Wilner, Arlene Fish, 288
Witek, Joseph, 290
Wittenberg, Yitzhak, 282
Wittgenstein, Ludwig Joseph Johann, 37
Woolf, Virginia, 242
Wordsworth, William, 18
World War I, 170

Y
Yad Vashem, 210
Yale University, 10
   Video Archives of Holocaust Testimo-
     nies, 10
Yeats, William Butler, 6
Young, James E., 13, 41-42, 196-197, 304

Z
Zionism, 17, 20, 64, 68, 170, 175, 226,
   234, 252, 269, 304